Who's Who in Dickens

Who's Who in Dickens is an accessible guide to the many characters in Charles Dickens's fiction. Dickens's characters are strikingly portrayed and have become a vital part of our cultural heritage – Scrooge has become a by-word for stinginess, Uriah Heep for unctuousness. From the much loved Oliver Twist to the fact-grubbing Mr Gradgrind, the obstinate Martin Chuzzlewit to the embittered Miss Havisham, this book covers the famous and lesser known characters in Dickens.

Who's Who in Dickens provides:
- an easy-to-use A-Z layout
- physical and psychological profiles of the characters
- a critical look at his characters by past and present influential commentators
- over forty illustrations of major characters drawn by Dickens's contemporaries
- an essential guide for students, teachers and the general reader alike

Donald Hawes has taught in schools and at the University of Westminster and the University of North London. He is presently a visiting lecturer at the University of Westminster and the Open University. He is co-author of *Thackeray: The Critical Heritage*, co-editor of *Villette*, author of *Poems Compared* and editor of volumes of *Pendennis*, *Henry Esmond* and *Barnaby Rudge*.

Who's Who in Dickens

Donald Hawes

London and New York

First published 1998
by Routledge
11 New Fetter Lane, London EC4P 4EE

Simultaneously published in the USA and Canada
by Routledge
29 West 35th Street, New York, NY 10001

© 1998 Donald Hawes

Typeset in Sabon by RefineCatch Limited, Bungay, Suffolk

Printed and bound in Great Britain by
Butler and Tanner Ltd., Frome and London

British Library Cataloguing in Publication Data
A catalogue record for this book is available from the British Library

Library of Congress Cataloguing in Publication Data
A catalogue record for this book has been requested

ISBN 0-415-1360-40 (hbk)
ISBN 0-415-1360-59 (pbk)

Contents

List of figures

Foreword

For many years, there has been a demand for books guiding readers through Charles Dickens's works. Dickens died in 1870 and 1878 saw the first publication to list and briefly describe the characters found in his books. Many such publications have followed. Dickens students and collectors know, to their frustration and to their cost, how quickly such works are snapped up when they become available, new or second-hand, and how well they hold their value, or indeed increase it. Paradoxically, a number of rare Dickens reference books of the past now cost the buyer more than first editions of some of the novels, a sign of just how useful readers find such works.

Dr Hawes's book will recommend itself to students because it is available, portable and affordable. But that is not all there is to recommend it. The predecessor, long out of print, to which it can most directly be compared is John Greaves's 1972 volume, also called *Who's Who in Dickens*. There is no denying the usefulness of the Greaves book, but Dr Hawes's book covers more of the fiction: the Christmas Stories, for instance, tales like 'George Silverman's Explanation' and 'Hunted Down', the children's stories which comprise 'A Holiday Romance', and 'The Mudfog Papers'. It covers material we might hesitate to classify as fiction, such as 'The Pantomime of Life' and *The Uncommercial Traveller*. It covers Dickens's plays and collaborative works such as some of the Christmas Stories and *Mr Nightingale's Diary*.

Dr Hawes's *Who's Who in Dickens* has the additional value of offering the reader scholarly background information, and critical judgements. School students and undergraduates with writing assignments can study entries, and use them as springboards for essays. General readers can discover the experiences that lie behind some of Dickens's creations, and how others have responded to them. Specialist scholars can quickly and conveniently remind themselves of such details. All will benefit from the way entries for characters from the longer works list each chapter in which the character appears or is mentioned. More than forty illustrations show how characters were understood by contemporaries and near contemporaries of Dickens.

One expert has identified more than 13,000 characters in Dickens's works. To include all of them in a book of this size would be to provide little more than a bare list. Through judicious selection, through the provision of background information and stimulating judgements, Dr Hawes has produced a book of great practical usefulness. *Who's Who in Dickens* is a valuable addition to the corpus of reference works on Dickens. Students and lovers of Dickens's works will find that it meets a clear need.

David Parker
Curator of the Dickens House Museum
London

Acknowledgements

I wish to thank the following people for their help in various ways in the preparation of this book: my daughter, Lucy, and Kevin Grant (for their assistance in preparing the typescript and disks); Michael Rogers (for checking the typescript); Andrew Xavier (for advice on illustrations); The Dickens House Museum, London, for providing the illustrations; and, as always, my wife, Pitsa, for her love, patience and support.

Note on texts and references

The Oxford Illustrated Dickens is an accessible and reasonably comprehensive edition of the works. The Clarendon Dickens (which began publication in 1966 and is still in progress) provides scholarly editions of the texts. There are also excellent separate editions of the works with introductions, explanatory notes and other information, in Penguin Classics, the World's Classics (Oxford University Press) and the Everyman Dickens (Dent). The numbers in parentheses after many of the entries in the *Who's Who* refer to the chapters in the novels in which the characters appear or are mentioned. References in the parentheses to the titles of short stories, sketches and articles are self-explanatory.

Abbreviations of Dickens's works cited

BH   *Bleak House* (1852–3)
BR   *Barnaby Rudge* (1841)
CB   *Christmas Books*, comprising *A Christmas Carol* (1843), *The Chimes* (1844), *The Cricket on the Hearth* (1845), *The Battle of Life* (1846), and *The Haunted Man* (1848)
CS   Christmas Stories, including 'The Poor Relation's Story' (1852), 'The School-boy's Story' (1853), 'Nobody's Story' (1852), 'The Seven Poor Travellers' (1854), 'The Holly-Tree Inn' (1855), 'The Wreck of the Golden Mary' (1856), 'The Perils of Certain English Prisoners' (1857), 'A House to Let' (1858), 'The Haunted House' (1859), 'A Message from the Sea' (1860), 'Tom Tiddler's Ground' (1861), 'Somebody's Luggage' (1862), 'Mrs Lirriper's Lodgings' (1863), 'Mrs Lirriper's Legacy' (1864), 'Doctor Marigold's Prescriptions' (1865), 'Mugby Junction' (1866), and 'No Thoroughfare' (1867). (Some of the Christmas Stories were written in collaboration with Wilkie Collins and others. Ruth Glancy's edition in the Everyman Dickens (see the Bibliography) gives full information on their authorship. The references in this *Who's Who* are to characters in the parts written by Dickens.)
DC   *David Copperfield* (1849–50)
DS   *Dombey and Son* (1846–8)
GE   *Great Expectations* (1860–1)
GSE   'George Silverman's Explanation' (1868)
HD   'Hunted Down' (1859)
HR   'A Holiday Romance' (1868)
HT   *Hard Times* (1854)
ISHW *Is She His Wife?* (1837)
L   *The Lamplighter* (1838)
LD   *Little Dorrit* (1855–7)
MED   *The Mystery of Edwin Drood* (1870)
MC   *Martin Chuzzlewit* (1843–44)
MHC   *Master Humphrey's Clock* (1840–1)
MND   *Mr Nightingale's Diary* (1851). Written by Mark Lemon; revised by Dickens
MP   'The Mudfog Papers' (1837–8)
NN   *Nicholas Nickleby* (1838–9)
OCS   *The Old Curiosity Shop* (1840–1)
OMF   *Our Mutual Friend* (1864–5)
OT   *Oliver Twist* (1837–9)
PL   'The Pantomime of Life' (1837)
PP   *Pickwick Papers* (1836–7)
RP   *Reprinted Pieces* (1858)

SB	*Sketches by Boz* (1836; 1839)
SG	*The Strange Gentleman* (1836)
SYC	*Sketches of Young Couples* (1840)
SYG	*Sketches of Young Gentlemen* (1838)
TTC	*A Tale of Two Cities* (1859)
UT	*The Uncommercial Traveller* (1861)
VC	*The Village Coquettes* (1836)

Lists of characters by work

The characters listed here do not necessarily comprise the complete *dramatis personae* of the works in question. But there are entries for all of those who appear in this *Who's Who*. Reference to some of the entries will sometimes lead to cross-references and to other characters.

Sketches by Boz (1836; 1839). The contents of the various collections that were published under this title appeared in various periodicals, including the *Monthly Magazine*, the *Morning Chronicle*, and *Bell's Life in London*.

'Our Parish': Brown, the Misses; Bung, Mr; Dawson, Mr; Fixem, Mr; Gubbins, Mr; Hopkins; Parker, Mrs Johnson; Purday, Captain; Robinson, Mr; Simmons; Spruggins, Thomas; Timkins; William; Willis, the Misses.

'Scenes': Alick; Barker, William; Bill, Uncle; Bumple, Michael; Clark, Betsy; Dando; George, Uncle and Aunt; Green, Mr; Henry, Mr; Jane; Jinkins, Mr and Mrs; Larkins, Jem; Loggins; Mackin, Mrs; Macklin, Mrs; Mary; Nathan, Mr; Nicholas; Peplow, Mrs; Sludberry, Thomas; Sluffen, Mr; Smith, Mr; Smuggins, Mr; Sullivan, Mrs; Tatham, Mrs; Walker, Mr; Walker, Mr and Mrs; White; Woolford, Miss.

'Characters': Bella; Billsmethi, Signor; Cooper, Augustus; Dobble, Mr; Dounce, John; Ellis, Mr; Emily; Evans, Miss Jemima; Harris, Mr; Jack; Jennings, Mr; Jones; Margaret, Aunt; Martin, Miss Amelia; Potter, Thomas; Rodolph, Mr and Mrs Jennings; Rogers, Mr; Smith, Mr; Smithers, Robert; Taplin, Harry; Tommy; Tupple, Mr; Wilkins, Samuel.

'Tales':
'The Boarding-House': Agnes; Bloss, Mrs; Calton, Mr; Evenson, John; Gobler, Mr; Hicks, Septimus; James; Maplesone, Mrs; O'Bleary, Frederick; Rampart, Sir Charles; Robinson; Simpson, Mr; Tibbs, Mrs; Tomkins, Alfred; Wisbottle, Mr; Wosky, Doctor.

'Mr Minns and his Cousin': Brogson, Mr; Budden, Octavius; Jones; Minns, Augustus.

'Sentiment': Butler, Theodosius; Crumpton, the Misses Amelia and Maria; Dadson, Mr; Dingwall, Cornelius Brook; Hilton, Mr; James; Lobskini, Signor; Muggs, Sir Alfred; Parsons, Miss Laetitia; Smithers, Miss Emily; Wilson, Miss Caroline.

'The Tuggses at Ramsgate': Amelia; Cower, Mr; Golding, Mary; Slaughter, Lieutenant; Tippin, Mr and Mrs, and family; Tuggs, Mr and family; Waters, Captain and Mrs.

'Horatio Sparkins': Barton, Jacob; Delafontaine, Mr; Flamwell, Mr; Gubbleton, Lord; John; Malderton, Mr and Mrs; Sparkins, Horatio.

'The Black Veil': Rose; Tom.

'The Steam Excursion': Briggs, Mr and Mrs, and family; Edkins, Mr; Fleetwood, Mr, Mrs and Master; Hardy, Mr; Helves, Captain; Noakes, Percy; Ram Chowder Doss Azuph Al Bowlar; Stubbs, Mrs; Taunton, Mrs and the Misses; Wakefield, Mr, Mrs and Miss.

'The Great Winglebury Duel': Brown, Emily; Cornberry, Mr; Hunter, Horace; Manners, Miss Julia; Overton, Joseph; Peter, Lord; Thomas; Trott, Alexander; Williamson, Mrs.

'Mrs Joseph Porter': Balderstone, Thomas; Brown, Mr; Cape, Mr; Evans, Mr; Gattleton, Sempronius, and family; Glumper, Sir Thomas; Harleigh, Mr; Jenkins, Miss; Porter, Mrs Joseph; Wilson, Mr.

'A Passage in the Life of Mr Watkins Tottle': Ikey; Jacobs, Solomon; Jem; John; Lillerton, Miss; Parsons, Gabriel; Ross, Frank; Timson, the Reverend Charles; Tottle, Watkins; Walker, Mr; Willis, Mr.

'The Bloomsbury Christening': Danton, Mr; Dumps, Nicodemus; Jane; Kitterbell, Mr and Mrs.

'The Drunkard's Death': Mary; Warden.

The Strange Gentleman (1836). Comic burletta.
Dobbs, Julia; John; Johnson, John; Noakes, Mrs; Overton, Owen; Sparks, Tom; Tomkins.

The Village Coquettes (1836). Comic operetta, with music by John Pyke Hullah.
Benson, Lucy; Benson, Old and Young; Edmunds, George; Flam, the Honourable Sparkins; Maddox, John; Norton, Squire; Rose; Stokes, Martin.

Pickwick Papers (1836–7). Novel. Serialised in monthly parts, April 1836–November 1837 (excluding June 1837).
Allen, Arabella; Allen, Benjamin; Ayresleigh, Mr; Bagman, the; Bamber, Jack; Bantam, Angelo Cyrus; Bardell, Mrs Martha; Beller, Henry; Betsey; Bill; Bladud, Prince; Blazo, Sir Thomas; Blotton, Mr; Boffer; Boldwig, Captain; Bolo, Miss; Brooks; Brown; Budger, Mrs; Bulder, Colonel; Bullman; Bunkin, Mrs; Burton, Thomas; Buzfuz, Serjeant; Charley; Clarke, Mrs Susan; Clubber, Sir Thomas; Cluppins, Mrs; Craddock, Mrs; Crawley, Mr; Cripps, Tom; Crookey; Crushton, the Honourable Mr; Cummins, Tom; Dodson and Fogg; Dowler, Mr and Mrs; Dubbley; Dumkins, Mr; Edmunds, John; Emma; Filletoville, the Marquess of; Fitz-Marshall, Captain Charles; Fizkin, Horatio; Fizzgig, Don Bolaro; Flasher, Wilkins; Fogg; Goodwin; Groffin, Thomas; Grub, Gabriel; Grummer, Daniel; Grundy, Mr; Gunter, Mr; Gwynn, Miss; Harris; Heyling, George; Hopkins, Jack; Humm, Anthony; Hunt; Hunter, Mrs Leo; Hutley, Jem; Isaac; Jane; Jackson; Jingle, Alfred; Jinkins, Mr; Jinks, Mr; Joe; John; John; Kate; Lobbs, Maria; Lowten, Mr; Lucas, Solomon; Lud Hudibras; Luffey, Mr;

Magnus, Peter; Mallard, Mr; Manning, Sir Geoffrey; Martin; Martin, Betsey; Martin, Jack; Martin, Tom; Mary; Matinter, the Misses; Miller, Mr; Mivins, Mr; Mordlin, Brother; Mudberry, Mrs; Mudge, Jonas; Mutanhed, Lord; Muzzle; Namby, Mr; Neddy; Noddy, Mr; Nupkins, Mr, Mrs and Miss; Payne, Doctor; Pell, Solomon; Perker, Mr; Phunky, Mr; Pickwick, Samuel; Pipkin, Nathaniel; Podder, Mr; Porkenham, Mr, Mrs, and family; Pott, Mr and Mrs; Price, Mr; Pruffle; Quanko Samba; Raddle, Mrs; Rogers, Mrs; Roker, Tom; Sam; Sanders, Mrs; Sawyer, Bob; Simmery, Frank; Simpson, Mr; Skimpin, Mr; Slammer, Doctor; Slasher, Mr; Slumkey, the Honourable Samuel; Slummintowkens, the; Slurk, Mr; Smangle, Mr; Smart, Tom; Smauker, John; Smiggers, Joseph, Esq; Smithers, Miss; Smithie, Mr, and family; Smorltork, Count; Smouch, Mr; Snicks, Mr; Snipe, the Hon. Wilmot; Snodgrass, Augustus; Snubbin, Serjeant; Snuphanuph, the Dowager Lady; Staple, Mr; Stareleigh, Mr Justice; Stiggins, Mr; Struggles, Mr; Tadger, Brother; Tappleton, Lieutenant; Thomas; Tomkins, Miss; Tomlinson, Mrs; Trotter, Job; Trundle, Mr; Tuckle, Mr; Tupman, Tracy; Upwitch, Richard; Walker, H.; Wardle, Mr, and family; Watty, Mr; Weller, Sam; Weller, Tony; Weller, Mrs Tony; Whiffers, Mr; Whiffin; Wicks, Mr; Wildspark, Tom; Wilkins; Winkle, Nathaniel; Winkle, Mr, senior; Witherfield, Miss; Wugsby, Mrs Colonel; Zephyr, the.

Is She His Wife? (1837). Comic burletta.
John; Limbury, Mr and Mrs Peter; Lovetown, Mr and Mrs Alfred; Tapkins, Felix.

'The Mudfog Papers' (1837–8). Published in *Bentley's Miscellany*.
Blank, Mr; Blubb, Mr; Blunderbore, Captain; Blunderum, Mr; Brown, Mr; Buffer, Doctor; Carter, Mr; Coppernose; Crinkles, Mr; Doze, Professor; Drawley, Mr; Dull, Mr; Dummy, Mr; Fee, Doctor W.R.; Flummery, Mr; Foxey, Dr; Greenacre, James; Grime, Professor; Grub. Mr; Grummidge, Doctor; Jennings, Mr; Jobba, Mr; Joltered, Sir William; Ketch, Professor John; Knight Bell, Mr; Kutankumagen, Dr; Kwakley, Mr; Leaver, Mr; Ledbrain, Mr X; Long Eers, the Honourable and Reverend; Mallett, Mr; Misty, Mr X. X.; Mortair, Mr; Muddlebranes, Mr; Muff, Professor; Mull, Professor; Neeshawts, Dr; Noakes, Mr; Nogo, Professor; Pessell, Mr; Pipkin, Mr; Prosee, Mr; Pumpinskull, Professor; Purblind, Mr; Queerspeck, Professor; Rummun, Professor; Scroo, Mr; Slug, Mr; Smith, Mr; Sniggs, Mr; Snivey, Sir Hookham; Snore, Professor; Snuffletoffle, Mr Q.J.; Soemup, Doctor; Sowster; Styles, Mr; Tickle, Mr; Timbered, Mr; Toorell, Doctor; Truck, Mr; Tulrumble, Mr; Twigger, Edward; Waghorn, Mr; Wheezy, Professor; Wigsby, Mr; Woodensconce, Mr.

'The Pantomime of Life' (1837). Published in *Bentley's Miscellany*.
Do'em; Fiercy, Captain the Honourable Fitz-Whisker.

Oliver Twist (1837–9). Novel. Serialised in monthly instalments in *Bentley's Miscellany*, February 1837–April 1839 (excluding June and October 1837 and September 1838).
Anny; Artful Dodger, the; Barker, Phil; Barney; Bates, Charley; Bayton, Mrs; Bedwin, Mrs; Bet; Blathers; Bolter, Morris; Brittles; Brownlow, Mr; Bull's-eye; Bumble, Mr; Charlotte; Chickweed, Conkey; Chitling, Tom; Claypole, Noah; Corney, Mrs; Crackit, Toby; Dawkins, Jack; Dick; Duff; Fagin; Fang, Mr; Fleming, Agnes; Gamfield, Mr; Giles; Grannett; Grimwig, Mr; Harry; Kags; Leeford, Edward; Leeford, Edwin; Limbkins, Mr; Lively, Mr; Losberne, Mr; Mann, Mrs; Martha; Maylie, Harry;

Maylie, Mrs; Maylie, Rose; Monks; Nancy; Ned; Sally; Sikes, Bill; Slout; Sowerberry, Mr and Mrs; Spyers, Jem; Twist, Oliver.

The Lamplighter (1838). Farce. Dickens later turned it into a short story, which was included in *The Pic-Nic Papers* (1841), a collection of pieces by various writers.
Brown, Fanny; Grig, Tom; Martin, Betsey; Mooney, Mr; Stargazer, Mr.

Sketches of Young Gentlemen (1838).
Balim, Mr; Barker, Mrs; Blake, Warmint; Boozle; Capper, Mr and Mrs; Caveton; Charles; Dummins; Fairfax, Mr; Greenwood, the Misses; Grey, the Misses; Griggins, Mr; Hopkins, Mr; Lambert, Miss; Lowfield, Miss; Martins, the; Milkwash, Mr; Mincin, Mr; Nixon, Felix; Thompson, Miss Julia; Watson, Mrs and the Misses.

Nicholas Nickleby (1838–9). Novel. Serialised in monthly parts, April 1838–October 1839.
Adams, Captain; Alice; Alphonse; Belling; Belvawney, Miss; Blockson, Mrs; Bobster, Cecilia; Bolder; Bonney, Mr; Borum, Mrs, and family; Bravassa, Miss; Bray, Madeline; Bray, Walter; Brooker, Mr; Browdie, John; Browndock, Mrs; Bulph, Mr; Cheeryble, Charles and Edwin; Cheeryble, Frank; Chowser, Colonel; Clark, Mrs; Cobbey; Cropley, Miss; Crowl, Mr; Crummles, Vincent, and family; Crummles, Ninetta; Curdle, Mr and Mrs; Cutler, Mr and Mrs; David; Dibabs, Jane; Dick; Dick; Dorker; Dowdles, the Miss; Fluggers; Folair, Mr; Gallanbile, Mr; Gazingi, Miss; Gentleman in Small Clothes; George; Glavormelly, Mr; Graymarsh; Gregsbury, Mr; Gride, Arthur; Grimble, Sir Thomas; Grogzwig, Baron of; Grudden, Mrs; Hannah; Hawk, Sir Mulberry; Hawkinses, the; Kenwigs, Mr and Mrs, and family; Knag, Miss; Knag, Mortimer; Koëldwithout, Baron von; La Creevy, Miss; Lane, Miss; Ledrook, Miss; Lenville, Mr and Mrs; Lillyvick, Mr; Linkinwater, Tim; Lukin; Lumbey, Doctor; Mallowford, Lord; Mantalini, Mr and Madame; Matthews; Mobbs; Muntle; Nickleby, Kate; Nickleby, Mrs; Nickleby, Nicholas; Nickleby, Ralph; Noggs, Newman; Peltirogus, Horatio; Petowker, Henrietta; Phoebe; Pitcher; Pluck, Mr; Price, Matilda; Pugstyles, Mr; Pupker, Sir Matthew: Pyke, Mr; Scaley, Mr; Simmonds, Miss; Sliderskew, Peg; Smike; Snawley, Mr; Snevellicci, Miss; Snewkes, Mr; Snobb, the Hon. Mr; Snuffim, Sir Tumley; Squeers, Fanny; Squeers, Mrs; Squeers, Wackford; Squeers, Wackford, junior; Swillenhausen, Baron von; Timberry, Snittle, Mr; Thomas; Tix, Tom; Tom; Tompkins; Trimmers, Mr; Verisopht, Lord Frederick; Watkins, Mr; Westwood, Mr; Wititterley, Henry and Julia; Wrymug, Mrs.

Sketches of Young Couples (1840).
Adams, Jane; Briggs, Mr and Mrs; Charles; Charlotte; Chirrup, Mr and Mrs; Chopper, Mrs; Clickit, Mr and Mrs; Crofts; Edward; Fielding, Emma; Finching, Mrs; Fithers, Mr; Glogwog, Sir Chipkins; Greenwood, the Misses; Harvey, Mr; Jenkins; Leaver, Mr and Mrs; Merrywinkle, Mr and Mrs; Parsons, Mrs; Saunders, Mr; Scuttlewig, the Duke of; Slang, Lord; Sliverstone, Mr and Mrs; Slummery, Mr; Snorflerer, the Dowager Lady; Starling, Mrs; Tabblewick, Mrs; Whiffler, Mr and Mrs; Widger, Mr and Mrs Bobtail.

Master Humphrey's Clock (1840–1). A weekly miscellany that originally included *The Old Curiosity Shop* and *Barnaby Rudge*.
Alice, Mistress; Belinda; Benton, Miss; Blinder, Bill; Deaf Gentleman, the; Gibbs, Villiam; Graham, Hugh; Humphrey, Master; Jinkinson; Marks, Will; Miles, Owen;

Pickwick, Samuel; Podgers, John; Redburn, Jack; Slithers; Toddyhigh, Joe; Weller, Sam.

The Old Curiosity Shop (1840–1). Novel. Serialised in weekly parts of *Master Humphrey's Clock*, 25 April 1840–6 February 1841.
Bachelor, the; Barbara; Brass, Sally; Brass, Sampson; Cheggs, Mr and Miss; Chuckster, Mr; Codlin, Thomas; David; Edwards, Miss; Evans, Richard; Foxey; Garland, Abel; Garland, Mr and Mrs; George; George, Mrs; Grandfather, Little Nell's; Grinder, Mr; Groves, James (Jem); Harris; Harry; Jarley, Mrs; Jerry; Jiniwin, Mrs; Jowl, Joe; List, Isaac; Losberne, Mr; Marchioness, the; Marton, Mr; Maunders; Monflathers, Miss; Morgan, Becky; Nell, Little; Nubbles, Kit; Nubbles, Mrs; Owen, John; Quilp, Daniel; Quilp, Mrs Betsy; Scott, Tom; Short; Simmons, Mrs Henrietta; Single Gentleman, the; Slum, Mr; Sphynx, Sophronia; Sweet William; Swiveller, Dick; Tomkinley, Mr; Trent, Frederick; Trent, Nell; Vuffin, Mr; Wackles, Sophia; West, Dame; Whisker; Witherden, Mr.

Barnaby Rudge (1841). Historical novel. Serialised in weekly parts of *Master Humphrey's Clock*, 13 February–27 November 1841.
Akerman, Mr; Black Lion, the; Chester, Mr (later, Sir) John; Chester, Edward; Cobb, Tom; Conway, General; Daisy, Solomon; Dennis, Ned; Fielding, Sir John; Gashford, Mr; Gilbert, Mark; Gordon, Colonel; Gordon, Lord George; Green, Tom; Grip; Haredale, Emma; Haredale, Geoffrey; Herbert, Mr; Hugh; Jones, Mary; Langdale, Mr; Miggs, Miss; Parkes, Phil; Peak; Percy, Lord Algernon; Philips; Rudge, Barnaby; Rudge, Mr; Rudge, Mrs; Stagg; Tappertit, Simon; Varden, Dolly; Varden, Gabriel; Varden, Mrs; Willet, Joe; Willet, John.

Christmas Books. Stories published in separate volumes at Christmas in the years indicated.
A Christmas Carol (1843): Belle; Cratchit, Bob, and family; Dilber, Mrs; Fan; Fezziwig, Mr; Fred; Joe; Marley, Jacob; Scrooge, Ebenezer; Tiny Tim; Topper, Mr; Wilkins, Dick.
The Chimes (1844): Bowley, Sir Joseph; Chickenstalker, Mrs Anne; Cute, Alderman; Deedles; Fern, Lilian; Fern, Will; Filer, Mr; Fish, Mr; Richard; Tugby; Veck, Meg; Veck, Trotty.
The Cricket on the Hearth (1845): Boxer; Fielding, May; Peerybingle, John and Mary; Plummer, Caleb; Slowboy, Tilly; Tackleton.
The Battle of Life (1846): Britain, Benjamin; Craggs, Thomas; Heathfield, Alfred; Jeddler, Doctor Anthony; Jeddler, Grace and Marion; Newcome, Clemency; Snitchey, Jonathan; Warden, Michael.
The Haunted Man (1848): Denham, Edmund; Longford, Edmund; Redlaw, Mr; Swidger, Milly; Tetterby, Adolphus.

Martin Chuzzlewit (1843–4). Novel. Serialised in monthly parts, January 1843–July 1844.
Bailey, Young; Bevan, Mr; Bib, Julius Washington Merryweather; Brick, Jefferson; Buffum, Oscar; Bullamy; Chiggle; Choke, General Cyrus; Chollop, Major Hannibal; Chuffey; Chuzzlewit, Anthony; Chuzzlewit, George; Chuzzlewit, Jonas; Chuzzlewit, Martin, junior; Chuzzlewit, Martin, senior; Chuzzlewit, Mrs Ned; Cicero; Codger, Miss; Crimple, David; Diver, Colonel; Dunkle, Doctor Ginery; Fips, Mr; Fladdock, General; Gamp, Mrs Sarah; Gander, Mr; Gill, Mrs; Graham, Mary; Groper, Colonel;

Hominy, Mrs; Izzard, Mr; Jane; Jinkins, Mr; Jobling, Doctor John; Jodd; Kedgick, Captain; Kettle, La Fayette; Lewsome; Lummy Ned; Lupin, Mrs; Moddle, Augustus; Montague, Tigg; Mould, Mr, and family; Mullit, Professor; Nadgett; Norris, Mr and Mrs, and family; Pawkins, Major and Mrs; Pecksniff, Charity; Pecksniff, Mercy; Pecksniff, Mr; Pinch, Ruth; Pinch, Tom; Pip, Mr; Piper, Professor; Pogram, Elijah; Prig, Mrs Betsey; Scadder, Zephaniah; Simmons, William; Slyme, Chevy; Smif, Putnam; Sophia; Spottletoe, Mr and Mrs; Sweedlepipe, Poll; Tacker; Tamaroo; Tigg, Montague; Todgers, Mrs; Toppit, Miss; Westlock, John; Wolf, Mr.

Dombey and Son (1846–8). Novel. Serialised in monthly parts, October 1846–April 1848.
Anne; Bagstock, Major Joseph; Baps, Mr; Berinthia; Bitherstone, Master; Blimber, Cornelia; Blimber, Doctor; Blimber, Mrs; Blockitt, Mrs; Bokum, Mrs; Briggs; Brogley, Mr; Brown, Mrs; Bunsby, Captain Jack; Burgess and Co.; Carker, Harriet; Carker, James; Carker, John; Chick, Mr; Chick, Mrs Louisa; Clark, Mr; Cuttle, Captain; Daws, Mary; Diogenes; Dombey, Edith; Dombey, Mrs Fanny; Dombey, Florence; Dombey, Mr Paul; Dombey, Paul; Feeder, B.A., Mr; Feenix, Cousin; Finchbury, Lady Jane; Flowers; Game Chicken, the; Gay, Walter; Gills, Solomon; Glubb, Old; Granger, Edith; Howler, the Reverend Melchisedech; Jemima; John; Johnson; Johnson, Tom; Kate; Larkey Boy; MacStinger, Mrs; Martha; Marwood, Alice; 'Melia; Miff, Mrs; Morfin, Mr; Native, the; Nipper, Susan; Pankey, Miss; Peps, Doctor (or, Sir); Perch, Mr and Mrs; Pilkins, Doctor; Pipchin, Mrs; Richards; Rob the Grinder; Robinson; Saxby, Long; Screwzer, Tommy; Skettles, Sir Barnet; Skewton, the Honourable Mrs; Smalder girls, the; Sownds, Mr; Toodle, Mr; Toodle, Polly; Toots, Mr; Towlinson, Mr; Tox, Lucretia; Tozer; Wickam, Mrs; Withers.

David Copperfield (1849–50). Novel. Serialised in monthly parts, May 1849–November 1850.
Adams; Babley, Richard; Bailey, Captain; Barkis, Mr; Charley; Chestle, Mr; Chillip, Doctor; Clickett; Copperfield, Mrs Clara (later, Mrs Murdstone); Copperfield, David; Copperfield, Dora; Creakle, Mr; Crewler, Sophie; Crupp, Mrs; Dartle, Rosa; Demple, George; Dick, Mr; Dolloby, Mr; Dora; Em'ly, Little; Endell, Martha; Fibbitson, Mrs; George; Grainger; Grayper, Mr and Mrs; Gregory; Gulpidge, Mr and Mrs; Gummidge, Mrs; Heep, Mrs; Heep, Uriah; Hopkins, Captain; Janet; Jip; Jones; Joram; Jorkins, Mr; Kidgerbury, Mrs; Kitt, Miss; Larkins, Miss; Littimer; Maldon, Jack; Markham; Markleham, Mrs; Mealy Potatoes; Mell, Charles; Micawber, Wilkins; Micawber, Mrs; Mills, Julia; Mithers, Lady; Mowcher, Miss; Murdstone, Edward; Murdstone, Jane; Nettingall, the Misses; Omer, Minnie; Paragon, Mary Anne; Passnidge, Mr; Peggotty, Clara; Peggotty, Daniel; Peggotty, Ham; Pyegrave, Charley; Quinion, Mr; Sharp, Mr; Shepherd, Miss; Spenlow, the Misses Clarissa and Lavinia; Spenlow, Dora (later, Dora Copperfield); Spenlow, Francis; Spiker, Mr and Mrs Henry; Steerforth, James; Steerforth, Mrs; Strong, Annie; Strong, Doctor; Tiffey, Mr; Tipp; Topsawyer; Traddles, Thomas; Trotwood, Miss Betsey; Tungay; Walker, Mick; Waterbrook, Mr and Mrs; Wickfield, Agnes; Wickfield, Mr; William; William; Yawler.

Bleak House (1852–3). Novel. Serialised in monthly parts, March 1852–September 1853.
Badger, Bayham; Badger, Mrs Bayham; Bagnet, Matthew; Bagnet, Mrs; Barbary, Miss; Blinder, Mrs; Blowers, Mr; Bogsby, James George; Boodle, Lord; Boythorn,

Lawrence; Bucket, Inspector; Bucket, Mrs; Buffy, the Right Honourable William; Carstone, Richard; Chadband, the Reverend Mr; Charley; Clare, Ada; Coavinses; Darby; Dedlock, Lady; Dedlock, Sir Leicester; Dedlock, Volumnia; Dingo, Professor; Donny, the Misses; Flite, Miss; George, Trooper; Gridley, Mr; Grubble, Mr; Guppy, Mrs; Guppy, William; Gusher, Mr; Guster; Hawdon, Captain; Hortense, Mademoiselle; James; Jarndyce, John; Jellyby, Caddy; Jellyby, Mrs; Jellyby, Peepy; Jenny; Jo; Jobling, Tony; Kenge, 'Conversation'; Krook; Lady Jane; Liz; Melvilleson, Miss M; Mercury; Mooney; Neckett; Neckett, Charlotte; Nemo; Pardiggle, Mrs, and family; Peffer; Perkins, Mrs; Piper, Mrs; Polly; Pouch, Mrs Joe; Priscilla; Quale, Mr; Rachael, Mrs; Rosa; Rouncewell, George; Rouncewell, Mr; Rouncewell, Mrs; Rouncewell, Watt; Skimpole, Harold; Sladdery, Mr; Smallweed, Bart; Smallweed, Grandfather, and family; Snagsby, Mr and Mrs; Squod, Phil; Stables, the Honourable Bob; Summerson, Esther; Swills, Little; Swosser, Captain; Tagle, Mr; Thomas; Tulkinghorn, Mr; Turveydrop, Mr; Turveydrop, Prince; Vholes, Mr; Weevle; Wisk, Miss; Woodcourt, Allan; Woodcourt, Mrs.

'To Be Read At Dusk' (1852). Two short stories, published in *The Keepsake* (an Annual).
Carolina; Clara; Dellombra, Signor; James; John; Wilhelm.

Christmas Stories. Tales and sketches written by Dickens and others (notably Wilkie Collins) for the Christmas numbers of *Household Words* and *All the Year Round.* The characters listed below are those who appear in the stories or parts of stories written by Dickens himself.

'The Poor Relation's Story' (1852): Chill, Uncle; Christiana; Frank, Little; Michael; Snap, Betsy; Spatter, John.

'The Schoolboy's Story' (1853): Cheeseman, Old; Pitt, Jane; Tarter, Bob.

'Nobody's Story' (1853): Bigwig family.

'The Seven Poor Travellers' (1854): Doubledick, Richard; Marshall, Mary; Taunton, Captain.

'The Holly-Tree Inn' (1855): Charley; Cobbs; Edwin; Emmeline; Leath, Angela; Louis; Macey, Mr and Mrs; Norah; Walmers, Harry.

'The Wreck of the Golden Mary' (1856): Atherfield, Mrs; Coleshaw, Miss; Mullion, John; Rames, William; Rarx, Mr; Ravender, Captain; Snow, Tom; Steadiman, John.

'The Perils of Certain English Prisoners' (1857): Carton, Captain George; Charker, Harry; Davis, Gill; Drooce, Sergeant; Fisher, Mr and Mrs; King, Christian George; Kitten, Mr; Linderwood, Lieutenant; Macey, Mr and Mrs; Maryon, Captain; Packer, Tom; Pordage, Commissioner; Tott, Mrs Isabella; Venning, Mrs.

'Going into Society', which was a part of 'A House to Let' (1858): Chops; Jarber; Magsman, Toby; Normandy; Tpschoffki; Trottle.

'The Haunted House' (1859): Bates, Belinda; Beaver, Nat; Bottles; Bule, Miss;

Governor, Jack; Greenwood; Griffin, Miss; Herschel, John; Ikey; Joby; John; Mesrour; Patty; Perkins; Pipson, Miss; Starling, Alfred; Streaker; Tabby; Undery, Mr.

'A Message from the Sea' (1860): Clissold, Lawrence; Jorgan, Captain Silas; Pettifer, Tom; Raybrock, Mrs; Tregarthen, Mr

'Tom Tiddler's Ground' (1861): Bella; Kimmeens, Kitty; Linx, Miss; Mopes, Mr; Pupford, Miss Euphemia; Traveller, Mr.

'Somebody's Luggage' (1862): Baptiste; Bebelle; Bouclet, Madame; Charles; Christopher; Click, Mr; Cour, Monsieur le Capitaine de la; Emile; Eugène; Gabrielle; Hyppolite, Private; Joseph; Langley, Mr; Martin, Miss; Mutuel, Monsieur; Pratchett, Mrs; Théophile, Corporal; Tom; Valentine, Private.

'Mrs Lirriper's Lodgings' (1863): Betley; Bobbo; Edson, Mr; George; Jackman, Major James; Jane; Lirriper, Mrs Emma; Maxey, Caroline; Perkinsop, Mary Anne; Seraphina; Sophy; Wozenham, Miss.

'Mrs Lirriper's Legacy' (1864): Buffle, Mr; Edson, Mr; George; Jackman, Major James; Madgers, Winifred; Rairyganoo, Sally; Wozenham, Miss.

'Doctor Marigold's Prescriptions' (1865). The title is often shortened to 'Doctor Marigold': Derrick, John; Harker, Mr; Marigold, Doctor; Mim; Pickleson; Sophy.

'Mugby Junction' (1866): Barbox Brothers; Ezekiel; Jackson, Mr; Lamps; Phoebe; Piff, Miss; Signalman, the; Sniff, Mr and Mrs; Tresham, Beatrice; Whiff, Miss.

'No Thoroughfare' (1867): Bintrey; Dor, Madame; Ganz, Doctor; Goldstraw, Sarah; Harker, the Reverend John; Jarvis; Ladle, Joey; Miller, Mrs Jane Ann; Obenreizer, Jules; Rolland, Monsieur; Vendale, George; Voigt, Maître; Wilding, Walter.

Mr Nightingale's Diary (1851). Farce written by Mark Lemon and extensively revised by Dickens.
Gabblewig; Lithers, Thomas; Nightingale, Rosina; Slap; Tip.

Hard Times (1854). Novel. Serialised in weekly instalments in Household Words, 1 April–12 August 1854.
Bitzer; Blackpool, Stephen; Bounderby, Josiah; Childers, E.W.B.; Gordon, Emma; Gradgrind, Louisa; Gradgrind, Mrs; Gradgrind, Thomas; Gradgrind, Tom; Harthouse, James; Jupe, Sissy; Kidderminster; M'Choakumchild, Mr; Merrylegs; Nickits; Pegler, Mrs; Rachael; Powlers, the; Scadgers, Lady; Slackbridge; Sleary, Mr; Sparsit, Mrs.

Little Dorrit (1855–7). Novel. Serialised in monthly parts, December 1855–June 1857.
Aunt, Mr F's; Bangham, Mrs; Barbary, Mrs Captain; Barnacles, the; Beadle, Harriet; Blandois; Bob; Casby, Christopher; Cavalletto, John Baptist; Barroneau, Madame; Chivery, Mr and Mrs John; Chivery, John; Clennam, Arthur; Clennam, Mrs; Cripples, Mr; Dawes, Mary; Dorrit, Amy; Dorrit, Edward; Dorrit, Fanny; Dorrit, Frederick; Dorrit, William; Doyce, Daniel; Finching, Flora; Flintwinch, Affery; Flintwinch,

Ephraim; Flintwinch, Jeremiah; General, Mrs; Gowan, Henry; Gowan, Mrs; Haggage, Doctor; Hawkins; Jenkinson; Lagnier; Lion; Maggy; Maroon, Captain; Martin, Captain; Meagles, Mr and Mrs; Meagles, Minnie (Pet); Merdle, Mr; Merdle, Mrs; Nandy, John Edward; Pancks, Mr; Physician; Plornish, Mr and Mrs; Rigaud; Rugg, Anastasia; Rugg, Mr; Slingo; Sparkler, Edmund; Stiltstalking, Lord Lancaster; Stiltstalking, Tudor; Tattycoram; Tickit, Mrs; Tinkler, Mr; Treasury; Wade, Miss; Wobbler, Mr.

Reprinted Pieces (1858). A collection of sketches, stories and essays (originally including some of the Christmas Stories) that were first published in *Household Words*. Only the pieces relevant to this *Who's Who* are listed.

'The Long Voyage': Brimer, Mr; Macmanus, Mr; Mansel, Miss; Meriton, Henry; Pierce, Captain; Rogers, Mr; Schutz, Mr.

'The Begging-Letter Writer': Southcote, Mr.

'Our English Watering-Place': Mills, Julia; Peepy, the Honourable Miss.

'Our French Watering-Place': Féroce, Monsieur; Loyal Devasseur, M.

'Births. Mrs Meek, of a Son': Bigby, Mrs; Meek, George; Prodgit, Mrs.

'The Ghost of Art': Julia; Parkins, Mrs.

'Out of the Season': Clocker, Mr; Wedgington, Mr and Mrs.

'A Poor Man's Tale of a Patent': Butcher, William; John; Joy, Thomas.

'A Flight': Diego, Don.

'The Detective Police' and 'Three Detective Anecdotes': Clarkson, Mr; Dornton, Sergeant; Dundey, Doctor; Fendall, Sergeant; Fikey; Grimwood, Eliza; Mesheck, Aaron; Mith, Sergeant; Phibbs, Mr; Shepherdson; Stalker, Inspector; Straw, Sergeant; Tatt, Mr; Thompson, Tally Ho; Trinkle, Mr; Wield, Inspector; Witchem, Sergeant.

'On Duty with Inspector Field:' Bark; Blackey; Click, Mr; Field, Inspector; Miles, Bob; Stalker, Mrs; Williams.

'Down with the Tide': Pea or Peacoat

'Prince Bull': Bear, Prince; Bull, Prince; Tape.

'Our Honourable Friend': Tipkisson.

'Our School': Blinkins; Dumbledon; Frost, Miss; Mawls and Maxby; Phil.

'Our Vestry': Banger, Captain; Chib, Mr; Dogginson; Magg, Mr; Tiddypot, Mr; Wigsby, Mr.

'Our Bore:' Blanquo, Pierre; Blumb, R.A.; Callow, Doctor; Clatter, Doctor; Fanchette; Jilkins; Moon; Our Bore; Parkins; Snugglewood.

'A Monument of French Folly': Doche, Madame; François, Monsieur.

A Tale of Two Cities (1859). Historical novel. Published in weekly instalments in *All the Year Round*, 30 April–26 November 1859.
Barsad, John; Carton, Sydney; Cly, Roger; Cruncher, Jerry, his wife and son; Darnay, Charles; Defarge, Ernest; Defarge, Madame Thérèse; Foulon; Gabelle, Théophile; Gaspard; Jacques; Joe; Lorry, Jarvis; Manette, Doctor; Manette, Lucie; Pross, Miss; Pross, Solomon; St Evrémonde; Stryver, Mr; Tom; Vengeance, the.

'Hunted Down' (1859). Short story, published in the *New York Ledger* (20 and 27 August 1859) and *All the Year Round* (4 and 11 April 1860).
Adams, Mr; Banks, Major; Beckwith, Alfred; Meltham, Mr; Niner, Margaret; Sampson, Mr; Slinkton, Julius.

Great Expectations (1860–1). Novel. Published in weekly instalments in *All the Year Round*, 1 December 1860–3 August 1861.
Aged Parent; Amelia; Avenger, the; Barley, Clara; Barley, Old; Biddy; Bill; Black Bill; Brandley, Mrs; Camilla; Clarriker, Mr; Coiler, Mrs; Compeyson; Drummle, Bentley; Dunstable; Estella; Flopson; Gargery, Joe; Gargery, Mrs Joe; Georgiana; Handel; Havisham, Miss; Hubble, Mr and Mrs; Jack; Jaggers, Mr; Lazarus, Abraham; Magwitch, Abel; Mary Anne; Mike; Millers; Molly; Orlick, Dolge; Pepper; Pip; Pocket, Herbert; Pocket, Mr and Mrs Matthew; Pocket, Sarah; Potkins, William; Provis; Pumblechook, Uncle; Raymond, Cousin; Skiffins, Miss; Startop; Trabb, Mr; Trabb's Boy; Waldengarver, Mr; Wemmick, John; Whimple, Mrs; Wopsle, Mr.

The Uncommercial Traveller (1861, and later editions). Papers from *All the Year Round*. As with *Reprinted Pieces*, above, only papers relevant to this *Who's Who* have been used.
Anderson, Mr and Mrs John; Angelica; Antonio; Battens, Mr; Bogles, Mrs; Bolier, the Reverend Boanerges; Bones, Mr and Mrs Banjo; Bullfinch; Carlavero, Giovanni; Chips; Cleverley, Susannah and William; Cobby; Cocker, Mr Indignation; Dibble, Mr Sampson and Mrs Dorothy; Face-Maker, Monsieur the; Flanders, Sally; Flipfield, Mr; Globson, Bully; Grazinglands, Mr and Mrs Alexander; Green, Lucy; Jack, Dark; Jack, Mercantile; Jobsons, the; Joseph and Celia; Kinch, Horace; Kindheart, Mr; Klem, Mr, Mrs and Miss; Mayday; Mellows, J.; Mercy; Miggott, Mrs; Mitts, Mrs; Murderer, Captain; Oakum-Head; Onowenever, Mrs; Pangloss; Parkle, Mr; Pegg; Quickear; Quinch, Mrs; Saggers, Mrs; Salcy, Monsieur P.; Sharpeye; Specks, Joe; Squires, Olympia; Straudenheim; Sweeney, Mrs; Testator, Mr; Timpson; Trampfoot; Uncommercial Traveller, the; Ventriloquist, Monsieur the; Victualler, Mr Licensed; Weedle, Anastatia; White, Betsey; Wiltshire.

Our Mutual Friend (1864–5). Novel. Published in monthly parts, May 1864–November 1865.
Akersham, Sophronia; Analytical Chemist, the; Bar; Blight; Bocker, Tom; Boffin, Nicodemus; Boffin, Mrs Henrietta; Boots and Brewer; Cleaver, Fanny; Dolls, Mr; Fledgeby, 'Fascination'; Glamour, Bob; Gliddery, Bob; Goody Mrs; Grompus, Mr; Gruff and Glum; Handford, Julius; Harmon, John; Harrison; Hawkinson, Aunt;

Headstone, Bradley; Hexam, Charley; Hexam, Gaffer; Hexam, Lizzie; Higden, Betty; Inspector, Mr; Joey, Captain; Johnny; Jonathan; Jones, George; Kibble, Jacob; Lammle, Alfred and Sophronia; Lightwood, Mortimer; Mary Anne; Milvey, the Reverend Frank, and family; Mullins, Jack; Peecher, Miss Emma; Podsnap, Georgiana; Podsnap, John; Podsnap, Mrs; Potterson, Miss Abbey; Riah; Riderhood, Pleasant; Riderhood, Rogue; Rokesmith, John; Sampson, George; Sloppy; Snigsworth, Lord; Sprodgkin, Mrs; Swoshle, Mrs Henry George Alfred; Tapkinses, the; Tippins, Lady; Toddles and Poddles; Tootle, Tom; Twemlow, Melvin; Veneering, Hamilton and Anastasia; Venus, Mr; Wegg, Silas; Wilfer, Bella; Wilfer, Lavinia; Wilfer, Mrs; Wilfer, Reginald; Williams, William; Wrayburn, Eugene; Wren, Jenny; Young Blight.

'George Silverman's Explanation' (1868). Short story. Published in *The Atlantic Monthly*, January–March 1868 and in *All the Year Round*, 1, 15 and 29 February 1868.
Fareway; Gimblet, Brother; Hawkyard, Verity; Parksop, Brother; Silverman, George; Sylvia; Wharton, Granville.

'A Holiday Romance' (1868). Four short stories, published in *Our Young Folks* (Boston, USA) in January, March, April and May 1868.
Alicia, Princess; Alicumpaine, Mrs; Ashford, Nettie; Black, Mrs; Boldheart, Captain; Boozey, William; Brown; Certainpersonio, Prince; Chopper, Mr; Drowvey, Miss; Emilia; Grandmarina, Fairy; Grimmer, Miss; Jane; Lemon, Mrs; Orange, Mrs; Peggy; Pickles; Rainbird, Alice; Redforth, Bob; Tinkling, William; Watkins the First; White.

The Mystery of Edwin Drood (1870). Unfinished novel. Published in monthly parts, April–September 1870. Only six of the projected twelve parts appeared.
Bazzard; Billickin, Mrs; Brobity, Miss; Bud, Rosa; Chinaman, Jack; Crisparkle, Mrs; Crisparkle, the Reverend Septimus; Datchery, Dick; Dean, the; Deputy; Drood, Edwin; Durdles; Ferdinand, Miss; Giggles, Miss; Grewgious, Hiram; Honeythunder, Luke; Jasper, John; Jennings, Miss; Joe; Landless, Neville and Helena; Lobley; Porters, Mr; Puffer, Princess; Reynolds, Miss; Rickitts, Miss; Sapsea, Thomas; Tartar, Lieutenant; Tisher, Mrs; Tope, Mr and Mrs; Twinkleton, Miss; Winks.

The principal non-fictional works by Dickens, not used in this *Who's Who*, are *American Notes* (1842), *Pictures from Italy* (1846), *The Life of our Lord* (written, 1846; published, 1934), and *A Child's History of England* (serialised in *Household Words*, 25 January 1851–10 December 1853). Other omissions are *The Lazy Tour of Two Idle Apprentices* (written jointly with Wilkie Collins and published in *Household Words*, October 1857) and later collections of Dickens's uncollected writings.

Introduction

Dickens enthusiastically created more memorable characters than any other English novelist. George Newlin, in his *Everyone in Dickens* (1995), calculates that there are 'a total of 3,592 name usages, and nearly that many named characters' in Dickens's fiction. When generic characters and the names of historical, mythical, biblical and other non-Dickensian characters are included, the total, according to Newlin, is '13,143 listings plus 95 documented, unused coinages' (I, p. xx). This *Who's Who in Dickens* includes about 1,650 personages (and a few animals and birds) from the main body of Dickens's work: the fiction and essays, as collected in the Oxford Illustrated Dickens and similar editions, and the plays. I have tried to include everyone of interest and importance and hope I have not omitted anyone's favourite character. My aim has been to give fuller accounts of the major characters than are found in many reference books, noting some of Dickens's possible sources and referring, in a limited way, to critical opinion, especially when questions of influence and interpretation have arisen (as in his depictions of Mr Boffin, Miss Mowcher, Riah and Harold Skimpole).

From the beginning of his career, Dickens's characters seized the imagination of his readers, who eagerly followed their fortunes and misfortunes as his serial stories unrolled. They rejoiced in Wellerisms and wept over the deaths of Little Nell and Paul Dombey. Some of the characters' names rapidly became household words to represent human traits or things and have remained part of our vocabulary: Gamp (an umbrella), Micawberism (jaunty improvidence), Podsnappery (British Philistinism) and Scrooge (a miser) can be found in current dictionaries. When Thackeray referred to 'Madame Mantalini's bill' in Chapter 10 of *The Great Hoggarty Diamond* (1841) and to 'old Weller' in Chapter 7 of *Vanity Fair* (1847–8), he took it for granted that his readers would recognise the allusions to *Nicholas Nickleby* and *Pickwick Papers*. John Leech, imitating George Cruikshank's illustration, drew Henry Brougham asking for more in a *Punch* cartoon on 30 March 1844, knowing that everyone was familiar with Oliver Twist's request. Frequent use was subsequently made in *Punch* (which had begun in July 1841) of Dickensian characters: the Artful Dodger, Mrs Gamp, Mr Bumble, Fagin, Mr Pecksniff, and so on. As Walter Dexter commented in the *Dickensian*, they 'are brought in over and over again to give point more surely than any amount of words could do' (1935, Vol. 31, p. 264).

Commemorations of Dickens inevitably, it seems, involve memories of his characters. Robert William Buss's popular (though unfinished) water-colour, 'Dickens's Dream', which he painted soon after the novelist's death and which now hangs in Dickens House, London, shows the novelist in his chair in his library at Gad's Hill Place with Little Dorrit on his knee, Paul Dombey and Little Nell on his immediate right, and many of the other creatures of his imagination around him. Almost a century later, when his house in Devonshire Terrace, London, was demolished in the early 1960s a sculptured panel by Estcourt J. Clack was placed on a wall near the site showing Dickens with characters who appeared in the fiction that he wrote there:

Little Nell and her grandfather, Barnaby Rudge, Scrooge, Mrs Gamp, Mr Dombey and Paul, and Mr Micawber. Citing these artists reminds us that Dickens's characters have fascinated and challenged numerous illustrators, some of whom are represented in this book. Actors have been similarly excited by them and have brought them memorably to life on stage and screen. Can we ever forget Bernard Miles's Joe Gargery in David Lean's film, *Great Expectations* (1946), David Threlfall's Smike in the Royal Shakespeare Company's production of *Nicholas Nickleby* (1980), or Sir John Mills's Chuffey in David Lodge's televised version of *Martin Chuzzlewit* (1994)?

Like his readers and the audiences at his public readings, with whom he constantly felt himself in sympathy, Dickens experienced deeply emotional affinities with his characters. On the day when he had written his account of the death of little Paul Dombey, he wandered through the streets of Paris on that night (14 January 1847) in a mood of desolation. On another occasion, his daughter, Mamie, resting unobserved on a sofa, remembered seeing him at work, going back and forth between his desk and a mirror, making facial contortions in front of the glass and talking to himself: she knew that 'with his natural intensity he had thrown himself completely into the character that he was creating, and that for the time being he had not only lost sight of his surroundings, but had actually become in action, as in imagination, the creature of his pen' (Collins 1981: 121–2). Dickens intensively gave voice, facial expression and gesture to his characters in the public readings he gave in Britain and America from the 1850s onwards. In his World's Classics edition of *Charles Dickens: Sikes and Nancy and Other Public Readings* (1983), Philip Collins quotes from an American observer writing in the *Portland (Maine) Transcript* on 4 February 1868:

> At one moment he is savage old Scrooge, at the next, his jolly nephew, and in the twinkling of an eye little timid, lisping Bob Cratchit appears. All this is effected by the play of features as well as the varying tones of voice. . . . And then he not only personates his characters, he performs their actions. . . . But then the man himself is also there. Dickens, the author, comes in at intervals to enjoy his own fun; you see him in the twinkle of the eye and the curve of the mouth.
>
> (p. 2)

Discussion of the reality or otherwise of Dickens's characters has always taken place. But no general definitions can possibly apply. Some of Dickens's personages are exaggerations (of virtue and vice, for example, as in Agnes Wickfield and Quilp), others are caricatures (of the aristocracy, for example, as represented by Sir Mulberry Hawk), others are Jonsonian embodiments of 'humours' (such as Pecksniff and Uriah Heep), and others have psychological complexity (such as Miss Dartle and Lizzie Hexam). Some have to be judged with reference to their social and cultural context: on the one hand, codes of Victorian morality may have inhibited Dickens on occasions (especially in his treatment of seduction and 'fallen women,' as in the story of Little Em'ly and Steerforth), and, on the other hand, the *laissez-faire* spirit of the age may have resulted in his depiction of colourful and resilient human traits that were necessary for survival in an environment much harsher than our present-day surroundings (as in his portrayals of Mr Jingle and Mr Micawber). We can note Dickens's powerful presentations of self-tormented men and women, like Bradley Headstone and Miss Wade; his relish of the grotesque and macabre, realised in his characterisation of Dennis, the hangman, and Grandfather Smallweed; his fascination with female role-reversal, seen in the parental concerns of young women such as Little Nell, Little Dorrit and Jenny Wren; his amused sympathies with poor clerks and men of similar social status, like Bob Cratchit, John Chivery and R.W. Wilfer; his many portraits of lawyers and others in the legal profession, including Sampson Brass, Mr Wickfield and Mr Tulkinghorn; his array of criminals, swindlers, misers and usurers, among whom Bill Sikes and Scrooge have become household words; his gallery of widows and landladies, such as Mrs Bardell, Mrs Gamp and Mrs Billickin; and his affectionate portrayals of the simple-minded (Barnaby Rudge, Mr Dick and Maggy). Then there are the orphaned, waif-like or pathetic children, who moved and saddened contemporary readers: among these children, of different social classes, were Oliver Twist, Dick (Oliver's friend), the boys at Dotheboys Hall, Paul Dombey and Johnny (Betty Higden's great-grandson).

Indeed, all the classes of Victorian urban society are to be found in his fiction: the old aristocracy (Cousin Feenix and Sir Leicester Dedlock), 'swells' (Jem Harthouse and Edmund Sparkler), the speculators and the nouveaux riches (the Merdles and the Veneerings), middle-class professional people (Doctor Strong, Allan Woodcourt and Mr Jaggers), self-made men (Mr Bounderby, on the one hand, and Mr Rouncewell, the northern ironmaster, on the other), lower middle-class shopkeepers and clerks (Mr Venus and Mr Guppy), shabby–genteel men (Dick Swiveller), the working class (Mr Toodle and Mr Plornish), fortune-hunters and adventurers (Montague Tigg and Rigaud), outcasts (Rudge and Martha Endell), and the downtrodden (the Marchioness and Jo). Rural characters are comparatively rare, though we remember John Browdie, the Peggotty family and Joe Gargery. Nearly all of these people have occupations. In his *Everyone in Dickens*, George Newlin lists 1024 occupations and vocations for males and 137 for females, noting that a few are pursued by both sexes (1995, volume III, pp. 214–20). Drawing on a more restricted range of Dickens's work (comparable to the range covered in this *Who's Who*), Gilbert A. Pierce and William A. Wheeler in their *Dickens Dictionary* (new edition, 1892) compiled 'A Classed List of Characters, Etc.' In that, about 150 professions, trades and occupations can be distinguished, including 47 clerks, 16 landladies, 13 merchants, 6 turnkeys, and 6 undertakers (ibid.: 577–86).

For a brief assessment of Dickens's achievement in characterisation, we can turn to John Forster's typically judicious observation on the subject. As *Pickwick Papers* developed, 'the art was seen [Forster writes] which can combine traits vividly true to particular men or women with propensities common to all mankind'. This was an art, so Forster goes on to say, that has its 'highest expression in Fielding' (1928: Book 9, Ch. 1). Fielding had argued in Book 3, Chapter 1 of *Joseph Andrews* (1742) that he described 'not men, but manners; not an individual, but a species'. The sharp-tongued Mrs Tow-wouse and her husband, the innkeeper (the kind of people Dickens put into his fiction a hundred years later), who had appeared in Book 1 of *Joseph Andrews*, represented certain general human characteristics:

> where extreme turbulency of temper, avarice, and an insensibility of human misery, with a degree of hypocrisy, have united in a female composition, Mrs Tow-wouse was that woman; and where a good inclination, eclipsed by a poverty of spirit and understanding, hath glimmered forth in a man, that man hath been no other than her sneaking husband.

Dickens's characters often strike us with their uniqueness rather than their representative qualities. But the combination of the individual and the general is sometimes encapsulated in the names Dickens gives them. A reviewer of *The Haunted Man*, writing in *Macphail's Edinburgh Ecclesiastical Journal* (January 1849), tartly observed that generally 'Mr Dickens, as if in revenge for his own queer name, does bestow still queerer ones upon his fictitious creations' (Collins 1971: 180). But he took much care over the choice of names. We know that he pondered over the name of the hero of his most famous novel. Dickens's first choice was Thomas Mag, which he changed to David Mag before hitting on David Copperfield. His Book of Memoranda contained Christian names of boys and girls from the Privy Council Education Lists and lists of other names of his own invention (some of which later appeared in his fiction). A few of the names he uses seem particularly eccentric, perhaps for comic or melodramatic effect or for the sake of memorability, such as Pickwick (although we know that an actual Moses Pickwick existed and is mentioned in Chapter 35 of *Pickwick Papers*), Nickleby and Chuzzlewit. At the other extreme, Dickens very occasionally uses unexceptional names for worthy people: Geoffrey Haredale, Mary Graham, Allan Woodcourt – but these are hard to find. A few are crude indications of 'humours' or occupations: Cheeryble, M'Choakumchild, and assorted members of the Mudfog Association. But many are brilliant inventions, which suggest through onomatopoeia, connotation or symbol the traits and function of the personage in question: Bounderby, Crisparkle, Nandy, Pumblechook and Scrooge. Echoes of his own name and initials, perhaps indicating wry self-reflection, may or may not be deliberate: David Copperfield, Mr Dick, Dick Swiveller, Richard Doubledick and Dick Datchery.

The names can startle, amuse or intrigue us when they are introduced. In any event, most of Dickens's characters spring to life as soon as we encounter them, by means of his sharply detailed and newly minted descriptions of their physical appearance and actions, their principal qualities of temperament, their occupations and their surroundings. It is relevant also to bear in mind his love of the theatre and his own vivacious accomplishments as actor, reader and public speaker. A striking entrance or beginning is an essential stage technique. His first published story ('A Dinner at Poplar Walk,' which was later entitled 'Mr Minns and his Cousin') opens with an economical and exact placing of the hero, whose name, with its combination of pompous Christian name and feeble-sounding surname, is in itself a perfect indication of the kind of man he is:

> Mr Augustus Minns was a bachelor, of about forty as he said – of about eight-and-forty as his friends said. He was always exceedingly clean, precise, and tidy; perhaps somewhat priggish, and the most retiring man in the world. He usually wore a brown frock-coat without a wrinkle, light inexplicables without a spot, a neat neckerchief with a remarkably neat tie, and boots without a fault; moreover, he always carried a brown silk umbrella with an ivory handle.

The amused perception (notice the silk and ivory in the umbrella), comedy and rhythm of these sentences from the earliest example of Dickens's fiction were repeated, with variations and refinements, in his portrayals of people throughout his work. In *Our Mutual Friend*, his last completed novel, he writes with splendidly suitable artifice of the guests at the Veneering's dinner table, whom we first see reflected in the 'great looking-glass:' the Veneerings themselves, Mr and Mrs Podsnap, Twemlow, Lady Tippins, and Mortimer Lightwood:

> Reflects Eugene, friend of Mortimer; buried alive in the back of his chair, behind a shoulder – with a powder-epaulette on it – of the mature young lady, and gloomily resorting to the champagne chalice proffered by the Analytical Chemist. Lastly, the looking-glass reflects Boots and Brewer, and two other stuffed Buffers interposed between the rest of the company and possible accidents.

(Book 1, Ch. 2)

Dickens's unflagging inventiveness is seen in some of the last pages he wrote, when he describes Mrs Billickin's coming to greet Mr Grewgious and Rosa: 'She came languishing out of her own exclusive back parlour, with the air of having been expressly brought-to for the purpose, from an accumulation of several swoons' (*The Mystery of Edwin Drood*, Ch. 22).

Many other instances will be found in the entries in this *Who's Who*, but there are hundreds more that are unrecorded here, since Dickens sees everybody, however infinitesimal his or her role, with unequalled clarity. Here are just two examples where he gives an immediate identity and emotional emphasis to unnamed people on the margins of his narrative. Just before little Paul Dombey is christened, a wedding is taking place in the cold church: 'The bride was too old and the bridegroom too young, and a superannuated beau with one eye and an eye-glass stuck in its blank companion, was giving away the lady, while the friends were shivering' (*Dombey and Son*, Ch. 5). Esther Summerson sees the apprentices 'to the trade of dancing' at Mr Turveydrop's academy:

> Besides the melancholy boy, who, I hoped, had not been made so by waltzing alone in the empty kitchen, there were two other boys, and one dirty little limp girl in a gauzy dress. Such a precocious little girl, with such a dowdy bonnet on (that, too, of a gauzy texture), who brought her sandalled shoes in an old threadbare velvet reticule. Such mean little boys, when they were not dancing, with string, and marbles, and cramp-bones in their pockets, and the most untidy legs and feet – and heels particularly.
>
> (*Bleak House*, Ch. 38)

Dickens hears as well as sees his characters. Again, the theatrical element comes to mind. His invention of distinctive and appropriate speech-patterns, or idiolects, has always struck commentators, who have, it must be admitted, sometimes found tiresome his use of catch-phrases and other repetitions (including gestures and involuntary bodily movements). He may have found some reiteration necessary because of the serialisation of his novels, which meant that he had to remind his readers each month or week of some salient characteristics of his men and women. In any case, many of us readers enjoy the device, in the same way as we enjoy hearing (in films, plays, broadcasts and friends' conversation) and saying such reassuring phrases ourselves. But apart from the familiar verbal tics of Captain Cuttle ('When found, make a note of'), Uriah Heep ('I'm a very umble person'), Mrs Micawber ('I never will desert Mr Micawber'), Mr Wemmick ('portable property') and others, there is his astounding linguistic inventiveness gloriously apparent in Sam Weller's spry observations, in the outpourings of Mrs Nickleby, Miggs, Mrs Gamp, Flora Finching and Mrs Lirriper, and in the near-apoplectic and self-congratulatory comments made by Major Bagstock. Dickens's scrupulously contrived phrasing of Miss Dartle's speech, with its cunningly naïve questions, precisely reflects her tortuous thoughts. Quotations from these idiolects and many others will be found in the accounts of characters in this book.

The complicated rhetoric, controlled and yet passionate, of the exchanges between Carker and Edith Dombey, especially in their final confrontation, may be called melodramatic by some critics, but it is fitting for a climactic occasion that is so intense and devious. Edith declaims to Carker:

> But if I tell you that the lightest touch of your hand makes my blood cold with antipathy; that from the hour when I first saw and hated you, to now, when my

instinctive repugnance is enhanced by every minute's knowledge of you I have since had, you have been a loathsome creature to me which has not its like on earth; how then?

(Dombey and Son, Ch. 54)

Dickens's rendering of Sir John Chester's conversation in *Barnaby Rudge* is a *tour de force*; his evasions, sneers and cool (even comic) utterances are consistently those of a gentleman in a Restoration or eighteenth-century play:

> Foh! . . . The very atmosphere that centaur [i.e., Hugh] has breathed, seems tainted with the cart and ladder. Here, Peak. Bring some scent and sprinkle the floor, and take away the chair he sat upon, and air it; and dash a little of that mixture upon me. I am stifled!

(Ch. 23)

In a quiet and non-theatrical mode, the sweet and self-effacing nature of Esther Summerson is conveyed in the easy syntax and vocabulary of her narrative (contrasted with the heightened, historic-present narrative of the other parts of *Bleak House*), despite the occasional presence of Dickensian wit and imagery:

> I don't know how it is, I seem to be always writing about myself. I mean all the time to write about other people, and I try to think about myself as little as possible, and I am sure, when I find myself coming into the story again, I am really vexed and say, 'Dear, dear, you tiresome little creature, I wish you wouldn't!' but it is all of no use.

(Ch. 9)

And so one can go on, demonstrating patterns of language that Dickens uses to identify his characters and maintain their existence.

Many biographers and commentators have suggested that a character's existence sometimes has its origins in the novelist's personal life. His first authoritative biographer, John Forster, discussed (particularly in Book 6, Ch. 7 of his *Life of Dickens*) a number of prototypes, including John Dickens (Dickens's father), Walter Savage Landor and Leigh Hunt as the bases of Mr Micawber, Lawrence Boythorn and Harold Skimpole respectively. Forster also tackled the problem of the relationship between David Copperfield and his creator, as we can see in the relevant entry in this book. Subsequent biographies (notably those by F.G. Kitton, Edgar Johnson, Fred Kaplan and Peter Ackroyd) and articles (especially in the *Dickensian*) have extended such explorations and at least two books have been written on the subject: Edwin Pugh's *The Dickens Originals* (1912) and Doris Alexander's *Creating Characters with Charles Dickens* (1991). A controversial area of influence is that concerning Dickens's portrayal of women. In *Dickens and Women* (1983), Michael Slater explains and discusses the relationships between the women in Dickens's life and the women in his fiction. There is little doubt that Dickens transformed his mother, Elizabeth Dickens, and the middle-aged Maria Winter (formerly Maria Beadnell) into Mrs Nickleby and Flora Finching. Memories of the youthful Maria, whom he had loved as a young man, inform other portrayals, possibly including Dora, David Copperfield's first wife. In 1837, Dickens's 17-year-old sister-in-law, Mary Hogarth, died in his arms. This death of a girl whom he loved and idealised haunted his memory. Her fictional counterparts include, with different emphases, Rose Maylie, Kate Nickleby, Little Nell and Agnes Wickfield. As for Ellen Ternan, the young actress with whom Dickens had a loving relationship in his later life, some biographers have seen her name and her supposed nature reflected in heroines of his later fiction: Estella, Bella Wilfer and Helena Land-less. Michael Slater argues, however, that such identifications are unsound, since (among other things) 'Estella and Bella, for example, are clearly developments or modifications of a certain type of female character which Dickens began to explore in Edith Dombey, long before Ellen entered his life' (p. 213). His comment reminds us that however fascinating (and occasionally productive) we may find aspects of Dickens's psychology and the relationships between his life and work, we need to take into account his art as a novelist as well as relevant literary, cultural and social conventions. Above all, we must remember the obvious fact that Dickens was creating imaginative worlds in his fiction.

Those worlds are populous. As Arthur Clennam, the Meagles family, Tattycoram, Miss Wade and their fellow-travellers disperse at the end of Book 1, Chapter 2 of *Little Dorrit*, Dickens comments:

And thus ever, by day and night, under the sun and under the stars, climbing the dusty hills and toiling along the weary plains, journeying by land and journeying by sea, coming and going so strangely, to meet and to act and react on one another, move all we restless travellers through the pilgrimage of life.

His own numerous 'restless travellers' come and go in the course of his narratives. Their meetings may be coincidental or arranged but are invariably purposeful. Dickens seems never to forget them, since they appear and reappear, weaving together the threads of plot, recalling important happenings, or serving new but convincing functions. Some of their family relationships derive from theatrical convention: the revelations concerning the parentage of Oliver Twist and Estella are the stuff of melodrama or popular comedy, although we should not overlook the ingenuity of Dickens's plots. His control over his characters remains firm and committed to the end of each work. The final chapters of the novels often give us the future fortunes of all the principal characters and some of the minor ones. The ending of *The Old Curiosity Shop* has an astonishing parade. We learn there what happened to Sampson and Sally Brass, Quilp's remains, Tom Scott, Mrs Quilp and Mrs Jiniwin, the Garlands, Whisker (the pony), Dick Swiveller and the Marchioness, Mr Chuckster, Isaac List, Jowl, James Groves, Frederick Trent, the Single Gentleman, the village schoolmaster, Mrs Jarley, Codlin and Short, Kit Nubbles, and Barbara. Other major or minor connections that Dickens surprises us with as his stories develop may please us with their appropriateness or annoy us by their coincidence. Jem Hutley turns out to be Job Trotter's brother. Edith Dombey turns out to be Alice Marwood's first cousin. Miss Murdstone becomes Dora's companion. Mr Creakle becomes a magistrate and shows David Copperfield two prisoners: Uriah Heep and Littimer. Mr Boythorn used to be in love with Miss Barbary. The Dorrits and Clennams have had former crucial mutual involvements. Mr Jingle keeps mischievously popping up, and Monks and Rigaud haunt the action of *Oliver Twist* and *Little Dorrit*. And so on. Dickens has, we feel, relished giving us in each work of fiction an intricate world, in which his characters have played indispensable parts, not merely in the plot but in the complete texture of every novel and story. Few – if any – of his personages are superfluous.

For a final assessment we can turn to George Santayana's appreciative essay on Dickens in his *Soliloquies in England* (1922). Santayana writes that Dickens

has held the mirror up to nature, and of its reflected fragments has composed a fresh world, where the men and women differ from real people only in that they live in a literary medium, so that all ages and places may know them. And they are worth knowing, just as one's neighbours are, for their picturesque characters and their pathetic fates. Their names should be in every child's mouth; they ought to be adopted members of every household. Their stories cause the merriest and the sweetest chimes to ring in the fancy, without confusing our moral judgement or alienating our interest from the motley commonplaces of daily life.

(p. 72)

A

Adams (DC) The head boy at Doctor Strong's school in Canterbury, where David Copperfield was a pupil. 'He looked like a young clergyman, in his white cravat, but he was very affable and good-humoured.' (16, 18)

Adams, Captain (NN) One of Lord Frederick Verisopht's seconds in his fatal duel with Sir Mulberry Hawk. The other second was Mr Westwood. (50)

Adams, Jane (SYC) The little housemaid's friend, who 'comes all out of breath to redeem a solemn promise of taking her in, under cover of the confusion, to see the breakfast table spread forth in state, and – sight of sights! – her young mistress [Miss Emma Fielding] ready dressed for church [for her wedding to young Mr Harvey].' ('The Young Couple')

Adams, Mr (HD) Mr Sampson's clerk in the Life Assurance Office.

Aged Parent (GE) Mr Wemmick's affectionate term for his father, with whom he lives at Walworth. He was 'a very old man in a flannel coat: clean, cheerful, comfortable, and well cared for, but intensely deaf'. He was proud of his son, who (in his opinion) 'is a wonderful hand at his business' (i.e., his work as clerk to Mr Jaggers, the solicitor), although he was originally 'brought up ... to the wine-coopering'. When giving away Miss Skiffins as his son's bride, he confuses the clergyman because his deafness prevents him from following the wedding ceremony. (25, 37, 45, 48, 51, 55)

Agnes (SB) Mrs Bloss's maid, who in her 'cherry-coloured merino dress, open-work stockings, and shoes with sandals' looked like 'a disguised Columbine'. She indignantly reported to her mistress that Mr Tibbs wanted to kiss her on the kitchen stairs. ('Tales: The Boarding-House')

Akerman, Mr (BR) Richard Akerman, who was an actual historical figure (1722–92), was the keeper of Newgate Prison from 1754 until his death. In the novel, he unsuccessfully exhorts the mob during the Gordon Riots to disperse when they threaten to attack the prison, which they go on to destroy by fire. (64, 77)

Akershem, Sophronia (OMF) *See* **Lammle, Alfred and Sophronia.**

Alice (NN) The youngest of 'The Five Sisters of York', in the grey-headed gentleman's story of that name. 'But if the four elder sisters were lovely, how beautiful was the youngest, a fair creature of sixteen!' (6)

Alice, Mistress (MHC) The Bowyer's daughter, who was the heroine of Magog's tale. (1)

Alicia, Princess (HR) The heroine of Miss Alice Rainbird's 'romance'.

Alick (SB) A 'damp earthy child in red socks', who attempts a dance on the Gravesend boat. ('Scenes: The River')

Alicumpaine, Mrs (HR) A friend of Mrs

Orange's in Miss Nettie Ashford's 'romance'.

Allen, Arabella (PP) Benjamin Allen's sister, whom he hoped to marry to his friend, Bob Sawyer. At the wedding of Mr Trundle and Isabella Wardle at Dingley Dell, she was the 'young lady with black eyes, an arch smile, and a pair of remarkably nice boots with fur round the tops', who captivates Mr Winkle. They eventually marry in secret. When old Mr Winkle, who disapproved of the match, meets her, he is immediately won over: 'You *are* a very charming little daughter-in-law, after all!' (28, 30, 38, 39, 47, 53, 54, 56, 57)

Allen, Benjamin (PP) A medical student and close friend of Bob Sawyer, to whom he plans to marry Arabella, his sister. He was 'a coarse, stout, thick-set young man, with black hair cut rather short, and a white face cut rather long. He was embellished with spectacles, and wore a white neckerchief. . . . He presented, altogether, rather a mildewy appearance, and emitted a fragrant odour of full-flavoured Cubas.' He and Bob Sawyer later take over a medical practice in Bath, but with no success ('Sawyer, late Nockemorf'). Mr Pickwick manages to reconcile him to Mr Winkle's marriage to Arabella. He and Bob Sawyer eventually gain medical appointments in India. (30, 32, 38, 48, 50–2, 54, 57)

Alphonse (NN) Mrs Wititterley's page. He was 'so little . . . that his body would not hold, in ordinary array, the number of small buttons which are indispensable to a page's costume, and they were consequently obliged to be stuck on four abreast'. As for his French name (which suits the pretensions of Mr and Mrs Wititterley), 'if ever an Alphonse carried plain Bill in his face and figure, that page was the boy'. (21, 28, 33)

Amelia (GE) The wife of Bill, whom Mr

Jaggers is defending. He peremptorily tells her that as long as she has paid Wemmick, his clerk, she has nothing else to do. (20)

Amelia (SB) One of a stout lady's four daughters playing a game of chance in the library at Ramsgate. Her mother commends her 'nice figure' to a thin youth. ('Tales: The Tuggses at Ramsgate')

Analytical Chemist, the (OMF) The Veneerings' 'melancholy retainer', who attends the dinner guests 'like a gloomy Analytical Chemist'. His silent presence is like that of a 'malignant star'. When Veneering wonders how people can live beyond their means, 'the Analytical Chemist going round with champagne, looks very much as if *he* could give them a pretty good idea how people did that, if he had a mind.' Dickens had created a similar ominous servant in Mr Merdle's butler in *Little Dorrit*: 'Mr Merdle didn't want him, and was put out of countenance when the great creature looked at him.' *See* also the Avenger, Pip's man-servant. All three employers – Veneering, Merdle, and Pip – are doomed to fail, in various degrees. (I: 2, 10, 17; II: 3, 16; III: 17)

Anderson, Mr and Mrs John (UT) A tramp and his wife, 'whose only improvidence appears to have been, that they spent the last of their little All on soap. They are a man and woman spotless to behold'. ('Tramps')

Angelica (UT) A sweetheart of the youthful Uncommercial Traveller, who remembers going with her to a City church 'on account of a shower'. ('City of London Churches')

Anne (DS) One of Mr Dombey's housemaids, who marries Towlinson, the butler. (31, 35, 39)

Anny (OT) An old crone, who was an inmate of the workhouse where Oliver Twist was born. She and Martha, another crone, looking and listening through chinks in the door, had witnessed Mrs Corney taking the pawnbroker's receipt from Sally, as she lay on her deathbed. (24, 51)

Antonio (UT) A swarthy young Spanish sailor, who plays the guitar. ('Poor Mercantile Jack')

Artful Dodger, the (OT) *See* **Dawkins, Jack**.

Ashford, Nettie (HR) A girl 'aged half-past six', who tells the story of Mrs Orange, Mrs Lemon and Mrs Alicumpaine.

Atherfield, Mrs (CS) A 'bright-eyed blooming young wife who was going out to join her husband in California'. She and her 3-year-old daughter, Lucy, are passengers on the *Golden Mary*. But Lucy dies of exposure in an open boat after the shipwreck. Dickens may have based Lucy on Lucy Stroughill, a friend of his childhood in Chatham. *See* **Manette, Lucie**. ('The Wreck of the Golden Mary')

Aunt, Mr F's (LD) The aunt of Flora Finching's late husband, who had bequeathed her to Flora in his will 'as a separate legacy'. She 'was an amazing little old woman, with a face like a staring wooden doll too cheap for expression, and a stiff yellow wig perched unevenly on the top of her head, as if the child who owned the doll had driven a tack through it anywhere, so that it only got fastened on. Another remarkable thing in this little old woman was, that the same child seemed to have damaged her face in two or three places with some blunt instrument in the nature of a spoon; her countenance, and particularly the tip of her nose, presenting the phenomena of several dints, generally answering to the bowl of that article.' Her 'major characteristics ... were extreme severity and grim taciturnity; sometimes interrupted by a propensity to offer remarks in a deep warning voice, which, being totally uncalled for by anything said by anybody, and traceable to no association of ideas, confounded and terrified the mind.' When, for example, Flora calls on Arthur Clennam to offer (in her usual confused manner) her congratulations and best wishes on his new business enterprise with Daniel Doyce, Mr F's Aunt suddenly exclaims, 'There's mile-stones on the Dover road!' Her final fierce and cryptic exclamation, made when she, Flora and Little Dorrit are in the pie-shop near the Marshalsea Prison, is, 'Bring him for'ard, and I'll chuck him out o' winder!' In his essay on *Little Dorrit*, Lionel Trilling says that Mr F's Aunt is 'one of Dickens's most astonishing ideas, the embodiment of senile rage and spite, flinging to the world the crusts of her buttered toast. "He has a proud stomach, this chap," she cries when poor Arthur hesitates over her dreadful gift. "Give him a meal of chaff!" It is the voice of one of the Parcae [i.e., the three Fates in classical mythology]' (1952: xiii-xiv). (I: 13, 23, 24, 35; II, 9, 34)

Avenger, the (GE) Pip's name for Pepper, his servant at Barnard's Inn, who 'haunted' his existence. (27, 28, 30, 34)

Ayresleigh, Mr (PP) A debtor Mr Pickwick met in Namby's sponging-house. He was 'a middle-aged man in a very old suit of black, who looked pale and haggard, and paced up and down the room incessantly; stopping, now and then, to look with great anxiety out of the window as if he expected somebody, and then resuming his walk'. (40)

B

Babley, Richard (DO) *See* **Dick, Mr.**

Bachelor, the (OCS) A 'little old gentleman', who had been a college friend of the clergyman of the village where Little Nell and her Grandfather finally found refuge and who had lived with him ever since the clergyman's wife had died. He was 'the active spirit of the place, the adjuster of all differences, the promoter of all merry-makings, the dispenser of his friend's bounty, and of no small charity of his own besides; the universal mediator, comforter, and friend'. He was always called the Bachelor, perhaps because of college honours or because he was unmarried. His letter to Mr Garland, his brother, leads to the journey to the village undertaken by Mr Garland, the Single Gentleman, and Kit Nubbles, and to their sad discoveries of Nell's death and her broken-hearted Grandfather. (52–55, 68, 69, 73)

Badger, Bayham (BH) A medical practitioner, 'who had a good practice in Chelsea, and attended a large public Institution besides' and who was a cousin of Mr Kenge, the solicitor. Thanks to the latter's recommendation, he supervises Richard Carstone's short-lived medical studies. He was 'a pink, fresh-faced, crisp-looking gentleman, with a weak voice, white teeth, light hair, and surprised eyes'. He admires his wife exceedingly, 'but principally, and to begin with, on the curious ground . . . of her having had three husbands'. Coincidentally or not, Mr Badger's Christian name is also the name of the London street where the Dickens family lived (at No. 16) in 1822–

3 on moving from Chatham. (13, 17, 30, 50)

Badger, Mrs Bayham (BH) The wife of the medical practitioner described above. 'She was a lady of about fifty . . . youthfully dressed, and of a very fine complexion', who used rouge a little. Her two previous husbands were Captain Swosser, RN and Professor Dingo. Because of her habits of observation formed during those marriages, she soon detected Richard Carstone's lack of commitment to his medical studies, as she revealed to Esther Summerson and Ada Clare. (13, 17)

Bagman, the (PP) A 'stout, hale personage of about forty, with only one eye – a very bright black eye, which twinkled with a roguish expression of fun and good humour'. He appears twice in the novel, first at the Peacock, Eatanswill and then at the Bush Inn, Bristol, telling a story on each occasion: 'The Bagman's Story' and 'The Bagman's Uncle'. (14, 48, 49)

Bagnet, Matthew (BH) 'An ex-artilleryman, tall and upright, with shaggy eyebrows, and whiskers like the fibres of a cocoa-nut, not a hair upon his head, and a torrid complexion. His voice, short, deep, and resonant, is not at all unlike the tones of the instrument to which he is devoted' (i.e., the bassoon). He keeps a musician's shop at the Elephant and Castle and is a trusted friend and adviser of Mr George. He implicitly follows his wife's advice on all matters, although he never owns to his obedience in front of her, for the sake of discipline. In fact, his advice is: 'Whatever the old girl says, do – do it!' She often calls her husband 'Lignum', 'on account, as it is supposed, of Lignum Vitae having been his old regimental nickname when they first became acquainted, in compliment to the extreme hardness and toughness of his physiognomy'. (Lignum Vitae is the hard wood of a tropical American tree). His devotion to his wife is humorously and affectionately shown in the importance he gives to organising her birthday dinner. They have named their children Woolwich, Quebec and Malta after the army stations where they were born. (27, 34, 49, 52, 66)

Bagnet, Mrs (BH) The 'soldierly-looking', tough, resourceful but affectionate wife of Matthew Bagnet, She was 'rather large-boned, a little coarse in the grain, and freckled by the sun and wind, which have tanned her hair upon the forehead; but healthy, wholesome, and bright-eyed. A strong, busy, active, honest-faced woman of from forty-five to fifty.' One of her constant occupations is washing greens. She is greatly admired by her husband, who unquestioningly accepts her judgement in everything: 'She is Colour-Serjeant of the Nonpareil battalion', in his words. It is through her that Mrs Rouncewell and her long-lost son, George, are brought together – in fact, she travels to Lincolnshire to fetch Mrs Rouncewell to London. John Butt and Kathleen Tillotson point out in *Dickens at Work* that 'a brief note in *Household Words* on 6 September 1851 [only a few months before the serialisation of *Bleak House* began] had drawn attention to the difficult conditions in which soldiers' wives were living', and that these were the conditions in which 'Mrs Bagnet had learned to practise her virtues' (1957: 198–9). (27, 34, 49, 53, 55, 66)

Bagstock, Major Joseph (DS) The apo-plectic, 'wooden-featured, blue-faced Major', who has retired from service in India and is attended by 'a dark servant' (*see* **Native, the**). He has arrived at 'what is called in polite literature, the grand meridian of life [i.e., the age of fifty]'. He constantly boastfully refers to himself in the third person as a tough and artful fellow: 'he's hard-hearted, Sir, is Joe – he's tough, Sir, tough, and de-vilish sly!' Annoyed at his neighbour Miss Tox's rejection of his various forms of 'Platonic dalliance' because she has hopes of ensnaring the newly widowed Mr Dombey, he cultivates Dombey's acquaintance and warns him against her. Having become Dombey's close companion, he accompanies him to Leamington Spa, where he introduces him to Edith Granger, the widowed daughter of Mrs Skewton, who is one of the Major's old flames. With the support of Mrs Skewton, he contrives the marriage between Dombey and Edith. But he is quick to desert Dombey at his downfall, angrily asserting that 'Joe had been deceived, Sir, taken in, hoodwinked, blindfolded.' Nevertheless, the Major nearly chokes himself to death with laughter when his servant, the Native, reports Miss Tox's continued fidelity to Mr Dombey. (7, 10, 20, 21, 26, 27, 29, 31, 36, 40, 51, 58, 59)

Bailey, Captain (DC) An army officer, who makes David Copperfield jealous by dancing with the eldest Miss Larkins. (18)

Bailey, Young (MC) The lively, impudent 'small boy with a large red head, and no nose to speak of', who was the boot-boy and 'youthful porter' at Mrs Todgers's Commercial Boarding House (known simply as Todgers's). 'Benjamin was supposed to be the real name of this young retainer, but he was known by a great variety of names . . . . At the period of which we write, he was generally known among the gentlemen [who lodged at Todgers's] as Bailey junior; a name bestowed upon him in contra-distinction, perhaps, to Old Bailey; and possibly as involving the recollection of an unfortunate lady of the same name, who perished by her own hand early in life, and has been immortalised in a bal-lad.' (The ballad is 'Unfortunate Miss Bailey', which tells of her seduction and her hanging herself in her garters). He is later employed as a groom by Montague Tigg and much fancies himself as a knowing man-about-town. 'There's nothin' he don't know; that's my opin-ion,' observed Mrs Gamp. 'All the wick-edness of the world is Print to him.' After being seriously injured in the accident to the carriage taking Jonas Chuzzlewit and Montague Tigg to Salisbury, Bailey makes a surprising recovery, to the de-light of his friend and admirer, Poll Sweedlepipe: ' "What a boy he is!" cried the tender-hearted Poll, actually sobbing over him. "I never see sech a boy! It's all his fun. He's full of it. He shall go into the business along with me. I am determined he shall. We'll make it Sweedlepipe and Bailey. He shall have the sporting branch (what a one he'll be for the matches!) and me the shavin".' (8, 9, 11, 26–29, 32, 38, 41, 42, 49, 52)

Balderstone, Thomas (SB) Mrs Gat-tleton's rich brother ('Uncle Tom'), who has a remarkable knowledge of Shake-speare's plays. ('Tales: Mrs Joseph Porter')

Balim, Mr (SYG) He was renowned as 'the young ladies' young gentleman'.

Bamber, Jack (PP) The attorney's clerk, whom Mr Pickwick met at the Magpie and Stump and who told the 'Tale of the Queer Client'. He was 'a little yellow high-shouldered man', with 'a fixed grim smile perpetually on his countenance'. (20, 21) Bamber is also mentioned in *Master Humphrey's Clock* (4).

Banger, Captain (RP) A member of the vestry, who ridicules Mr Tiddypot's claim that water is not a necessary of life. ('Our Vestry')

Bangham, Mrs (LD) The charwoman and messenger at the Marshalsea Prison, who attended Mrs Dorrit at the birth of Amy. She 'was not a prisoner (though she had been once), but was the popular me-dium of communication with the outer world'. (I: 6, 7, 14; II: 19)

Banks, Major (HD) One of the names assumed by Meltham in tracking down Slinkton.

Bantam, Angelo Cyrus (PP) The Master of Ceremonies at Bath. He was 'a charm-ing young man of not much more than fifty', elegantly dressed and with much gold about his person. 'His features were contracted into a perpetual smile.' (35, 37)

Baps, Mr (DS) The dancing master at Doctor Blimber's school. (14)

Baptista, Giovanni The Genoese courier who tells the story of Clara and Signor Dellombra. ('To be Read at Dusk')

Baptiste (CS) A soldier billeted on the poor water-carrier in the French town where Mr The Englishman (i.e., Mr Langley) found Bebelle. ('Somebody's Luggage')

Bar (LD) A barrister, who is a regular guest at Mr Merdle's social gatherings. He has a 'little insinuating Jury-droop' and a 'persuasive eye-glass'. Based on Sir Fitzroy Kelly (1796–1880). (I: 21; II: 12, 16, 25)

Barbara (OCS) The Garlands' 'little servant-girl, very tidy, modest, and de-mure, but very pretty too'. When Kit Nubbles enters the Garlands' service, she is often jealously upset by his frequent expressions of admiration for Little Nell. But the 'sly little Barbara' eventually gets her reward: she and Kit marry and have several children (including Barbara, Abel, Dick and Jacob). Her mother became friendly with Mrs Nubbles when Kit took them to Astley's and went with her to visit him in prison. (22, 38–40, 68, 69, 73)

Barbary, Miss (BH) Lady Dedlock's harsh and secretive sister, who brings up Esther Summerson, claiming to be her godmother. In a 'cold, low voice', she tells Esther: 'Your mother, Esther, is your disgrace, as you were hers.' In his youth, Mr Boythorn had loved her, but (in Mr Jarndyce's words) she 'died to him'. (3, 29, 43)

Barbary, Mrs Captain (LD) In his account of the negotiations concerning Tip Dorrit's release from the Marshalsea Prison, Mr Plornish tells Arthur Clennam that she sold 'a remarkably fine grey gelding' for only £20 because it had run away with her at Cheltenham. Her husband, Captain Barbary, was a private friend of Captain Maroon's. (I: 12)

Barbox Brothers (CS) *See* **Jackson, Mr.**

Bardell, Mrs Martha (PP) Mr Pickwick's landlady in Goswell Street. She was 'the relict and sole executrix of a deceased custom-house officer' and 'a comely woman of bustling manners and agreeable appearance, with a natural genius for cooking, improved by study and long practice, into an exquisite talent'. She has one son, Tommy, an unpleasant boy of 10 or 11 years old. When Mr Pickwick broaches the subject of employing Sam Weller as his manservant, Mrs Bardell mistakes his words for a proposal of marriage and flings her arms round his neck, 'with a cataract of tears and a chorus of sobs'. She sues him for breach of promise and damages of £1500 and wins the case. Mr Pickwick is sent to prison, but she herself is also imprisoned in the Fleet for the costs. She is released when Mr Pickwick is persuaded to pay all the legal bills. Afterwards, she 'let lodgings to many conversable single gentlemen, with great profit, but never brought any more actions for breach of promise of marriage'. (12, 18, 20, 22, 26, 31, 34, 46, 47, 57)

Bark (RP) A 'lodging-house keeper and receiver of stolen goods' in Wentworth Street, Whitechapel. His 'kitchen is crammed full of thieves, holding a *conversazione* there by lamp-light' when the two policemen, Black and Green, look in. ('On Duty with Inspector Field')

Barker, Mrs (SYG) A lady of whom Mr Fairfax's opinion is asked. ('The Censorious Young Gentleman')

Barker, Phil (OT) A drunken criminal at The Three Cripples, which Fagin visits. (26)

Barker, William (SB) An omnibus 'cad' (i.e., conductor). ('Scenes: The Last Cab-Driver, and The First Omnibus Cad')

Barkis, Mr (DC) The carrier between Blunderstone (David Copperfield's childhood home) and Yarmouth. He was 'of a phlegmatic temperament, and not at all conversational'. He courts Peggotty, David's nurse, by using David as an intermediary. When taking David on the way to Mr Creakle's school, he makes a request: 'If you was writin' to her, p'raps you'd recollect to say that Barkis was willin'; would you?' He and Peggotty have a quiet wedding, while David and Little Em'ly wait outside the church: 'I have often thought, since, what an odd, innocent, out-of-the-way kind of wedding it must have been!' As time goes on, Barkis becomes 'a little nearer' than he used to be, keeping his money in a box under his bed and opening it only in secret. He dies embracing it and saying 'Barkis is willin'!' As Mr Peggotty had prophesied, 'he went out with the tide'. (2–5, 8, 10, 17, 21–23, 28, 30, 31, 51)

Barley, Clara (GE) Herbert Pocket's fiancée, who is 'rather below [his] mother's nonsensical family notions' since her father 'had to do with the victualling of passenger-ships'. She was 'a very pretty, slight, dark-eyed girl of twenty or so', who Pip thought 'might have passed for a captive fairy, whom that truculent Ogre, Old Barley, had pressed into his service'. She devotedly tends her father until his death. She and Herbert marry, and Pip happily lives with them as a lodger. (30, 46, 55, 58)

Barley, Old (GE) Clara's father, an unseen 'sad old rascal' (in Herbert Pocket's words), who used to be a ship's purser and who drinks rum and constantly growls and roars in an upstairs room: 'Ahoy! Bless your eyes, here's old Bill Barley. Here's old Bill Barley, bless your eyes. Here's old Bill Barley on the flat of his back, by the Lord. Lying on the flat of his back, like a drifting old dead flounder, here's your old Bill Barley, bless your eyes. Ahoy! Bless you.' (30, 46, 55, 58)

Barnacles, the (LD) 'The Barnacle family had for some time helped to administer the Circumlocution Office. The Tite Barnacle Branch, indeed, considered themselves in a general way as having vested rights in that direction, and took it ill if any other family had much to say to it. The Barnacles were a very high family, and a very large family. They were dispersed all over the public offices, and held all sorts of public places.' Arthur Clennam's attempts to investigate the situation of the Dorrit family and Daniel Doyce's attempts to patent his invention are constantly frustrated by the inertia and obstruction of the Circumlocution Office. Lord Decimus Tite Barnacle had 'the very smell of Despatch-Boxes upon him'. His nephew, Mr Tite Barnacle, was 'more flush of blood than money. As a Barnacle he had his place, which was a snug thing enough; and as a Barnacle he had of course put in his son Barnacle Junior, in the office. But he had intermarried with a branch of the Stiltstalkings, who were also better endowed in a sanguineous point of view than with real or personal property, and of this marriage there had been issue, Barnacle Junior, and three young ladies.' Tite Barnacle was 'the express image and presentment of How not to do it'; he 'wound and wound folds of white cravat round his neck, as he wound and wound folds of tape and paper round the neck of the country'. Barnacle Junior had a languid demeanour, 'a youthful aspect, and the fluffiest little whisker, perhaps, that ever was seen', and found it impossible to keep his eyeglass in his eye. He remonstrates with Arthur Clennam: 'Look here. Upon my soul, you mustn't come into the place saying you want to know, you know.' Ferdinand Barnacle, however, 'was a vivacious, well-looking, well-dressed, agreeable young fellow ... on the more sprightly side of the family'. When visiting Arthur Clennam in prison, Ferdinand frankly confesses 'his faith as the head of the rising Barnacles': 'We must have humbug, we all like humbug, we couldn't get on without humbug. A little humbug, and a groove, and everything goes on admirably, if you leave it alone.' Yet another member of the family, William Barnacle, 'had made the ever-famous coalition with Tudor Stiltstalking' and 'always kept ready his own particular recipe for How not to do it'. Mrs Gowan also disparagingly alludes to John Barnacle, who had conciliated 'the mob'. James Fitzjames Stephen, in his review of *Little Dorrit* in the *Edinburgh Review* (July 1857), took strong exception to Dickens's portrayal of the British system of government: 'Messrs Tite Barnacle and Stiltstalking are uniformly put forward as the representatives of the twenty or thirty permanent undersecretaries and heads of departments, by whom so large a portion of the public affairs is conducted, and every species of meanness, folly, and vulgarity is laid to their charge' (Collins 1971: 371). (I: 9, 10, 17, 26, 34; II: 12, 24, 28)

Barney (OT) The Jewish waiter at The Three Cripples public house, who helped Bill Sikes and Toby Crackit to plan their burglary of Mrs Maylie's house. (15, 22, 26, 42, 45)

Barronneau, Madame (LD) The widow whom Rigaud married and was accused of murdering. But he claimed that during a violent quarrel between them she leapt over a cliff-top and dashed herself to death on the rocks below. (I: 1)

Barsad, John (TTC) The name adopted by Solomon Pross, the brother of Miss Pross. Defarge describes him as follows: 'Age, about forty years; height, about five feet nine; black hair; complexion dark; generally, rather handsome visage; eyes dark, face thin, long, and sallow; nose aquiline, but not straight, having a peculiar inclination towards the left cheek; expression, therefore, sinister.' As Mr Lorry knows, he is 'a heartless scoundrel', who has 'stripped [Miss Pross] of everything' and abandoned her, although she remains faithful to his memory. He is a spy who works successively for the English government, the pre-revolutionary French government and the republican French government. We first encounter him giving evidence in the trial of Charles Darnay for treason. He is the one who tells the Defarges of the forthcoming marriage of Charles Darnay and Lucie Manette. During the French Revolution, he is employed at the Conciergerie as a turnkey and 'a sheep of the prisons' (i.e., a spy on the prisoners). Miss Pross recognises him in Paris. Sydney Carton, having discovered the truth about Cly, Barsad's accomplice, forces Barsad to help him gain access to the prison to engineer the release of Darnay. (II: 3, 6, 16; III: 8,9, 11, 13–15)

Barton, Jacob (SB) A grocer, who is the brother of Mrs Malderton, whom he embarrasses in society by openly referring to his trade. ('Tales: Horatio Sparkins')

Bates, Belinda (CS) A 'most intellectual, amiable, and delightful girl', who was one of the guests at the Haunted House. She goes in for 'Woman's mission, Woman's rights, Woman's wrongs, and everything that is woman's with a capital W'. Dickens is referring here to Adelaide Anne Procter (1825–64), the popular poet, whom he admired and who contributed a poem to this particular story (Glancy 1996: 815). ('The Haunted House')

Bates, Charley (OT) One of Fagin's gang of boy thieves, he is 'a very sprightly young friend of the Artful Dodger'. Like the Artful Dodger, he is a knowing and accomplished thief full of comic insolence and facetiousness. He advises Oliver Twist to put himself under Fagin's tuition in order to make his fortune: 'And so be able to retire on your property, and do the genteel: as I mean to, in the very next leap-year but four that ever comes, and the forty-second Tuesday in Trinity-week.' But he is horrified by Sikes's murder of Nancy, physically attacks him and does all that he can to hand him over to those who have come to arrest him. Charley resolves to amend his way of life and eventually succeeds after moving to the countryside: 'from being a farmer's drudge, and a carrier's lad, he is now the merriest young grazier in all Northamptonshire'. (8, 9, 10, 12, 13, 16, 18, 25, 39, 43, 50, 53)

Battens, Mr (UT) The oldest pensioner in Titbull's Alms-Houses. He is a 'virulent old man'. ('Titbull's Alms-Houses')

Bayton, Mrs (OT) A wretchedly poor woman, whose parochial funeral Mr

Bumble indignantly arranges with Mr Sowerberry. (6)

Bazzard (MED) Mr Grewgious's clerk. He was 'a pale, puffy-faced, dark-haired person of thirty, with big dark eyes that wholly wanted lustre, and a dissatisfied doughy complexion that seemed to ask to be sent to the baker's'. He seems to possess 'some strange power over Mr Grewgious'. Grewgious tells Rosa Bud that Bazzard has written a tragic drama, 'The Thorn of Anxiety', which nobody will produce. Because Bazzard's father, a Norfolk farmer, was furious that his son wished to be a playwright, Grewgious employed him to save him from starvation. He is one of the many characters in *The Mystery of Edwin Drood* about whom there has been much speculation. Is he Datchery, for example? Mr Grewgious says in Chapter 20 that he is absent from the office at a time that would suit that speculation. In his Introduction to *Edwin Drood*, Michael Innes observes: 'Similarly the information that Bazzard has written a tragedy prompts the notion that he may have unsuspected powers and an interest in the technique of impersonation' (1950: xiii). (11, 20)

Beadle, Harriet (LD) *See* **Tattycoram**.

Bear, Prince (RP) Prince Bull's enemy, who symbolises Russia in the Crimean War (1854–6). ('Prince Bull. A Fairy Tale')

Beaver, Nat (CS) A ship's captain 'with a thick-set wooden face and figure', who is a guest in the Haunted House. ('The Haunted House')

Bebelle (CS) The pet name of Gabrielle, the little orphan protected by Corporal Théophile and then adopted by Mr Langley. ('Somebody's Luggage')

Beckwith, Alfred (HD) A name used by Meltham to help him entrap Slinkton.

Bedwin, Mrs (OT) A 'motherly old lady', who is Mr Brownlow's housekeeper and who tenderly cares for Oliver Twist when he is brought to the house after fainting outside Mr Fang's courtroom. She remains firm in her belief in his honesty even when Mr Brownlow and Mr Grimwig state their mistaken opinion that he was an imposter. (12, 14, 15, 17, 41, 51)

Belinda (MHC) A lovelorn correspondent of Master Humphrey's. She writes to him, with a sad tale of a faithless lover, 'on strongly-scented paper, and sealed in light-blue wax, with the representation of two very plump doves interchanging beaks'. (2)

Bella (CS) Miss Pupford's housemaid, who Miss Kitty Kimmeens insists should leave her on her own in the house when the other pupils have left for the midsummer holidays. ('Tom Tiddler's Ground')

Bella (SB) A weeping girl, not yet 14, who is taken away with her shameless elder sister, Emily, in the prisoners' van. Both are presumably prostitutes. ('Characters: The Prisoners' Van')

Belle (CB) The youthful Scrooge's girlfriend, who sorrowfully accuses him of displacing her with the 'Idol' of gold. (*A Christmas Carol*)

Beller, Henry (PP) A former toastmaster, who has become a member of the Brick Lane Branch of the United Grand Junction Ebenezer Temperance Association. (33)

Belling (NN) A boy from Taunton, who became a pupil at Dotheboys Hall. (4, 5)

Bellows, Brother (LD) A barrister, who is a guest at Mr Merdle's. (I: 21)

Belvawney, Miss (NN) An actress in Mr

Crummles's company. She 'seldom aspired to speaking parts, and usually went on as a page in white silk hose, to stand with one leg bent, and contemplate the audience'. (23, 24, 29)

Bench (LD) A guest at Mr Merdle's. (I: 21)

Benson, Lucy (VQ). Although she flirts with Squire Norton, she goes back to her true sweetheart, George Edmunds.

Benson, Old and Young (VQ). Respectively the father and brother of Lucy. *See* the previous entry.

Benton, Miss (MHC) Master Humphrey's housekeeper. (5, 6)

Berinthia (DS) Mrs Pipchin's niece, always called Berry, who was 'her good-natured and devoted slave, but possessing a gaunt and iron-bound aspect, and much afflicted with boils on her nose'. (8, 11, 59)

Berry (DS) *See* **Berinthia**.

Bet (OT) A friend of Nancy's in Fagin's gang of thieves and prostitutes. She is the sweetheart of Tom Chitling, who says that the sight of Nancy's dead body sent her mad and that she had to be taken to hospital in a straitjacket. (9, 13, 16, 18, 25, 50)

Betley (CS) One of Mrs Lirriper's lodgers, who 'loved his joke'. ('Mrs Lirriper's Lodgings')

Betsy (PP) Mrs Raddle's dirty and slipshod maid. (32)

Bevan, Mr (MC) An honest and kind American physician, who sent Martin Chuzzlewit money when he and Mark Tapley were in distress in Eden so that they could return to New York. (16, 17, 21, 33, 34, 43)

Bib, Julius Washington Merryweather (MC) A 'gentleman in the lumber line ... and much esteemed', who is one of the boarders at the National Hotel who attend the 'le-vee' for Elijah Pogram. (34)

Biddy (GE) She was 'Mr Wopsle's great-aunt's grand-daughter'. Like Pip, she was an orphan, who 'had been brought up by hand'. She tries to help Mr Wopsle's great-aunt in running her chaotic village school and as she was, in Pip's opinion, 'the most obliging of girls', she imparts everything she knows to him. After Mrs Gargery is incapacitated by Orlick's brutal attack, she takes charge of the household. Pip notes that she becomes neat in appearance: 'She was not beautiful – she was common, and could not be like Estella – but she was pleasant and wholesome and sweet-tempered.' He tells her of his social ambitions and his admiration for Estella and in general treats her in a patronising and even disparaging way, ignoring her quiet wisdom and implied criticism of his behaviour. After his humiliation and illness, Pip at last fully realises her worth and resolves to ask her to marry him, imagining himself saying the following words: 'if you can tell me that you will go through the world with me, you will surely make it a better world for me, and me a better man for it, and I will try hard to make it a better world for you'. But on going back to his old home, he finds that he has arrived on the day of her wedding to Joe. He sincerely congratulates them as he is aware how truly honest and loving they are. (7, 10, 12, 15–19, 35, 57–59)

Bigby, Mrs (RP) Mr Meek's mother-in-law, who in his opinion 'would storm a town, single-handed, with a hearth-broom, and carry it'. ('Births. Mrs Meek of a Son')

Bigwig family (CS) A family who were 'composed of all the stateliest people' in the neighbourhood where 'Nobody' lived and who sought to control all that he did. ('Nobody's Story')

Bill (GE) Amelia's husband, whom Mr Jaggers is defending. (20)

Bill (PP) The turnkey in Sam Weller's story of 'the little dirty-faced man in the brown coat', who was imprisoned for debt. (41)

Bill, Uncle (SB) He is among those enjoying themselves in the tea-gardens. 'Observe the inexpressible delight of the old grandmother, at Uncle Bill's splendid joke of "tea for four: bread-and-butter for forty;" and the loud explosion of mirth which follows his wafering a paper "pigtail" on the waiter's collar.' ('Scenes: London Recreations')

Billickin, Mrs (MED) The landlady of a lodging-house in Southampton Street, Bloomsbury Square, where Mr Grewgious found apartments for Rosa Bud and Miss Twinkleton (on the latter of whom Mrs Billickin declares war). 'Personal faintness, and an overpowering personal candour, were distinguishing features of Mrs Billickin's organisation.' She refuses to use a Christian name and title, not wishing to commit herself to 'a solitary female statement'. The brass door-plate on her house therefore simply states, Billickin. (22)

Billsmethi, Signor (SB) The proprietor of a dancing academy, who threatens Augustus Cooper with an action for breach of promise on behalf of his daughter, Miss Billsmethi. His real name is, of course, Bill Smith. ('Characters: The Dancing Academy')

Bintrey (CS) A solicitor for Wilding and Co., who helps to trace Obenreizer. ('No Thoroughfare')

Bishop (LD) A church dignitary, who is

one of Mr Merdle's guests. (I: 21; II: 12, 16, 25)

Bitherstone, Master (DS) One of Mrs Pipchin's boarders, whose father was an old army friend of Major Bagstock's. It was this friendship that enabled the Major to make the acquaintance of Mr Dombey. (8, 10, 11, 41, 60)

Bitzer (HT) When we first meet him, he is a model pupil at the school owned by Mr Gradgrind, described in terms that directly contrast with the description of Sissy Jupe, one of his fellow-pupils. 'But, whereas the girl was so dark-eyed and dark-haired, that she seemed to receive a deeper and more lustrous colour from the sun, when it shone upon her, the boy was so light-eyed and light-haired that the self-same rays appeared to draw out of him what little colour he ever possessed. His cold eyes would hardly have been eyes, but for the short ends of lashes which, by bringing them into immediate contrast with something paler than themselves, expressed their form. His short-cropped hair might have been a continuation of the sandy freckles on his forehead and face. His skin was so unwholesomely deficient in the natural tinge, that he looked as though, if he were cut, he would bleed white.' When Mr Gradgrind asks him for his definition of a horse, he can concisely supply all the facts, which Gradgrind values above all else in a system of education: ' "Quadruped. Graminivorous. Forty teeth, namely twenty-four grinders, four eye-teeth, and twelve incisive. Sheds coat in the spring; in marshy countries, sheds hoofs, too. Hoofs hard, but requiring to be shod with iron. Age known by marks in mouth." Thus (and much more) Bitzer'. He becomes the 'light porter' (Dickens's pun is intentional) at the Bank in Coketown, where 'he held the respectable office of general spy and informer in the establishment, for which volunteer service he received a present at Christmas, over and above his weekly wage. . . . All his proceedings were the result of the nicest and coldest calculation' – including having his widowed mother shut up in the workhouse. He spies on Tom Gradgrind and seizes him at Sleary's circus, intending to take him back to Coketown and deliver him to Mr Bounderby. When Mr Gradgrind pleads with him, asking him whether he has a heart, Bitzer smiles at the oddity of the question, since, as he points out, the circulation 'couldn't be carried on without one'. In any case, he asserts that his heart is accessible only to reason. Sleary, however, frustrates his attempted arrest of Tom by means of a circus-trained pony and dog. For more on the contrast between Bitzer and Sissy Jupe, see the entry for the latter. (I: 2, 5; II: 1, 4, 6, 8, 9, 11; III: 7–9)

Black (RP) An imperturbable policeman, who meets Inspector Field in Whitechapel. ('On Duty with Inspector Field')

Black, Mrs (HR) A pupil of Mrs Lemon's in Miss Nettie Ashford's 'romance'. She is 'always gadding about and spoiling her clothes'.

Black Bill (GE) A prisoner Mr Wemmick recognises in Newgate Prison 'behind the cistern' when he takes Pip on a visit to the prison. (32)

Black Lion, The (BR) The landlord of the inn of the same name in Whitechapel visited by Joe Willet. He 'was called both man and beast, by reason of his having instructed the artist who painted his sign, to convey into the features of the lordly brute whose effigy it bore, as near a counterpart of his own face as his skill could compass and devise'. He swigged such copious draughts of beer 'that most of his faculties were utterly drowned and washed away, except the one great faculty of sleep, which he retained in surprising perfection'. (31)

Blackey (RP) A beggar, 'who has stood near London Bridge these five-and-twenty years, with a painted skin to represent disease'. ('On Duty with Inspector Field')

Blackpool, Stephen (HT) A power-loom weaver in Mr Bounderby's mill at Coketown. Although he was only 40 years old, he looked older because of the hard life he had experienced. He was 'a rather stooping man, with a knitted brow, a pondering expression of face, and a hard-looking head sufficiently capacious, on which his iron-grey hair lay long and thin'. He has been married for nineteen years to a wife who has become a drunken and worthless woman. But because of the existing laws, which would require him to pay exorbitant legal fees (as Bounderby triumphantly explains to him), he is unable to divorce her and to marry the virtuous Rachael. Trapped in the social and legal system of the 1850s, Stephen feels desperate but sees no hope of amelioration: 'Let everything be. Let all sorts alone. 'Tis a muddle, and that's aw.' But he refuses to join the workers' union, as a result of a promise he made to Rachael, and is consequently ostracised by his fellow-workers. He leaves Coketown to try to find work elsewhere, but owing to Tom Gradgrind's machinations he is suspected of robbing the bank. Returning in order to clear his name, he falls down a disused mine (symbolically named the Old Hell Shaft), is found by Rachael and Sissy Jupe, but dies soon after being rescued. His surname is meant to emphasise his Lancashire associations, and his Christian name may be intended to suggest martyrdom. Mrs Jane Sinnett, in the *Westminster Review* (October 1854), thought that 'Stephen Blackpool, with his rugged steadfastness, sturdy truth, upright bearing, and fine Northern English dialect, smacking strongly of the old Saxon, is a noble addition to the gallery which already contained the bluff John Browdie [in *Nicholas Nickleby*], the Yarmouth boatmen [Daniel and Ham Peggotty in *David Copperfield*], and so many other fine portraits' (Collins 1971: 306–7). (I: 10–13; II: 4–6, 8; III: 4–7, 9)

Bladud, Prince (PP) The legendary founder of Bath, the subject of 'The True Legend of Prince Bladud', which Mr Pickwick reads in his bedroom. (36)

Blake, Warmint (SYG) An 'out-and-out young gentleman'.

Blandois (LD) *See* **Rigaud**.

Blank, Mr (MP) At the second meeting of the Mudfog Association, he exhibited at the Display of Models and Mechanical Science 'a model of a fashionable annual, composed of copper-plates, gold leaf, and silk boards, and worked entirely by milk and water'.

Blanquo, Pierre (RP) A Swiss guide who accompanies 'Our Bore' on an expedition to the mountains. ('Our Bore')

Blathers (OT) A Bow Street Runner, who (with Duff) unsuccessfully investigates the attempted burglary at Mrs Maylie's house. He was a 'stout personage of middle height, aged about fifty: with shiny black hair, cropped pretty close; half-whiskers, a round face, and sharp eyes'. (31)

Blazo, Sir Thomas (PP) Mr Jingle claims that he played a single-wicket cricket match with him on a blazingly hot day in the West Indies. (7, 53)

Blight (OMF) Mortimer Lightwood's appropriately named 'dismal' office boy, often referred to as 'young Blight'. (I: 8, 12; III: 17; IV: 9, 16)

Blimber, Cornelia (DS) The daughter of Dr and Mrs Blimber. 'There was no light nonsense about Miss Blimber. She kept her hair short and crisp, and wore spectacles. She was dry and sandy with working in the graves of deceased languages. None of your live languages for Miss Blimber. They must be dead – stone dead – and then Miss Blimber dug them up like a Ghoul.' When Paul Dombey joins the school, her father at first gives him into her charge: 'Bring him on, Cornelia, bring him on.' At her wedding to Mr Feeder, B.A., she 'looked, as of old, a little squeezed in appearance, but very charming', and 'with her crisp little curls, "went in", as the Chicken [a pugilist] might have said, with great composure'. (11, 12, 14, 41, 60)

Blimber, Doctor (DS) The pompous and pedantic headmaster and proprietor of the school in Brighton where Paul Dombey was a pupil. His 'establishment was a great hot-house, in which there was a forcing apparatus incessantly at work'. He 'was a portly gentleman in a suit of black, with strings at his knees, and stockings below them. He had a bald head, highly polished; a deep voice; and a chin so very double, that it was a wonder how he ever managed to shave into the creases. He had likewise a pair of little eyes that were always half shut up, and a mouth that was always half expanded into a grin, as if he had, that moment, posed a boy, and were waiting to convict him from his own lips. Insomuch, that when the Doctor put his right hand into the breast of his coat, and with his other hand behind him, and a scarcely perceptible wag of his head, made the commonest observation to a nervous stranger, it was like a sentiment from the sphynx, and settled his business.' When he retires, he hands over the school to Mr Feeder, B.A., his assistant, who marries Cornelia, his daughter. Philip Collins sees Doctor Blimber as the 'respectable equivalent in the world of education' of the respectable Mr Dombey: 'impercipient men, no doubt, and thus cruel, but without the consciousness or the odium of wickedness' (1963: 141). (11, 12, 14, 24, 28, 41, 60)

Blimber, Mrs (DS) She is the proud and devoted wife of Doctor Blimber. She 'was not learned herself, but she pretended to be, and that did quite as well. She said at evening parties, that if she could have known Cicero, she thought she should have died contented. It was the steady joy of her life to see the Doctor's young gentlemen go out walking, unlike all other young gentlemen, in the largest possible shirt-collars, and the stiffest possible cravats. It was so classical, she said.' She is horrified at Paul's asking whether old Glubb could come to see him: ' "What a dreadful low name!" said Mrs Blimber. "Unclassical to a degree! Who is the monster, child?" ' (11, 12, 14, 24, 28, 41, 60)

Blinder, Bill (MHC) An ostler who leaves his stable lantern to Tony Weller in his will. (4)

Blinder, Mrs (BH) The kindly old woman who took care of the Neckett children. (15, 47)

Blinkins (RP) A Latin master, whom the headmaster caught asleep while taking a class. He is perhaps based on a Mr Manville, who was the Latin master at the Wellington House Academy, where Dickens was a pupil in 1824–7. ('Our School')

Blockitt, Mrs (DS) The first Mrs Dombey's nurse, who was a 'simpering piece of faded gentility'. (1)

Blockson, Mrs (NN) The Knags' charwoman. (18)

Blogg, Mr (OMF) The beadle who permitted Betty Higden to adopt Sloppy. (I: 16)

Bloss, Mrs (SB) A wealthy widow who

boarded at Mrs Tibbs's and who married Mr Gobler, a hypochondriac like herself. ('Tales: The Boarding-House')

Blotton, Mr (PP) A member of the Pickwick Club, until he is expelled for revealing the origin of Bill Stumps's inscription. (1, 11)

Blowers, Mr (BH) A QC in the case of Jarndyce v. Jarndyce. (1)

Blubb, Mr (MP) At the Umbugology and Ditchwaterisics session at the second meeting of the Mudfog Association, he lectured on the characteristics of the supposed cranium of Mr Greenacre (q.v.), only to have it exposed by Professor Ketch as a 'coker-nut'.

Blumb, R.A. (RP) A Royal Academician whom Our Bore took to see a painting of the Virgin and Child, 'the finest picture in Italy', which deeply affected him. 'He cried like a child!' ('Our Bore')

Blunderbore, Captain (MP) An officer of the Horse Marines, who was an authority on equine matters.

Blunderum, Mr (MP) He delighted the Zoology and Botany section of the Mudfog Association at their first meeting with a paper 'on the last moments of the learned pig'.

Bob (LD) The kindly turnkey at the Marshalsea Prison, who is Little Dorrit's godfather and friend. As a bachelor, Bob wants to leave her his 'little property of savings', but can never make the necessary arrangements and dies intestate. (I: 6, 7; II: 19)

Bobbo (CS) A friend of the schoolboy hero of Jemmy Lirriper's story. ('Mrs Lirriper's Lodgings')

Bobster, Cecilia (NN) A young woman whom Newman Noggs mistook for

Madeline Bray. Just when Nicholas Nickleby discovered the mistake, Mr Bobster, her tyrannical father, arrived on the scene, but Nicholas and Noggs managed to escape. (40, 51)

Bocker, Tom (OMF) A 19-year-old orphan, whom the Reverend Frank Milvey suggested that the Boffins could adopt. (I: 9)

Boffer (PP) A Stock Exchange broker, on whose probable methods and timing of committing suicide Wilkins Flasher and Frank Simmery placed bets. (55)

Boffin, Mrs Henrietta (OMF) She was 'a stout lady of a rubicund and cheerful aspect', who, in her husband's words, was 'a highflyer at Fashion'. When Mr Boffin inherited Harmon's property, she was determined that they should 'act up to it', which meant 'a good house in a good neighbourhood, good things about us, good living, and good society. I say, live like our means, without extravagance, and be happy.' They therefore move to Cavendish Square, into the house about which Silas Wegg used to fantasise. She was kind-hearted and benevolent, insisting that Bella Wilfer should live with them because she had apparently been disappointed of a husband and riches, wanting to adopt an orphan child in commemoration of John Harmon (though the orphan, by happy coincidence named Johnny, who was Betty Higden's great-grandson, died in hospital), and visibly showing her distress at Mr Boffin's apparently miserly behaviour. (I: 5, 8, 9, 15–17; II: 8–10, 14; III: 4, 5, 7, 9, 12, 15, 16; IV: 2, 3, 12–14, 16)

Boffin, Nicodemus (OMF) He had been employed by the late John Harmon as his foreman. Because Harmon's son, also named John, has apparently died, Boffin has inherited his former employer's property worth upwards of £100,000.

Harmon had made his fortune dealing in refuse in the form of huge dust heaps and so Boffin becomes known as the 'Golden Dustman'. He was a 'broad, round-shouldered, one-sided old fellow. . . . Both as to his dress and to himself, he was of an overlapping rhinoceros build, with folds in his cheeks, and his forehead, and his eyelids, and his lips, and his ears; but with bright, eager, childishly-inquiring grey eyes, under his ragged eyebrows, and broad-brimmed hat.' He and his wife live comfortably in 'Boffin's Bower' but on coming into their money move to a fashionable mansion in Cavendish Square. Boffin is illiterate and hires the rascally Silas Wegg to read to him; thanks to Mr Venus and John Harmon, he foils Wegg's blackmailing plot against him. The Boffins adopt Bella Wilfer and employ John Harmon (who is pretending to be John Rokesmith) as a secretary. After a while, Mrs Boffin realises Rokesmith's true identity. Perhaps alarmed by Bella's mercenary attitude and sympathetic to John Harmon's love for her, Mr Boffin apparently becomes a merciless miser and dismisses Harmon from his employment. Bella therefore learns the error of her ways, leaves the Boffins, and marries John. In due course, Boffin delightedly reveals his deception to them, but some critics have speculated whether this revelation was a change of intention on Dickens's part, as Boffin's miserliness had seemed so convincing. George Gissing felt that 'Dickens originally meant Mr Boffin to suffer a real change of character, to become in truth the miserly curmudgeon which we are told he only pretended to be', but admits that a change of plan could be justified, since it was much better 'to choose the Mr Boffin who will end in hearty laughter and overflowing benevolence!' (1974: 79). In any case, Dickens makes clear fairly early on in the novel the admiration we should feel for the Boffins: 'These two ignorant and unpolished people had guided themselves so far on in their journey of life, by

Figure 1 Mr Boffin and Bella Wilfer by Marcus Stone

a religious sense of duty and desire to do right.' Edwin Pugh suggests that Boffin is based on a Mr Dodd, a dust contractor of the period (1912: 280). (I: 5, 8, 9, 15–17; II: 7, 8, 10, 14, 16; III: 4–7, 9, 12, 14, 15; IV: 2, 3, 12–14, 16)

Bogles, Mrs (UT) A boarding-house keeper. ('Refreshments for Travellers')

Bogsby, James George (BH) The 'highly respectable' landlord of the Sol's Arms. (33)

Boiler, the Reverend Boanerges (UT) A 'powerful' preacher of 'lumbering jocularity'. His biblical Christian name signifies 'sons of thunder'. ('City of London Churches')

Bokum, Mrs (DS) A widow, who was the 'dearest friend' of Mrs MacStinger. She kept a close eye on Captain Bunsby on his way to his wedding to Mrs MacStinger in case he tried to escape. (60)

Bolder (NN) One of Squeers's pupils, whose father was 'two pound ten short' in the payment of his fees. Bolder has warts all over his hands. Calling him 'an incorrigible young scoundrel', Squeers soundly canes him. (7, 8)

Boldheart, Captain (HR) The pirate captain of *The Beauty* in Lieutenant-Colonel Robin Redforth's 'romance'.

Boldwig, Captain (PP) 'A little fierce man in a stiff black neckerchief and blue surtout.' On discovering Mr Pickwick asleep on his property in a wheelbarrow after drinking a considerable quantity of cold punch, he orders Wilkins, one of his gardeners, to wheel him to the pound. (19)

Bolo, Miss (PP) Mr Pickwick's partner in whist at Bath. He played so badly that she 'went straight home, in a flood of tears, and a sedan chair'. (35)

Bolter, Morris (OT) *See* **Claypole, Noah.**

Bones, Mr and Mrs Banjo (UT) Entertainers in a Liverpool 'singing-house'. ('Poor Mercantile Jack')

Bonney, Mr (NN) The promoter of The United Metropolitan Hot Muffin and Crumpet Baking and Punctual Delivery Company. He was 'a pale gentleman in a violent hurry', who took off 'a white hat which was so full of papers that it could scarcely stick upon his head'. (2)

Boodle, Lord (BH) A politician, 'of considerable reputation with his party', who is one of Sir Leicester Dedlock's regular guests. He speculates (in a celebrated satirical passage) on the formation of a new Ministry, involving Lord Coodle and Sir Thomas Doodle, and so on through the alphabet up to Quoodle. *See* **Buffy.** (12, 28)

Boots and Brewer (OMF) Guests at the Veneerings' social gatherings. (I: 2, 10; II: 3, 16; III: 17; IV: 17)

Boozey, William (HR) The captain of the foretop on *The Beauty* in Lieutenant-Colonel Robin Redforth's 'romance'.

Boozle (SYG) An actor in melodrama at the Surrey Theatre. ('The Theatrical Young Gentleman')

Borum, Mrs and family (NN) A Portsmouth family, who patronise Mr Crummles's stage productions. Mrs Borum says, however, that she will take only two of her six children to Miss Snevellici's 'bespeak'. (24)

Bottles (CS) A deaf stableman at the Haunted House. ('The Haunted House')

Bouclet, Madame (CS) Mr Langley's landlady. ('Somebody's Luggage')

Bounderby, Josiah (HT) 'He was a rich man: banker, merchant, manufacturer, and what not. A big loud man, with a stare, and a metallic laugh. A man made out of a coarse material, which seemed to have been stretched to make so much of him. A man with a great puffed head and forehead, swelled veins in his temples, and such a strained skin to his face that it seemed to hold his eyes open and lift his eyebrows up. A man with a pervading appearance on him of being inflated like a balloon, and ready to start. A man who could never sufficiently vaunt himself a self-made man. A man who was always proclaiming, through that brassy speaking-trumpet of a voice of his, his old ignorance and his old poverty. A man who was the Bully of humility.' He is in his late forties but looks older. He delights in boasting of his poverty to Mrs Sparsit, his housekeeper (who has come down in the world): 'You were coming out of the Italian Opera, ma'am, in white satin and jewels, in a blaze of splendour, when I hadn't a penny to buy a link to light you.' He has the utmost contempt for the 'Hands', such as Stephen Blackpool, although he admits that the latter is not as 'unreasonable' as the others: 'You don't expect to be set up in a coach and six, and to be fed on turtle soup and venison, with a gold spoon as a good many of 'em do!' He employs Tom Gradgrind at the Bank and marries the young Louisa Gradgrind, who leaves him and returns to her father's house. He assumes that Stephen Blackpool has stolen money from the Bank and is relentless in trying to bring about his arrest. Bounderby is publicly embarrassed when his mother, Mrs Pegler, makes herself known and reveals that his stories of childhood neglect were fictitious, showing that 'he had built his windy reputation upon lies'. Five years later, he dies 'of a fit in the Coketown street', leaving a 'vainglorious' will that begins 'its long career of quibble, plunder, false pretences, vile example, little service and much law'. It

may be worth noting that the first example in the *OED* of 'bounder' meaning 'a person of objectionable manners or anti-social behaviour; a cad' is dated 1889. (I; 3–9, 11–12, 14–16; II: 1–12; III: 2–9)

Bowley, Sir Joseph (CB) A pompous philanthropist, who boasts to Trotty Veck that he is the 'Poor Man's Friend'. His wife, Lady Bowley, is a 'stately lady'. He boastfully anticipates that his 12-year-old son, William, will have a brilliant future in Parliament and elsewhere. (*The Chimes*)

Boxer (CB) John Peerybingle's dog, known by everybody. (*The Cricket on the Hearth*)

Boythorn, Lawrence (BH) He is a close friend of Mr Jarndyce, whom he has known since they were at school together forty-five years previously. He is an elderly, boisterous, hearty, impetuous man, handsome, upright and stalwart, 'with a massive grey head, [and] a fine composure of face when silent'. His warm-heartedness is symbolised by his tender regard for his pet canary. Sir Leicester Dedlock's estate adjoins his property, and both men are engaged in legal proceedings regarding a right of way. Boythorn was based on Walter Savage Landor (1775–1864), one of Dickens's friends and the godfather to his second son. (9, 12, 13, 15, 18, 23, 35, 36, 43, 66)

Brandley, Mrs (GE) A friend of Miss Havisham's, with whom Estella boarded at Richmond. (38)

Brass, Sally (OCS) The sister of Sampson Brass, to whom she was 'clerk, assistant, housekeeper, secretary, confidential plotter, adviser, intriguer, and bill of cost increaser'. She was 'a lady of thirty-five or thereabouts, of a gaunt and bony figure, and a resolute bearing . . . [which] certainly inspired a feeling akin to awe in the breasts of those male strangers who had the happiness to approach her'. Although she resembles her brother in appearance, she is far tougher and more resolute: she refuses to confess her part in the conspiracy against Kit Nubbles when confronted by Mr Witherden and others, calling her brother a 'pitiful dastard' for doing so and sending a letter of warning to Quilp. (33, 34, 37, 50, 51, 56–60, 62–64, 66, 67, 73)

Brass, Sampson (OCS) He was 'an attorney of no very good repute, from Bevis Marks in the city of London'. He was 'a tall, meagre man, with a nose like a wen, a protruding forehead, retreating eyes, and hair of a deep red . . . He had a cringing manner, but a very harsh voice.' As the servile and ingratiating legal adviser to Quilp, who delights in tormenting him, he helps to gain possession of Nell's grandfather's house, plots against Kit Nubbles, and hires and dismisses Dick Swiveller. But he later admits that he has always hated Quilp wholeheartedly and (to the disgust of his sister, Sally) reveals the truth about the conspiracy against Kit. In that last confession, he 'really seemed to have changed sexes with his sister, and to have made over to her any spark of manliness he might have possessed'. Dickens describes his sentence to penal servitude in remarkably 'sportive vein' (his own phrase). Sampson and his sister end as 'two wretched people' shuffling along the London streets, 'looking into the roads and kennels as they went in search of refuse food or disregarded offal'. (11–13, 33–38, 49, 51, 56–60, 62–64, 66, 67, 73)

Bravassa, Miss (NN) A 'beautiful' actress in Mr Crummles's company. She 'had once had her likeness taken "in character" by an engraver's apprentice, whereof impressions were hung up for sale in the pastry-cook's window, and the greengrocer's, and at the circulating library, whenever the announce bills came out for her annual night'. (23–25, 29)

Bray, Madeline (NN) A girl with a 'very slight and delicate figure, but exquisitely shaped' and a 'countenance of most uncommon beauty', whom Nicholas Nickleby sees first at the General Agency Office and then at the Cheerybles' office. Seeing her, 'he loved and languished after the most orthodox models'. He eventually marries her, thanks to the failure of the plot contrived by Arthur Gride and Ralph Nickleby to marry her to the former, who is the only one who knows that she is the heiress to a fortune of £12,000 left by her maternal grandfather. (16, 40, 46–48, 51–57, 63–5)

Bray, Walter (NN) Madeline Bray's father, a petulant, sick man of 'scarce fifty, perhaps, but so emaciated as to appear much older'. Because he is in debt to Arthur Gride and Ralph Nickleby, he somewhat reluctantly agrees to the marriage of his daughter to Gride. But his sudden death on the morning of the wedding day prevents the plan from being carried out. (46, 47, 53, 54)

Brewer (OMF) *See* **Boots and Brewer.**

Brick, Jefferson (MC) The war correspondent on Colonel Driver's *New York Rowdy Journal*. His wife, 'a sickly little girl with tight round eyes', was an enthusiastic lecture-goer. (16, 17)

Briggs (DS) One of Paul Dombey's fellow-pupils at Doctor Blimber's school. His 'learning, like ill-arranged luggage, was so tightly packed that he couldn't get at anything he wanted'. (12, 14, 41, 60)

Briggs, Mr and Mrs (SYC) Friends of the egotistical couple. ('The Egotistical Couple')

Briggs, Mrs, and family (SB) Mrs Briggs, a widow, had two sons in the legal profession and three daughters. The daughters' vocal and guitar trio defeats the

Tauntons' efforts on board the *Endeavour*. ('Tales: The Steam Excursion')

Brimer, Mr (RP) The fifth mate of the *Halsewell*. ('The Long Voyage')

Britain, Benjamin (CB) Doctor Jeddler's manservant, who later marries Clemency Newcome. (*The Battle of Life*)

Brittles (OT) A 'lad of all work' (but aged over 30) at Mrs Maylie's. (28–31, 53)

Brobity, Miss (MED) The proprietor of a school in Cloisterham, who married Mr Sapsea. (4)

Brogley, Mr (DS) The 'sworn broker and appraiser' who took possession of the Wooden Midshipman when Solomon Gills fell into debt. He was 'a moist-eyed, pink-complexioned, crisp-haired man, of a bulky figure and an easy temper'. (9, 48, 49)

Brogson, Mr (SB) An 'elderly gentleman in a black coat, drab knee-breeches, and long gaiters', who was one of the guests at the Buddens' dinner to which Mr Minns was invited. ('Tales: Mr Minns and his Cousin')

Brook Dingwall (SB) *See* **Dingwall, Cornelius Brook.**

Brooker, Mr (NN) Ralph Nickleby's former clerk, who took charge of his employer's son, named him Smike, and left him at Dotheboys Hall. Returning to England, having served an eight-year sentence of transportation, he is angered by Ralph Nickleby's refusal to help him and in revenge reveals the story of Smike's origins. (44, 58, 60, 61)

Brooks (NN) A boy who shares his bed with Jennings, little Bolder, Graymarsh and 'what's his name' at Dotheboys Hall. (7)

Brooks (PP) A pieman and a fellow-lodger of Sam Weller's at one time, who could 'make pies out o' anything', including cats. (19)

Browdie, John (NN) A bluff Yorkshire corn factor, who was 'something over six feet high, with a face and body rather above the due proportion than below it' and who speaks in a broad Yorkshire accent. He is a stalwart friend to Nicholas Nickleby and others: he gives Nicholas a sovereign and a stick to help him on his escape from Dotheboys Hall, releases Smike from Squeers's London lodgings, and urges the boys to run away 'like men' from Dotheboys Hall after Squeers's downfall (though typically offering to help Mrs Squeers and Fanny if they need anything). He marries Matilda Price. In his Preface to the first cheap edition of *Nicholas Nickleby* (1848), Dickens implies that he based John Browdie on 'a jovial, ruddy, broadfaced man', whom he questioned about Yorkshire schools when he and Phiz visited that county to gather information for the novel. (9, 13, 39, 42, 43, 45, 64)

Brown (HR) A greedy and gouty pupil of Mrs Lemon's in Miss Nettie Ashford's 'romance'.

Brown (PP) The Muggleton shoemaker, whose name on Miss Rachel Wardle's shoes, which had been left with Sam Weller for cleaning, showed Mr Wardle and the others that she was staying at the White Hart. (10)

Brown, Conversation (DS) One of Cousin Feenix's acquaintances, who was a 'four-bottle man at the Treasury Board'. (61)

Brown, Emily (SB) She was the innocent cause of Horace Hunter's challenge to Alexander Trott. She subsequently married Hunter at Gretna Green. ('Tales: The Great Winglebury Duel')

Brown, Fanny (L) Mr Stargazer's niece, whom he wishes to marry Tom Grig.

Brown, the Misses (SB) The three Miss Browns were 'enthusiastic admirers' of the curate and taught classes of charity children. ('Our Parish: The Beadle. The Parish Engine. The Schoolmaster; The Ladies' Societies')

Brown, Mr (MP) A member of the Mudfog Association from Edinburgh.

Brown, Mr (SB) The near-sighted cellist at the Gattletons' Private Theatricals who could only play 'a bar now and then in the wrong place, and put the other performers out'. ('Tales: Mrs Joseph Porter')

Brown, Mrs (DS) She calls herself 'Good Mrs Brown' and is the mother of Alice (known as Alice Marwood), as the result of her seduction as a young woman by the uncle of the future Edith Dombey. She appears at various points in the novel as an ominous presence. 'She was a very ugly old woman, with red rims round her eyes, and a mouth that mumbled and chattered of itself when she was not speaking.' When Florence Dombey gets lost in the London streets, she seizes her and robs her of her clothes. In her own words to Alice, she 'hangs about the Dombeys'. Alone or with Alice she watches and curses Mr Carker, who had seduced Alice. Together they force Rob the Grinder to tell them all he knows about Carker and Edith's apparent elopement, while Mr Dombey listens concealed. (6, 27, 34, 40, 46, 52, 58)

Browndock, Miss (NN) Mr Nickleby's cousin's sister-in-law, who (according to Mrs Nickleby) 'was taken into partnership by a lady that kept a school at Hammersmith, and made her fortune in no time at all'. Mrs Nickleby thinks she was 'the same lady that got the ten thousand pounds in the lottery'. (17)

Brownlow, Mr (OT) A kindly, elderly gentleman, 'with a powdered head and gold spectacles', with a heart 'large enough for any six ordinary old gentlemen of humane disposition'. After Oliver Twist has been wrongfully accused of picking his pocket, he takes the little boy into his house. 'Deep affliction' has strengthened and refined his affections, which he is disposed to bestow on Oliver. But after Oliver's recapture, he is temporarily persuaded by Mr Bumble into believing that Oliver is an imposter, despite his housekeeper Mrs Bedwin's protestations. Rose Maylie reveals Oliver's story to him, and with her he meets Nancy on London Bridge. He has Monks seized, lays bare all the villainies in Monks's past life and compels him to restore to Oliver all the wrongly appropriated property. Finally, he adopts Oliver as his son. (10–12, 14, 15, 17, 32, 41, 46, 49, 51–53)

Bucket, Inspector (BH) He is almost certainly the first police detective in English fiction. He 'is a stoutly built, steady-looking, sharp-eyed man in black, of about the middle age'. His 'fat forefinger' seems like a 'familiar demon': 'He puts it to his ears, and it whispers information; he puts it to his lips, and it enjoins him to secrecy; he rubs it over his nose, and it sharpens his scent; he shakes it before a guilty man, and it charms him to his destruction.' He is active in a number of different investigations. Employed by Mr Tulkinghorn, he pursues Gridley to his hiding place in George's Shooting Gallery; he arrests George, mistakenly, for the murder of Tulkinghorn, but subsequently arrests Mlle Hortense for the crime (in a scene of confrontation and painstaking explanation, like those found in detective novels in the 1930s); with Esther Summerson and Allan Woodcourt, he traces Lady Dedlock's route to her death at the gate of the graveyard; and he compels Smallweed to hand over the vital bill to Mr Jarndyce.

He habitually addresses Sir Leicester Dedlock as 'Sir Leicester Dedlock, Baronet'. He relishes his work and brings to it a dry and sometimes sardonic humour, as in his reply to Hortense's wish to tear his wife limb from limb: ' "Bless you, darling", says Mr Bucket, with the greatest composure; "I'm fully prepared to hear that. Your sex have such a surprising animosity against one another, when you do differ. You don't mind me half so much do you?" ' Bucket was modelled on Inspector Charles Frederick Field (q.v.) of the Metropolitan Police Department, an officer Dickens much admired. Although Dickens implicitly denied in a letter to *The Times* that Inspector Field was the original of Inspector Bucket, his 'mannerisms, appearance, habits, qualities, personality and speech-idiom are all very close to ... descriptions of Bucket' (Collins 1964: 206–7). (22, 24, 25, 46, 47, 49, 53, 54, 56, 57, 59, 61, 62)

Bucket, Mrs (BH) Inspector Bucket's wife, who was 'a lady of a natural detective genius, which if it had been improved by professional exercise, might have done great things, but which has paused at the level of a clever amateur'. She keeps Mlle Hortense under close observation when the French maid lodges in the Buckets' house and helps her husband to prove her guilt. (53, 54)

Bud, Rosa (MED) 'The pet pupil of the Nuns' House [i.e., Miss Twinkleton's Seminary for Young Ladies in Cloisterham] is Miss Rosa Bud, of course called Rosebud; wonderfully pretty, wonderfully childish, wonderfully whimsical.' Her father and Edwin Drood's father had been close friends and under the terms of her father's will she was to marry Edwin when she came of age. She and Edwin amicably agree, however, to break the engagement and to 'change to brother and sister'. After Edwin's unexplained disappearance, John Jasper passionately avows to her that he has always loved her 'madly'. Terrified by his declaration and suspecting that he has murdered Edwin, she takes refuge in London with her guardian, Mr Grewgious. She meets Mr Tartar and it seems as if they are falling in love. Forster clearly states that 'Rosa was to marry Tartar' (1928: Book 11, Ch. 2). (2, 3, 7–9, 11, 13, 15, 19–23)

Budden, Octavius (SB) A retired cornchandler and the cousin of Mr Minns, whose visit to him was the subject of Dickens's first published story (originally entitled 'A Dinner at Poplar Walk', published in the *Monthly Magazine* in December 1833). Mr Budden 'had purchased a cottage in the vicinity of Stamford Hill, whither he retired with the wife of his bosom, and his only son, Master Alexander Augustus Budden'. ('Tales: Mr Minns and his Cousin')

Budger, Mrs (PP) An elderly widow, with whom Mr Jingle (in Mr Winkle's dress-suit) danced at the Rochester ball, to the jealous fury of Doctor Slammer, who consequently challenges the unfortunate Mr Winkle to a duel. (2)

Buffer, Doctor (MP) A member of the Mudfog Association.

Buffle, Mr (CS) A disagreeable collector of assessed taxes. His wife gives herself important airs and his daughter, Robina, is in love with George. ('Mrs Lirriper's Legacy')

Buffum, Oscar (MC) One of the deputation who arranged the 'le-vee' in honour of Elijah Pogram at the National Hotel in an American town. (34)

Buffy, the Right Honourable William (BH) An MP, who attends Sir Leicester Dedlock's social gatherings. Like Boodle, he speculates on governmental machinations, including Cuffy, Duffy and so on through the alphabet up to Puffy. (12, 28, 53, 58, 66)

Bulder, Colonel (PP) The head of the Rochester garrison, who is a guest, with his wife and daughter, at the charity ball at the Bull attended by the Pickwickians. He commands the military review at Chatham when Mr Pickwick gets in the way. (2, 4)

Bule, Miss (CS) An 8- or 9-year old girl in Miss Griffin's school. ('The Haunted House')

Bull, Prince (RP) A 'powerful Prince', who symbolises England during the Crimean War (1854–6). ('Prince Bull. A Fairy Tale')

Bullamy (MC) The porter at the offices of Montague Tigg's fraudulent Anglo-Bengalee Disinterested Loan and Assurance Company. After Tigg's murder, he and David Crimple make off with the firm's money. (27, 51)

Bullfinch (UT) The Uncommercial Traveller's friend, who unfortunately proposes that they should dine at the Temeraire. ('A Little Dinner in an Hour')

Bullman (PP) The plaintiff in the case discussed by Dodson and Fogg's clerks in the hearing of Mr Pickwick and Sam Weller. (20)

Bull's-eye (OT) Bill Sikes's 'white shaggy dog, with his face scratched and torn in twenty different places'. He falls to his death at the same time as Sikes accidentally hangs himself on Jacob's Island. (13, 15, 16, 18, 19, 39, 48, 50)

Bulph, Mr (NN) A pilot, in whose house the Crummles lodge when they visit Portsmouth. (23, 30)

Bumble, Mr (OT) The beadle of the parish where Oliver Twist is born in the workhouse. He is a fat, choleric and pompous man with a harsh contempt for all orphans and paupers. He 'invented' Oliver Twist's name: 'We name our foundlings in alphabetical order. The last was a S – Swabble, I named him. This was a T, – Twist I named *him*. The next one as comes will be Unwin, and the next Vilkins. I have got names ready to the end of the alphabet, and all the way through it again, when we come to Z.' He marries Mrs Corney, the matron of the workhouse, after taking care to count her teaspoons, weigh her sugar-tongs, and ascertain the genuineness of her silver tea-pot, but it is a marriage that he quickly regrets, especially when his wife violently assaults him. He becomes the Master of the Workhouse. He and his wife are dismissed from parochial office when Mr Brownlow discovers that she was guilty of obtaining, from a pawnbroker, the locket and gold ring that belonged to Oliver Twist's mother (from whom Sally had taken them) and selling them to Monks in her husband's presence. When Mr Brownlow points out to Bumble that 'the law supposes that your wife acts under your direction', he makes the famous retort: 'If the law supposes that . . . the law is a ass – a idiot.' Deprived of their situations, Mr and Mrs Bumble 'were gradually reduced to great indigence and misery, and finally became paupers in that very same workhouse in which they had once lorded it over others'. As Kathleen Tillotson observes in her Introduction to *Oliver Twist*, Mr Bumble's name 'has become a type of the petty tyrant and jack-in-office' (1982: viii). *See* **Simmons**. (2–5, 7, 17, 23, 27, 37, 38, 51, 53)

Bumple, Michael (SB) A plaintiff in a case of alleged brawling. Thomas Sludberry had applied to him the words, 'You be blowed.' ('Scenes: Doctors' Commons')

Bung, Mr (SB) A broker's man, who is elected the beadle of 'our parish'. ('The Election for Beadle' and 'The Broker's Man')

Bunkin, Mrs (PP) A woman 'which clear-starched' and who was one of those who had told Mrs Sanders that Mr Pickwick would marry Mrs Bardell, according to Mrs Sanders's evidence at the trial of Bardell v. Pickwick. (34)

Bunsby, Captain Jack (DS) He is the commander of the *Cautious Clara* and is greatly admired by his friend, Captain Cuttle, who says that Bunsby could deliver an opinion on any subject 'as could give Parliament six and beat 'em'. He had 'one stationary eye in [his] mahogany face, and one revolving one, on the principle of some lighthouses'. His utterances are so cryptic that 'students of the sage's precepts [are] left to their own application of his wisdom upon a principle which was the main leg of the Bunsby tripod, as it is perchance of some other oracular stools', as when he gives his opinion on the possible fate of the *Son and Heir* (the ship on which Walter Gay has sailed): 'Do I believe that this here Son and Heir's gone down, my lads? Mayhap. Do I say so? Which? If a skipper stands out by Sen' George's Channel, making for the Downs, what's right ahead of him? The Goodwins. He isn't forced to run upon the Goodwins, but he may. The bearings of this observation lays in the application of it. That an't no part of my duty. Awast then, keep a bright look-out for'ard, and good luck to you!' He rescues Captain Cuttle from the irascible Mrs MacStinger, whom he placates ('Awast, my lass, awast!') but who succeeds in dominating him and in leading him to the altar. (15, 23, 39, 60)

Burgess and Co. (DS) Mr Toots's tailors, who were 'fash'nable but very dear'. (12, 18, 41, 48)

Burton, Thomas (PP) A 'purveyor of cat's meat to the Lord Mayor and Sheriffs, and several members of the Common Council'. He has become a member of the Brick Lane Branch of the United Grand Junction Ebenezer Temperance Association. (33)

Butcher, William (RP) A Chartist, who explained to 'old John' the 'cruel wrong' of the law of Patent. ('A Poor Man's Tale of a Patent')

Butler, Theodosius (SB) The Misses Crumpton's cousin, who eloped with Lavinia Brook Dingwall. He is a conceited young man, who imagines that he is a genius. ('Tales: Sentiment')

Buzfuz, Serjeant (PP) The prosecuting counsel in the trial of Bardell v. Pickwick. (A Serjeant was a barrister of the highest rank.) He has a fat body and a red face, an histrionic manner and volubility of speech. Sam Weller's cool impertinence, however, discomposes him. He was based on Serjeant Bompas. (34)

C

Callow, Doctor (RP) 'One of the most eminent physicians in London'. He diagnoses Our Bore's illness as 'Liver!' and prescribes rhubarb and calomel. ('Our Bore')

Calton, Mr (SB) A 'superannuated old beau', who is one of Mrs Tibbs's boarders. Mrs Maplesone sues him for breach of promise. ('Tales: The Boarding-House')

Camilla (GE) Matthew Pocket's sister, who is one of the relatives who assiduously attend on Miss Havisham, hoping for a legacy. According to Joe Gargery, Miss Havisham left her £5 in her will, 'to buy rushlights to put her in spirits when she wake [sic] up in the night'. (11, 25, 34, 57)

Cape, Mr (SB) A violinist in the orchestra at the Gattletons' evening of Private Theatricals. ('Tales: Mrs Joseph Porter')

Capper, Mr and Mrs (SYG) The host and hostess of Mr Mincin, 'the very friendly young gentleman'.

Carker, Harriet (DS) The sister of James and John Carker. She is devoted to her 'outcast brother', John, and is a 'slight, small, patient figure, neatly dressed in homely stuffs, and indicating nothing but the dull, household virtues, that have so little in common with the received idea of heroism and greatness'. She takes pity on Alice Marwood, who calls at her house by chance, but is later spurned by her when Alice learns that Harriet is James Carker's sister. But Alice gets to know her true worth and Harriet lovingly visits her on her deathbed. Harriet marries Mr Morfin, the assistant manager of Dombey and Son. (22, 33, 34, 53, 58, 62)

Carker, James (DS) The Manager of Dombey and Son. He was 'a gentleman thirty-eight or forty years old, of a florid complexion, and with two unbroken rows of glistening teeth, whose regularity and whiteness were quite distressing. It was impossible to escape the observation of them, for he showed them whenever he spoke; and bore so wide a smile upon his countenance (a smile, however, very rarely, indeed, extending beyond his mouth), that there was something in it like the snarl of a cat. He affected a stiff white cravat, after the example of his principal, and was always closely buttoned up and tightly dressed.' Outwardly subservient to Mr Dombey, he nevertheless deliberately brings him to personal and financial ruin. When Mr Dombey employs him to convey messages to Edith, he contrives to persuade her to escape from her unhappy marriage and to join him in France, where, however, he discovers that she has no intention of being his mistress. His methodical and secret policy of overextending the financial commitments of Dombey and Son brings about the bankruptcy of the firm. Carker had previously seduced Alice Marwood and then cast her off, hence incurring her mother's hatred of him and desire for revenge. He treats his elder brother, John, with contempt, because of the latter's previous imprudence. He employs Rob the Grinder as his spy, who reveals (to Mrs Brown and Alice) Carker's whereabouts in France in the hearing of Mr Dombey. In flight from Dombey, Carker staggers, slips, and falls to his death under a train 'that spun him round and round, and struck him limb from limb, and licked his stream of life up with its fiery heat, and cast his mutilated fragments in the air'. Doris Alexander argues that Carker was based on John Wilson Croker (1780–1857), the critic and politician (1991: 27–9). (10, 13, 17, 18, 22, 24, 26–28, 31–34, 36, 37, 40, 42, 43, 45–47, 51–55)

Carker, John (DS) Although he is the elder brother of James Carker, the Manager, he is in a junior position in the office of Dombey and Son. 'He was not old, but his hair was white; his body was bent, or bowed as if by the weight of some great trouble: and there were deep lines in his worn and melancholy face. The fire of his eyes, the expression of his features, the very voice in which he spoke, were all subdued and quenched, as if the spirit within him lay in ashes.' He takes a friendly interest in Walter and wishes him well in all he undertakes to do. As a young employee of the firm, John Carker had stolen money from them, had been found out and had, nevertheless, been mercifully treated by Mr Dombey's father. But his brother James never lets him forget this shameful action, which he sincerely repents. He is devoted to his sister, Harriet, and despite his dismissal from the firm after his brother's villainous action he agrees, with her, to help the ruined Mr Dombey with money inherited from James. (6, 13, 19, 22, 33, 34, 46, 53, 58, 62)

Carlavaro, Giovanni (UT) The keeper of a small wine-shop. ('The Italian Prisoner')

Carolina The maid to Clara, the young bride. ('To be Read at Dusk')

Carstone, Richard (BH) 'A handsome youth, with an ingenuous face, and a most engaging laugh', who is a ward of Mr Jarndyce and a suitor in Chancery. He is a feckless young man, careless with money, who tries various professions (medicine, the law and the army) but never settles down in any of them. He is carelessly confident that money will come to him from the Chancery suit and is encouraged in this belief by Mr Skimpole. Esther Summerson agrees with Mr Jarndyce in thinking that 'the uncertainties and delays of the Chancery suit had imparted to his nature something of the careless spirit of the gamester, who felt that he was part of a great gaming system'. He becomes estranged from Mr Jarndyce, whose cautions he ignores, and falls under the influence of Vholes. He secretly marries Ada Clare, Mr Jarndyce's other ward, who has long loved him. Broken in spirits and health by his disappointments, which culminate in the absorption in legal costs of all the money at issue in Jarndyce v. Jarndyce, he dies, leaving Ada and her unborn child in the care of Mr Jarndyce. (1–6, 8, 9, 13, 14, 17, 18, 20, 23, 24, 35, 37, 39, 43, 51, 59–62, 64, 65)

Carter, Mr (MP) The President of the Mechanical Science session at the first meeting of the Mudfog Association.

Carton, Captain George (afterwards, **Admiral Sir George Carton, CB**) (CS) The leader of the expedition that drove the pirates from Silver-Store Island. He later married Miss Marion Maryon. ('The Perils of Certain English Prisoners')

Carton, Sydney (TTC) A barrister, who was 'the idlest and most unpromising of men' and the 'great ally' of Stryver. 'Stryver never had a case in hand, anywhere, but Carton was there, with his hands in his pockets, staring at the ceiling of the court; they went the same Circuit, and

even there they prolonged their usual or-
gies late into the night, and Carton was
rumoured to be seen at broad day, going
home stealthily and unsteadily to his
lodgings, like a dissipated cat. At last, it
began to get about, among such as were
interested in the matter, that although
Sydney Carton would never be a lion, he
was an amazingly good jackal, and that
he rendered suit and service to Stryver in
that humble capacity.' Carton, in fact, is
the one who works hard on Stryver's
cases and gives him invaluable advice. He
is, by the way, one of the few characters
in Dickens's work who went to a public
school – Shrewsbury, where he 'did exer-
cises for other boys, and seldom did [his]
own'. He is a 'man of good abilities and
good emotions, incapable of their directed exercise, incapable of his own help
and his own happiness, sensible of the
blight on him, and resigning himself to
let it eat him away'. His remarkable physical likeness to Charles Darnay is noted
at the trial of the latter for treason, with
the result that a witness for the prosecu-
tion is so disconcerted about the question of identity that the jury acquits
Darnay. Through his involvement in the
trial, he meets and falls in love with Lucie
Manette and confesses to her her good
influence upon him; she is sure, in her
turn, that he is capable of good things.
He realises, however, the depth of the
love between her and Darnay and seeks
not to disturb this in any way. His love
for Lucie is shown in his final self-
sacrifice. When Darnay is imprisoned
and condemned to death by the revolutionaries in France, Carton, with the
help of Barsad, contrives to take his
place in the prison cell and is guillotined
in his place. His final thoughts at the
scaffold include visions of a favourable
future for France and of the particular
destinies of the men and women he knew.
His last words of all form the famous last
sentence of the novel: 'It is a far, far better thing that I do, than I have ever done;
it is a far, far better rest that I go to than I

have ever known.' Carton may be based
on Gordon or George Allen, who helped
Edwin James, the original of Stryver. (II:
2–6, 11, 13, 20, 21; III: 8, 9, 11–13, 15)

Casby, Christopher (LD) The landlord
of Bleeding Heart Yard, formerly Town-
agent to Lord Decimus Tite Barnacle,
and the father of Flora Finching. In appearance, he still has some of the characteristics of a boy. 'There was the same
smooth face and forehead, the same calm
blue eye, the same placid air. The shining
bald head, which looked so very large because it shone so much; and the long grey
hair at its side and back, like floss silk or
spun glass, looked so very benevolent
because it was never cut; were not, of
course, to be seen in the boy as in the old
man.' Many people delighted to give him
the designation of 'Patriarch': 'Various
old ladies in the neighbourhood spoke of
him as The Last of the Patriarchs'. But as
Arthur Clennam had long suspected, his
benevolent air was deceptive, since Casby
was, in fact, 'a crafty imposter' and 'a
heavy, selfish, drifting Booby'. He was a
ruthless landlord, but he employed
Pancks to do his dirty work – that is, to
collect the rents from his tenants without any mercy. One can compare this
arrangement with Fledgeby's use of Riah
in *Our Mutual Friend*. Casby is responsible for Miss Wade's finances but refuses
to give Arthur Clennam any information
about them. In the end, Pancks confronts
him in public in Bleeding Heart Yard. He
'shoots off' Casby's hat, calls him a 'sug-
ary swindler', and snips off his hair,
much to the delight of the onlookers. (I:
12, 13, 23, 24, 35; II: 9, 23, 32)

Cavaletto, John Baptist (LD) When we
first meet him as a fellow-prisoner of
Rigaud in the prison at Marseilles, he is
'a sunburnt, quick, lithe, little man,
though rather thick-set. Earrings in his
brown ears, white teeth lighting up his
grotesque brown face, intensely black
hair clustering about his brown throat, a

ragged red shirt open at his brown breast. Loose, seamanlike trousers, decent shoes, a long red cap, a red sash round his waist, and a knife in it.' His catchword is 'Altro!' (hence Pancks addresses him as 'Altro'). On his arrival in London, he is knocked down in the street by a mail cart and taken to Saint Bartholomew's Hospital by Arthur Clennam, who finds accommodation for him in the house where the Plornish family live in Bleeding Heart Yard. He makes a living as a wood-carver and a part-time watchman. He is constantly singing and laughing and is therefore one of the liveliest presences in the rather sombre narrative of *Little Dorrit*. He also plays quite an important part in the complex plot, since he tracks down Rigaud for Arthur Clennam. When Arthur becomes ill in the Marshalsea Prison, Cavaletto helps to take care of him. (I: 1, 11, 13, 23, 25; II: 9, 13, 22, 23, 28, 30, 33)

Caveton (SYG) The 'throwing-off' (i.e., boastful) young gentleman.

Certainpersonio, Prince (HR) Alicia's bridegroom in Miss Alice Rainbird's 'romance'.

Chadband, the Reverend Mr (BH) He is a minister who is attached to no particular denomination and is greatly admired by Mrs Snagsby. He was 'a large yellow man, with a fat smile, and a general appearance of having a great deal of train oil in his system'. In his hypocritical sermonising, he piles 'verbose flights of stairs, one upon the other', as on one occasion when he addresses Jo and others at the Snagsbys' on the subject of 'Terewth': 'Say not to me it is *not* the lamp of lamps. I say to you, it is. I say to you, a million times over, it is. It is! I say to you that I will proclaim it to you, whether you like it or not; nay, that the less you like it, the more I will proclaim it to you. With a speaking-trumpet! I say to you that if you rear yourself against it,

you shall fall, you shall be bruised, you shall be battered, you shall be flawed, you shall be smashed.' With his wife, Mrs Snagsby and Smallweed, he becomes involved in a scheme, which is thwarted by Inspector Bucket, for extorting money from Sir Leicester Dedlock. Mr Chadband's wife, formerly called Mrs Rachael, had been the stern nurse of Esther Summerson's childhood. Dennis Walder suggests in *Dickens and Religion* (1981: 166) that Chadband's prototype may have been the Reverend Edward Irving (1792–1834). (3, 19, 22, 24, 25, 44, 54)

Charker, Harry (CS) A corporal in the Royal Marines and a comrade of Gill Davis. ('The Perils of Certain English Prisoners')

Charles (CS) 'Old Charles', according to Christopher, the narrator, was 'long eminent at the West Country Hotel' and was 'by some considered the Father of Waiting'. ('Somebody's Luggage')

Charles (SYC) He and his wife, Louisa, were the 'cool couple'.

Charley (BH) Her full name was Charlotte Neckett and she was the eldest daughter of Neckett, the bailiff's man (whom Skimpole calls Coavinses, after the sponging-house that employs him). After her widowed father's death, she has to look after her little brother and sister. When Esther Summerson first sees her, she is 'a very little girl, childish in figure but shrewd and older-looking in the face – pretty-faced too'. She works as a servant at the Smallweeds', but is then employed by Mr Jarndyce as Esther's personal maid. She is devoted to Esther, who has so much affection for her that the two become virtually inseparable. Esther nurses her through smallpox, and then she in turn tends Esther, who has caught the disease from her. After seven years, 'Charley (round-eyed still, and not at all grammatical)' gets married 'to a miller in the neighbourhood'. (15, 21, 23, 30, 31, 35–37, 44, 45, 51, 57, 61, 62, 64, 67)

Charley (CS) A guest at the Holly-Tree Inn, who narrates the story. He eventually marries Angela Leath. ('The Holly-Tree Inn')

Charley (DC) The 'dreadful old man' who owned a marine-store shop at Chatham and to whom David Copperfield sold his jacket for eighteen pence. (13)

Charley (PP) The shambling red-headed pot-boy at the Magpie and Stump where Mr Pickwick and Sam Weller go in search of Mr Lowten. (20)

Charlotte (LD) The 'false young friend' of Miss Wade when they were schoolgirls. (II: 21)

Charlotte (OT) The maidservant to Mr and Mrs Sowerberry, the undertakers. She is very fond of Noah Claypole, whom she feeds with oysters ('I like to see you eat 'em, Noah dear, better than eating 'em myself'), and – according to Noah – 'makes all manner of love to him'. Having taken money from the till for Noah's sake, she accompanies him to London. (4–6, 27, 42, 53)

Charlotte (SYC) She and her husband, Edward, are the 'contradictory couple'.

Cheeryble, Charles and Edwin (NN) The benevolent, elderly twins, self-made wealthy 'German merchants', who take Nicholas Nickleby into their employment and do all they can to help Madeline Bray and Nicholas's mother and sister. When Nicholas accidentally first encounters Charles Cheeryble, he is principally attracted by 'the old gentleman's eye, – never was such a clear, twinkling, honest, merry, happy eye, as that'. He also has 'such a pleasant smile

playing about his mouth, and such a comical expression of mingled slyness, kind-heartedness, and good-humour, lighting up his jolly old face, that Nicholas would have been content to have stood there, and looked at him until evening, and to have forgotten, meanwhile, that there was such a thing as a soured mind or a crabbed countenance to be met with in the whole wide world'. The brothers help to bring about the happy resolution of the difficulties and crises faced by the principal characters: the revelation of Ralph Nickleby's evil past, the restoration of Madeline Bray's inheritance, and their nephew Frank's engagement to Kate Nickleby. Dickens based them on William and Daniel Grant, calico printers in Manchester, whom he had met in 1838. He pointed out in his Preface to the first edition of the novel (1839) that the brothers were drawn from life: 'those who take an interest in this tale, will be glad to learn that the Brothers Cheeryble live; that their liberal charity, their singleness of heart, their noble nature, and their unbounded benevolence, are no creations of the Author's brain; but are prompting every day (and oftenest by stealth) some munificent and generous deed in that town of which they are the pride and honour'. (35, 37, 40, 43, 46, 48, 49, 55, 57, 61, 63, 65)

Cheeryble, Frank (NN) The nephew of the Cheeryble brothers. He was 'a sprightly, good-humoured, pleasant fellow ... good-looking and intelligent [with] a plentiful share of vivacity'. He falls in love with Kate Nickleby, marries her, and becomes a partner with Nicholas in his uncles' business. (43, 46, 48, 49, 55, 57, 61, 63, 65)

Cheeseman, Old (CS) A boarding-school boy, who becomes an unpopular schoolmaster, inherits a fortune, and marries Jane Pitt. ('The School-Boy's Story')

Cheggs, Mr and Miss (OCS) Friends of Sophy Wackles, Dick Swiveller's sweetheart. Cheggs, who is a market gardener, eventually marries Sophy, much to Dick's distress. (8, 21, 50)

Chester, Edward (BR) The son of Mr (later, Sir) John Chester. When we first see him in the Maypole Inn, he is 'a young man of about eight-and-twenty, rather above the middle height, and though of a somewhat slight figure, gracefully and strongly made... But travel-stained though he was, he was well and even richly attired, and without being over-dressed looked a gallant gentleman.' On his way back to London, he is attacked, wounded and robbed by the Stranger (i.e., Rudge), and is found by Barnaby Rudge and Gabriel Varden, who take him to Mrs Rudge's house. He and Emma Haredale are in love. His father casts him out after he expresses his indignation at the deception practised on Emma to make her break off the affair and makes clear his refusal to sacrifice his self-respect at his father's bidding. Returning from the West Indies to England at the time of the Gordon Riots, he helps Joe Willet and Gabriel Varden to rescue Dolly Varden, Emma Haredale and Miggs in the nick of time from their captivity. He marries Emma, and 'when the Riots were many years old' they come back to England 'with a family almost as numerous as Dolly's'. (1, 3–6, 12, 14, 15, 19, 20, 24, 27, 29, 32, 67, 71, 72, 78, 79, 82)

Chester, Mr (later, Sir) John (BR) Modelled to some extent on the fourth Earl of Chesterfield (1694–1773), who is remembered particularly for his worldly-wise *Letters* to his natural son, Chester is 'a soft-spoken, delicately made, precise, and elegant' gentleman, cold, calculating and scheming. A 'deep and bitter animosity' exists between him and Mr Geoffrey Haredale, exacerbated by the fact that Chester is a Protestant whereas Haredale is a Roman Catholic (a significant cause of hostility in 1775–80, the period in which *Barnaby Rudge* is set). He ruthlessly determines to break up the love affair between Edward, his son, and Emma Haredale, Mr Haredale's niece, using Hugh as his agent. When Edward expresses his suspicions of deception and is evidently determined to be honourably independent, his father expels him from his house. Chester becomes an MP and a knight: 'Such elegance of manner, so many graces of deportment, such powers of conversation, could never pass unnoticed ... He caught the fancy of the king [George III], knelt down a grub, and rose a butterfly. John Chester, Esquire, was knighted and became Sir John.' When Gabriel Varden confronts him with Dennis's revelation that Hugh was his illegitimate son by a gipsy woman whom he had abandoned (and who had been hanged for petty theft), he remains outwardly unruffled, 'the same imperturbable, fascinating gentleman' of previous days. But in an angry encounter, Haredale kills him with his sword. (5, 10–12, 14, 15, 23, 24, 26–30, 32, 40, 43, 53, 75, 81, 82)

Chestle, Mr (DC) An elderly Kentish hop-grower, who marries the eldest Miss Larkins. (18)

Chib, Mr (RP) The 82-year-old father of the vestry. ('Our Vestry')

Chick, Mr (DS) Mr John Chick was the husband of Mrs Louisa Chick and hence Mr Dombey's brother-in-law. He was 'a stout bald gentleman, with a very large face, and his hands continually in his pockets, . . . who had a tendency in his nature to whistle and hum tunes'. He makes a memorable suggestion concerning the feeding of the infant Paul on the death of Mrs Dombey: 'Couldn't something temporary be done with a teapot?' Although Mrs Chick treats this suggestion with 'silent resignation', at other times 'he was often in the ascendant himself, and at those times punished Louisa soundly'. (2, 5, 8, 29, 31, 36)

Chick, Mrs Louisa (DS) She is Mr Dombey's sister, who is 'a lady rather past the middle age than otherwise'. She typically tells the first Mrs Dombey, as she lies dying after giving birth to Paul, 'It's necessary for you to make an effort, and perhaps a very great and painful effort which you are not disposed to make; but this is a world of effort you know, Fanny, and we must never yield, when so much depends upon us.' She similarly blames Mr Dombey after his downfall for not making an effort. With Miss Tox, she oversees little Paul's upbringing, but scornfully casts her off when she discovers her matrimonial ambitions concerning herself and Mr Dombey: 'To think . . . that she should ever have conceived the base idea of connecting herself with our family by a marriage with Paul!' She is outraged at not being invited to the dinner given by Mr Dombey and Edith soon after their marriage and at being ignored at the subsequent reception. (1, 2, 5–8, 10, 14, 16, 18, 19, 29, 31, 36, 51, 58, 59)

Chickenstalker, Mrs Anne (CB) A shopkeeper, who was one of Trotty Veck's creditors. In Trotty's dream, she marries Tugby, Sir Joseph Bowley's porter. (*The Chimes*)

Chickweed, Conkey (OT) According to Blathers, he was a publican who committed a fake burglary on himself, although the deception was detected by Jem Spyers, a Bow Street runner. (31)

Chiggle (MC) An 'immortal' American sculptor, who made a statue of Elijah Pogram. (34)

Childers, E.W.B. (HT) A young man, who was an equestrian in Mr Sleary's circus. 'His face, close-shaven, thin, and sallow, was shaded by a great quantity of dark hair, brushed into a roll all round his head, and parted up the centre. His legs were very robust, but shorter than legs of good proportions should have been. His chest and back were as much too broad, as his legs were too short.' He was 'justly celebrated for his daring vaulting act as the Wild Huntsman of the North American Prairies'. When Mr Bounderby and Mr Gradgrind enquire about Sissy Jupe and her missing father, he speaks bluntly to Bounderby but is anxious to conciliate Gradgrind for the sake of Sissy's welfare. When Tom Gradgrind takes refuge in the circus, E.W.B. Childers smuggles him away to Liverpool. Childers marries Josephine, Sleary's daughter, and has a son, who at 3 years old is already (according to Sleary) 'The Little Wonder of Thcolathtic Equitation'. (I: 6; III: 7,8)

Chill, Uncle (CS) Michael's avaricious old uncle. ('The Poor Relation's Story')

Chillip, Doctor (DC) The doctor who attends Mrs Copperfield at David's birth. 'He was the meekest of his sex, the mildest of little men.' He is kind to David after his mother's death, although (in David's words) 'it was but seldom that I enjoyed the happiness of passing an afternoon in his closet of a surgery; reading some book that was new to me, with the smell of the whole pharmacopoeia coming up my nose, or pounding something in a mortar under his mild direction'. He is a widower, but gets married again, to a 'tall, raw-boned, high-nosed wife', with whom he has a 'weazen little baby'. Towards the end of the narrative, Chillip gives David news of Mr Murdstone's second marriage. (1, 2, 9, 10, 22, 30, 59)

Chinaman, Jack (MED) The keeper of a London opium den, which he ran in opposition to Princess Puffer's den. (1, 23)

Chips (UT) A shipwright who made a bargain with the Devil in a story told by Mercy. ('Nurse's Stories')

Chirrup, Mr and Mrs (SYC) The 'nice little couple'. He has 'something of the brisk, quick manner of a small bird' and she is 'the prettiest of all little women'.

Chitling, Tom (OT) A thief in Fagin's gang and Bet's sweetheart. He was about 18 years old, but showed deference to the Artful Dodger, who was younger. 'He had small twinkling eyes, and a pock-marked face; wore a fur cap, a dark corduroy jacket, greasy fustian trousers, and an apron'. (18, 25, 39, 50)

Chivery, John (LD) The 'sentimental son' of the turnkey at the Marshalsea Prison. He was 'small of stature, with rather weak legs and very weak light hair. One of his eyes . . . was also weak, and looked larger than the other, as if it couldn't collect itself. Young John was gentle likewise. But he was great of soul. Poetical, expansive, faithful.' He is hopelessly and pathetically in love with Little Dorrit. 'It was an instinctive testimony to Little Dorrit's worth, and difference from all the rest [of her family], that the poor young fellow honoured and loved her for being simply what she was.' When he declares his love for her, she gently but firmly rejects him, leading him to compose one of the epitaphs he frequently imagines: 'Here lie the mortal remains of JOHN CHIVERY. Never anything worth mentioning. Who died about the end of the year one thousand eight hundred and twenty-six, Of a broken heart, Requesting with his last breath that the word AMY might be inscribed over his ashes, Which was accordingly directed to be done, BY his afflicted Parents.' He helped Pancks in his investigations into the Dorrits' rights to a fortune. With the best intentions, he pays his respects and offers a gift of cigars to Mr Dorrit when the latter visits London in his days of prosperity but thereby causes the elderly man acute embarrassment at being reminded of their acquaintance in the Marshalsea Prison. John Chivery is the one who reveals to Arthur Clennam in prison that Little Dorrit loves him. (I: 18, 19, 22, 25, 31, 35, 36; II: 18, 26, 27, 29, 31, 33, 34)

Chivery, Mr and Mrs John (LD) Mr John Chivery was a turnkey at the Marshalsea Prison. 'He locked himself up as carefully as he locked up the Marshalsea debtors' and never opened his mouth 'without occasion'. His wife kept a tobacco shop. She 'was a comfortable-looking woman, much respected about Horsemonger Lane for her feelings and her conversation'. (I: 18, 19, 22, 25, 31, 35, 36; II: 26, 27, 29, 31, 34)

Choke, General Cyrus (MC) An American swindler, who introduced Martin Chuzzlewit to Scadder, the agent of the Eden Land Corporation. (21)

Chollop, Major Hannibal (MC) An American 'worshipper of freedom', who met Martin Chuzzlewit and Mark Tapley in Eden and who was 'a splendid sample of our na-tive raw material, sir'. (33, 34)

Chopper, Mr (HR) Master William Tinkling's great-uncle.

Chopper, Mrs (SYC) The mother of Mrs Merrywinkle, one of the 'couple who coddle themselves'.

Chops (CS) A dwarf, whose name was Stakes but whose professional name was Major Tpschoffki. He was in Toby Magsman's show, having been cheated out of the £12,000 he won in a lottery. ('Going into Society')

Chowser, Colonel (NN) One of Ralph Nickleby's disreputable acquaintances. He was a Colonel 'of the Militia – and the race-courses'. (19, 50)

Christiana (CS) Michael's former sweetheart. ('The Poor Relation's Story')

Christopher (CS) The head waiter who narrates 'Somebody's Luggage'.

Chuckster, Mr (OCS) Mr Witherden's clerk, who affects the airs of a man-about-town, looks down on Kit Nubbles (calling him a 'snob', i.e., a low and vulgar fellow), and boasts a sophisticated knowledge of fashionable scandals, 'in which [knowledge] he was justly considered by his friends to shine prodigiously'. Like his friend, Dick Swiveller, Mr Chuckster is a member of the Glorious Apollos. As he claims to be 'perfectly acquainted with all those little artifices which find the readiest road' to women's hearts, he is infuriated when he sees Kit and Barbara (whom Mr Chuckster considers to be a 'devilish pretty girl') waving affectionately to each other. (14, 20, 38, 40, 56, 60, 64, 65, 69, 73)

Chuffey (MC) The clerk in the 'old-established firm of Anthony Chuzzlewit and Son, Manchester Warehousemen'. He was 'a little blear-eyed, weazen-faced, ancient man ... He was of a remote fashion, and dusty, like the rest of the furniture; he was dressed in a decayed suit of black; with breeches garnished at the knees with rusty wisps of ribbon, the very paupers of shoe-strings; on the lower portion of his spindly legs were dingy worsted stockings of the same colour. He looked as if he had been put away and forgotten half a century before, and somebody had just found him in a lumber-closet.' Chuffey was devoted to Anthony Chuzzlewit, after whose death he went to live with Jonas Chuzzlewit and his wife (formerly Mercy Pecksniff). Jonas handed him over to Mrs Gamp, whose reports of Chuffey's remarks make Jonas think that Chuffey knows that Jonas murdered his father. But Chuffey later reveals the way in which

Jonas's murderous plot was known to Anthony Chuzzlewit. (11, 18, 19, 25, 26, 46, 48, 49, 51, 52, 54)

Chuzzlewit, Anthony (MC) The younger brother of old Martin Chuzzlewit and the father of Jonas. When the Chuzzlewits and others assemble at Mr Pecksniff's house, old Anthony Chuzzlewit's face is 'so sharpened by the wariness and cunning of his life, that it seemed to cut him a passage through the crowded room, as he edged away behind the remotest chairs'. He makes no bones on that occasion about calling Pecksniff a hypocrite. When Pecksniff and his daughters, Charity and Mercy, are travelling in the coach to London, they hear his 'thin sharp voice' uttering a typical demand: 'Now mind ... I and my son go inside, because the roof is full, but you agree only to charge us outside prices. It's quite understood that we won't pay more. Is it?' Not surprisingly, Anthony exults in his son Jonas's slyness, cunning and covetousness and he urges Pecksniff to persuade Charity to marry Jonas. He dies after suffering a series of seizures, having discovered the poison Jonas had prepared for him to drink, as he tells Chuffey: 'It's a dreadful thing to have my own child thirsting for my death. But I might have known it. I have sown, and I must reap.' (4, 8, 11, 18, 19, 48, 51)

Chuzzlewit, George (MC) A 'gay bachelor cousin [of old Martin Chuzzlewit], who claimed to be young but had been younger, and was inclined to corpulency, and rather over-fed himself'. (4, 54)

Chuzzlewit, Jonas (MC) The only son of Anthony Chuzzlewit, who had trained and encouraged him in all kinds of villainy. At the Pecksniff 'family council', he is seen as having 'so well profited by the precept and example of the father, that he looked a year or two the elder of the twain, as they stood winking their red eyes, side by side, and whispering to each other softly'. After his father's death (which he mistakenly thought he had brought about by means of poison), he marries Mercy Pecksniff – a surprising choice, since it was thought by many (including Charity) that he would marry Charity, and subjects her to brutal mistreatment. He becomes involved in Montague Tigg's fraudulent insurance company. Nadgett, employed by Tigg, discovers his plan to poison his father and in fear that he will be exposed as a murderer he is compelled to get more deeply involved in Tigg's shady business. In despair, he murders Tigg, is arrested thanks to Nadgett's investigations, and commits suicide by poison. In his Preface to the first cheap edition of the novel (1849), Dickens defended his characterisation of Jonas Chuzzlewit: 'I claim him as the legitimate issue of the father upon whom those vices [i.e., cunning, treachery and avarice] are seen to recoil.' (4, 8, 11, 18–20, 24–28, 38, 40–44, 46–48, 51)

Chuzzlewit, Martin, junior (MC) The eponymous hero of the novel, he is the grandson of old Martin Chuzzlewit, who has bred and reared him. At first, he is a complacent and selfish young man, who becomes Mr Pecksniff's pupil in architecture and treats Tom Pinch condescendingly, although his love for Mary Graham is genuine. When Pecksniff turns him out of his house (on old Martin Chuzzlewit's orders), he goes to America with Mark Tapley, with a vague idea of practising domestic architecture there but in any case with the belief that he has 'great prospects of doing well'. He is disillusioned in America when he discovers that the land he has invested in, ironically called Eden, is little more than a swamp. When he and Mark Tapley fall desperately ill with fever, he reflects on his personal deficiencies, concluding that 'selfishness was in his breast, and must be rooted out'. Returning to England as a reformed character, he regains his grand-

father's favour and marries Mary Graham. (2, 5–7, 10, 12–17, 21–23, 31, 33–35, 43, 48–50, 52, 53)

Chuzzlewit, Martin, senior (MC) The head of the Chuzzlewit family, 'he was a strong and vigorous old man, with a will of iron, and a voice of brass'. He is suspicious of the doings and motives of all the Chuzzlewits: 'Ugh! What a calendar of deceit, and lying, and false-witnessing, the sound of any word of kindred opens before me!' Mary Graham is his paid companion, but he has made it clear to her that she will inherit nothing from him. He tests and observes young Martin and Mr Pecksniff. He has Pecksniff expel Martin from his house and then he himself goes to live with Pecksniff, whom he deceives into thinking that he will inherit his money. But after young Martin's return from America, he exposes and denounces Pecksniff as a scoundrel, striking him to the ground with his walking stick and saying that he had always hoped that 'love might grow up between Mary and Martin'. (3, 4, 6, 10, 14, 24, 30, 31, 43, 44, 50–54)

Chuzzlewit, Mrs Ned (MC) A 'strong-minded woman', who was the widow of a deceased brother of old Martin Chuzzlewit and the mother of three spinster daughters. (4, 54)

Cicero (MC) A former black slave, who had bought his liberty and was saving money in order to buy his daughter's liberty. (17)

Clara A young English bride, who is haunted by Signor Dellombra, who makes off with her when she is staying at Genoa. ('To be Read at Dusk')

Clare, Ada (BH) She and her cousin, Richard Carstone, are two wards in Chancery under the guardianship of Mr Jarndyce, who chooses Esther Summerson as Ada's companion. She is, says

Esther, 'such a beautiful girl! With such rich golden hair, such soft blue eyes, and such a bright, innocent, trusting face!' She falls in love with Richard, whom she secretly marries after that young man's disagreement with Mr Jarndyce. After Richard's death, Esther and Mr Jarndyce care for her; they give her baby, 'born before the turf was planted on its father's grave', his father's name. (1, 3–6, 8, 9, 13–15, 17, 18, 23, 24, 30, 31, 35–37, 43, 45, 50, 51, 59–62, 64, 65, 67)

Clark, Betsy (SB) A housemaid. ('Scenes: The Streets – Morning')

Clark, Mr (DS) A stout man employed at a wharf, who puts Florence Dombey into the charge of Walter Gay when she is lost in the London streets after her frightening encounter with Mrs Brown. (6)

Clark, Mrs (NN) The lady whom the proprietress of a registry office recommended as an employer for Madeline Bray. (16)

Clarke, Mrs Susan (PP) See **Weller, Mrs Tony.**

Clarkson, Mr (RP) The counsel for the defence in the story told by Sergeant Mith. Clarkson was, in fact, a prominent barrister in the 1840s and 1850s. ('The Detective Police')

Clarriker, Mr (GE) A 'worthy young merchant or shipping broker', whom Mr Wemmick recommended to Pip, who buys Herbert Pocket a partnership in his business. Pip is also eventually employed in the firm. (37, 52, 58)

Clatter, Doctor (RP) One of Our Bore's medical men. He says that Our Bore's illness is due to 'Accumulation of fat about the heart!' ('Our Bore')

Claypole, Noah (OT) The 'large-headed, small-eyed youth', a charity boy, who worked for Mr Sowerberry, the undertaker. He cruelly taunts Oliver Twist by saying that the latter's late mother was 'a regular right-down bad 'un', with the result that Oliver knocks him down in a fury. With Charlotte, who is devoted to him, he later goes to London, where he falls in with Fagin, calls himself Morris Bolter, and becomes a thief. On Fagin's instructions, he spies on Nancy's meeting with Mr Brownlow and Rose Maylie on London Bridge and reports what he overheard to Fagin and Bill Sikes. Having turned King's evidence against Fagin, he is pardoned and goes into business as an Informer, 'in which calling he realizes a genteel subsistence'. (5, 6, 27, 42, 43, 45–47, 53)

Cleaver, Fanny (OMF) See **Wren, Jenny.**

Cleaver, Mr (OMF) See **Dolls, Mr.**

Clennam, Arthur (LD) A 40-year old man, who has returned to England after twenty years in business in China. He immediately finds the English Sunday and his mother (who had adopted him) forbiddingly dreary, austere and harsh and determines to renounce any part in the family business. He becomes fascinated by the demeanour and plight of Little Dorrit, who is working as a seamstress at his mother's house, and finds employment for her with Flora Finching. He is greatly attracted by the beautiful and youthful Pet Meagles but realises that he cannot permit himself to fall in love with her. He is shocked and disappointed when he meets Flora, who used to be his youthful sweetheart and is now 'broad', short of breath and voluble. He becomes a partner in Daniel Doyce's business but unwisely invests money in Merdle's enterprises. When the financial crash comes, Clennam is ruined and imprisoned for debt in the Marshalsea. While in prison, he learns from young John Chivery of Little Dorrit's love for him. After his release, thanks to Doyce, he marries her, in one of the most unusual matches in Dickens's fiction. But his quiet sincerity and recognition of his own fallibility make it a convincing partnership, as the final words of the novel beautifully express: 'They went quietly down into the roaring streets, inseparable and blessed; and as they passed along in sunshine and shade, the noisy and the eager, and the arrogant and the froward and the vain, fretted, and chafed, and made their usual uproar'. Doris Alexander suggests that Arthur Clennam 'embodies Dickens's mature self in his early forties' (1991: 120). (I: 2, 3, 5, 7–10, 12–17, 22–28, 31–36; II: 3, 4, 8–11, 13, 17, 20, 22, 23, 26–34)

Clennam, Mrs (LD) The supposed mother of Arthur Clennam, she is a grim, unyielding woman, who abides by harsh, Calvinistic religious beliefs. On his return to England, Arthur recalls 'the interminable Sunday of his nonage; when his mother, stern of face and unrelenting of heart, would sit all day behind a bible – bound, like her own construction of it, in the hardest, barest, and straitest boards.' She herself declares that she justifies all her actions by the authority of 'these Books'. She has lost the use of her limbs ('what with . . . rheumatic affection, and what with its attendant debility and nervous weakness') and has been confined to her room for a dozen years. Nevertheless, she is still intent on increasing the profits of the family business. When Arthur first sees her again after his long absence abroad, she is seated, dressed in a widow's dress, 'on a black-bier-like sofa . . . propped up behind with one great angular black bolster, like the block at a state execution in the good old times'. At the end of the novel, Rigaud, with confirmation from Affery Flintwinch, reveals the complex secrets of her past life: 'a history of a strange marriage, and a strange mother, and revenge, and a suppression'. She had

compelled her husband to yield to her his child, Arthur, the mother of whom was a poor singer he had truly loved. She was determined that Arthur might 'work out his release in bondage and hardship'. Frederick Dorrit had been helping the young girl, who died of a broken heart because of Mrs Clennam's cruelty. Mrs Clennam had suppressed a codicil in the will of Gilbert Clennam, her husband's uncle, who had compelled Arthur's father to marry her. In his remorse for bringing about that marriage, Gilbert had left 'one thousand guineas to the little beauty [whom Mrs Clennam] slowly hunted to death' and 'one thousand guineas to the youngest daughter her patron [Frederick Dorrit] might have at fifty, or (if he had none) brother's youngest daughter, on her coming of age'. As Frederick Dorrit was unmarried and childless, Little Dorrit should have received the thousand guineas. When Mrs Clennam is faced with Rigaud's threats to inform Arthur Clennam of these facts, she staggers to her feet, makes her way to the Marshalsea Prison, where she kneels at Little Dorrit's feet to ask her forgiveness. Then, on seeing her house collapse in ruins, she suffers a severe stroke, is confined paralysed and dumb in a wheelchair for three years, and 'lived and died a statue'. (I: 3–5, 8, 14, 15, 29, 30; II: 10, 17, 20, 23, 28, 30, 31)

Cleverly, Susannah and William (UT) A sister and brother who are Mormon emigrants. ('Bound for the Great Salt Lake')

Click (RP) A suspicious character told to 'hook it' by Rogers, one of Inspector Field's men. ('On Duty with Inspector Field')

Click, Mr (CS) A gas-fitter who has 'a theatrical turn . . . and wishes to be brought out in the character of Othello'. ('Somebody's Luggage')

Clickett (DC) Mrs Micawber's maid,

who was 'a dark-complexioned young woman, with a habit of snorting' and who told David Copperfield that she was an 'Orfling' (i.e., orphan) from St Luke's Workhouse. (11, 12)

Clickit, Mr and Mrs (SYC) Friends of the Bobtail Widgers, the 'plausible young couple'.

Clissold, Lawrence (CS) A clerk in Dringworth Brothers, who stole £500 and put the blame on Tregarthen, a fellow-clerk. He was 'a long, lean, wiry man, with some complaint in his eyes which forced him to wear spectacles of blue glass'. He was at least 52 years old, with 'a suspicious morning-tremble in his hands'. ('A Message from the Sea')

Clive, Mr (LD) An official in the Circumlocution Office, to whom Mr Wobbler refers Arthur Clennam. (I: 10)

Clocker, Mr (RP) A grocer in a seaside resort. ('Out of the Season')

Clubber, Sir Thomas (PP) The head of Chatham Dockyard. He, his wife and daughters were guests at the ball attended by the Pickwickians at the Bull Inn, Rochester. (2)

Cluppins, Mrs (PP) A 'little, brisk, busy-looking woman', who was a close friend of Mrs Bardell's and the sister of Mrs Raddle. She gave evidence in support of Mrs Bardell in the trial of Bardell v. Pickwick. (26, 34, 46)

Cly, Roger (TTC) A criminal associate of Barsad, Cly, as 'a virtuous servant', gives evidence against Charles Darnay at his trial at the Old Bailey for treason. Because of his 'unpopularity with the blackguard multitude' (in Barsad's words), who detest spies, he feigns death and arranges a mock funeral for himself. He works with Barsad as a spy in Paris but his previous deception is revealed by

Jerry Cruncher, who as a 'Resurrection man' had opened his supposed coffin only to find paving-stones and earth instead of a body. This revelation gives Sydney Carton an additional hold on Barsad, who is therefore compelled to help Carton in his efforts to rescue Charles Darnay. (I: 3, 14, II: 8, 15)

Coavinses (BH) *See* **Neckett**.

Cobb, Tom (BR) The 'general chandler and post-office keeper' at Chigwell and one of John Willet's regular customers at the Maypole Inn. Angered by Cobb's taunts, in support of John Willet's rebukes to Joe, Joe Willet knocks him into a heap of spittoons, where he lies 'stunned and motionless'. (1, 30, 33, 54, 56, 82)

Cobbey (NN) A boy at Dotheboys Hall, whose sister sends him eighteen pence. On her husband's instructions, Mrs Squeers takes this to pay for a broken square of glass. (8)

Cobbs (CS) The boots at the Holly-Tree Inn, who tells the story of the attempted 'elopement' by the children, Master Harry and Miss Norah. ('The Holly-Tree Inn')

Cobby (UT) The 'Giant' tramp who was sharing his meal with the White-haired Lady with pink eyes. ('Tramps')

Cocker, Mr Indignation (UT) An irate diner at the Temeraire Inn, Namelesston. ('A Little Dinner for an Hour')

Codger, Miss (MC) A Transcendental Literary Lady presented to Elijah Pogram with Miss Toppit. 'Sticking on her forehead . . . by invisible means, was a massive cameo, in size and shape like the raspberry tart which is ordinarily sold for a penny, representing on its front the Capitol at Washington'. (34)

Codlin, Thomas (OCS) With Short, his partner, he is an itinerant Punch and Judy showman. He has 'a surly, grumbling manner' and, according to Short, he is 'a universal mistruster'. Hoping to be rewarded for restoring Nell and her Grandfather to their friends, he tries to ingratiate himself with Nell, urging her to recollect that 'Codlin's the friend, not Short.' But Nell and her Grandfather give him and Short the slip at a race-meeting. (16–19, 37, 73)

Coiler, Mrs (GE) A widow, who was a 'toady neighbour' of the Matthew Pockets. (23)

Cole, King (PP) The father of Prince Bladud, in the story read by Mr Pickwick at Bath. (36)

Coleshaw, Miss (CS) A 'sedate young woman in black', who was a passenger on the *Golden Mary*. ('The Wreck of the Golden Mary')

Compeyson (GE) According to Magwitch, Compeyson 'set up fur a gentleman ... and he'd been to a public boarding-school and had learning. He was a smooth one to talk, and was a dab at the ways of gentlefolk. He was good-looking too.' He persuades Magwitch to become his partner in crime, particularly in 'swindling, handwriting forging, stolen bank-note passing, and such-like'. Magwitch becomes Compeyson's bitter enemy when he receives a lighter sentence 'on account of good character and bad company' and vows revenge. They escape separately from the prison ship, are found by the military search-party (accompanied by Pip, Joe and Mr Wopsle) furiously fighting each other in the marshes, and are re-arrested. Previously, Compeyson, in collusion with Miss Havisham's half-brother, Arthur, had pretended to love her (because they wished to cheat her out of money), but had jilted her on the wedding morning, with the

consequence that she had become the heart-broken, revengeful recluse whom Pip encounters. As Magwitch tells Pip, 'Him [Arthur, Miss Havisham's half-brother] and Compeyson had been in a bad thing with a rich lady ... and they'd made a pot of money by it'. Compeyson's wife, Sally, is ill-treated by him (he often kicks her). When Magwitch illegally returns to England, Compeyson informs on him. During Magwitch's attempted escape, Compeyson is drowned when they both fall into the river, 'fiercely locked in each other's arms' and struggling under the water. (3, 5, 42, 45, 47, 50, 53–55)

Conway, General (BR) An army officer and Member of Parliament, who protested against Lord George Gordon's petition to Parliament. He lived from 1721 to 1795. (49)

Cooper, Augustus (SB) A young man 'in the oil and colour line' who, to his bewilderment, is threatened with an action of breach of promise by Signor Billsmethi on behalf of his daughter. But his mother 'compromised the matter with twenty pounds from the till'. ('Characters: The Dancing Academy')

Copperfield, Mrs Clara (later, Mrs **Murdstone**) (DC) David Copperfield's mother, who is a very young widow when he is born. ' "Why, bless my heart!" exclaimed Miss Betsey [Trotwood]. "You are a very Baby!" ' As Quinion, Mr Murdstone's friend says, she is 'bewitching' and 'a pretty little widow', a description that delights her when David repeats it to her. After Mr Murdstone marries her, he and his sister immediately subjugate her to their will and forbid her from showing any softness and affection for David. She and her baby boy (Mr Murdstone's son) die not long afterwards. (1–4, 8, 9, 13, 14)

Copperfield, David (DC) The hero and

first-person narrator of what is probably Dickens's most popular novel. His opening sentence is modest and disarming: 'Whether I shall turn out to be the hero of my own life, or whether that station will be held by anybody else, these pages must show.' David's earliest days are spent in blissful happiness with his young widowed mother and his affectionate nurse, Peggotty. But he soon experiences hard and miserable times after his widowed mother marries Mr Murdstone: the Murdstones' harshness, Mr Creakle's school, his mother's death, and his degrading work in Murdstone and Grinby's warehouse. But once he is adopted by his great-aunt, Miss Betsey Trotwood, he receives a good education at Dr Strong's school, begins work in the legal profession, and eventually becomes a successful author. David's personal relationships are sometimes marked by imprudence, as in his admiring friendship with Steerforth and in his first marriage (though he and Dora, his 'child–wife', truly love each other). Thanks partly to the influence of his affectionate but resolute great-aunt, Miss Trotwood, he is determined, however, to make a success of his life and become a worthy husband: 'What I had to do, was, to take my woodman's axe in my hand, and clear my own way through the forest of difficulty, by cutting down the trees until I came to Dora.' Another beneficent influence upon him was Agnes Wickfield, who was in love with him, although he was unaware of this: 'She filled my heart with such good resolutions, strengthened my weakness so, by her example, so directed ... the wandering ardour and unsettled purpose within me, that all the little good I have done, and all the harm I have forborne, I solemnly believe I may refer to her.' Annie Strong's words to her husband also make a powerful impression on him when he reflects on his own marriage to Dora, including her reference to 'the first mistaken impulse of an undisciplined heart'. After the deaths of

Dora, Steerforth and Ham, David's sense of 'loss and sorrow' cast him in the depths of despair. But a period abroad, the healing influence of Nature and a letter from Agnes enable him to reach a true recognition of his real self and of his defects and errors. Returning to England after three years, he finds happiness and certainty in marriage to Agnes. Some likenesses are obvious between aspects of David Copperfield's life and career and Dickens's own, but John Forster's judicious comments on any possible comparisons should be borne in mind: 'many as are the resemblances in Copperfield's adventures to portions of those of Dickens, and often as reflections occur to David which no one intimate with Dickens could fail to recognise as but the reproduction of his, it would be the greatest mistake to imagine anything like a complete identity of the fictitious novelist with the real one, beyond the Hungerford scenes [in Murdstone and Grinby's warehouse]; or to suppose that the youth, who then received his first harsh schooling in life, came out of it as little harmed or hardened as David did. The language of the fiction reflects only faintly the narrative of the actual fact' (1928: Book 6, Ch. 7) (*passim*).

Copperfield, Dora (DC) *See* **Spenlow, Dora**.

Coppernose, Mr (MP) He puts forward suggestions at the Display of Models and Mechanical Science at the second meeting of the Mudfog Association concerning the provision of 'some harmless and wholesome relaxation for the young gentlemen of England'.

Cornberry, Mr (SB) The wealthy old gentleman to whom Julia Manners was engaged. On his death, he left her all his property. ('Tales: The Great Winglebury Duel')

Corney, Mrs (later, Mrs Bumble)

(OT) The matron of the workhouse where Oliver Twist was born. She gains possession of the jewellery that belonged to Oliver Twist's deceased mother. *See* **Bumble, Mr.** (23, 24, 27, 37, 38, 51)

Cour, Monsieur le Capitaine de la (CS) The commanding officer in the French town where Mr The Englishman (i.e., Mr Langley) found Bebelle. ('Somebody's Luggage')

Cower, Mr (SB) A solicitor in the Temple, who sends news to Mr Joseph Tuggs that he has inherited £20,000. ('Tales: The Tuggses at Ramsgate')

Crackit, Toby (OT) One of Fagin's gang of thieves, he was Bill Sikes's accomplice in their attempted burglary of Mrs Maylie's house. 'He was dressed in a smartly-cut snuff-coloured coat, with large brass buttons; an orange neckerchief; a coarse, staring, shawl-pattern waistcoat; and drab breeches. Mr Crackit . . . had no very great quantity of hair upon his head or face; but what he had, was of a reddish dye, and tortured into long corkscrew curls.' (19, 22, 25, 26, 28, 39, 50)

Craddock, Mrs (PP) The landlady of a house in the Royal Crescent, Bath, where the Pickwickians take lodgings. (36, 37)

Craggs, Thomas (CB) A partner in the law firm of Snitchey and Craggs, Doctor Jeddler's solicitors. He 'seemed to be represented by Snitchey, and to be conscious of little or no separate existence or personal individuality'. He was 'a cold, hard, dry man, dressed in grey and white, like a flint; with small twinkles in his eyes, as if something struck sparks out of them'. His wife, Mrs Craggs, 'was on principle suspicious of Mr Snitchey'. (*The Battle of Life*)

Cratchit, Bob and family (CB) Scrooge's clerk, who is paid fifteen shillings a week, works in a 'dismal little cell . . . a sort of

tank', and is grudgingly given the day off to celebrate Christmas (though Scrooge warns him to be at work 'all the earlier next morning'). But he is a devoted family man with a loving wife and six children (including Martha, Belinda and Peter) and has a special affection for his little crippled son, Tiny Tim. The Cratchits' Christmas dinner is a justly popular episode in Dickens's fiction. Despite Mrs Cratchit's disapproval, Bob is kind-hearted enough to propose drinking a toast to 'Mr Scrooge, the Founder of the Feast'. After Scrooge's conversion, he promises to raise Bob's salary and to assist his 'struggling family'. (*A Christmas Carol*)

Crawley, Mr (PP) Mrs Wugsby forbids her daughter Jane from dancing with him at the Assembly Rooms in Bath since he cannot inherit his father's eight hundred a year. (35)

Creakle, Mr (DC) The proprietor of Salem House, the school David Copperfield is sent to by Mr Murdstone. David recalled that 'Mr Creakle's face was fiery, and his eyes were small, and deep in his head; he had thick veins in his forehead, a little nose, and a large chin. He was bald on the top of his head . . . But the circumstance about him which impressed me most, was, that he had no voice, but spoke in a whisper. The exertion this cost him, or the consciousness of talking in that feeble way, made his angry face so much more angry, and his thick veins so much thicker, when he spoke, that I am not surprised, on looking back, at this peculiarity striking me as his chief one.' He is accompanied by a wooden-legged man, Tungay, who acts as his 'interpreter', repeating Mr Creakle's words and gestures. Creakle was an ignorant man, who used to be a dealer in hops, before being made bankrupt. 'He laid about him, right and left, every day of his life, charging in among the boys like a trooper, and slashing away unmercifully.' To the distress of his wife and daughter, he had turned his own son out of his house when he remonstrated with his father. Creakle later became a Middlesex Magistrate and was one of the group of officials who showed David Copperfield and Traddles round the prison where Heep and Littimer were confined. Creakle was possibly based on Mr William Jones, the proprietor of the Wellington House Academy, where Dickens was a pupil in 1824–7. (5–7, 9, 13, 27, 61)

Crewler, Sophie (DC) She is the daughter ('one of ten') of the Reverend Horace Crewler, a curate in Devonshire, and the fiancée of Tommy Traddles, to whom 'she's the dearest girl!' They eventually marry. 'And a more cheerful, amiable, honest, happy, bright-looking bride, I [i.e., David Copperfield] believe (as I could not help saying on the spot) the world never saw.' (27, 28, 34, 41, 43, 59, 61, 64)

Crimple, David (MC) Originally a pawnbroker, he changed his name from 'Crimp' to 'Crimple'. He became the secretary of Montague Tigg's fraudulent Anglo-Bengalee Disinterested Loan and Assurance Company at 'eight hundred pounds per annum, with his house-rent, coals, and candles free'. After Tigg's murder, Crimple and Bullamy, the porter, made off with the firm's money. (13, 27, 28, 49, 51)

Crinkles, Mr (MP) At the Display of Models and Mechanical Science at the second meeting of the Mudfog Association, he exhibited 'a most beautiful and delicate machine, of little larger size than an ordinary snuff-box, manufactured entirely by himself, and composed exclusively of steel, by the aid of which more pockets could be picked in one hour than by the present slow and tedious process in four-and-twenty'.

Cripples, Mr (LD) The proprietor of an Academy that gave Evening Tuition in the house where Frederick and Fanny Dorrit lodged. His son was a 'little white-faced boy'. (I: 9)

Cripps, Tom (PP) Bob Sawyer and Benjamin Allen's errand-boy, dressed in grey livery, who leaves the medicines at all the wrong houses. (38, 48, 50)

Crisparkle, Mrs (MED) The Reverend Septimus Crisparkle's mother, with whom he lives. 'What is prettier than an old lady – except a young lady – when her eyes are bright, when her figure is trim and compact, when her face is cheerful and calm, when her dress is as the dress of a china shepherdess: so dainty in its colours, so individually assorted to herself, so neatly moulded on her?' (6, 7, 10)

Crisparkle, the Reverend Septimus (MED) A Minor Canon in Cloisterham, he is 35 years old and lives with his widowed mother. He is 'fair and rosy, and perpetually pitching himself headforemost into all the deep running water in the surrounding country; Mr Crisparkle, Minor Canon, early riser, musical, classical, cheerful, kind, good-natured, social, contented, and boy-like'. He takes in Neville Landless as a pupil and in his gentle, sympathetic way endeavours to calm his passionate nature and to bring about a reconciliation with Edwin Drood after their quarrel. After the disappearance of Edwin Drood, Crisparkle, convinced of Neville's innocence and believing in his good qualities, consults Mr Grewgious about clearing him from suspicion. (2, 6–8, 10, 12–17, 19, 21–23)

Crofts (SYC) The barber who shaved old Mr Harvey. ('The Old Couple')

Crookey (PP) A servant at Namby's sponging-house. In dress and general appearance he 'looked something between

Figure 2 Mr Crummles and Nicholas Nickleby by Thomas Onwhyn

a bankrupt grazier, and a drover in a state of insolvency'. (40)

Cropley, Miss (NN) A former friend at Exeter of Mrs Nickleby's. (33)

Crowl, Mr (NN) A 'hard-featured square-faced man, elderly and shabby', who wears a 'wig of short, coarse, red hair' (which he takes off with his hat) and who lodges in the next garret to Newman Noggs. (14, 15, 32)

Crummles, Ninetta (NN) The so-called 'Infant Phenomenon'. *See* **Crummles, Vincent and family.**

Crummles, Vincent, and family (NN) Mr Vincent Crummles was the actor–manager of a touring theatrical company. He was 'a large heavy man' with 'a very full under-lip, a hoarse voice, as though he were in the habit of shouting very much, and very short black hair, shaved off nearly to the crown of his head – to admit . . . of his more easily wearing character wigs of any shape or pattern'. On meeting Nicholas Nickleby and Smike near Portsmouth, he gives them employment in his company. Nicholas's 'Romeo was received with hearty plaudits and unbounded favour, and Smike was pronounced unanimously, alike by audience and actors, the very prince and prodigy of Apothecaries.' When Nicholas leaves the company, Mr Crummles takes an imposing, public farewell of him, 'inflicting upon him a rapid succession of stage embraces'. His wife and three children are also actors. Of these, the most remarkable was Miss Ninetta Crummles, the Infant Phenomenon, whose talent, according to her father, 'is not to be imagined.' She is supposedly 10 years of age, but 'though of short stature, had a comparatively aged countenance, and had moreover been precisely the same age – not perhaps to the full extent of the memory of the oldest inhabitant, but certainly for five good years'. Mr Crummles and his family emigrate to America, a move which is announced in the newspapers: 'The talented Vincent Crummles, long favourably known to fame as a country manager and actor of no ordinary pretensions, is about to cross the Atlantic on an histrionic expedition. Crummles is to be accompanied, we hear, by his lady and gifted family.' Mr Crummles and the Infant Phenomenon are probably based on T.D. Davenport (1792–1851), an actor–manager, and his daughter, Jean (1829–1903). (22–25, 29, 30, 48)

Crumpton, the Misses Amelia and Maria (SB) They were 'two unusually tall, particularly thin, and exceedingly skinny personages: very upright, and very yellow', who are the proprietors of Minerva House, Hammersmith, a 'finishing establishment for young ladies'. Miss Lavinia Brook Dingwall elopes from there with Theodosius Butler. ('Tales: Sentiment')

Cruncher, Jerry, his wife and son (TTC) During the day he is the 'odd-job-man' and 'occasional porter and messenger' at Tellson's Bank and during the evenings he is a 'Resurrection Man', secretly removing corpses from burial grounds and selling them for dissection. At home, he is perpetually annoyed by his wife's kneeling in prayer: 'What are you up to, Aggerawayter? . . . Saying your prayers! You're a nice woman! What do you mean by flopping yourself down and praying agin me?' He has a son, also named Jerry, who is curious about his father's part-time occupation. Because of his activities as a Resurrection Man, Jerry Cruncher is aware that Cly's supposed coffin was filled with paving-stones and earth and so enables Sydney Carton to increase his hold over Cly and Barsad. Frightened by his dangerous situation in revolutionary Paris, Jerry cryptically vows to Miss Pross that he will relinquish his grave-robbing activities and his interfering with Mrs Cruncher's 'flopping'. (I: 2, 3; II: 1–3, 14, 24; III: 3, 7–9, 14)

Crupp, Mrs (DC) David Copperfield's landlady in Buckingham Street, Adelphi. She calls him 'Mr Copperfull' ('firstly, no doubt, because it was not my name; and secondly, I am inclined to think, in some indistinct association with a washing day'). David discovers that she is 'a martyr to a curious disorder called "the spazzums", which was generally accompanied with inflammation of the nose, and required to be constantly treated with peppermint'. She is 'a woman of penetration', who realises that David is love-sick over Dora Spenlow and whose 'advice . . . is, to cheer up, sir, and keep a good heart, and to know your own walue'. But she establishes a tyranny over David, who says that 'she was the terror of [his life]'. She is, however, worsted by Betsey Trotwood: 'rather than encounter my aunt upon the staircase, she would endeavour to hide her portly form behind doors – leaving visible, however, a wide margin of flannel petticoat – or would shrink into dark corners'. (23–26, 28, 34, 35, 37, 44)

Crushton, the Honourable Mr (PP) He is a gentleman in a 'red waistcoat and dark moustache', the 'bosom friend' of Lord Mutanhed, both of whom are among those in the Assembly Rooms at Bath when Mr Pickwick is there. (35, 36)

Cummins, Tom (PP) He was in the chair when Dodson and Fogg's clerks spent a convivial evening. (20)

Curdle, Mr and Mrs (NN) After some hesitation, they agree to be among the patrons of Miss Snevellici's 'bespeak'. Mrs Curdle 'was supposed, by those who were best informed on such points, to possess quite the London taste in matters relating to literature and the drama'. Mr Curdle 'had written a pamphlet of sixty-four pages, post octavo, on the character of the Nurse's deceased husband in *Romeo and Juliet*'. (24)

Curzon, Thomas (BR) A London hosier, to whom Mark Gilbert, an initiate in the 'Prentice Knights, is bound apprentice. He pulled Gilbert's ears for looking at his daughter, and for this and other ill-treatment he is denounced by Sim Tappertit. (8)

Cute, Alderman (CB) Despite his easy and affable manner, he declares his determination in his capacity as a Justice to 'put down' such poor people as 'distressed wives' and 'boys without shoes and stockings'. Above all, he has made up his mind to 'Put suicide Down'. Dickens based him on Sir Peter Laurie, the Lord Mayor of London in 1832–33. (*The Chimes*)

Cutler, Mr and Mrs (NN) They are among the friends invited to the party given by Mr and Mrs Kenwigs to celebrate their wedding anniversary. (14)

Cuttle, Captain (DS) The devoted friend of Sol Gills, Walter Gay, and Florence Dombey. He had 'a hook instead of a hand attached to his right wrist; very bushy black eyebrows, and a thick stick in his left hand, covered all over (like his nose) with knobs . . . He was usually addressed as Captain . . . and had been a pilot, or a skipper, or a privateers-man, or all three perhaps; and was a very salt-looking man indeed.' He lodges with a widow, Mrs MacStinger, of whom he goes in great trepidation. His conversation is full of wise and hearty precepts, one of the most memorable of which is 'When found, make a note of.' But he places great confidence in the advice of his friend, Captain Bunsby. When Sol Gills goes away in search of Walter, Captain Cuttle secretly escapes from Mrs MacStinger's lodgings and takes charge of the Wooden Midshipman, Sol Gills's shop. He takes care of Florence Dombey, when she seeks refuge there after fleeing from her father. When she kisses his hand, so many feelings and memories 'all so rushed upon the good Captain together, that he fairly overflowed with compassion and gentleness'. On Sol Gills's return, Captain Cuttle goes into partnership with him: 'His delight in his own name over the door, is inexhaustible. He crosses the street, twenty times a day, to look at it from the other side of the way, and invariably says, on these occasions, "Ed'ard Cuttle, my lad, if your mother could ha' know'd as you would ever be a man o' science, the good old creetur would ha' been took aback indeed!"' Kitton says that Captain Cuttle may have been based on David Mainland, a merchantman, who was once introduced to Dickens, and also notes that Samuel Pepys met a Captain Cuttle (1906: 163). (4, 9, 10, 15, 17, 19, 23, 25, 31, 32, 38, 39, 48–50, 56, 57, 60, 62)

D

Dadson, Mr (SB) The writing-master at Minerva House, the Misses Crumpton's school in Hammersmith. ('Tales: Sentiment')

Daisy, Solomon (BR) The parish clerk who frequents the Maypole and who relates at the outset of *Barnaby Rudge* the story of the murder of Reuben Haredale at the Warren and of the discovery of the supposed body of Rudge, the steward, twenty-two years previously. 'By dint of relating the story very often, and ornamenting it (according to village report) with a few flourishes suggested by the various hearers from time to time, he had come by degrees to tell it with great effect.' Five years later, in 1775, on the anniversary of the murders, Daisy bursts into the Maypole in terror, having seen what he takes to be Rudge's ghost. When the Gordon Riots break out, he and his two cronies, Cobb and Parkes, defy Mr Willet, the landlord of the Maypole, by walking from Chigwell to London to see for themselves what is happening there. (1–3, 11, 30, 33, 54, 56, 82)

Dando (SB) The head boatman at Searle's yard on the banks of the Thames. ('Scenes: The River')

Danton, Mr (SB) A friend of Mr Kitterbell's. 'He had acquired, somehow or other, the reputation of being a great wit, and, accordingly, whenever he opened his mouth, everybody who knew him laughed very heartily.' ('Tales: The Bloomsbury Christening')

Darby (BH) A police constable on duty in Tom-all-Alone's, who accompanies Inspector Bucket and Mr Snagsby in their investigations in that area. (22)

Darnay, Charles (TTC) He was the nephew of the Marquis St Evrémonde, but he had adopted the name of Darnay, an Anglicised version of D'Aulnay, his mother's maiden name. He was 'a young man of about five-and-twenty, well-grown and well-looking, with a sunburnt cheek and a dark eye. His condition was that of a young gentleman.' He is tried at the Old Bailey on a false charge of treason, but he is cleared when his remarkable likeness to Sydney Carton is adduced as evidence of the uncertainty of his identity. Darnay detests the aristocratic family and system to which he belongs by birth. In conversation with his uncle, the Marquis, he recalls that 'we did a world of wrong, injuring every human creature who came between us and our pleasure [including Doctor Manette, although Darnay is unaware of this]'. The consequence is that Darnay, as he says, is 'bound to a system that is frightful to [him], responsible for it, but powerless in it'. He works in England, where he has sought refuge from the abhorred system, as a French tutor. Having fallen in love with Lucie Manette, he marries her. During the French Revolution, he goes to France, in response to a plea for help from Gabelle, an old servant of the St Evrémonde family, who has been imprisoned. Darnay himself is imprisoned but is released owing to the intervention of Doctor Manette. But he is rearrested, imprisoned again, and condemned to death, because of Doctor

Figure 3 Doctor Manette, little Lucie and Charles and Lucie Darnay by Hablot K. Browne (Phiz)

Manette's written testimony of the wrongs committed by the St Evrémonde family. He is saved when Sydney Carton, his double, takes his place in the prison cell and allows himself to be executed in Darnay's place. For the possible significance of his initials, which are the same as Charles Dickens's, *see* **Doubledick, Richard**. (II: 2–4, 6, 9, 10, 16–18, 20, 21, 24; III: 1, 3–13)

Dartle, Rosa (DC) Mrs Steerforth's companion. She was 'of a slight short figure, dark, and not agreeable to look at, but with some appearance of good looks too, who attracted my [i.e., David Copperfield's] attention . . . She had black hair and eager black eyes, and was thin, and had a scar upon her lip. It was an old scar – I should rather call it, seam, for it was not discoloured, and healed years ago – which had once cut through her mouth, downward towards the chin . . . I concluded in my own mind that she was about thirty years of age, and that she wished to be married. She was a little

dilapidated – like a house – with having been so long to let; yet had, as I have said, an appearance of good looks. Her thinness seemed to be the effect of some wasting fire within her, which found a vent in her gaunt eyes.' David is fascinated by her to the extent that he even finds himself 'a little in love' with her. Miss Dartle is a young woman of sarcastic penetration, who indirectly makes her opinions clear by a process of asking for information, as when she asks Steerforth about the Peggotty family and household: 'That sort of people. Are they really animals or clods, and things of another order? I want to know *so* much.' As Steerforth tells David, 'she brings everything to a grindstone . . . and sharpens it, as she has sharpened her own face and figure these years past. She has worn herself away by constant sharpening. She is all edge.' When Steerforth was a boy, he was so exasperated by her on one occasion that he threw a hammer at her and it was this that had scarred her lip. Despite that incident, she is passionately in love with him and therefore rages against him, Emily and Daniel Peggotty when she hears of the elopement: 'They are a depraved, worthless set. I would have her whipped.' In a highly melodramatic confrontation with Emily, after the latter's return to England, she mercilessly excoriates her. She later pitilessly hurls verbal abuse at Mrs Steerforth after Steerforth's death: 'My love would have been devoted – would have trod your paltry whimpering under foot!' Nevertheless, she remains with Mrs Steerforth, by turns caressing her and quarrelling with her. In her torments and frustrations, Miss Dartle can be compared with Miss Wade. A possible model for Miss Dartle is Miss Meredith, who was the companion of Miss Burdett Coutts, one of Dickens's close acquaintances. (20, 21, 24, 29, 32, 36, 46, 50, 56, 64)

Datchery, Dick (MED) He is a mysterious stranger who appears in Cloisterham. He was 'a white-haired personage, with black eyebrows. Being buttoned up in a tightish blue surtout, with a buff waistcoat and gray trousers, he had something of a military air. . . This gentleman's white head was unusually large, and his shock of white hair was unusually thick and ample.' He lodges with the Topes, is very interested in John Jasper, and questions Princess Puffer and Deputy. Dickens evidently destined Datchery to play an important part in the novel. Commentators are generally agreed that he is a character in disguise – but who? Candidates include Helena or Neville Landless, Bazzard, Grewgious, Tartar, and Edwin Drood himself. (18, 23)

David (NN) The Cheerybles' 'ancient butler of apoplectic appearance . . . with very short legs'. (37, 63)

David (OCS) The elderly, deaf gravedigger in the village where Little Nell and her Grandfather find refuge. (54)

Davis, Gill (CS) A private in the Royal Marines, who is the narrator of the events on Silver-Store Island. ('The Perils of Certain English Prisoners')

Dawes, Mary (LD) The nurse in the poor nobleman's household where Miss Wade was employed for a time as a governess. Miss Wade typically misinterpreted her benevolent actions as a form of exulting over her. (II: 21)

Dawkins, Jack (OT) The young pickpocket, always called the Artful Dodger, whom Oliver Twist encounters in Barnet, on the road to London. 'He was a snubnosed, flat-browed, common-faced boy enough; and as dirty a juvenile as one would wish to see; but he had about him all the airs and manners of a man.' His speech is full of ironical remarks and the vivid slang known as 'thieves' cant', as when he talks to Oliver at their first meeting: 'But come . . . you want grub, and you shall have it. I'm at low-water-mark myself – only one bob and a magpie; but, *as* far *as* it goes, I'll fork out and stump. Up with you on your pins. There! Now then! Morrice!' He takes Oliver to Fagin's den, and it's the Dodger's theft of Mr Brownlow's handkerchief that leads to Oliver's wrongful arrest. Regarded by Fagin as his 'best hand', the Dodger is finally convicted of stealing a silver snuff-box from a gentleman's pocket, which does not prevent him from treating the court officials with grinning impudence: 'for this ain't the shop for justice; besides which, my attorney is a-breakfasting this morning with the Wice President of the House of Commons'. (8–10, 12, 13, 16, 18, 19, 25, 39, 43)

Daws, Mary (DS) A 'young kitchenmaid of inferior rank' in Mr Dombey's household. After the failure of Dombey's firm, she unexpectedly utters the words, 'Suppose the wages shouldn't be paid!' and is consequently rebuked by the Cook. (59)

Dawson, Mr (SB) The surgeon in 'Our Parish'. As was customary, he 'displays a large lamp, with a different colour in every pane of glass, at the corner of the row'. ('Our Parish: The Four Sisters')

Deaf Gentleman, the (MHC) A dear friend of Master Humphrey's, who trusts and believes that their attachment 'will only be interrupted by death, to be re-newed in another existence'. (2)

Dean, the (MED) A 'modest and worthy gentleman', who is the Dean of Cloister-ham Cathedral. (2, 4, 12, 16)

Dedlock, Lady (BH) Honoria Dedlock was the proud and elegant wife of Sir Leicester Dedlock. Although her origins were reputed to be humble, 'she had beauty, pride, ambition, insolent resolve, and sense enough to portion out a legion of fine ladies. Wealth and station, added to these, soon floated her upward; and for years, now, my Lady Dedlock has been at the centre of the fashionable in-telligence, and at the top of the fashion-able tree . . . She has beauty still, and, if it be not in its heyday, it is not yet in its autumn. She has a fine face – originally of a character that would be rather called very pretty than handsome, but improved into classicality by the acquired expres-sion of her fashionable state.' But her guilty, secret past is gradually uncovered, mostly by her lawyer, Mr Tulkinghorn, and Mr Guppy: as a young woman, she had a child, Esther Summerson, by her lover, Captain Hawdon. Wrongly de-nounced in a letter as the murderess of Tulkinghorn and having heard from Guppy that her secrets will be exposed, she takes flight. Her route is traced by Esther and Inspector Bucket, who (with Mr Woodcourt) find her lying dead at the gate of the burial ground where Hawdon was interred. Michael Slater, in *Dickens and Women*, sees her as Edith Dombey's successor: 'the "Bought Bride" [Edith Dombey] is succeeded by the Great Lady

with a Guilty Secret, a figure belonging more to the world of melodrama (Miss Braddon was to give Victorian readers a definitive embodiment of the role in *Lady Audley's Secret* ten years later) than the Bought Bride, who was so much closer to contemporary social realities. Yet Lady Dedlock seems, on the whole, less jarringly melodramatic than Edith [partly because of the terser language she speaks]' (1983: 261). (2, 7, 9, 12, 16, 18, 23, 28, 29, 33, 36, 37, 40, 41, 43, 48, 53–59)

Dedlock, Sir Leicester (BH) 'Sir Leices-ter Dedlock is only a baronet, but there is no mightier baronet than he. His family is as old as the hills, and infinitely more respectable. He has a general opinion that the world might get on without hills, but would be done up without Dedlocks . . . Sir Leicester is twenty years, full measure, older than my Lady [whom he married for love]. He will never see sixty-five again, nor perhaps sixty-six, nor yet sixty-seven. He has a twist of the gout now and then, and walks a little stiffly. He is of a worthy presence, with his light grey hair and whiskers, his fine shirt-frill, his pure white waistcoat, and his blue coat with bright buttons always but-toned.' Mr Boythorn, his neighbour, an-grily exclaims that Sir Leicester and his family 'are the most solemnly conceited and consummate blockheads!' In his aristocratic pride, Sir Leicester scorns all social classes below his own and any moves towards democratic parliamentary elections. He considers that the whole country is going to pieces. After the rev-elations concerning Lady Dedlock's past and present conduct, he is so shocked that he has a stroke, and becomes 'in-valided, bent, and almost blind, but of worthy presence yet'. He nevertheless asks Volumnia Dedlock, Mrs Rouncewell and George to witness that he asserts no cause of complaint against Lady Ded-lock and that he retains an undiminished affection for her. G.K. Chesterton makes a typically paradoxical comparison between Sir Leicester Dedlock and Harold Skimpole: they 'are alike in accepting with a royal unconsciousness the anomaly and evil of their position. But the idleness and insolence of the aristocrat is human and humble compared to the idleness and insolence of the artist' (1933: 158). (2, 7, 9, 12, 16, 18, 27–29, 40, 41, 43, 48, 49, 53–56, 58, 63, 66)

Dedlock, Volumnia (BH) A cousin of Sir Leicester Dedlock's. She was 'a young lady (of sixty)', who has retired to Bath, 'where she lives slenderly on an annual present from Sir Leicester, and whence she makes occasional resurrections in the country houses of her cousins'. After Lady Dedlock's death, she remains with Sir Leicester, where she 'has alighted on a memorandum concerning herself, in the event of "anything happening" to her kinsman, which is handsome compensation for an extensive course of reading, and holds even the dragon Boredom at bay'. (28, 40, 53, 56, 58, 66)

Deedles (CB) A friend of Alderman Cute, he was a banker who put 'a double-barrelled pistol to his mouth, in his own counting house . . . and blew his brains out'. (*The Chimes*)

Defarge, Ernest (TTC) A wine-shop keeper in Paris. He 'was a bull-necked, martial-looking man of thirty, and he should have been of a hot temperament, for, although it was a bitter day, he wore no coat, but carried one slung over his shoulder. His shirt-sleeves were rolled up, too, and his brown arms were bare to the elbows. Neither did he wear anything more on his head than his own crisply-curling short dark hair. He was a dark man altogether, with good eyes and a good bold breadth between them. Good-humoured-looking on the whole, but implacable-looking, too; evidently a man of a strong resolution and a set purpose; a man not desirable to be met, rushing

down a narrow pass with a gulf on either side, for nothing would turn the man.' As Doctor Manette's former servant, he gives him refuge after his release from the Bastille. Unlike his wife, he becomes discouraged by the apparently slow progress of the revolutionary cause. But when the Revolution comes, he is one of the leaders of the assault on the Bastille (where he retrieves from a chimney Doctor Manette's written testimony concerning the evil doings of the St Evrémonde family) and is one of the participants in the hanging of Foulon. At Charles Darnay's second trial, he produces Doctor Manette's incriminating evidence and thus brings about Darnay's condemnation. He nevertheless urges Madame Defarge and others to spare Doctor Manette and Lucie out of sympathy for their emotional anguish. (I: 5, 6; II: 7, 15, 16, 21, 22; III: 1, 3, 6, 7, 9, 10, 12, 14)

Defarge, Madame Thérèse (TTC) The wife of Defarge, the wine-shop keeper. She 'was a stout woman of about his own age [thirty], with a watchful eye that seldom seemed to look at anything, a large hand heavily ringed, a steady face, strong features, and a great composure of manner'. She is constantly knitting 'with the steadfastness of Fate', keeping thereby a register 'in her own stitches and her own symbols'. (This is Dickens's imaginative heightening of the well-known figure of the *tricoteuse* during the French Revolution.) With even more determination than her husband, she relentlessly prepares, in the pre-revolutionary days, for 'vengeance and retribution', however long they may take. In his admiring opinion, she is 'a great woman . . . a strong woman, a grand woman, a frightfully grand woman!' Armed with an axe, she leads the women in the assault on the Bastille and hews off the head of the governor of the prison. She rejoices in the capture and execution of Foulon, clapping her hands 'as at a play'. She reveals a personal motive for her bloodthirsty fervour in that she was the sister of the woman and boy killed by the Evrémondes: 'imbued from her childhood with a brooding sense of wrong, and inveterate hatred of a class, opportunity had developed her into a tigress. She was absolutely without pity. If she had ever had the virtue in her, it had quite gone out of her.' Hunting down Lucie Darnay, her child and Doctor Manette, whom she has resolved must die, she accidentally shoots herself dead in a struggle with Miss Pross. (I: 5, 6; II: 7, 15, 16, 21, 22; III: 3, 5, 6, 8–10, 12, 14)

Delafontaine, Mr (SB) A gentleman who lived in Bedford Square with whom Horatio Sparkins claimed to have exchanged cards. ('Tales: Horatio Sparkins')

Dellombra, Signor He 'was dressed in black, and had a reserved and secret air, and was a dark remarkable-looking man, with black hair and a grey moustache'. He haunts Clara, a young English bride, in dreams and in reality, and is later reported to have made off with her in a carriage. ('To be Read at Dusk')

Demple, George (DC) A doctor's son, who was one of David Copperfield's fellow-pupils at Salem House. (5, 7)

Denham, Edward (CB) The assumed name of Edmund Longford. (*The Haunted Man*)

Dennis, Ned (BR) The public hangman, who eagerly becomes one of the ringleaders of the Gordon Riots. He 'was a squat, thickset personage, with a low retreating forehead, a coarse shock head of hair, and eyes so small and near together, that his broken nose seemed to prevent their meeting and fusing into one of the usual size'. His motive for joining the anti-Catholic movement led by Lord George Gordon is that his work is 'sound, Protestant, constitutional, English work'. If, he exclaims with grim relish, 'these Papists gets into power and begins to boil and roast instead of to hang, what becomes of my work!' He takes a blackly jocular pride in making cryptic references to his occupation. One of the many people he had previously hanged was Hugh's mother. But he shows abject cowardice when he himself is arrested, condemned to death and hanged for his prominent part in the Riots. Dickens based him on the actual hangman of the same name, who held the office from 1771 to 1786 and who was active in the Riots. He was, however, reprieved from execution. There were also literary antecedents: 'the first chapter of Charles Whitehead's *Autobiography of Jack Ketch* [1834] and, more generally . . . the irony of [Fielding's] *Jonathan Wild* [1743]' (Tillotson 1954a: xi). (36–40, 44, 49, 50, 52–54, 59, 60, 63–65, 69–71, 74–77)

Deputy (MED) Also known as Winks, he was a 'hideous small boy', who, in his own words, was 'man-servant up at the Travellers' Twopenny in Gas Works Garding'. Durdles pays him a halfpenny 'to pelt him home' if Deputy catches him out late. Deputy chants, 'like a little savage', a strange rhyme that begins 'Widdy widdy wen!' (5, 12, 18, 23)

Derrick, John (CS) The 'trusty and attached servant for more than twenty years' of the narrator of 'To be Taken with a Grain of Salt'. ('Doctor Marigold')

Dibabs, Jane (NN) A former acquaintance of Mrs Nickleby, who cites her as an example of a woman who 'married a man who was a great deal older than herself'. (55)

Dibble, Mr Sampson and Mrs Dorothy (UT) An aged, blind Mormon emigrant and his wife. ('Bound for the Great Salt Lake')

Dick (NN) A 'stout old Yorkshireman', who was the guard on the coach that took Mr Squeers and Nicholas Nickleby to Greta Bridge. (5)

Dick (NN) Tim Linkinwater's blind blackbird, which he kept in the Brothers Cheeryble's counting-house. 'There was not a bird of such methodical and business-like habits in all the world, as the blind blackbird, who dreamed and dozed away his days in a large snug cage, and had lost his voice, from old age, years before Tim first bought him.' Dickens's daughters had a pet canary named Dick. (37)

Dick (OT) A pathetic, half-starved, little pauper boy, who was a friend of Oliver Twist's at Mrs Mann's baby-farm. When Oliver determines to go away and seek his fortune, he bids farewell to Dick, who exclaims, 'God bless you!' This was the first blessing that Oliver had received, and 'through the struggles and sufferings, and troubles and changes, of his after life, he never once forgot it'. At the end of the novel, Oliver learns that Dick has died. (7, 17, 51)

Dick, Mr (DC) The name by which Mr Richard Babley was known. He was an amiable, simple-minded gentleman, who lived with Miss Trotwood, of whom he was a 'sort of distant connexion'. When David arrives at Miss Trotwood's house in Dover, he looks at an upstairs window, where he sees 'a florid, pleasant-looking gentleman, with a grey head, who shut up one eye in a grotesque manner, nodded his head at me several times, shook it at me as often, laughed, and went away'. Mr Dick's submission to Miss Trotwood and 'his childish delight when she praised him' made David suspect that he was 'a little mad'. According to Miss Trotwood, who shows him great devotion, he was made ill by his sister's wretched marriage and fear of his brother-in-law. She refuses to acknowledge that he is mentally

defective in any way, and turns to him for advice in practical matters. When she asks him what should be done with David, who has so unexpectedly arrived from London, he immediately replies, 'I should put him to bed', which gives her a feeling of 'complacent triumph' in his good judgement. Mr Dick is perpetually engaged in writing a Memorial for the legal authorities but can never keep out of it his obsession with King Charles I (hence, the phrase 'King Charles's head'). One of his pleasures is flying a great kite made out of old leaves of the Memorial. Having always venerated Dr Strong, he becomes a sympathetic link between him and Annie, helping to bring about a full understanding between them. Dickens's presentation of Mr Dick, and the relationship between him and Aunt Betsey, is markedly sympathetic and forward-looking, as John Forster pointed out: 'By a line thrown out in *Wilhelm Meister*, that the true way of treating the insane, was, in all respects possible, to act to them as if they were sane, Goethe anticipated what it took a century to apply to the most terrible disorder of humanity; and what Mrs [sic] Trotwood does for Mr Dick goes a step further, by showing how often asylums might be dispensed with, and how large might be the number of deficient intellects manageable with patience in their own homes.' (1928: Book 6, Ch. 7). For Dickens's use of the name 'Dick', *see* **Doubledick, Richard**. (13–15, 17–19, 23, 34–38, 40–43, 45, 49, 52, 54, 59, 60, 62, 64)

Diego, Don (RP) The 'inventor of the last new Flying Machines, price so many francs for ladies, so many more for gentlemen'. ('A Flight')

Dilber, Mrs (CB) A laundress, whom Scrooge sees in his vision of the future selling some of his possessions after his death. (*A Christmas Carol*)

Figure 4 Mr Dick by Harry Furniss

Dingo, Professor (BH) Mrs Bayham Badger's second husband, who (according to Mr Bayham Badger) had been 'of European reputation'. (13)

Dingwall, Cornelius Brook (SB) An MP, who was 'very haughty, solemn and portentous'. He sends his daughter, Lavinia, to the Miss Crumptons' finishing school, whence she elopes with Theodosius Butler. ('Tales: Sentiment')

Diogenes (DS) The Blimbers' dog, with a fully appropriate classical name. Because Paul had been fond of him, Toots gives him, with the Blimbers' approval, to Florence. Although he 'was as ridiculous a dog as one would meet with on a summer's day', Florence loves and cherishes him. (14, 18, 22, 23, 28, 30, 31, 35, 41, 44, 48–50, 56)

Diver, Colonel (MC) The editor of the *New York Rowdy Journal*. He was a 'sallow gentleman, with sunken cheeks, black hair, small twinkling eyes . . . [and] a mixed expression of vulgar cunning and conceit'. (16)

Dobble, Mr (SB) The host of a New Year's Eve quadrille party. He is a clerk with a wife, son and daughter. ('Characters: The New Year')

Dobbs, Julia (SG) The heroine of the play.

Doche, Madame (RP) A dealer in the Calf Market at Poissy. ('A Monument of French Folly')

Dodson and Fogg (PP) Mrs Bardell's attorneys, whose offices were in 'a dingy house, at the very furthest end of Freeman's Court, Cornhill'. Fogg was 'an elderly, pimply-faced, vegetable-diet sort of man', who seemed 'to be an essential part of the desk at which he was writing', whereas Dodson was 'a plump, portly, stern-looking man, with a loud voice'.

They 'are universally considered among the sharpest of the sharp', and have no hesitation in committing to prison their own client, Mrs Bardell, in execution of costs. In his Preface to the first cheap edition of *Pickwick Papers* (1847), written ten years after its first publication, Dickens noted with satisfaction that 'legal reforms have pared the claws of Messrs Dodson and Fogg'. (18, 20, 22, 26, 31, 35, 46, 47, 53, 57)

Do'em (PL) The livery servant who attends the Honourable Captain Fitz-Whisker Fiercy.

Dogginson (RP) A member of the vestry, who is regarded as 'a regular John Bull'. ('Our Vestry')

Dolloby, Mr (DC) A dealer in old clothes in the Kent Road, to whom David Copperfield sells his waistcoat for ninepence when he is starting his journey to Dover. (13)

Dolls, Mr (OMF) Called thus by Eugene Wrayburn, he is the wretched, drunken father of Jenny Wren, the dolls' dressmaker (his real name is Cleaver). Jenny, who is in reality devoted to him, treats him as a naughty child, typically addressing him as 'You bad old boy!' In response, 'the shaking figure, unnerved and disjointed from head to foot, put out its two hands a little way, as making overtures of peace and reconciliation. Abject tears stood in its eyes, and stained the blotched red of its cheeks. The swollen lead-coloured under lip trembled with a shameful whine. The whole indecorous threadbare ruin, from the broken shoes to the prematurely-grey scanty hair, grovelled. Not with any sense worthy to be called a sense, of this dire reversal of the places of parent and child, but in a pitiful expostulation to be let off from a scolding.' After Lizzie Hexam's disappearance, Eugene Wrayburn persuades him to give him her address by promising

Figure 5 James Carker and Edith Dombey by Hablot K. Browne (Phiz)

to give him money for rum. Mr Dolls, on his way to a licensed victualler's and to 'bestow some maudlin remorse on Mr Eugene Wrayburn', collapses and dies outside the latter's chambers in the Temple. (II; 1, 2; III: 10, 17; IV: 9)

Dombey, Edith (DS) The daughter of Mrs Skewton, she was first married at the age of eighteen to Colonel Granger, who died two years later. Major Bagstock tells Mr Dombey that their son was drowned at four or five years old. When Mr

Dombey and Major Bagstock meet her with her mother at Leamington Spa, they are immediately struck by 'the proud beauty of the daughter with her graceful figure and erect deportment'. She scornfully agrees to marry Mr Dombey, despising herself for doing so, and blaming her ambitious mother for her attitude towards life. On the eve of her wedding, she reproaches her: 'Oh mother, mother, if you had but left me to my natural heart when I too was a girl – a younger girl than Florence – how different I might have been!' Edith refuses to bow her will to Mr Dombey's, and in her hatred of his domineering behaviour she runs away to join Carker in Dijon. But she then makes contemptuously clear to Carker that she has used him merely as an instrument of revenge: 'I single out in you the meanest man I know, the parasite and tool of the proud tyrant [Dombey], that his wound may go the deeper and may rankle more.' When Florence Dombey, for whom Edith had always had a tender and sympathetic affection, pleads with her at Cousin Feenix's house, on her return from France, she moves towards a kind of forgiveness of Dombey's treatment of her. Edith Dombey is often considered to be a melodramatic figure, an opinion reinforced by Phiz's theatrical drawings of her. In his *Charles Dickens*, K.J. Fielding comments, however, that 'Edith was meant to be regarded with some sympathy, and to accomplish this she is deliberately conventionalised, made more "distant" from the reader, and shown as a sort of tragedy queen' (1965: 118). See also Michael Slater's comparison with Lady Dedlock, in the entry for that character, above. (21, 26–31, 35–37, 40–43, 45–47, 54, 61)

Dombey, Mrs Fanny (DS) Mr Dombey's first wife, the mother of Florence and Paul. She dies in giving birth to Paul: she 'drifted out upon the dark and unknown sea that rolls all round the world'. *See*

Chick, Mrs Louisa and **Dombey, Mr Paul.** (1)

Dombey, Florence (DS) Mr Dombey's daughter, whom he despises and neglects as a being inferior to Paul, his son and heir. 'But what was a girl to Dombey and Son! In the capital of the House's name and dignity, such a child was merely a piece of base coin that couldn't be invested – a bad Boy – nothing more.' She is, nevertheless, the loving centre of the narrative, the means of reconciliation and redemption. Her little brother, Paul, is devoted to her, calling her 'Floy', and dies affectionately clasping her. Edith, too, is sympathetically fond of her, recognising in her an innocent goodness she herself has long lost, in her opinion. When Edith leaves Dombey, he strikes Florence to the ground, bidding her 'follow her, since they had always been in league'. The early mutual affection between Florence and Walter Gay deepens into love on his return from sea, and they are married, in a delightful scene, in the presence of Captain Cuttle, Sol Gills, Mr Toots (who had had an unrequited love for Florence), and Susan Nipper. In *Novels of the Eighteen Forties*, Kathleen Tillotson has suggested that one fruitful approach to Dickens's characterisation of Florence Dombey is by way of fairy tale: 'If we can see Florence as the princess under a spell, or the unrecognised child of royal birth from whom a strange light shines, or even as Spenser's Una, we may come nearer to Dickens's own intention' (1954: 175). (1, 3–6, 8–12, 14, 16–20, 22–24, 26, 28–32, 35–37, 39–45, 47–50, 56, 57, 59–62)

Dombey, Mr Paul (DS) The proud and wealthy City merchant, whose family firm, established by his father, is Dombey and Son. He 'was about eight-and-forty years of age... [he] was rather bald, rather red, and though a handsome well-made man, too stern and pompous in appearance, to be prepossessing'. He had been the 'sole representative of the firm' for almost twenty years. 'Of those years he had been married, ten – married, as some said, to a lady with no heart to give him; whose happiness was in the past, and who was content to bind her broken spirit to the dutiful and meek endurance of the present. Such idle talk was little likely to reach the ears of Mr Dombey, whom it nearly concerned; and probably no one in the world would have received it with such utter incredulity as he, if it had reached him. Dombey and Son had often dealt in hides, but never in hearts.' He exults in the birth of a son and heir, coolly regrets the death in childbirth of his first wife as the loss of a household possession, and treats his daughter, Florence, with cold contempt. After his son's death in early childhood, he marries the equally proud Edith, whom he sees primarily as a means of enhancing his own authority and pride: 'It flattered him to picture to himself, this proud and stately woman doing the honours of his house, and chilling his guests after his own manner. The dignity of Dombey and Son would be heightened and maintained, indeed, in such hands.' But he is doubly humiliated, first by Edith's apparent elopement with Carker and second by the bankruptcy of his firm maliciously brought about by Carker's financial schemes. He becomes fully and movingly repentant, thanks to Florence's deeply felt, sympathetic pleas. A reviewer in *The Economist* (10 October 1846) thought that 'there was urgent need to paint such a man as Dombey. The world of London is filled with cold, pompous, stiff, purse-proud men like this' (Collins 1971: 215). In his Prefaces to later editions of the novel, Dickens wrote: 'Mr Dombey undergoes no violent change, either in this book, or in real life. A sense of his injustice is within him, all along. The more he represses it, the more unjust he necessarily is. Internal shame and external circumstances bring the contest to

a close in a week, or a day; but, it has been a contest for years, and is only fought out after a long balance of victory.' Dickens was particularly anxious that Phiz (Hablot K. Browne), the illustrator of the novel, should depict Dombey accurately: 'The man for Dombey, if Browne could see him, the class man to a T, is Sir A – E –, of D – 's' (Forster 1928: Book 5, Ch. 3). This possible source has not been identified. Edgar Johnson thinks this allusion was a disguise and observes that 'when the book began to appear there were readers who were sure they recognised the character as Thomas Chapman, in whose Leadenhall Street business Dickens's young brother Augustus was employed' (1953:596). Forster reproduces in the *Life* a page of Phiz's trial sketches, which Forster sent to Dickens so that he could choose the most appropriate. (1–6, 8–11, 13–16, 18, 20, 21, 23, 26–31, 35–37, 40–45, 47, 51–55, 58, 59, 61, 62)

Dombey, Paul (DS) The son and heir of Mr Dombey, who takes an enormous pride in him. But he is a frail child: 'The chill of Paul's christening had struck home, perhaps to some sensitive part of his nature, which could not recover itself in the cold shade of his father; but he was an unfortunate child from that day.' At the age of 5, 'he was childish and sportive enough at times, and not of a sullen disposition; but he had a strange, old-fashioned, thoughtful way, at other times, of sitting brooding in his miniature arm-chair, when he looked (and talked) like one of those terrible little Beings in the Fairy tales, who, at a hundred and fifty or two hundred years of age, fantastically represent the children for whom they have been substituted.' He memorably questions his father about the meaning of money and disconcerts Mrs Pipchin with his strange, independent manner, when he is sent to stay with her at Brighton for his health. When taken in a little carriage, pulled by old

Figure 6 Preliminary sketches for Mr Dombey by Hablot K. Browne (Phiz)

Glubb, to the margin of the sea every day, he is fascinated by the sea and the sounds it makes. He asks his sister, 'The sea, Floy, what is it that it keeps on saying?' His education at Dr Blimber's school in Brighton ends after only a year because of his ill health. Paul has a vivid imagination and premonitions of death.

He dies peacefully, entwined with his loving sister, and with images in his mind of flowing water and of a divine being on the bank with light shining about the head. Paul's death caused emotional responses among readers like those aroused by the death of Little Nell in *The Old Curiosity Shop*. Lord Jeffrey 'so cried and sobbed over [the fifth monthly number, Chapters 14–16] last night, and again this morning . . . . Since that divine Nelly was found dead on her humble couch, beneath the snow and the ivy, there has been nothing like the actual dying of that sweet Paul, in the summer sunshine of that lofty room' (Collins 1971: 217). Like Tiny Tim, Paul may have been based on Harry Burnett, Dickens's crippled nephew. (1–3, 5–8, 10–12, 14–16)

Donny, the Misses (BH) Twin sisters who ran Greenleaf, the boarding school near Reading that Esther Summerson attended. (3)

Dor, Madame (CS) Jules Obenreizer's Swiss housekeeper, who protects his niece, Marguerite. ('No Thoroughfare')

Dora (DC) *See* **Spenlow, Dora**.

Dorker (NN) A boy who had died at Dotheboys Hall. (4)

Dornton, Sergeant (RP) A sergeant in the Detective Force, who was 'about fifty years of age, with a ruddy face and a high sunburnt forehead' and who related the Adventures of a Carpet Bag. ('The Detective Police')

Dorrit, Amy (LD) Always called Little Dorrit, after whom the novel is named. She was the youngest child of William Dorrit and had been born in the Marshalsea, with Bob, the turnkey, as her godfather. When she was 8 years old, her mother died, and Amy Dorrit became known as the Child of the Marshalsea. 'What her pitiful look saw, at that early time, in her father, in her sister, in her brother, in the jail; how much, or how little of the wretched truth it pleased God to make visible to her; lies hidden with many mysteries. It is enough that she was inspired to be something which was not what the rest were, and to be that something, different and laborious, for the sake of the rest.' Arthur Clennam takes an interest in her when he finds her working for his mother as a seamstress. He 'found that her diminutive figure, small features, and slight spare dress, gave her the appearance of being much younger than she was. A woman, probably of not less than two-and-twenty, she might have been passed in the street for little more than half that age.' He finds work for her with Flora Finching. Little Dorrit acts as 'Little Mother' to Maggy, the poor, half-witted girl. John Chivery, the son of the turnkey, is hopelessly in love with her, but she gently rejects his suit. She herself falls in love with Arthur, who, not knowing of her feelings towards him, unwittingly hurts her when he confides to her his disappointment over Pet Meagles: 'O! If he had known, if he had known! If he could have seen the dagger in his hand, and the cruel wounds it struck in the faithful bleeding breast of his Little Dorrit!' When her father comes into his fortune, she displeases him by not adapting herself as he feels she should to their new social status. She offers money to help Arthur Clennam when he is imprisoned for debt and, by the means of John Chivery, sends her 'undying love' to him. After the loss of her own money in the general crash of Merdle's enterprises, she marries Arthur. Some similarities between Dickens's portrayals of her and Little Nell are obvious: each is 'Little' and each embodies virtue among surroundings inimical to it. But Philip Collins points out that 'Little Dorrit herself never became a cult-figure, as her similarly-named predecessor Little

Nell had been; perhaps the time had passed for such a figure to appeal so widely, and Dickens had now certainly got past his great juvenile-deathbed phase. So Little Dorrit is not killed off' (1971: 357). (I: 3, 5–9, 12–15, 18–20, 22–25, 27, 29, 31, 32, 35, 36; II: 1, 3–8, 11, 14, 15, 17–19, 24, 27, 29–31, 33, 34)

Dorrit, Edward (LD) The son of William Dorrit. 'His name was Edward, and Ted had been transformed into Tip, within the walls [of the Marshalsea Prison].' He is a ne'er-do-well young man, who tries various occupations, becomes a horse-dealer, but ends up imprisoned for debt, like his father. Arthur Clennam obtains his discharge and he becomes a billiard-marker. After the family comes into its fortune, Tip continues to lead a dissolute life. Not surprisingly, when the money is lost he becomes 'a weak, proud, tipsy, young old man'. (I: 6–8, 12, 20, 22, 24, 31, 35, 36; II: 1, 3, 5, 7, 11, 14, 15, 19, 24, 29, 33, 34)

Dorrit, Fanny (LD) The elder daughter of William Dorrit. A dancer at the theatre where her uncle, Frederick, plays in the orchestra, she is 'pretty, and conscious, and rather flaunting'. She attracts Edmund Sparkler, but boldly stands up to Mrs Merdle, his mother, who buys her off with a bracelet. She patronisingly points out to her sister, Little Dorrit, that while the latter has been 'domestic and resignedly shut up there [in the Marshalsea Prison]' she has been 'moving more in Society and may have been getting proud and spirited – more than I ought to be, perhaps?' When the Dorrits come into their money, she determines to capture Edmund Sparkler and make him 'fetch and carry'. Furthermore, she will submit neither to Mrs General nor to Mrs Merdle. She and Edward marry in Rome and establish themselves unhappily in London. After the loss of the family money, she has, in the end, to rely on her husband. (I: 6–9, 14, 20, 31, 33, 35,

36; II: 1, 3, 5–7, 11, 12, 14–16, 18, 19, 24, 33, 34)

Dorrit, Frederick (LD) William Dorrit's brother, who had been financially ruined by him, 'and knowing no more how than his ruiner did, but accepting the fact as an inevitable certainty'. 'He stooped a good deal, and plodded along in a slow preoccupied manner, which made the bustling London thoroughfare no very safe resort for him. He was dirtily and meanly dressed ... Under one arm he carried a limp and worn-out case, containing some wind instrument.' He plays the clarionet six nights a week at a theatre where he has worked for many years and lives in squalid lodgings, where he is cruelly teased. His brother derives pleasure from patronising him. When the family comes into its money and travels abroad, he shuffles into picture galleries in Italy and passes 'hours and hours before the portraits of renowned Venetians'. He angrily rebukes his brother and Fanny for their setting up 'superiorities' over the affectionate Little Dorrit. He dies immediately after his brother, kneeling on the floor and drooping over the deathbed. After his death, it was revealed that he had been the kind 'patron' of the young woman who became Arthur Clennam's mother. (I: 7–9, 19, 20, 35, 36; II: 1, 3, 5, 19, 30)

Dorrit, William (LD) According to Ferdinand Barnacle, Mr Dorrit was 'a partner in a house on some large way ... and the house burst'. The Barnacles were among the creditors. Dorrit was consequently imprisoned for debt in the Marshalsea, where he remained for over twenty years. When he was first imprisoned, he was 'a shy, retiring man; well-looking though in an effeminate style; with a mild voice, curling hair, and irresolute hands – rings upon the fingers in those days – which nervously wandered to his trembling lip a hundred times, in the first half-hour of his acquaintance with the jail. His principal anxiety was about his wife.' As the years went by, he became proud of the title of 'Father of the Marshalsea'. Dependent on his children and on gifts from departing 'collegians' (i.e., fellow-prisoners), he nevertheless preserved an air of 'forlorn gentility' and independence. Especially when seen in company with his humble brother, Frederick, he was 'so courtly, condescending, and benevolently conscious of a position' of superiority. On inheriting the money that led to his release, he left the prison with a great show of pomp and patronage. But he was always afraid on the Continent and in London that the secret of his past would emerge. Mr Merdle persuaded him to invest in his enterprises, with the result that all the family money was lost, though he did not live to see this. He seemed about to propose marriage to Mrs General (as Fanny had feared), but soon after he collapsed and died after making an incoherent speech, full of references to his past life, at a dinner given by Mrs Merdle in Rome. 'Various external details in the portrayal of William Dorrit – his insistence on being taken as a gentleman, his pompous speech, his ornately ringed fingers, and, in the days when he is first in the Marshalsea, the way his nervous hands wander to his trembling lips – indubitably derive from John Dickens [Dickens's father] and his son's memories of the prison experience' (Johnson 1953: 898–9). (I: 6–10, 12, 18–20, 22, 23, 31, 32, 35, 36; II: 1–3, 5–7, 12, 15–19)

Doubledick, Richard (CS) A wild young soldier in the Napoleonic wars. After being severely wounded at Waterloo, he marries his sweetheart, Mary Marshall. Ruth Glancy comments on the name in her edition of the *Christmas Stories*, noting that 'Dickens frequently used variations of his own name for his characters, often with the implication of doubles or doppelgangers'. She also adduces the names of Mr Dick and Charles

Darnay (1996: 802). ('The Seven Poor Travellers')

Dounce, John (SB) A 'retired glove and braces maker, a widower, resident with three daughters – all grown up, and all unmarried – in Cursitor Street, Chancery Lane'. He becomes infatuated with a 25-year-old young lady who works in an oyster shop. She rejects his proposal of marriage. Dounce then made offers to other women, who also rejected them, and was eventually accepted by a cook, 'with whom he now lives, a henpecked husband'. ('Characters: The Misplaced Attachment of Mr John Dounce')

Dowdles, the Miss (NN) According to Mrs Nickleby, they were 'the most accomplished, elegant, fascinating creatures', who were pupils at the school in Devonshire that Kate Nickleby attended as a girl. (26)

Dowler, Mr and Mrs (PP) A fierce, 45-year-old former army officer and his wife, who travelled with the Pickwickians to Bath. Mr Winkle confusedly jumps one evening into a sedan chair carrying Mrs Dowler, with the result that her husband threatens to cut his throat. But the misunderstandings are soon happily cleared up. (35–38)

Doyce, Daniel (BH) Doyce is a smith and engineer, who has perfected (in his friend Mr Meagles's words) 'an invention (involving a very curious secret process) of great importance to his country and his fellow-creatures', but who is perpetually frustrated by the Government in his attempts to get it accepted and developed. (Dickens does not define Doyce's invention.) 'The ingenious culprit was a man of great modesty and good sense; and, though a plain man, had been too much accustomed to combine what was original and daring in conception with what was patient and minute in execution, to be by any means an ordinary man.' Arthur Clennam goes into business partnership with him with the result that the firm of Doyce and Clennam is established. Doyce goes abroad in the service of 'a certain barbaric Power with valuable possessions on the map of the world', which needed and honoured engineers. Although he counselled Clennam against speculation, Clennam invested in Merdle's enterprises with disastrous results. Clennam expresses his abject grief to Pancks at ruining Doyce, 'the honest, self-helpful, indefatigable old man, who has worked his way all through his life'. Meanwhile, however, Doyce in his overseas employment is 'medalled and ribboned, and starred and crossed ... like a born nobleman'. On his return to England, he forgives Clennam, obtains his release from the Marshalsea, and takes him back into his business. For a comparison with Doyce's early difficulties, *see* **John** (RP). (I: 10, 12, 16, 17, 23, 26, 28, 34; II: 8, 13, 22, 26, 33, 34)

Doze, Professor (MP) A vice-president of the Zoology and Botany section of the Mudfog Association at their first meeting.

Drawley, Mr (MP) A vice-president of the Zoology and Botany section of the Mudfog Association at their second meeting

Drooce, Sergeant (CS) A sergeant in the Royal Marines, who was the 'most tyrannical non-commissioned officer in His Majesty's service'. ('The Perils of Certain English Prisoners')

Drood, Edwin (MED) A young man who is John Jasper's nephew and who is engaged to Rosa Bud, in fulfilment of the terms of his father's will. At his uncle's rooms, he violently quarrels with Neville Landless, who thinks that he prizes Rosa too lightly and is exasperated by his 'air of leisurely patronage and indifference'.

Neville flings the dregs of his wine at him after Edwin's insulting allusion to his dark skin. Edwin and Rosa amicably agree to terminate their engagement since they recognise that they do not love each other. Jasper yields to Crisparkle's entreaties and persuades Edwin to agree to a reconciliation with Neville. But having left Jasper's rooms with Neville on Christmas Eve, Edwin Drood disappears. The river is dragged, 'but no trace of Edwin Drood revisited the light of the sun'. At the Weir, Mr Crisparkle finds a gold watch engraved with the initials, E.D. But because the novel is unfinished, the mystery of his disappearance is not explained, although the usual interpretation is that he was murdered by John Jasper. (2, 3, 7–11, 13–16, 19, 23)

Drowvey, Miss (HR) Miss Grimmer's partner in the ownership of the girls' school attended by Nettie Ashford and Annie Rainbird (1)

Drummle, Bentley (GE) A fellow-pupil of Pip's at Mr Matthew Pocket's. He was 'the next heir but one to a baronetcy'. 'Heavy in figure, movement, and comprehension – in the sluggish complexion of his face, and in the large awkward tongue that seemed to loll about in his mouth as he himself lolled about in a room – he was idle, proud, niggardly, reserved, and suspicious.' Mr Jaggers is intrigued by him ('I like the look of that fellow'), calling him 'the Spider'. Pip is elected to a club, the Finches of the Grove, of which Drummle is a member, and is infuriated when Drummle publicly drinks a toast there to Estella. Drummle doggedly pursues her, and she agrees to marry him, despite Pip's pleas. He treats her cruelly, they separate, and he dies 'from an accident consequent on his ill-treatment of a horse'. (23, 25, 26, 34, 38, 43, 44, 48, 59)

Dubbley (PP) A 'dirty-faced man, something over six feet high, and stout in proportion', who was one of the officials under Mr Grummer's command who arrested Mr Pickwick and his friends at Ipswich. (24, 25)

Duff (OT) A Bow Street officer, who helped Blathers to investigate the attempted burglary at Mrs Maylie's house. He was a 'red-headed, bony man; in top-boots; with a rather ill-favoured countenance, and a turned-up sinister-looking nose'. (31)

Dull, Mr (MP) A vice-president of Umbugology and Ditchwaterisics section at the second meeting of the Mudfog Association.

Dumbledon (RP) An 'idiotic goggle-eyed boy, with a big head and half-crowns without end, who suddenly appeared as a parlour-boarder' at Our School. ('Our School')

Dumkins, Mr (PP) A redoubtable cricketer who played for the All-Muggleton club. (7)

Dummins (SYG) An 'out-and-out young gentleman'.

Dummy, Mr (MP) A vice-president of the Umbugology and Ditchwaterisics section at the second meeting of the Mudfog Association.

Dumps, Nicodemus (SB) He was a 'bachelor, six feet high, and fifty years old; cross, cadaverous, odd, and ill-natured', who reluctantly agrees to be a godfather to his nephew Charles Kitterbell's baby son. On the way to the christening he is robbed of the mug he was

going to give his godson. His speech at the 'sit-down supper' after the ceremony casts a gloom on the proceedings, an effect which apparently amuses him. ('Tales: The Bloomsbury Christening')

Dundey, Doctor (RP) He robbed an Irish bank, but was tracked down and arrested in America by Sergeant Dornton. ('The Detective Police')

Dunkle, Doctor Ginery (MC) A 'shrill boy', who is a 'gentleman of great poetical elements'. He acts as the spokesman of the committee that welcomes Elijah Pogram. (34)

Dunstable (GE) The butcher mentioned by Mr Pumblechook at the Gargerys' Christmas dinner. He points out that if Pip had been born a pig ('a Squeaker') the butcher would have cut his throat with a penknife. (4)

Durdles (MED) A stonemason in Cloisterham. 'He is the chartered libertine of the place. Fame trumpets him a wonderful workman – which, for aught that anybody knows, he may be (as he never works); and a wonderful sot – which everybody knows he is. With the Cathedral crypt he is better acquainted than any living authority; it may even be than any dead one.' He used to pay Deputy a halfpenny to pelt him home if he stayed out late. For some reason, Jasper asks Durdles to take him on 'a moonlight expedition . . . among the tombs, vaults, towers, and ruins' of the cathedral. Datchery, too, seems to be about to make a similar appointment with him. (4, 5, 12, 14, 18)

E

Edkins, Mr (SB) One of the party on the steam excursion on the Thames. He was a 'pale young gentleman, in a green stock and spectacles of the same, a member of the honourable society of the Inner Temple'. He rashly attempts to propose a toast despite the storm and the onset of seasickness among many of the passengers, including himself. ('Tales: The Steam Excursion')

Edmunds, George (VQ) The farm labourer who is Lucy Benson's sweetheart.

Edmunds, John (PP) The main character in 'The Convict's Return', the story told by the clergyman at Dingley Dell. His father and mother are also prominent in the story. (6)

Edson, Mr (CS) One of Mrs Lirriper's lodgers. He deserts his wife, who dies after giving birth to a son. Mrs Lirriper adopts the child. When Edson lies on his deathbed in France, he sends for her and so sees his son. *See* **Jackman, Major James**. ('Mrs Lirriper's Lodgings' and 'Mrs Lirriper's Legacy')

Edward (SYC) The husband of Charlotte in the 'Contradictory Couple'.

Edwards, Miss (OCS) A pupil–teacher at Miss Monflathers's Boarding and Day Establishment. 'This young lady, being motherless and poor, was apprenticed at the school – taught for nothing – teaching others what she learnt, for nothing – boarded for nothing – lodged for nothing – and set down and rated as something

immeasurably less than nothing, by all the dwellers in the house.' (31, 32)

Edwin (CS) Charley's supposed rival in Angela Leath's affections. ('The Holly-Tree Inn')

Ellis, Mr (SB) A 'sharp-nosed, light-haired man in a brown surtout reaching nearly down to his heels' and smoking a pipe, who is one of the company in an old public house near the City Road. ('Characters: The Parlour Orator')

Emile (CS) A soldier billeted at the Clock-maker's in the French town where Mr The Englishman (i.e., Mr Langley) found Bebelle. ('Somebody's Luggage')

Emilia (HR) Mrs Orange's baby in Miss Nettie Ashford's 'romance'.

Emily (SB) A teenage girl, obviously a prostitute, taken away with other prisoners in the prisoners' van. With her younger sister, Bella, she 'had been thrown upon London streets, their vices and debauchery, by a sordid and rapacious mother'. ('Characters: The Prisoners' Van')

Em'ly, Little (DC) The orphaned niece and adopted daughter of Mr Peggotty. As a young boy, David Copperfield immediately falls in love with that 'blue-eyed mite of a child', who even in her earliest childhood wants to be 'a lady'. She is apprenticed to Mr Omer as a dressmaker. Although she is full of self-torment over her moral weaknesses and unworthiness, she succumbs to Steerforth and abandons the worthy and honest Ham Peggotty, to whom she was engaged and who truly loves her. She goes abroad with Steerforth, hoping to be brought back to England as a lady, but (according to Littimer, Steerforth's manservant) he tires of 'her low spirits and tempers of that kind' and deserts her in Italy, suggesting that she should marry Littimer. Fully repentant, Em'ly makes her way back to England, where, thanks to Martha Endell's help, she is saved from a life of vice and is found by David and Mr Peggotty, who rescue her from the fury of Rosa Dartle. She emigrates to Australia, with Mr Peggotty, Mrs Gummidge, and Martha. In *The Dickens World*, Humphrey House provocatively argued that everything 'shows Emily worthy to become the lady she hoped to be. Even Pamela [the eponymous heroine of Samuel Richardson's novel] only did better in being more cunning' (1942: 162). (3, 7, 10, 17, 21–23, 30, 31, 40, 46, 47, 50, 51, 55, 57, 63)

Emma (PP) One of the 'buxom' maidservants at the Manor Farm, Dingley Dell. (5, 8, 9, 11, 28)

Emmeline (CS) Angela Leath's cousin, who eloped with Edwin to Gretna Green. 'She was wrapped in soft white fur, like the snowy landscape: but was warm, and young, and lovely.' ('The Holly-Tree Inn')

Endell, Martha (DC) A 'fallen woman', originally an apprentice dressmaker at Mr Omer's, whom David Copperfield and Steerforth first see in Yarmouth: 'she was lightly dressed, looked bold, and haggard, and flaunting, and poor'. Em'ly gives her money and she goes to London, presumably working there as a prostitute. But (like Em'ly) she is ashamed of her conduct. Mr Peggotty and David find her in suicidal mood by the Thames, and persuade her to help them find Em'ly, to shelter her, and to take them to her. She emigrates to Australia with Mr Peggotty,

Mrs Gummidge, and Em'ly, and marries a farm labourer there. (22, 40, 46, 47, 50, 51, 57, 63)

Estella (GE) The girl adopted by Miss Havisham. Pip meets her when he is summoned to play at Satis House: 'She seemed much older than I, of course, being a girl, and beautiful and self-possessed; and she was as scornful of me as if she had been one-and-twenty, and a queen.' When they play cards, for example, she utters contemptuous words: ' " He calls the knaves, Jacks, this boy!" said Estella with disdain, before our first game was out. "And what coarse hands he has! And what thick boots!" ' But from that time on, Pip remains hopelessly in love with her. As a young woman, she bitterly attributes her pride and hardness to her upbringing by Miss Havisham, who has, as it were, trained her to break men's hearts, because of the suffering she has herself endured: 'Estella [as Pip realises] was set to wreak Miss Havisham's revenge on men.' Estella herself reproaches Miss Havisham: 'I am what you have made me. Take all the praise, take all the blame; take all the success, take all the failure.' When Pip declares his love for her (although he has no hope that this can be fulfilled), she calmly says, in Miss Havisham's presence: 'When you say you love me, I know what you mean, as a form of words; but nothing more. You address nothing in my breast, you touch nothing there.' Despite Pip's passionate pleas to her not to fling herself away 'upon a brute', she defiantly marries Bentley Drummle, is cruelly used by him, and separates from him. Drummle dies in an accident caused by his ill-treatment of a horse. Pip has discovered that Estella was the illegitimate daughter of Magwitch and Molly, a reprieved murderess, whom Mr Jaggers employs as a housekeeper. Jaggers had therefore arranged her adoption by Miss Havisham. Estella, however, remains in ignorance of her humble and shameful origins, which obviously form a parallel with the origins of Pip's fortune and snobbishness. Eleven years or so after their last meeting, Pip encounters Estella by chance at the site of the now-demolished Satis House. In the ambiguous conclusion to the novel, with which Dickens (acting on Bulwer Lytton's suggestion) had replaced a conclusion in which Pip and Estella remain separated, Estella says that they 'will continue friends apart'. But Pip's last words are that he 'saw no shadow of another parting from her'. Many commentators have argued that Estella was based on Ellen Ternan, the young actress with whom Dickens had a long and close relationship, although Michael Slater, in *Dickens and Women*, argues that a more likely source was Maria Beadnell, whom Dickens had loved as a young man (1983: 73–6). (7, 8, 11–15, 22, 29, 30, 32, 33, 38, 44, 48–51, 56, 59)

Eugène (CS) A soldier billeted at the Tinman's in the French town where Mr The Englishman (i.e., Mr Langley) found Bebelle. ('Somebody's Luggage')

Evans, Miss Jemima (SB) 'Miss Evans (or Ivins, to adopt the pronunciation most in vogue with her circle of acquaintance)' was a shoe-binder and straw-bonnet maker, who lived with her mother and two sisters in Camden Town. She goes out one evening with Samuel Wilkins (her young man) and another pair, but a fight ensues with a 'waistcoat and whiskers', who makes impudent remarks about the ankles of Jemima and her friend. ('Characters: Miss Evans and the Eagle')

Evans, Mr (SB) A 'tall, thin, pale young gentleman, with extensive whiskers' who plays the part of Roderigo in the Gattletons' amateur production of *Othello*. ('Tales: Mrs Joseph Porter')

Evans, Richard (OCS) One of Mr Marton's pupils in the village school. According to the Bachelor, he is 'an amazing boy to learn ... [but] he's always falling asleep in sermon-time'. (52)

Evenson, John (SB) One of the lodgers at Mrs Tibbs's boarding-house. He was about 50, 'very morose and discontented', and 'a thorough radical [who] used to attend a great variety of public meetings, for the express purpose of finding fault with everything that was proposed'. ('Tales: The Boarding-House')

Ezekiel (CS) The boy at Mugby Junction, who narrates the third chapter of the story. ('Mugby Junction')

F

Face-Maker, Monsieur the (UT) An entertainer at the Fair, who 'transforms the features that Heaven has bestowed on him into an endless succession of surprising and extraordinary visages'. ('In the French-Flemish Country')

Fagin (OT) 'A very old shrivelled Jew, whose villainous-looking and repulsive face was obscured by a quantity of matted red hair.' He is a fence, who organises and trains a group of young pickpockets (including the Artful Dodger and Charley Bates), into whose company Oliver Twist innocently falls. Fagin also employs Bill Sikes, a burglar, and Nancy, a prostitute, on criminal activities of various kinds. Monks makes him his accomplice in his unsuccessful endeavours to get Oliver convicted and transported. He indirectly brings about Nancy's murder by Bill Sikes because he tells the latter that Noah Claypole has seen her talking to Mr Brownlow and Rose Maylie on London Bridge and that he therefore suspects that she is informing on them. Immediately after the murder, Fagin is arrested. Noah Claypole (under the name of Morris Bolter) turns king's evidence, Fagin is found guilty of being an accessory before the fact, and is condemned to death. On the eve of his execution, he is visited in the condemned cell by Oliver Twist and Mr Brownlow, who makes him tell them the hiding place where Monks had concealed vital papers concerning Oliver. Oliver, bursting into tears, prays God to forgive the wretched Fagin, who is in dreadful torment. Apart from Dickens's verbal evocations of Fagin's appearance and

behaviour and of his feelings of horror on his 'last night alive', two visual images remain in the reader's mind: George Cruikshank's drawings of him and Monks peering through the window at Oliver Twist asleep ('Monks and the Jew') and of him in the condemned cell. Fagin is based on Ikey Solomon, a notorious fence of the period. Dickens borrowed the name, Fagin, from Bob Fagin, a youth who worked with him in Warren's Blacking warehouse. *See* **Riah**. (8, 9, 12, 13, 15, 16, 19, 20, 25, 26, 34, 39, 42–45, 47, 53)

Fairfax, Mr (SYG) A 'censorious young gentleman'. ('The Censorious Young Gentleman')

Fan (CB) Scrooge's sister, who comes to bring him home from boarding-school. The Ghost of Christmas Past reminds him that she was 'delicate' and 'had a large heart'. She 'died a woman', and had one child, Scrooge's nephew. (*A Christmas Carol*)

Fanchette (RP) The 'charming daughter' of the hostess of the Swiss inn where 'Our Bore' was taken ill. ('Our Bore')

Fang, Mr (OT) The choleric and arbitrary police magistrate who hears the charge of theft against Oliver, whom he summarily commits 'for three months – hard labour of course', before the fortunate intervention of the bookstall owner clears Oliver of the accusation. When Mr Brownlow admits he had forgotten to pay for the book he was reading when Oliver was supposed to have picked his

Figure 7 Fagin by George Cruikshank

pocket, Fang turns on him as well, much to Brownlow's indignation. The original of Fang was Allan Stewart Laing, a magistrate at Hatton Garden Police Court. (II)

Fareway, Mr (GSE) Mr Fareway was an idle pupil of George Silverman's at Cambridge. Lady Fareway, his mother, presents Silverman to a church living,

provided that he acts as tutor to her daughter, Adelina. Although Silverman falls in love with Adelina, he feels that he is unworthy of her and so manages to turn her affections towards Granville Wharton. He marries them in secret, with the consequence that Lady Fareway dismisses him.

Fee, Dr W.R. (MP) A member of the

medical section of the Mudfog Association.

Feeder, B.A., Mr (DS) The assistant master at Dr Blimber's school, where little Paul Dombey was a pupil. He was 'a kind of human barrel-organ, with a little list of tunes at which he was continually working, over and over again, without any variation. He might have been fitted up with a change of barrels, perhaps, in early life, if his destiny had been favourable; but it had not been; and he had only one, with which, in a monotonous round, it was his occupation to bewilder the young ideas of Doctor Blimber's young gentlemen.' He 'was in the habit of shaving his head for coolness'. Paul has 'free right of entry' to Mr Feeder's snug room, which contains an assortment of objects, including 'a beautiful little curly secondhand key-bugle, a chess-board and men, a Spanish Grammar, a set of sketching materials, and a pair of boxing-gloves'. Mr Feeder takes over the school on Doctor Blimber's retirement and is married to Miss Cornelia Blimber by his brother, the Reverend Alfred Feeder, MA. (11, 12, 14, 41, 60)

Feenix, Cousin (DS) Always called Cousin Feenix (he is, in fact, Lord Feenix), he is Mrs Skewton's aristocratic nephew, whom we first encounter at the wedding of Mr Dombey and Edith, which he has come from abroad to attend. He 'was a man about town, forty years ago; but he is still so juvenile in figure and in manner, and so well got up, that strangers are amazed when they discover latent wrinkles in his lordship's face, and crows' feet in his eyes; and first observe him, not exactly certain when he walks across a room, of going straight to where he wants to go'. He delightfully and inconsequentially rambles in his speech, but he is a kindly gentleman, who seeks Edith out in France after her disgrace and offers a refuge in his London house to his 'lovely and accomplished relative'. (21, 31, 36, 41, 51, 61)

Fendall, Sergeant (RP) A 'light-haired, well-spoken, polite person, [who] is a prodigious hand at pursuing private inquiries of a delicate nature'. He was based on Inspector Edward Kendall. ('The Detective Police')

Ferdinand, Miss (MED) A lively, mischievous girl at Miss Twinkleton's school. (9, 13)

Fern, Lilian (CB) Will Fern's niece. (*The Chimes*)

Fern, Will (CB) A poor labourer who, accompanied by Lilian, his niece, seeks work in London. He is brought before Alderman Cute, who is determined to 'put him down'. But he is helped by Trotty Veck and discovers an old friend in Mrs Chickenstalker. In his New Year vision, Trotty Veck sees Will as a rick-burner and Lilian falling into a life of prostitution. (*The Chimes*)

Féroce, Monsieur (RP) A bathing-machine proprietor. 'How he ever came by his name we cannot imagine', since he is gentle, polite, stout and 'of a beaming aspect'. ('Our French Watering-Place')

Fezziwig, Mr (CB) The employer to whom Scrooge was apprenticed as a young man. He is 'an old gentleman in a Welsh wig', full of benevolence and joviality, and with a 'comfortable, oily, rich, fat, jovial voice'. He, his wife, and three daughters happily and vigorously join in the Christmas ball he organises for his employees. Scrooge's former self and his fellow-apprentice, Dick, pour out 'their hearts in praise of Fezziwig'. (*A Christmas Carol*)

Fibbitson, Mrs (DC) An elderly inmate of the almshouses where Mrs Mell lives. When David Copperfield saw her, she was sitting by the fire and 'was such a bundle of clothes that I feel grateful to this hour for not having sat upon her by mistake'. (5)

Field, Inspector (RP) Inspector Charles Frederick Field was in the London Detective Department and was much admired by Dickens, who makes him the hero of 'On Duty with Inspector Field'. Inspector Wield and Inspector Bucket were also modelled on him. For a full account and discussion, see Philip Collins, *Dickens and Crime*, 1964: 206–11.

Fielding, Emma (SYC) The young woman who marries Mr Harvey. ('The Young Couple'). She reappears as the great-grandmother in 'The Old Couple'.

Fielding, Sir John (BR) The magistrate who immediately commits Rudge to Newgate at Mr Haredale's request. Dickens has here introduced an actual historical figure: Fielding, the blind half-brother of Henry Fielding, the novelist, was the chief magistrate at Bow Street from 1754 to 1780. But Fielding was, in fact, lying seriously ill at Brompton at the time of the Gordon Riots. (58, 66)

Fielding, May (CB) Believing that her lover, Edward Plummer, has died, she agrees to marry Tackleton, a surly toy-maker. But Edward reappears, and she marries him on the day planned for her wedding to Tackleton. Her mother, Mrs Fielding, is a 'little querulous chip of an old lady with a peevish face'. (*The Cricket on the Hearth*)

Fiercy, Captain the Honourable Fitz-Whisker (PL) Attended by his servant, Do'em, he 'struts and swaggers about'. But the two of them turn out to be imposters and swindlers.

Fikey (RP) A forger of South-Western Railway debentures arrested by Inspector Wield. ('The Detective Police')

Filer, Mr (CB) A friend of Alderman Cute's, he is a 'low-spirited gentleman of middle age, of a meagre habit, and a disconsolate face', who relies on statistics to prove his arguments about the improvidence of the poor. (*The Chimes*)

Filletoville, the Marquess of (PP) The father of the 'young gentleman in sky-blue' who abducted the lady rescued by the Bagman's Uncle. (49)

Finchbury, Lady Jane (DS) An acquaintance of Cousin Feenix's. According to him, she was a 'woman with tight stays', who made an admirable sketch of an Anglo-Norman church. (41)

Finching, Flora (LD) As Flora Casby, the daughter of Christopher Casby, she was the 'beloved of [Arthur Clennam's] boyhood', although Mrs Clennam had prevented their marriage. When Arthur meets her again after his twenty-five years' residence in China, she is the widow of Mr Finching. But 'Clennam's eyes no sooner fell upon the subject of his old passion, than it shivered and broke to pieces. . . Flora, always tall, had grown to be very broad, too, and short of breath; but that was not much. Flora, whom he had left a lily, had become a peony; but that was not much. Flora, who had seemed enchanting in all she said and thought, was diffuse and silly. That was much. Flora, who had been spoiled and artless long ago, was determined to be spoiled and artless now. That was a fatal blow'. Her speech is characterised by 'disjointed volubility', which Dickens presents in what can be called some of the earliest examples of 'stream of consciousness'. Here she is, for example, in a pie-shop offering Little Dorrit her rather tearful good wishes, mingled with her habitual sad reminiscences of the fondness that existed between her and Arthur in their youthful days: 'If Fancy's fair dreams . . . have ever pictured that when Arthur – cannot over-

Figure 8 Mr Casby, Mr Pancks, Mr F's Aunt, Flora Finching and Arthur Clennam by
Hablot K. Browne (Phiz)

come it pray excuse me – was restored to freedom even a pie as far from flaky as the present and so deficient in kidney as to be in that respect like a minced nutmeg might not prove unacceptable if offered by the hand of true regard such visions have for ever fled and all is cancelled but being aware that tender relations are in contemplation beg to state that I heartily wish well to both and find no fault with either not the least, it may be withering to know that ere the hand of Time had made me much less slim than formerly and dreadfully red on the slightest exertion particularly after eating I well know when it takes the form of a rash it might have been and was not through the interruption of parents and mental torpor succeeded until the mysterious clue was held by Mr F still I would not be ungenerous to either and I heartily wish well to both.' Flora's constant kindness is shown in her employing Little Dorrit for a while (at Arthur Clennam's request) and in her uncomplaining toleration of Mr F's Aunt. Dickens based Flora's characterisation and Arthur's sense of disillusion on his own experiences in early 1855, not long before the publication of *Little Dorrit* began. It was then that he renewed his acquaintance with Maria Winter (née Beadnell), his own childhood sweetheart, after an interval of ten years or so. Michael Slater points out that 'it says much for the good humour of Flora's original that she seems not to have resented Dickens's caricature', and quotes from a letter Dickens wrote to the Duke of Devonshire: 'I am so glad you like Flora. It came into my head one day that we have all had our Floras (mine is living, and extremely fat), and that it was a half serious half ridiculous truth which had never been told' (Slater 1983: 71). (I: 13, 23, 24, 35; II: 9, 17, 23, 34)

Finching, Mrs (SYC) A friend of the Bobtail Widgers. ('The Plausible Couple')

Fips, Mr (MC) A lawyer in Austin Friars, who was secretly commissioned by old Martin Chuzzlewit to employ Tom Pinch to arrange and catalogue books at £100 a year. Mr Fips was 'small and spare, and looked peacable, and wore black shorts [i.e., knee-breeches] and powder [on his hair]'. (39, 40, 53)

Fish, Mr (CB) Sir Joseph Bowley's confidential secretary, who was a 'not very stately gentleman in black'. (*The Chimes*)

Fisher, Mr and Mrs (CS) Residents on Silver-Store Island. Mrs Fisher, in the opinion of Gill Davis, the narrator, 'was a delicate little baby-fool'. ('The Perils of Certain English Prisoners')

Fithers, Mr (SYC) A painter, who is a friend of the Bobtail Widgers. ('The Plausible Couple')

Fitz-Marshall, Charles (PP) An alias used by Mr Jingle.

Fixem, Mr (SB) The broker who used to employ Bung. ('Our Parish: The Broker's Man')

Fizkin, Horatio (PP) The Buff candidate in the Eatanswill election, who was defeated by the Hon. Samuel Slumkey. (13, 18)

Fizzgig, Don Bolaro (PP) According to one of Jingle's tall stories, he was a Spanish grandee, whose daughter, Christina, loved Jingle to distraction. His initial disapproval eventually led to Christina's death, so that in remorse he committed suicide by sticking his head in the main pipe of a fountain 'with a full confession in his right boot'. (2)

Fladdock, General (MC) After condemning the exclusiveness, pride and the 'artificial barriers set up between man and man' in Europe, which he has just visited, the General is appalled to learn that Martin Chuzzlewit had taken his passage in the steerage on *The Screw*: 'And meeting that fellow in the very sanctuary of New York fashion, and nestling in the bosom of the New York aristocracy! He almost laid his hand upon his sword.' (17)

Flam, the Honourable Sparkins (VQ) Squire Norton's friend, whose scheme to abduct Rose is foiled by Martin Stokes.

Flamwell, Mr (SB) He was 'one of those gentlemen of remarkably extensive information whom one occasionally meets in society, who pretend to know everybody but in reality know nobody'. When Mr Malderton questions him about Horatio Sparkins, he thinks from his description that 'he bears a strong resemblance to the Honourable Augustus Fitz-Edward Fitz-John Fitz-Osborne'. ('Tales: Horatio Sparkins')

Flanders, Sally (UT) The Uncommercial Traveller's nurse. When her husband, a small master builder, died, the Traveller attended the funeral, which was the first he had been to. ('Medicine Men of Civilisation')

Flasher, Wilkins (PP) The broker who arranged the transfer of the late Mrs Weller's stock to her widower, Tony Weller. When Sam Weller and his father go into his office, 'Wilkins Flasher, Esquire, was balancing himself on two legs of an office stool, spearing a wafer-box with a pen-knife, which he dropped every now and then with great dexterity into the very centre of a small red wafer that was stuck outside.' He was also engaged in betting with Mr Simmery on Boffer's possible suicide. (55)

Fledgeby, 'Fascination' (OMF) The proprietor of Pubsey and Co., a firm of money-lenders and bill-brokers, but he deviously conducts all the business through Mr Riah, his agent, who is therefore thought to be its ruthless owner. 'Young Fledgeby had a peachy cheek, or a cheek compounded of the peach and the red red red wall on which it grows, and was an awkward, sandy-haired, small-eyed youth, exceeding slim (his enemies would have said lanky), and prone to self-examination in the articles of whisker and moustache.' He lives in chambers in Albany, Piccadilly. 'He was sensible of the value of appearances as an investment, and liked to dress well; but he drove a bargain for every moveable about him, from the coat on his back to the china on his breakfast-table; and every bargain, by representing somebody's ruin or somebody's loss, acquired a peculiar charm for him.' He promises the Lammles a thousand pounds if they can arrange a marriage between him and Georgiana Podsnap for the sake of her money, but Mrs Lammle eventually regrets trying to do this, asking Twemlow to warn Podsnap against Fledgeby. By means of Riah, Fledgeby ruthlessly insists that Lammle and Twemlow must pay their debts. Mrs Lammle comes to realise that 'Mr Riah is his mask', as she informs Twemlow. Lammle violently assaults Fledgeby in his Albany rooms, beating him up and cramming salt and snuff into his mouth. In the end, 'the accessibility of Riah proving very useful as to a few hints towards the disentanglement of [Eugene Wrayburn's] affairs, [Mortimer] Lightwood applied himself with infinite zest to attacking and harassing Mr Fledgeby; who, discovering himself in danger of being blown into the air by certain explosive transactions in which he had been engaged, and having been sufficiently flayed under his beating, came to a parley and asked for quarter'. (II: 4, 5, 16; III: 1, 12, 13, 17; IV: 8, 9, 16)

Fleetwood, Mr, Mrs and Master (SB) A family who arrive late with the Wakefields on a wherry to join the excursion on the Thames. ('Tales: The Steam Excursion')

Fleming, Agnes (OT) Oliver Twist's mother, who dies in the workhouse after she has given birth to him. She had been seduced by Edwin Leeford, the father of Monks. Her sister was Rose Maylie. (1, 49, 51, 53)

Flintwinch, Affery (LD) The wife of Jeremiah Flintwinch, she is a 'tall hardfavoured sinewy woman, who in her youth might have enlisted in the Foot Guards'. But she goes in fear of 'them two clever ones', Jeremiah and Mrs Clennam, who had both forced her into the marriage. She used to be Arthur Clennam's childhood nurse. She constantly sees and hears disturbing things in the old house that she cannot explain and so assumes that she must have dreamt them. These phenomena include strange noises and movements in the building, which are at last explained at the end of the narrative when the house collapses. 'In the vagueness and indistinctness of all her new experiences and perceptions, as everything about her was mysterious to herself, she began to be mysterious to others; and became as difficult to be made out to anybody's satisfaction, as she found the house and everything in it difficult to make out to her own.' Affery becomes more and more bewildered, is too frightened to tell Arthur what 'whisperings and counsellings' she has overheard, but finally defiantly confronts Mrs Clennam by supplementing Rigaud's revelations with her own evidence. (I: 3–5, 14, 15, 29, 30; II: 10, 17, 23, 30, 31)

Flintwinch, Ephraim (LD) Jeremiah Flintwinch's brother, who is his double. (I: 4; II: 30)

Flintwinch, Jeremiah (LD) Mrs Clennam's confidential clerk and business partner. 'He was a short, bald old man, in a high-shouldered black coat and waistcoat, drab breeches, and long drab gaiters. He might, from his dress, have been either clerk or servant, and in fact had long been both. There was nothing about him in the way of decoration but a watch, which was lowered into the depths of its proper pocket by an old black ribbon, and had a tarnished copper key moored above it, to show where it was sunk. His head was awry, and he had a one-sided, crab-like way with him, as if his foundations had yielded at about the same time as those of the house, and he ought to have been propped up in a similar manner.' His wife, Affery, is terrified of him. Jeremiah knows the secret of Mrs Clennam's suppression of the codicil in Gilbert Clennam's will and gives the relevant papers into the keeping of his 'Double' (i.e., his brother, Ephraim), until Rigaud somehow gains possession of them. He was not in Mrs Clennam's house when it collapsed, as he 'had been rather busy elsewhere, converting securities into as much money as could be got for them on the shortest notice', and apparently made his way to Holland, where he 'consorted with the Dutchmen on the quaint banks of the canals at the Hague, and in the drinking-shops of Amsterdam, under the style and designation of Mynheer von Flyntevyge'. (I: 3–5, 14, 15, 29, 30; II: 10, 17, 23, 28, 30, 31)

Flipfield, Mr (UT) The Uncommercial Traveller's friend, who gives a birthday party at which his long-lost brother is a guest. The other members of the Flipfield family are Miss Flipfield (his elder sister), Mr Tom Flipfield (his brother) and Mrs Flipfield (his mother). ('Birthday Celebrations')

Flite, Miss (BH) 'A curious little old woman', who befriends Esther Summerson, Ada Clare and Richard Carstone and who regularly attends the Court of Chancery with her documents:

'I expect a judgment. Shortly. On the Day of Judgment.' She lodges over Krook's shop and keeps a collection of caged birds to be liberated, in Krook's words, 'when my noble and learned brother gives his Judgment'. The birds' names are Hope, Joy, Youth, Peace, Rest, Life, Dust, Ashes, Waste, Want, Ruin, Despair, Madness, Death, Cunning, Folly, Words, Wigs, Rags, Sheepskin, Plunder, Precedent, Jargon, Gammon, and Spinach, to which she later adds the Wards in Jarndyce. Although Miss Flite's family had all been brought to ruin by the Court of Chancery, she feels that 'there's a dreadful attraction to the place'. After the end of the Jarndyce case and the death of Richard, whom Miss Flite had thought of making her executor because of his own assiduous attendance in the Court, Esther tells us that 'poor Miss Flite came weeping to me, and told me she had given her birds their liberty'. (1, 3, 5, 11, 14, 20, 23, 24, 33, 35, 45, 47, 50, 60, 65)

Flopson (GE) She and Millers are the two nursemaids employed by Mrs Matthew Pocket to look after her seven little children. (22, 23)

Flowers (DS) Mrs Skewton's personal maid. (27, 30, 36, 37, 40)

Fluggers (NN) An actor in Mr Crummles's company, who 'does the heavy business'. (30)

Flummery, Mr (MP) At the second meeting of the Mudfog Association, he spoke at the Zoology and Botany session, exhibiting 'a twig, claiming to be a veritable branch of that noble tree known to naturalists as the Shakespeare'.

Fogg (PP) *See* **Dodson and Fogg.**

Folair, Mr (NN) A 'pantomimist' in Mr Crummles's company. He was known to delight in mischief 'and was by no means scrupulous'. He brought Nicholas Mr Lenville's 'challenge'. (23–25, 29, 30)

Foulon (TTC) Joseph-François Foulon (1715–89), an unscrupulous financier of the *ancien régime*, who had notoriously said on one occasion, 'The people may eat grass'. He is seized by a mob, in which the Defarges are prominent, has bunches of straw and grass thrust into his face, is hanged on a lamp post, and decapitated. Dickens's account closely follows Carlyle's account in *The French Revolution* (1837), Part 1, 5:9. (II: 22)

Foxey (OCS) The 'revered father' of Sampson and Sally Brass. His maxim was 'Always suspect everybody'. (66)

Foxey, Dr (MP) A member of the Mudfog Association. At its second meeting, his 'brown silk umbrella and white hat [became] entangled in the machinery while he was explaining to a knot of ladies the construction of the steam-engine'.

François, Monsieur (RP) A butcher who comes from Paris to buy at the Calf Market in Poissy. ('A Monument of French Folly')

Frank, Little (CS) The son of Michael's first cousin. He has a particular affection for him, although 'he is a diffident boy by nature'. ('The Poor Relation's Story')

Fred (CB) Scrooge's nephew, who invites his uncle to Christmas dinner. Scrooge contemptuously rejects this, but the Ghost of Christmas Present shows him Fred and his wife holding a happy party, in which Fred has some good-natured things to say about him. (*A Christmas Carol*)

Frost, Miss (RP) A teacher at 'our' preparatory school, whose name and black dress 'hold an enduring place in our remembrance'. ('Our School')

G

Gabblewig (MND) The suitor of Rosina Nightingale.

Gabelle, Théophile (TTC) The postmaster 'and some other taxing functionary united' in the St Evrémonde village. When the French Revolution breaks out, the village people raze his house to the ground and take him to the Prison of the Abbaye in Paris because of his service to the St Evrémonde family. In response to his urgent pleas for help, Charles Darnay travels to Paris and is himself arrested. Dickens names him after the salt tax which was imposed in the pre-revolutionary days. (II: 8, 9, 23, 24; III: 1, 6)

Gabrielle (CS) *See* Bebelle.

Gallanbile, Mr (NN) An MP, whose family is seeking a cook through the General Agency Office which Nicholas Nickleby uses. The conditions of service include: 'Fifteen guineas, tea and sugar, and servants allowed to see male cousins, if godly. Note. Cold dinner in the kitchen on the Sabbath, Mr Gallanbile being devoted to the Observance question. No victuals whatever cooked on the Lord's day, with the exception of dinner for Mr and Mrs Gallanbile, which, being a work of piety and necessity, is exempted. Mr Gallanbile dines late on the day of rest, in order to prevent the sinfulness of the cook's dressing herself.' (16)

Game Chicken, the (DS) A pugilist employed by Mr Toots in the 'cultivation of those gentle arts which refine and humanise existence'. The Game Chicken was 'always to be heard of at the bar of the Black Badger, wore a shaggy white great-coat in the warmest weather, and knocked Mr Toots about the head three times a week, for the small consideration of ten and six per visit'. He is finally appalled by Mr Toots's 'mean' behaviour in relinquishing all hopes of marrying Florence and insists on being paid off with a 'fi'typunnote' (which Toots gladly agrees to). (22, 28, 31, 32, 41, 44, 56)

Gamfield, Mr (OT) A cruel chimney sweep, who thinks that a good blaze is humane for his apprentices: 'even if they've stuck in a chimbley, roasting their feet makes 'em struggle to hextricate themselves'. He arranges to take Oliver Twist, but the magistrates refuse to sanction the indentures when they see that Oliver is terror-stricken at the prospect. (3, 51)

Gamp, Mrs Sarah (MC) One of the greatest of all Dickens's comic characters, Mrs Gamp is a midwife and nurse, who first appears in the novel when Mr Pecksniff hires her to lay out the body of Anthony Chuzzlewit. 'She was a fat old woman, this Mrs Gamp, with a husky voice and a moist eye, which she had a remarkable power of turning up, and only showing the white of it. Having very little neck, it cost her some trouble to look over herself, if one may say so, at those to whom she talked. She wore a very rusty black gown, rather the worse for snuff, and a shawl and bonnet to correspond . . . The face of Mrs Gamp – the nose in particular – was somewhat red and swollen, and it was

Figure 9 Mrs Betsey Prig and Mrs Gamp by Hablot K. Browne (Phiz)

difficult to enjoy her society without becoming conscious of the smell of spirits.' She carries 'a species of gig umbrella; the latter article in colour like a faded leaf, except where a circular patch of a lively blue had been dexterously let in at the top' (hence the popular word, 'gamp', for 'umbrella'). Perhaps because of her close and constant acquaintance with matters of birth, sickness and death, Mrs Gamp is given to philosophising about 'this wale of life' mixed with personal reminiscences, as when she archly alludes to Mr Mould the undertaker's daughters' possible thoughts of marriage: 'the blessing of a daughter was denied me; which if we had had one, Gamp would certainly have drunk its little shoes right off its feet, as with our precious boy he did, and arterwards sent the child a errand to sell his wooden leg for any money it would fetch as matches in the rough, and bring it home in liquor: which was truly done beyond his years, for ev'ry individgle penny that child lost at toss or buy for kidney ones; and come home arterwards quite bold, to break the news, and offering to drown himself if that would be a satisfaction to his parents ... There's something [i.e., marryings] besides births and berryins in the newspapers, an't there, Mr Mould?' By listening to the ramblings of two of her patients, Lewsome and Chuffey, she learns enough to help to bring about the exposure of Jonas Chuzzlewit's plan to poison his father. Her prime concern when looking after the sick (whom she deals with briskly and callously) is her own comfort and the plentiful supply of good food and drink. She constantly alludes to her supposed friend, Mrs Harris: 'Mrs Harris ... leave the bottle on the chimney-piece, and don't ask me to take none, but let me put my lips to it when I am so dispoged, and then I will do what I'm engaged to do, according to the best of my ability.' She quarrels with her fellow-nurse, Mrs Betsey Prig, who finally infuriates her by suggesting that Mrs Harris is an imaginary woman: 'I don't believe there's no sich a person!' Two observations can be made about Dickens's portrayal of Mrs Gamp. The first is the wonderful inventiveness of language in her speech, based on Cockney usage and pronunciation. Second, despite the rich comedy in all her actions and words, Dickens had a serious social purpose in presenting her to his readers. In his Preface to the Cheap Edition of the novel (November 1849), he wrote: 'In all the tales comprised in this cheap series, and in all my writings, I hope I have taken every possible opportunity of showing the want of sanitary improvements in the neglected dwellings of the poor. Mrs Sarah Gamp is a representation of the hired attendant on the poor in sickness.' Dickens is said to have based her on a nurse whom his friend, Miss Burdett Coutts, had described to him. (19, 25, 26, 29, 38, 40, 46, 48, 49, 51, 52)

Gander, Mr (MC) One of the boarders at Todgers's, who is 'remarkable for his ready wit'. (9)

Ganz, Doctor (CS) A Swiss physician, who helps to prove George Vendale's identity. ('No Thoroughfare')

Gargery, Joe (GE) The village blacksmith, married to Pip's sister and hence a kind of father to Pip. 'Joe was a fair man, with curls of flaxen hair on each side of his smooth face, and with eyes of such a very undecided blue that they seemed to have somehow got mixed with their own whites. He was a mild, good-natured, sweet-tempered, easy-going, foolish, dear fellow – a sort of Hercules in strength, and also in weakness.' He is very fond of Pip and does all that he can to shelter him from the sometimes fierce attentions of Mrs Gargery, to whom Joe is a submissive husband. He explains his reasons to Pip: 'I see so much in my poor mother, of a woman drudging and slaving and breaking her honest hart and never getting no peace in her mortal days, that I'm dead affeered of going wrong in the way of not doing what's right by a woman, and I'd fur rather of the two go wrong the t'other way, and be a little ill-conwenienced myself.' Under the influence of Estella and his 'great expectations', Pip becomes ashamed of Joe, urging Biddy to help him on: 'Joe is a dear good fellow – in fact, I think he is the dearest fellow that ever lived – but he is rather backward in some things. For instance, Biddy, learning and manners'. He is further embarrassed when Joe pays him and Herbert Pocket a visit in London, since Joe behaves on that occasion with gauche and stiff attempts at polite behaviour. But on Joe's concluding admission that he knows he is 'wrong out of the forge, the kitchen, or off th' meshes [marshes]', Pip realises that 'there was a simple dignity in him'. When Pip fell ill after the ruin of his 'expectations', Joe gently tended him, paid his debts, and ('not wishful to intrude') quietly went away. Soon afterwards, Joe marries Biddy; they name their son Pip. (2, 4–7, 9, 10, 12, 16, 18, 19, 27, 35, 57–59)

Gargery, Mrs Joe (GE) Pip's sister (whose Christian names were Georgiana Maria), who is married to Joe Gargery, the village blacksmith. Twenty years older than Pip, she has brought him up 'by hand'. 'She was not a good-looking woman, my sister; and I had a general impression that she must have made Joe Gargery marry her by hand . . . [She] had such a prevailing redness of skin, that I sometimes used to wonder whether it was possible that she washed herself with a nutmeg-grater instead of soap. She was tall and bony, and almost always wore a coarse apron, fastened over her figure behind with two loops, and having a square impregnable bib in front, that was stuck full of pins and needles.' When she cut bread-and-butter, 'she jammed the loaf hard and fast against her bib – where it sometimes got a pin into it, and sometimes a needle, which we afterwards got into our mouths'. She treats Pip harshly, often using what Joe calls 'Tickler', which 'was a wax-ended piece of cane, worn smooth by collision with [Pip's] tickled frame'. She calls Orlick, Joe's journeyman, 'the blackest-looking and the worst rogue between this and France' and angrily incites Joe to knock him down. Not long afterwards, she is found lying terribly injured on the floor, having been struck on the head and spine with a convict's leg-iron. As a result, her sight, hearing and speech are impaired, so that she has to try to communicate by writing on a slate. But 'her temper was greatly improved, and she was patient'. When she dies, Pip notes that 'it was the first time that a grave had opened in [his] road of life, and the gap it made in the smooth ground was wonderful'. He feels 'a shock of regret which may exist [he supposes] without much tenderness'. It later transpires that Orlick had been Mrs Gargery's assailant. (2, 4–7, 9, 10, 12–18, 24, 25)

Garland, Abel (OCS) Mr and Mrs Garland's 28-year-old son, 'who had a quaint old-fashioned air about him, looked nearly the same age as his father . . . [and had] a timid reserve'. Like Mr Garland, he had a club foot. He was articled to Mr Witherden, the solicitor. (14, 20, 21, 38–41, 57, 60, 63–66, 68, 69, 73)

Garland, Mr and Mrs (OCS) Mr Garland, 'a little fat placid-faced old gentleman', and Mrs Garland, 'a little old lady, plump and placid like himself', are a benevolent couple who employ Kit Nubbles as 'a good lad' in their house, Abel Cottage, Finchley, for six pounds a year, 'over and above his board and lodging'. Mr Garland, who is the Bachelor's brother, is active with others in clearing Kit Nubbles's name and in finding the village where Nell and her Grandfather have sought refuge. John Forster tells us that in portraying the Garlands, Dickens was remembering a kindly family in whose house he lodged when his father and family were confined in the Marshalsea (1928: Book 1, Ch. 2). (14, 20–22, 38–40, 57, 60, 63, 66, 68–71, 73)

Gashford (BR) Secretary to Lord George Gordon, whom he encourages in his anti-Catholic campaign. He had been a schoolfellow of Mr Geoffrey Haredale and Sir John Chester at St Omer's, the Jesuit college in Northern France. Under the influence of Lord George's eloquence, he had 'abjured the errors of the Romish church'. He was 'taller [than Lord George], angularly made, high-shouldered, bony, and ungraceful. His dress, in imitation of his superior, was demure and staid in the extreme; his manner, formal and constrained. This gentleman had an overhanging brow, great hands and feet and ears, and a pair of eyes that seemed to have made an unnatural retreat into his head, and to have dug themselves a cave to hide in. His manner was smooth and humble, but very sly and slinking.' He cunningly instigates Hugh and his associates to perform acts of violence during the Riots, including the burning down of The War-ren, Haredale's house. Under the pre-tence of rescuing Emma Haredale from captivity, he attempts to seize her for himself but is prevented at the last min-ute by Joe Willet, Edward Chester and others. After the suppression of the Riots, Gashford 'subsisted for a time upon his traffic in his master's secrets' and then became a Government spy. Years later, he was found dead in an inn in the Borough, having poisoned himself. Dickens may have partly based Gashford on Robert Watson (1746–1838), the biog-rapher of Lord George Gordon. He claimed that he had been Lord George's secretary. This claim has, however, been disputed. But on 20 November 1838, just over two years before the beginning of the serialisation of *Barnaby Rudge*, an inquest was held on the body of Watson, who had committed suicide by strangling himself. After the inquest, about nine-teen scars were found on his body. J.P. De Castro, in *The Gordon Riots* (1926: 226–9), suggested that this discovery may have been responsible for Dickens's choice of name for his character, whose personality and behaviour are in any case the novelist's own invention. (35–38, 43, 44, 48–50, 52, 53, 57, 71, 81, 82)

Gaspard (TTC) A Parisian, whose child is run over and killed by the Marquis St Evrémonde's coach as it drives furiously through the streets. In revenge, he stabs the Marquis to death on his bed in his château and is hanged on a 40-foot-high gallows. (I: 5; II, 7, 9, 15, 16)

Gattleton, Sempronius, and family (SB) Mr Gattleton was a 'stock-broker in especially comfortable circumstances' who lived with his family at Rose Villa, Clapham Rise. His wife 'was a kind, good-tempered, vulgar soul, exceedingly fond of her husband and children, and entertaining only three dislikes': any-body else's unmarried daughters, ridi-cule, and Mrs Joseph Porter. The 'whole

family was infected with the mania for Private Theatricals'. But their produc-tions of *Othello* and *Masaniello* were disastrous, much to the delight of the audience. ('Tales: Mrs Joseph Porter')

Gay, Walter (DS) He is the appropriately-named, 'cheerful looking, merry boy . . . fair-faced, bright-eyed, and curly-haired', the nephew of Solomon Gills. He works as an office-boy in the firm of Dombey and Son. Angered by the warm feelings Florence and Paul Dombey show towards Walter, Mr Dombey sends him to the West Indies aboard the *Son and Heir*. When news comes that the ship is lost at sea, Solomon Gills leaves home in search of Walter. But Walter has survived the shipwreck, returns to England, and mar-ries Florence, whom he has loved ever since he found her wandering frightened in the streets after her encounter with Good Mrs Brown. He and Florence sail to China, where he has been given a post. After the fall of Dombey and his firm, they return to England, become recon-ciled with him and take him to live with them and their children. Dickens had first intended to show Walter 'trailing away . . . into negligence, idleness, dissi-pation, dishonesty and ruin' (which probably accounts' for John Carker's friendly concern for his welfare). But John Forster evidently dissuaded him from this plan of development: 'For reasons that need not be dwelt upon here, but in which Dickens ultimately acqui-esced, Walter was reserved for a happier future; and the idea thrown out took modified shape, amid circumstances bet-ter suited to its excellent capabilities, in the striking character of Richard Carstone in the tale of *Bleak House*' (1928: Book 6, Ch. 2). (4, 6, 9, 10, 13, 15–17, 19, 22, 23, 32, 35, 49, 50, 56, 57, 59, 61, 62)

Gazingi, Miss (NN) An actress in Mr Crummles's company, whom Nicholas Nickleby sees 'with an imitation ermine boa tied in a loose knot round her neck, flogging Mr Crummles, junior, with both ends, in fun'. (33)

General, Mrs (LD) The chaperone and companion Mr Dorrit engages after he has come into his fortune to complete his two daughters' education. 'Mrs General was the daughter of a clerical dignitary in a cathedral town, where she had led the fashion until she was as near forty-five as a single lady can be. A stiff commissariat officer of sixty, famous as a martinet, had then become enamoured of the gravity with which she drove the proprieties four-in-hand through the cathedral town society, and had solicited to be taken beside her on the box of the cool coach of ceremony to which that team was harnessed. His proposal of marriage being accepted by that lady, the commissary took his seat behind the proprieties with great decorum, and Mrs General drove until the commissary died.' As an impoverished widow, Mrs General undertook the formation of young women's minds and manners for remuneration, the amount of which she considered it ungenteel to discuss. She believed in suppressing all opinions and difficulties and 'was not to be told of anything shocking', since it was her province to 'varnish' everything. Her most famous precept, which she divulged to Amy Dorrit, was that 'Papa, potatoes, poultry, prunes, and prism, are all very good words for the lips: especially prunes and prism. You will find it serviceable, in the formation of a demeanour, if you sometimes say to yourself in company – on entering a room, for instance, Papa, potatoes, poultry, prunes and prism, prunes and prism.' Mr Dorrit treats Mrs General with deference, unlike his elder daughter, Fanny, who rightly suspects that she has matrimonial designs on her father. After Mr Dorrit's death and the crash of Merdle's enterprises, she sent a 'Prune and Prism by post every other day, demanding a new Testimonial by way of

recommendation to some vacant appointment or other'. Like Mr Podsnap, Mrs General represents the prudish codes of morality that had become prevalent in mid-Victorian England. (II: 1–7, 11, 15, 19, 24, 33)

Gentleman in Small Clothes, the (NN) A crazy old gentleman, looked after by a keeper, who lives next door to Mrs Nickleby and Kate at their cottage in Bow. He throws cucumbers and vegetable marrows over the garden wall and proposes marriage to Mrs Nickleby, who is flattered by his attentions. He comes down the chimney of the Nicklebys' house and is immediately infatuated with Miss La Creevy. Urged on by Frank Cheeryble, he follows her out of the room, 'strongly guarded by Tim Linkinwater on one side, and Frank himself on the other'. (37, 41, 49)

George. Dickens gives this name to coach guards (DC 5 and 'The Holly-Tree Inn') and to Tony Weller's friend, an insolvent coachman (PP 43). *See* also **George** (OCS), below.

George (CS) A weak-headed young man articled to Mr Buffle, the tax collector. ('Mrs Lirriper's Lodgings')

George (NN) A 'young man, who had known Mr Kenwigs when he was a bachelor, and was much esteemed by the ladies, as bearing the reputation of a rake'. (14, 15)

George (OCS) Mrs Jarley's van driver, who eventually married her. (26, 28, 47)

George, Mrs (OCS) A stout lady, who is a friend of Mrs Jiniwin's and who expresses her indignation at Quilp's treatment of his wife: 'before I'd consent to stand in awe of a man as she does of him, I'd – I'd kill myself, and write a letter first to say he did it!' (4)

George, Trooper (BH) *See* **Rouncewell, George.**

George, Uncle and Aunt (SB) They hold an annual, festive Christmas party for the family. ('Scenes: A Christmas Dinner')

Georgiana (GE) One of the 'toadies and humbugs' who hung around Miss Havisham. 'She was a cousin – an indigestive single woman, who called her rigidity religion, and her liver love'. Miss Havisham left her £20 in her will. (11, 25, 57)

Gibbs, Villiam (MHC) The young barber whose story Sam Weller relates in *Master Humphrey's Clock*. (5)

Giggles, Miss (MED) One of the pupils at Miss Twinkleton's school so 'deficient in sentiment' that she professes to make faces at any young men paying homage to her. (9, 13)

Gilbert, Mark (BR) An apprentice bound to Thomas Curzon, hosier, and in love with Curzon's daughter. He is initiated into the 'Prentice Knights and later becomes one of Sim Tappertit's two lieutenants during the Gordon Riots, when the 'Prentice Knights have renamed themselves the United Bull-dogs. (8, 39)

Giles (OT) Mrs Maylie's butler and steward. Rather a cowardly man, he shoots and wounds Oliver Twist in the attempted burglary of her house. (28–31, 34–36, 53)

Gill, Mrs (MC) One of Mrs Gamp's clients, who could calculate exactly when the birth of her babies was due. She 'wos never wrong with six', and Mr Gill 'would back his wife agen Moore's almanack, to name the very day and hour, for ninepence farden'. (29)

Gills, Solomon (DS) The proprietor of the Wooden Midshipman, a ship's instrument store, where he lives with his beloved nephew, Walter Gay. His closest friend is Captain Cuttle. He 'was far from having a maritime appearance', wore a 'plain and stubborn' Welsh wig, and was 'a slow, quiet-spoken, thoughtful old fellow, with eyes as red as if they had been small suns looking at you through a fog . . . He wore a very precise shirt-frill, and carried a pair of first-rate spectacles on his forehead, and a tremendous chronometer in his fob'. But his business (presumably made virtually obsolete by the new industrial and commercial developments of the 1840s) is doing so badly that Mr Brogley, a broker, takes possession of it in execution of an overdue bond debt. Captain Cuttle and Walter, helped by Paul's pleas to his father, persuade an extremely reluctant Mr Dombey to lend money to Gills (who manages somehow to pay it off). When Walter is lost at sea, Solomon Gills goes in search of him, leaving a message for Captain Cuttle, whom he asks to take care of 'the little Midshipman'. He travels to the West Indies, learns that Walter has sailed for England, and returns in time for Walter and Florence's wedding. He makes Captain Cuttle a partner in his business, with the result that above the effigy of the Wooden Midshipman the names of Gills and Cuttle 'shine refulgent'. According to Kitton, 'Sol Gills found his prototype in Mr Norie, of the firm of Norie & Wilson, nautical instrument makers, of Leadenhall Street, outside whose shop might be observed the carved sign of the Little Wooden Midshipman' (1906: 163). (4, 6, 9, 10, 15, 17, 19, 22, 23, 25, 39, 50, 56, 57, 62)

Gimblet, Brother (GSE) An elderly drysalter and an 'expounder' in a Dissenting congregation. He discovers that Hawkyard, his rival, is cheating George Silverman out of his inheritance and blackmails him.

Glamour, Bob (OMF) A regular customer at the Six Jolly Fellowship-Porters. (I: 6; III: 3)

Glavormelly, Mr (NN) A deceased actor, who had been a friend of Miss Snevellici's papa, who thought it a shame that he was not buried in Westminster Abbey. (30)

Gliddery, Bob (OMF) The 'sapient' potboy at the Six Jolly Fellowship-Porters. (I: 6, 13; III: 2, 3)

Globson, Bully (UT) A 'big fat boy, with a big fat head and a big fat fist', who was a schoolfellow of the Uncommercial Traveller. He apologised for hitting the latter as soon as he heard that he was expecting a hamper of delicacies from the Western Indies. ('Birthday Celebrations')

Glogwog, Sir Chipkins (SYC) He told a 'capital story about the mashed potatoes' to the Egotistical Couple. ('The Egotistical Couple')

Glubb, Old (DS) A 'weazen, old, crab-faced man, in a suit of battered oilskin, who had got tough and stringy from long pickling in salt water, and who smelt like a weedy sea-beach when the tide was out'. He draws Paul's wheeled 'couch' on the shore at Brighton and tells him stories of fish and sea monsters. To the Blimbers' horror, Paul thinks him 'a very nice old man' and tells Miss Blimber that if he might sometimes talk a little with old Glubb he would do better at his lessons. In his depiction of Glubb, Dickens therefore conveys the importance, as he saw it, of imagination in the education of the young, as opposed to the approach used by the Blimbers. He treated this principle more extensively a few years later in *Hard Times*, in which Sissy Jupe and Mr Sleary are contrasted in this respect with Bitzer and Mr Gradgrind. (8, 12)

Glumper, Sir Thomas (SB) He was among the 'rank and fashion of Clapham and its vicinity' who attended the Gattletons' Private Theatricals. Others who were there included 'the Smiths, the Gubbinses, the Nixons, the Dixons, the Hicksons, people with all sorts of names [and] two aldermen'. ('Tales: Mrs Joseph Porter')

Gobler, Mr (SB) A hypochondriac boarder at Mrs Tibbs's, who marries Mrs Bloss, another hypochondriac, whom he meets there. They go to live in 'a secluded retreat in Newington Butts', and are 'happy in their complaints, their table, and their medicine'. ('Tales: The Boarding-House')

Golding, Mary (SB) A young lady bathing in the sea at Ramsgate seen by Captain and Mrs Waters. She looked in her bathing costume 'as if she was enveloped in a patent Mackintosh, of scanty dimensions'. ('Tales: The Tuggses at Ramsgate')

Goldstraw, Sarah (CS) Formerly a nurse at the Foundling Hospital, she becomes Mr Wilding's housekeeper. She tells him of the mistake that was made concerning his identity. ('No Thoroughfare')

Goodwin (PP) Mrs Pott's maid, who acted as her body-guard. Her 'ostensible employment was to preside over her toilet, but [she] rendered herself useful in a variety of ways, and in none more so than in the particular department of constantly aiding and abetting her mistress in every wish and inclination opposed to the desires of the unhappy Pott'. Goodwin can be seen as a forerunner of Miggs in *Barnaby Rudge*. (18, 51)

Goody, Mrs (OMF) The Reverend Mr Milvey suggests that the Boffins could adopt her grandchild but Mrs Milvey disagrees, since Mrs Goody is an 'inconvenient woman', who drank eleven cups of tea the previous Christmas 'and grumbled all the time'. (I: 9)

Gordon, Colonel (BR) Lord Adam Gordon (1726?-1801), a kinsman of Lord George Gordon. He swears to run his sword through Lord George Gordon's body if any man among the rioters 'crosses the threshold of the House of Commons'. (49)

Gordon, Emma (HT) A tightrope lady (in the family way) who comforts Sissy Jupe when her father disappeared. Later, her first husband died as a result of falling off an elephant and she married (in Mr Sleary's words) 'a Cheethemonger ath fell in love with her from the front'. (I: 6; III: 7)

Gordon, Lord George (BR) Lord George Gordon (1751–93), the third son of the third Duke of Gordon, was a Member of Parliament and the President of the Protestant Association. He was the instigator of the Riots that broke out in June 1780 in London in protest against the Catholic Relief Act of 1778. Dickens describes him as a man 'about the middle height, of a slender make, and sallow complexion, with an aquiline nose, and long hair of a reddish brown, combed perfectly straight and smooth about his ears, and slightly powdered, but without the faintest vestige of a curl . . . As he stood musing in the red glow of the fire [at the Maypole Inn], it was striking to observe his very large bright eye, which betrayed a restlessness of thought and purpose, singularly at variance with the studied composure and sobriety of his mien, and with his quaint and sad apparel. It had nothing harsh or cruel in its expression; neither had his face, which was thin and mild, and wore an air of melancholy; but it was suggestive of an indefinable uneasiness, which infected those who looked upon him, and filled them with a kind of pity for the man: though why it did so, they would have some trouble to

explain.' John Forster objected to Dickens's favourable view of 'this madman', but in a letter to Forster Dickens defended his portrayal of Lord George: 'he must have been at heart a kind man, and lover of the despised and rejected, after his own fashion'. (Forster 1928: Book 2, Ch. 9). Dickens had evidently been influenced by some of his sources for *Barnaby Rudge*, including Robert Watson's *Life of Lord George Gordon* (1795) and Thomas Holcroft's *A Plain and Succinct Narrative of the Late Riots* (1780). Apart from this controversial interpretation of his character and descriptions of his encounters with fictional personages, Dickens's presentation of Lord George's part in the Gordon Riots follows the accepted historical facts. (35–37, 43, 48–51, 57, 73, 82)

Governor, Jack (CS) A naval officer, who was a guest at the Haunted House. He was a 'portly, cheery, well-built figure of a broad-shouldered man, with a frank smile, a brilliant dark eye, and a rich dark eyebrow'. He is said to be based on Clarkson Stanfield (1793–1867), the painter, who was one of Dickens's friends. ('The Haunted House')

Gowan, Henry (LD) He is a gentleman barely 30 years old, 'well dressed, of a sprightly and gay appearance, a well-knit figure, and a rich dark complexion'. When Arthur first encounters him beside the Thames, 'the lounger glanced at him for a moment, and then resumed his occupation of idly tossing stones into the water with his foot. There was something in his way of spurning them out of their places with his heel, and getting them into the required position, that Clennam thought had an air of cruelty about it. . . [Gowan] took no notice of a fine Newfoundland dog [named Lion], who watched him attentively, and watched every stone too, in its turn, eager to spring into the river on receiving his master's sign'. Gowan, who is distantly related to the Barnacles, is always affable and careless. Much to the misgivings of Clennam, Daniel Doyce, and Mr and Mrs Meagles, he wins the affections of Pet Meagles, whom he marries. In Italy, Mr Dorrit commissions him to paint his portrait. Gowan moves in high society there, and frequently neglects his wife, although they have a baby son. Little Dorrit reports in a letter to Arthur Clennam that she fancies that Mr and Mrs Meagles are 'under a constraint with Mr Gowan, and that they feel as if his mocking way with them was sometimes a slight given to their love for her'. In fact, he eventually tells Mr Meagles that he thought 'it would be a good thing if – politely, and without any scene, or anything of that sort – they agreed that they were the best fellows in the world, but were best apart'. Gowan, however, is gratified that as a result Mr Meagles is even more liberal in providing Pet with an allowance. John Forster points out that the 'Circumlocution heroes [i.e., the Barnacles and Lord Stiltstalking] led to the Society scenes, the Hampton Court dowager-sketches [of Mrs Gowan, for example], and Mr Gowan; all parts of one satire levelled against prevailing political and social vices' (1928, Book 8, Ch, 1). Hesketh Pearson thought that Thackeray 'must have perceived what no one else has been able to see: that the character of Henry Gowan, though not a portrait of him in the sense that Skimpole was a portrait of Hunt, contained Dickens's opinion of him' – notably that he was cynical (1949: 227). (I: 17, 26–28, 33, 34; II: 1, 3–9, 11, 14, 20, 21, 28, 33)

Gowan, Mrs (LD) The widowed mother of Henry Gowan. Her husband had been 'a commissioner of nothing in particular, [who had died] at his post with his drawn salary in his hand'. She is 'a courtly old lady', who lives in Hampton Court (in a 'grace-and-favour' residence). She disdains and patronises the Meagles family (whom she calls 'the Miggles people'),

but is quietly pleased with the marriage between Henry and Pet for financial reasons, although she snobbishly pretends otherwise to her friend, Mrs Merdle. When she later calls on Mr and Mrs Meagles, she is at pains to remind them such a marriage is inappropriate: 'this kind of thing never answers – as my poor fellow [her son] himself would say, that it never pays – in one word, that it never does'. (I: 17, 26, 33; II: 5, 8)

Gradgrind, Louisa (HT) The daughter of Mr Thomas Gradgrind. 'There was an air of jaded sullenness in them both [Louisa and her brother, Tom], and particularly in the girl: yet, struggling through the dissatisfaction of her face, there was a light with nothing to rest upon, a fire with nothing to burn, a starved imagination keeping life in itself somehow, which brightened its expression.' Looking at his pretty teenage daughter, Mr Gradgrind reflects: 'Would have been self-willed (he thought in his eminently practical way) but for her bringing up.' Dickens presents her always in a state of tension between the constraints upon her and her innermost emotions, significantly conveyed in images of fire and smoke. Louisa agrees to a loveless marriage to Mr Bounderby for the sake of her brother's advancement. When Tom gets into debt she still does all she can to help him. Unlike the harsh Bounderby, she shows compassion for Stephen Blackpool's plight. Although she finds James Harthouse attractive, she runs away from her marital home to her father. She finds salvation in Sissy Jupe; she falls on her knees in front of her, asks for pity and compassion, and physically and symbolically lays her head upon Sissy's 'loving heart'. (I: 3, 4, 7–9, 14–16; II: 1–3, 5–12; III: 1–9)

Gradgrind, Mrs (HT) Mr Gradgrind's wife and the mother of his five children. She was 'a little, thin, white, pink-eyed bundle of shawls, of surpassing feebleness, mental and bodily'. Bewildered by her husband's unyielding principles and by all the tensions in the family, Mrs Gradgrind utters memorable words just before she dies: 'I think there's a pain somewhere in the room . . . but I couldn't positively say that I have got it'. She also realises (as she tells Louisa) that 'there is something – not an Ology at all – that [Mr Gradgrind] has missed, or forgotten'. (I: 4, 9, 15; II: 9)

Gradgrind, Thomas (HT) A retired wholesale hardware merchant of Coketown and the local MP. In his seminal essay on *Hard Times* in *The Great Tradition*, F.R. Leavis states that in the novel Dickens is 'for once possessed by a comprehensive vision, one in which the inhumanities of Victorian civilisation are seen as fostered and sanctioned by a hard philosophy, the aggressive formulation of an inhumane spirit', and that this philosophy is represented by Gradgrind (1962: 250–1). Dickens makes this clear in his opening description: 'Thomas Gradgrind, Sir. A man of realities. A man of facts and calculations. A man who proceeds upon the principle that two and two are four, and nothing over, and who is not to be talked into allowing anything over. Thomas Gradgrind, Sir – peremptorily Thomas – Thomas Gradgrind. With a rule and a pair of scales, and the multiplication table always in his pocket, Sir, ready to weigh and measure any parcel of human natire, and tell you exactly what it comes to. It is a mere question of figures, a case of simple arithmetic.' He is married to the mentally and physically feeble Mrs Gradgrind. Their five children (Louisa, Tom, Adam Smith, Malthus and Jane) 'had been lectured at, from their tenderest years; coursed, like little hares' – with tragic consequences as far as Louisa and Thomas are concerned. Gradgrind therefore excludes all imagination from life ('Louisa, never wonder!'). But he is humbled and enlightened by the disasters that befall Louisa and Tom and his future redemption is hinted at: 'How much of futurity did he see? Did he see himself, a white-haired decrepit man, bending his hitherto inflexible theories to appointed circumstances; making his facts and figures subservient to Faith, Hope, and Charity; and no longer trying to grind that Heavenly trio in his dusty little mills?' Parallels are obvious between Gradgrind and Mr Dombey in many general and particular respects. (I: 1–9, 14–16; II: 1, 2, 11, 12; III: 1–9)

Gradgrind, Tom (HT) The eldest son of Mr Gradgrind. He is sulky and desperate because of his upbringing: 'If father was determined to make me either a Prig or a Mule, and I am not a Prig, why, it stands to reason, I must be a Mule.' Knowing his sister Louisa's love for him, he persuades her to accept Mr Bounderby's proposal of marriage in order to smooth his career at Bounderby's bank ('What a game girl you are, to be such a first-rate sister, Loo!'). But he soon becomes 'a dissipated, extravagant idler' (in Bitzer's words), appropriately called the 'Whelp' by James Harthouse. Tom robs the bank of £150, successfully throwing the blame on Stephen Blackpool. When his guilt is about to be exposed, he takes refuge in Sleary's circus, where Mr Gradgrind, Louisa and Sissy Jupe find him disguised as a black-faced clown – a grotesque and telling transformation: 'And one of [Mr Gradgrind's] model children had come to this!' With Sleary's help, Tom is taken to Liverpool and thence abroad. (I: 3, 4, 7–9, 14, 16; II: 1–3, 6–8, 10–12; III: 2, 4–9)

Graham, Hugh (MHC) A young apprentice in Elizabethan London in love with his master's daughter, Alice, who is seduced by a nobleman. Hugh kills the nobleman but is himself shot dead in the riot that ensues. Alice is found lying dead at the scene. (1)

Graham, Mary (MC) The companion of old Martin Chuzzlewit, 17 years old, timid and yet self-controlled, she was short, slight and charming. 'Her attire was that of a lady, but extremely plain; and in her manner, even when she sat as still as she did then [by Chuzzlewit's sickbed], there was an indefinable something which appeared to be in kindred with her scrupulously unpretending dress.' Old Martin tells Pecksniff that Mary is an orphan, whom he has adopted but who will inherit no money from him. He is angered by young Martin's love for her but by the end of the story gives his blessing to their union. Tom Pinch fell hopelessly in love with her at first sight, when he saw her standing in the church porch listening to him playing the organ. Mr Pecksniff forces his attentions on her with a view to marriage, as he thinks that she will, after all, inherit old Martin's money, but she rebuffs him. (3–6, 12, 14, 24, 30, 31, 33, 35, 43, 48, 52, 53)

Grainger (DC) One of Steerforth's friends who attend David Copperfield's dinner-party. (24)

Grandfather, Little Nell's (OCS) When Master Humphrey, the narrator, first sees Little Nell's grandfather, who is the proprietor of the Old Curiosity Shop, he notes 'his haggard face, his wandering manner, his anxious looks'. At the end of the story, the Single Gentleman, who is his long-lost brother, Master Humphrey, reveals the grandfather's sad history: the early death of his wife, his daughter's wretched marriage to a man who beggars him, and the waywardness of Fred, his grandson. 'Crushed and borne down less with the weight of years than by the hand of sorrow . . . he began to trade – in pictures first, and in curious ancient things.' Dreading that poverty and want will be the lot of Little Nell, his beloved and tenderly affectionate grand-daughter, he starts to gamble, is forced to borrow money from Quilp, gets deeper and deeper into debt, and has his house and possessions seized by Quilp. In his subsequent wanderings with Little Nell, he still succumbs to the temptations of gambling, taking all of Little Nell's money. Tempted by gamblers to rob Mrs Jarley, he is urged by Nell to flee; he finds a peaceful refuge, with her, in a village. After Little Nell's death, he is 'a stricken figure', who has lost his wits and who daily sits by her grave, where he is found one spring day 'lying dead upon the stone'. (1–3, 6, 7, 9–13, 15–19, 24–32, 40, 42–46, 52, 54, 55, 69, 71, 72)

Grandmarina, Fairy (HR) In Miss Alice Rainbird's 'romance', she is Princess Alicia's godmother, who says she should clean and prepare a fishbone, which will then have magical powers. (2)

Granger, Edith (DS) *See* **Dombey, Edith.**

Grannett (OT) A hard-hearted overseer in the workhouse, whose cruel treatment of a pauper is praised by Mrs Corney. (23)

Graymarsh (NN) One of the boys at Dotheboys Hall. His 'maternal aunt' (who is, presumably, his mother) sends her 'respectful compliments to Mrs Squeers, and thinks she must be an angel'. (7, 8)

Grayper, Mr and Mrs (DC) Neighbours of the Copperfields at Blunderstone, who later go to South America. (2, 9, 22)

Grazinglands, Mr and Mrs Alexander (UT) They come to London on business from the Midland Counties and are disillusioned by their experiences at a pastry-cook's and an hotel. ('Refreshments for Travellers')

Green (RP) An 'imperturbable' police officer, who is waiting in Whitechapel for Inspector Field. ('On Duty with Inspector Field')

Green, Lucy (UT) The childhood sweetheart of the Uncommercial Traveller, who he finds in later life has married Specks. ('Dullborough Town')

Green, Mr (SB) Charles Green (1785–1870), a celebrated aeronaut. Dickens describes ascents made by him and his son in two balloons at Vauxhall Gardens. ('Scenes: Vauxhall Gardens by Day')

Green, Tom (BR) The name Joe Willet assumes when he becomes a soldier. *See* **Willet, Joe.**

Greenacre, James (MP) Greenacre (1785–1837) was a murderer hanged at Newgate on 2 May 1837. At the second meeting of the Mudfog Association, Professor John Ketch exhibits what the members think is Greenacre's skull, which leads to an animated discussion. He then reveals that it is 'a coker-nut.'

Greenwood (CS) *See* **Joby.**

Greenwood, the Misses (SYG) One of them wonders whether Mr Fairfax will ever be married. ('The Censorious Young Gentleman')

Gregory (DC) The foreman of the packers at Murdstone and Grinby's warehouse. *See* **Tipp.** (11)

Gregsbury, Mr (NN) A self-satisfied MP, who refuses to resign despite the protests of a deputation that accuses him of breaking his election promises. He would require Nicholas Nickleby, who has applied to be his secretary, to supply him with detailed information, to write him 'a few little flourishing speeches, of a patriotic cast', and to perform other duties. Nicholas refuses because he fears to undertake such heavy duties, for which he would be paid only fifteen shillings a week. (16)

Grewgious, Hiram (MED) Rosa Bud's guardian. He is the Receiver and Agent 'to two rich estates', and has chambers in

Staple Inn, Holborn. He is 'a man of incorruptible integrity'. Although he is 'an arid, sandy man', awkward, shambling, and near-sighted, he 'still had some strange capacity in him of making on the whole an agreeable impression'. In discharge of a trust, Grewgious hands over to Edwin Drood the ring that belonged to Rosa Bud's deceased mother. After the disappearance of Edwin, he reveals to John Jasper the decision made by Edwin and Rosa to break off their engagement. Rosa Bud goes to him when she flees from John Jasper; he is sympathetically attentive to her, finding her lodgings with Mrs Billickin. (9, 11, 14–17, 20, 23)

Grey, the Misses (SYG) Two young sisters, who are acquaintances of Mrs Nixon and her son, Felix. ('The Domestic Young Gentleman')

Gride, Arthur (NN) A lean, bent money-lender in his seventies, 'the whole expression of [whose] face was concentrated in a wrinkled leer, compounded of cunning, lecherousness, slyness and avarice'. With the help of Ralph Nickleby, he plans to marry the 19-year-old Madeline Bray in order to gain control of the property to which the 'pretty chick' is entitled. But his plans are frustrated by Nicholas and Kate Nickleby's angry, determined confrontation with him and Ralph Nickleby, and by Mr Bray's death just before the wedding was due to take place – followed by Nicholas's carrying off Madeline to safety. Gride is appropriately murdered in his bed by robbers. (47, 51–54, 56, 59, 65)

Gridley (BH) 'The man from Shropshire' driven to angry desperation (including imprisonment for contempt of court) by twenty-five years' entanglement in legal proceedings in the Court of Chancery. He would sometimes visit George's Shooting Gallery to relieve his feelings by paying for fifty shots and firing away 'till he was red hot'. In order to avoid arrest, he hides in the Shooting Gallery, where Inspector Bucket discovers him. Just as Bucket is in the process of arresting him, he collapses and dies. Dickens stated in his Preface to *Bleak House* that 'the case of Gridley is in no essential altered from one of actual occurrence, made public by a disinterested person who was professionally acquainted with the whole of the monstrous wrong from beginning to end'. Dickens is referring to a pamphlet by William Challinor: *The Court of Chancery; its inherent defects . . . with suggestions for a remedy* (1849). (1, 15, 24, 27)

Griffin, Miss (CS) The headmistress of an 'establishment by Hampstead Ponds', who was 'bereft of human sympathies'. ('The Haunted House')

Grig, Tom (L) The lamplighter, who at first agrees to marry Fanny Brown, Mr Stargazer's niece, but then refuses when the philosopher's stone does not materialise. He also refuses to marry Betsy Martin when he learns that he is destined to live a long life.

Griggins, Mr (SYG) A 'droll dog', who continually jokes and plays tricks at a Christmas party. ('The Funny Young Gentleman')

Grimble, Sir Thomas (NN) Apparently a former acquaintance of Mrs Nickleby's. He was a 'very proud man . . . with six grown-up and most lovely daughters, and the finest park in the county' (of Yorkshire). (35)

Grime, Professor (MP) A prominent member of the Mudfog Association. Because he has lost his teeth, he is unable to eat his crusts 'without previously soaking them in bottled porter'.

Grimmer, Miss (HR) With Miss Drowvey she is the co-proprietor of the girls' school in the 'Introductory Romance' by William Tinkling.

Grimwig, Mr (OT) The irascible bachelor friend of Mr Brownlow's, whose brusqueness conceals a kind heart. He classifies all boys as either 'mealy' or 'beef-faced', and habitually promises to 'eat his head' if certain events should occur. He suspects that Oliver Twist is untrustworthy, a suspicion that seems to be confirmed when Oliver fails to return from the errand on which Mr Brownlow sends him. At the end of the story, Mr Brownlow rallies him on his prophecy, but 'Mr Grimwig contends that he was right in the main, and, in proof thereof, remarks that Oliver *did not come back*, after all; which always calls forth a laugh on his side, and increases his good humour'. (14, 15, 17, 41, 51, 53)

Grimwood, Eliza (RP) A young woman, commonly called the Countess, whose murder was investigated by Inspector Wield. ('Three "Detective" Anecdotes')

Grinder, Mr (OCS) An itinerant entertainer, whose 'lot' consisted of 'a young gentleman and a young lady [dressed in Highland costume] on stilts'. He accompanied them on foot with a drum on his back. (17)

Grip (BR) Barnaby Rudge's pet raven, his inseparable companion. The bird seems to have a preternatural knowingness and to incarnate a spirit of diabolical mischief. 'The raven, with his head very much on one side, and his bright eye shining like a diamond', speaks in a hoarse and distant voice, as in his first utterance in the story: 'Halloa, halloa, halloa! What's the matter here! Keep up your spirits. Never say die. Bow bow bow. I'm a devil, I'm a devil, I'm a devil. Hurrah!' As Gabriel Varden observes, 'The bird has all the wit', in contrast to Barnaby's simple-mindedness. Dickens bluntly explained in a letter of 28 January 1841 to George Cattermole, one of the two illustrators of the novel, that 'Barnaby being an idiot my notion is to have him always in company with a pet raven who is immeasurably more knowing than himself' (House *et al.* 1965. vol. II, p.197). After Barnaby's experiences in the Gordon Riots, Grip loses his ability to speak for a time. When he recovers the skill, 'he constantly practised and improved himself in the vulgar tongue', and (in the final words of the novel) 'has very probably gone on talking to the present day'. Dickens told his readers in his Preface to the first cheap edition of the novel (1849) that 'the raven in this story is a compound of two great originals, of whom I have been, at different times, the proud possessor'. A.W. Ward suggested that a literary antecedent was Ralpho, the raven who frightened Roderick Random and Strap in Smollett's novel, *Roderick Random*, Chapter 13 (1882: 47n). (5, 6, 10, 17, 25, 45–47, 57, 58, 62, 68, 73, 76, 77, 79, 82)

Groffin, Thomas (PP) A chemist, who unsuccessfully asks to be excused from jury duty at the trial of Bardell v. Pickwick. He has left his errand boy in charge, who thinks that 'Epsom salts means oxalic acid; and syrup of senna, laudanum'. (34)

Grogzwig, Baron of (NN) The Baron von Koëldwithout, who was the hero of the merry-faced gentleman's story. (6)

Grompus, Mr (OMF) One of the guests at the party the Podsnaps give for their daughter's eighteenth birthday. He is an 'Ogre' and 'complacent monster', who dances with her and bores her with a long account of an archery meeting. (I: 11)

Groper, Colonel (MC) One of the deputation that greet Elijah Pogram. (34)

Groves, James (Jem) (OCS) The landlord of the Valiant Soldier, who, with his confederates, List and Jowl, inveigles Nell's grandfather into gambling at cards. (29, 30, 73)

Grub, Gabriel (PP) An 'ill-conditioned, cross-grained, surly fellow', who is the subject of 'The Story of the Goblins who stole a Sexton', related by Mr Wardle. He is tormented by goblins in a dream he has in a churchyard on Christmas Eve. When he wakes up, he is shamefully aware of his misanthropic behaviour, wanders around for about ten years, and returns as a 'ragged, contented, rheumatic old man'. To some extent, therefore, Gabriel Grub and his visions foreshadow Scrooge and his experiences. (29)

Grub, Mr (MP) The president of the Umbugology and Ditchwaterisics session at the second meeting of the Mudfog Association.

Grubble, Mr (BH) The landlord of the Dedlock Arms. He was a 'pleasant-looking, stoutish, middle-aged man, who never seemed to consider himself cosily dressed for his own fireside without his hat and top-boots, but who never wore a coat except at church'. According to Charley, 'his wife is a beautiful woman, but she broke her ankle, and it never joined'. (37)

Grudden, Mrs (NN) A member of Mr Crummles's company. She 'assisted Mrs Crummles in her domestic affairs, and took money at the doors, and dressed the ladies, and swept the house, and held the prompt book when everybody else was on for the last scene, and acted any kind of part on any emergency without ever learning it, and was put down in the bill under any name or names whatever, that occurred to Mr Crummles as looking well in print'. (23–25, 29, 30, 48)

Grueby, John (BR) Servant to Lord George Gordon. 'He was a square-built, strong-made, bull-necked fellow, of the true English breed. . . [and] was one of those self-possessed, hard-headed, imperturbable fellows, who, if they are ever beaten at fisticuffs, or other kind of warfare, never know it, and go on coolly to win.' He is opposed to the fanatical excesses of Lord George's followers and is instrumental in rescuing Mr Haredale from an angry anti-Catholic mob. After making an implicit comparison between the 'mad' Barnaby Rudge and Lord George, he is dismissed by Lord George and becomes Langdale the distiller's servant and helper during the Riots. Nevertheless, Grueby maintains that Lord George was 'a misled man – a kind-hearted man', whom he goes back to tend some years later in Newgate Prison, remaining with him until his death. Grueby was Dickens's own fictional creation, as Lord George's personal servant was John M'Queen. (35, 37, 38, 43, 57, 66, 67, 82)

Gruff and Glum (OMF) An old pensioner with two wooden legs, who is present at the wedding of John Harmon and Bella Wilfer. (IV: 4)

Grummer, Daniel (PP) An elderly gentleman with a 'bottle-nose, a hoarse voice, a snuff-coloured surtout, and wandering eye'. He was the Ipswich 'peace-officer' who (with Dubbley and a body of 'specials') arrested Mr Pickwick and Mr Tupman for committing a breach of the peace and brought them (and the other Pickwickians and Sam Weller) before Mr Nupkins. When Mr Tupman identifies himself, Mr Grummer replies, 'My name's Law'. In his *Dickens Companion*, Norman Page suggests that there is 'some affinity with Dogberry and Verges', in *Much Ado About Nothing* (1984: 76). (24, 25)

Grummidge, Doctor (MP) A member of the Mudfog Association, who spoke on 'a most interesting case of monomania' at the Anatomy and Medicine session at the second meeting of the Mudfog Association.

Grundy, Mr (PP) A gentleman who abruptly refuses 'to oblige the company with a song' at the Magpie and Stump, where Mr Pickwick and Sam Weller have gone to meet Mr Lowten. (20)

Gubbins, Mr (SB) The ex-churchwarden who presented the silver inkstand to the curate 'as a mark of esteem for his services to the parish'. ('Our Parish: The Curate. The Old Lady. The Half-Pay Captain')

Gubbleton, Lord (SB) A 'devilish good fellow', with whom Mr Flamwell claims an intimate friendship. ('Tales: Horatio Sparkins')

Gulpidge, Mr and Mrs (DC) Guests at the Waterbrooks' dinner party to which David Copperfield was invited. Mr Gulpidge 'had something to do at second hand ... with the law business of the Bank'. (25)

Gummidge, Mrs (DC) The widow of Mr Peggotty's 'partner in a boat'. She is Mr Peggotty's housekeeper. 'Mrs Gummidge's was rather a fretful disposition, and she whimpered more sometimes than was comfortable for other parties in so small an establishment [as the converted boat].' Her frequent complaint is that 'I am a lone lorn creetur' ... and everythink goes contrairy with me.' Still, she is delighted at Ham and Emily's engagement, 'clapping her hands like a madwoman'. David Copperfield is astonished at the change in her when Daniel Peggotty decides to leave in search of Emily: she becomes 'the prop and staff of Mr Peggotty's affliction' and hence affords David a salutary lesson in self-reliance and determination. She insists on accompanying Mr Peggotty and others when they emigrate to Australia. When there, she angrily rejects an offer of marriage, and turns out to be (in Mr Peggotty's words) 'the willingest, the trewest, the honestest-helping woman ... as ever

Figure 10 Mr Jobling, Mr Guppy and Bart Smallweed by Hablot K. Browne (Phiz)

draw'd the breath of life'. (3, 7, 10, 17, 21, 22, 31, 32, 40, 51, 57, 63)

Gunter, Mr (PP) One of the guests at Bob Sawyer's supper party in his lodgings. He and Mr Noddy have a fierce quarrel, which is quite quickly resolved with both of them shaking hands. (32)

Guppy, Mrs (BH) William Guppy's mother, who lives with her son in the Old Street Road. 'She was an old lady in a large cap, with rather a red nose and rather an unsteady eye, but smiling all over'. But when Mr Jarndyce rejects Guppy's second offer of marriage to Esther Summerson, Mrs Guppy becomes angry and abusive: 'Ain't my son good enough for you?' (8, 9, 64)

Guppy, William (BH) The young, vulgar

and unintentionally comic clerk in the law firm of Kenge and Carboy. Soon after meeting Esther Summerson, he makes a declaration of love to her, which she gently but firmly rejects. He hastily retracts his declaration, however, when he sees her face disfigured after her near-fatal attack of smallpox. In a spirit of magnanimity, he later renews his proposals concerning Esther, only to have them this time peremptorily rejected by Mr Jarndyce. Early in the story, Guppy had been struck by the resemblance between Esther and the portrait of Lady Dedlock he saw on a visit to Chesney Wold. Eager to serve Esther's interests, he investigates the secrets of her birth. During the course of his investigations, Guppy and his friend Weevle (the name he had suggested that Jobling should adopt) discover Krook's death by 'spon-

taneous combustion'. His revelations distress Lady Dedlock and eventually bring
about her flight. (3, 4, 7, 9, 13, 14, 19, 20,
24, 29, 32, 33, 38, 39, 44, 55, 62, 64)

Gusher, Mr (BH) One of Mrs Pardiggle's evangelical friends, who (according
to her) 'is a very impassioned speaker –
full of fire!' He is a 'flabby gentleman
with a moist surface' and with very small
eyes in a moon-like face. (8, 15)

Guster (BH) The Snagsbys' servant, 'a
lean young woman from a workhouse
(by some supposed to have been
christened Augusta)'. She is in her early
twenties but looks older, and is subject
to fits. In her eyes, the law-stationer's
establishment is 'a Temple of plenty
and splendour'. (10, 11, 19, 25, 42,
59)

Gwynn, Miss (PP) The 'writing and
ciphering governess' at the Westgate
House Establishment for Young Ladies.
(16)

H

Haggage, Doctor (LD) The prisoner who attends at the birth of Little Dorrit. When the turnkey goes to fetch him he finds him playing all-fours (a card-game) with a friend in an ill-smelling little room: 'The doctor's friend was in the positive degree of hoarseness, puffiness, red-facedness, all-fours, tobacco, dirt, and brandy; the doctor in the comparative – hoarser, puffier, more red-faced, more all-fourey, tobaccoer, dirtier, and brandier'. But he eagerly obeys the turnkey's summons: ' "Childbed?" said the doctor. "I'm the boy!" ' (I: 6, 7)

Handel (GE) Herbert Pocket's name for Pip. *See* **Pocket, Herbert.**

Handford, Julius (OMF) The name used by John Harmon when he went to see the body of the drowned man which was thought to be his. (I: 3, 16; II: 13; IV: 12)

Hannah (NN) Miss La Creevy's 'servant girl with an uncommonly dirty face'. (3)

Hardy, Mr (SB) Mr Percy Noakes's bosom friend, who takes part in the steam excursion. He was 'a practical joker, immensely popular with married ladies, and a general favourite with young men. He was always engaged in some pleasure excursion or other, and delighted in getting somebody into a scrape on such occasions. He could sing comic songs, imitate hackney-coachmen and fowls, play airs on his chin, and execute concertos on the Jews'-harp.' ('Tales: The Steam Excursion')

Haredale, Emma (BR) The beautiful daughter of the murdered Reuben Haredale, she is brought up by her uncle, Geoffrey Haredale. She and Edward Chester love each other but any relationship between them is forbidden by her uncle on personal and religious grounds. Dolly Varden acts as a go-between and is later asked by Mr Haredale to be Emma's companion. When she, Dolly Varden and Miggs are captured by Hugh and Sim Tappertit, Gashford attempts to carry her off, under the pretence of taking her to safety. But Edward, who opportunely appears with other rescuers, fells him 'like an ox in the butcher's shambles'. Soon afterwards, Mr Haredale agrees to her marriage to Edward. (1, 4, 12–15, 20, 25, 27–29, 32, 41, 59, 70, 71, 79, 82)

Haredale, Geoffrey (BR) A Catholic squire and the younger brother of the murdered Reuben Haredale, he lives at the Warren, near Chigwell, Essex, taking affectionate care of his niece, Emma, Reuben's daughter. He broods over the mysterious murder, of which he himself has been vaguely suspected. In contrast to Mr Chester, whose smooth sophistication and cynicism he detests, he is 'a burly square-built man, negligently dressed, rough and abrupt in manner, stern, and [sometimes] forbidding both in look and speech'. He agrees with Chester, however, that the relationship between his niece and Edward Chester must cease, although five years later, when Edward's worth has been fully proved, he agrees to their marriage. Ever since the supposed death of Mrs Rudge's husband, he has paid her a small annuity;

he is perturbed by her refusal to continue accepting the money and by her disappearance. He comes gradually to realise that the Stranger who has ominously come upon the scene is Rudge and that he was the murderer. After Haredale's house is burnt by a mob during the Gordon Riots, he returns to the ruins, discovers Rudge there, seizes him and has him imprisoned, tried, and executed. In a duel with Sir John Chester, Haredale kills him with his sword, flees the country, and finds refuge in a religious establishment in Europe. (1, 10–12, 14, 15, 20, 25–27, 29, 34, 42–44, 56, 61, 66, 67, 71, 76, 79, 81, 82)

Harker, Mr (CS) The officer in charge of the jury in the murder trial. 'He had an agreeable presence, good eyes, enviable black whiskers, and a fine sonorous voice.' ('Doctor Marigold')

Harker, the Reverend John (CS) A clergyman, later martyred in New Zealand, who supplied a reference for Mrs Miller when she adopted an orphan foundling. ('No Thoroughfare')

Harleigh, Mr (SB) The singer of the part of Masaniello at the Gattletons' evening of Private Theatricals. But he 'was hoarse, and rather unwell, in consequence of the great quantity of lemon and sugar-candy he had eaten to improve his voice'. Dickens named him after John Pritt Harley (*c*. 1790–1858), the manager and principal actor at the St James's Theatre, London, where Dickens's comic burletta, *The Strange Gentleman*, was performed. ('Tales: Mrs Joseph Porter')

Harmon, John (OMF) He was the only son of John Harmon, 'a tremendous old rascal who made his money by Dust' (i.e., dealing in refuse). As a 14-year-old boy, he pleaded his sister's cause with his father (who had turned her out because he was angered by her engagement to be married), was himself turned out, and

went to work in South Africa. His inheritance from his late father was dependent on his marrying Bella Wilfer, whom he had not even seen. On returning to England, he tells George Radfoot, the third mate on the ship, that he would like to land incognito: 'So the plot was made out of our getting common sailors' dresses (as he was able to guide me about London), and throwing ourselves in Bella Wilfer's neighbourhood, and trying to put ourselves in her way, and doing whatever chance might favour on the spot, and seeing what came of it.' But Radfoot double-crosses him, drugs and attacks him, gets involved in a further mêlée, is thrown with Harmon into the Thames, and is drowned. Harmon swims ashore, adopts the name of Julius Handford and identifies Radfoot's body as his own. Adopting a second name, John Rokesmith, he takes lodgings with the Wilfers, who see him as 'A dark gentleman. Thirty at the utmost. An expressive, one might say, handsome, face. A very bad manner. In the last degree constrained, reserved, diffident, troubled.' He becomes Secretary to Mr Boffin, and genuinely falls in love with Bella (who at first rejects him). When Boffin expels him (as part of his plan), Bella realises that she loves him, leaves the Boffin household, and happily marries John. Meanwhile, Mrs Boffin has recognised John Rokesmith as John Harmon, although he himself does not reveal his identity, even to his wife, until he is on the point of being arrested on suspicion of murder. In conversation with the Wilfers, Mr Boffin refers to John Harmon as 'Our Mutual Friend', an ungrammatical phrase (as has often been pointed out) but nevertheless a clear indication of the part he plays in one of the main plots of the novel. 'Upon no hypothesis, however,' G.K. Chesterton argued, 'can he be made one of the more impressive figures of Dickens. It is true that it is an unfair criticism to object, as some have done, that Dickens does not succeed in disguising the identity of John Harmon with John Rokesmith. Dickens never intended to disguise it; the whole story would be mainly unintelligible and largely uninteresting if it had been successfully disguised. But though John Harmon or Rokesmith was never intended to be merely a man of mystery, it is not quite so easy to say what he was intended to be' (1933: 216). (I: 2, 3, 4, 6, 8, 9, 12, 15–17; II: 7–10, 12–14; III: 4, 5, 9, 15, 16; IV: 4, 5, 11–14, 16)

Harris (OCS) *See* **Short**

Harris (PP) The greengrocer in whose shop the Bath footmen hold their 'swarry', to which Sam Weller is invited. (37)

Harris, Mr (SB) A law-stationer, who is one of Mr John Dounce's friends. ('Characters: The Misplaced Attachment of Mr John Dounce')

Harris, Mrs (MC) Mrs Gamp's supposed friend, in whose existence Mrs Betsey Prig memorably expresses her disbelief. *See* **Gamp, Mrs Sarah** and **Prig, Mrs Betsey**. (19, 25, 29, 40, 46, 49, 51, 52)

Harrison (OMF) A little boy, whom the Reverend Frank Milvey suggests as a suitable orphan for the Boffins to adopt. He is overruled by his wife, who says the child squints '*so* much'. (I: 9)

Harry (OCS) Mr Marton's favourite pupil, who falls sick and dies. His grandmother blames the schoolmaster for his death since she claims that he studied too hard for fear of him. (24, 25)

Harry (OT) The 'half pedlar and half mountebank' who offers to remove the bloodstain from Bill Sikes's hat when he is fleeing after murdering Nancy. (48)

Harthouse, James (HT) A handsome man, 35 years old, who comes to Coketown with a view to being its Member of Parliament. He 'was a thorough gentle-

man, made to the model of the time; weary of everything, and putting no more faith in anything than Lucifer'. He had tried various occupations and activities, including army service, the diplomatic service, travelling to Jerusalem, and yachting round the world, but had found everything 'a bore'. His brother then suggested that he should stand for Parliament: 'Jem, there's a good opening among the hard Fact fellows, and they want men.' Harthouse is attracted by Mrs Bounderby (Mr Gradgrind's daughter, Louisa) and cultivates the friendship of her brother, Tom, whom he calls the 'Whelp'. He is ready to elope with her, but she resists temptation, leaves her husband, and returns to her father's home. Sissy Jupe persuades Harthouse to leave Coketown, saying, 'I am quite sure that you can mitigate in no other way the wrong and harm you have done'. He accepts defeat, sees himself as 'a Great Pyramid of failure', decides to go up the Nile, and writes to his brother accordingly: 'Dear Jack, – All up at Coketown. Bored out of the place, and going in for camels. Affectionately, Jem'. In his Introduction to *Hard Times* (1913), Bernard Shaw saw Harthouse as a typical Victorian 'swell'. '[He] reappears, more seriously and kindly taken, as Eugene Wrayburn and Mortimer Lightwood in *Our Mutual Friend*. He reappears as a club in The Finches of the Grove in *Great Expectations*. He will reappear in all his essentials in fact and fiction until he is at last shamed or coerced into honest industry and becomes not only unintelligible but inconceivable' (Laurence and Quinn 1985: 35). (II: 1–3, 5, 7–12; III: 2, 3)

Harvey, Mr (SYC) The 'angel of a gentleman' who marries Miss Emma Fielding. ('The Young Couple')

Havisham, Miss (GE) The old lady who lives as a recluse in Satis House. Having been jilted on her wedding day by Com-

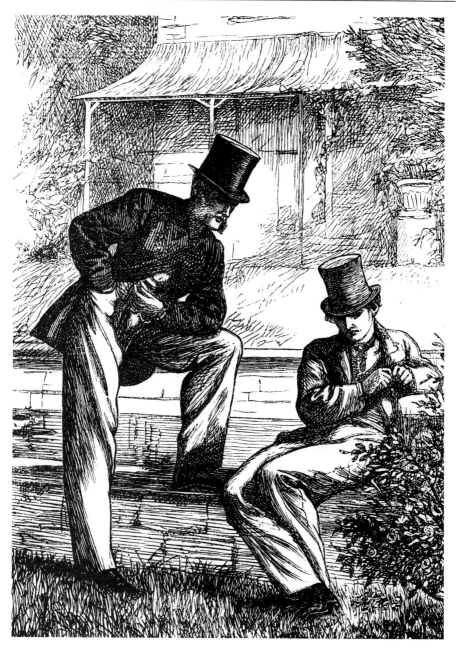

Figure 11 James Harthouse and Tom Gradgrind by Frederick Walker

peyson many years previously, she is broken-hearted and vengeful. She remains dressed in her bridal gown and has kept everything in her room exactly as it was on the day meant for her marriage. She summons Pip to play in the house as a diversion, since she has 'done with men and women'. Pip recollects his first sight

Figure 12 Pip and Miss Havisham by Marcus Stone

of her: 'I saw that the bride within the bridal dress had withered like the dress, and like the flowers, and had no brightness left but the brightness of her sunken eyes. I saw that the dress had been put upon the rounded figure of a young woman, and that the figure upon which it now hung loose, had shrunk to skin and bone.' Through the agency of Mr Jaggers, her lawyer, she has adopted Estella, whom she brings up as her instrument of revenge on men; she takes pleasure in the torments Pip suffers in his love for her beautiful protégée. She pays for Pip's indentures to Joe, the blacksmith. Pip naturally thinks that she must be the secret source of his 'great expectations', a belief that she does nothing to disabuse him of. Shortly before her marriage to Bentley Drummle, Estella coolly reminds Miss Havisham of the way she has been brought up, greatly to the distress of Miss Havisham: 'Did I never give her love! . . . Did I never give her a burning love, inseparable from jealousy at all times, and from sharp pain, while she speaks thus to me!' She gives Pip £900 to pass on to Herbert Pocket to finance his partnership with Clarriker. Then she drops to her knees at his feet, raises her folded hands to him, and utters words of despair and remorse concerning Estella's upbringing: 'I stole her heart away and put ice in its place.' Immediately afterwards, her clothes catch fire, and despite Pip's efforts to smother the flames she is seriously injured, and dies shortly afterwards. Various sources have been suggested for Dickens's depiction of Miss Havisham, including his description of the 'White Woman' in 'When We Stopped Growing' (an article in *Household Words*, 1 January 1853) and Wilkie Collins's recently published novel, *The Woman in White* (1860). But, as Humphry House commented in *All in Due Time*, 'it seems clear that Miss Havisham is another example of Dickens's regular habit of fusing together items from a number of different sources, remembered over a considerable time' (1955: 213). (8, 9, 11–13, 17, 19, 22, 29, 38, 44, 49, 57)

Hawdon, Captain (BH) Using the name of Nemo, Hawdon works as a law writer and lodges over Krook's shop, where Tulkinghorn finds him dead; he had apparently accidentally taken an overdose of opium, to which he was addicted. As a military officer, he had known George Rouncewell and he had also somehow fallen into the clutches of Grandfather Smallweed. Before her marriage to Sir Leicester, Lady Dedlock was engaged to him and bore his child, Esther Summerson. He was one of the few people to show kindness to Jo, the crossing-sweeper. On her final despairing journey, Lady Dedlock made her way to the graveyard where he was buried and was found dead at the gate by Esther Summerson, Inspector Bucket and Allan Woodcourt. (5, 10–12, 16, 21, 26, 27, 29, 32, 40)

Hawk, Sir Mulberry (NN) A dissolute man-about-town, who was 'remarkable for his tact in ruining, by himself and his creatures, young gentlemen of fortune'. Kate Nickleby indignantly resists his amorous advances. Nicholas, in defence of his sister's honour, strikes him with a whip handle, laying open one side of his face and causing him to fall from his cabriolet. Sir Mulberry kills Lord Verisopht in a duel, after the latter has turned against him in disgust at his behaviour. After a period abroad, Sir Mulberry 'was thrown into jail for debt, and there perished miserably, as such high spirits generally do'. (19, 26–28, 32, 38, 50, 65)

Hawkins (LD) A middle-aged baker, whom Miss Rugg had successfully sued for damages for breach of promise. (I: 25)

Hawkinses, the (NN) A gentlemanly family in Taunton Vale, whom Mrs Nickleby said she visited at least twice every half-year when she was at school. (35)

Hawkinson, Aunt (OMF) Georgiana Podsnap's aunt, who left her a necklace, which she offers to Mrs Lammle. (IV: 2)

Hawkyard, Verity (GSE) A 'yellow-faced, peak-nosed gentleman, clad all in iron grey to his gaiters'. He is the self-righteous leader of a Dissenting congregation, who becomes George Silverman's guardian and cheats him out of his inheritance.

Headstone, Bradley (OMF) Charley Hexam's schoolmaster. 'Bradley Headstone, in his decent black coat and waistcoat, and decent white shirt, and decent formal black tie, and decent pantaloons of pepper and salt, with his decent silver watch in his pocket and his decent hair-guard round his neck, looked a thoroughly decent young man of six-and-twenty ... Suppression of so much to make room for so much [i.e., a store of teacher's knowledge], had given him a constrained manner, over and above. Yet there was enough of what was animal, and of what was fiery (though smouldering), still visible in him, to suggest that if young Bradley Headstone, when a pauper lad, had chanced to be told off for the sea, he would not have been the last man in a ship's crew.' He bitterly resents Eugene Wrayburn's attentions to Lizzie Hexam, with whom Bradley Headstone has fallen in love at first sight. (Bradley himself is secretly loved by Miss Peecher, the schoolmistress). He passionately declares his love to Lizzie, who firmly rejects it. As he speaks, he grips a coping-stone so hard that 'the powdered mortar from under the stone at which he wrenched, rattled on the pavement to confirm his words'. After Lizzie's refusal, Headstone 'hated his rival [Eugene Wrayburn] with his strongest and worst forces'. Disguised in Rogue Riderhood's clothes, he attacks Wrayburn, who falls into the river, terribly injured, but is rescued by Lizzie. When Bradley hears that Eugene and Lizzie have married, he suffers further torments and fits. Rogue Riderhood, who has fished his clothes out of the river, attempts to blackmail him. Bradley grapples with him by the riverside, and both drown. Apart from

Dickens's penetrating presentation in Bradley Headstone of obsessive, frightening passion, there is his presentation in him of a narrow philosophy of education, continuing one of the themes of *Hard Times*: 'The intellectual insecurity of Headstone ("a kind of settled trouble in the face") replaces the relentless confidence of M'Choakumchild [in *Hard Times*], and is connected with the social unease which provides the new theme in this later study of the new-style schoolmaster' (Collins 1963: 150). (II: 1, 6, 11, 14, 15; III: 9–11; IV: 1, 6, 7, 10, 11, 15)

Heathfield, Alfred (CB) Doctor Jeddler's ward. He falls in love with Marion Jeddler, who disappears when she realises that her sister, Grace, loves Heathfield. Heathfield and Grace marry and he becomes the village doctor. (*The Battle of Life*)

Heep, Mrs (DC) Uriah Heep's widowed mother, with whom he lives. She 'was the dead image of Uriah, only short. She received me [David Copperfield] with the utmost humility, and apologised to me for giving her son a kiss, observing that, lowly as they were, they had their natural affections, which they hoped would give no offence to any one.' Mrs Heep is as ingratiating and hypocritical as her son. When Uriah is imprisoned, he asks permission to write to her so that he can urge her to save herself from sin. (17, 39, 42, 52, 54, 61)

Heep, Uriah (DC) The clerk in Mr Wickfield the lawyer's office. When David Copperfield first meets him, he is aged 15, but he looks much older. He had a cadaverous face and was 'a red-haired person ... whose hair was cropped as close as the closest stubble; who had hardly any eyebrows, and no eyelashes, and eyes of a red-brown, so unsheltered and unshadowed, that I remember wondering how he went to sleep. He was high-shouldered and bony; dressed in decent black, with a white wisp of a neckcloth, buttoned up to the throat; and had a long, lank, skeleton hand, which particularly attracted my attention, as he stood at the pony's head, rubbing his chin with it, and looking up at us [David and his aunt] in the chaise'. He has perpetually damp palms and notably 'snaky twistings of his throat and body'. He lives with his widowed mother, who was 'the dead image of Uriah, only short' and is equally hypocritical. Under the guise of being 'a very umble person', a self-description he frequently repeats, he gradually gains power over Mr Wickfield, establishes himself as his business partner, and aims to make Agnes, Mr Wickfield's daughter, his wife. He also attempts to poison Dr Strong's mind against Annie, his young wife, and to implicate David in the suspicions he attempts to arouse. Enraged, David strikes him on 'his lank cheek', an action for which, in his hypocritical way, Uriah Heep is, he says, determined to forgive. Thanks to Mr Micawber, with assistance from Traddles, Uriah Heep's machinations and fraud are exposed. David and Traddles later meet him as prisoner Number Twenty-Seven, in gaol for 'fraud, forgery, and conspiracy', awaiting transportation for life. Doris Alexander, in *Creating Characters with Dickens*, startlingly suggests that Dickens modelled Uriah Heep partly on Hans Christian Andersen (1805–75), whom he first met in 1847 (1991: 78–81). (15–17, 19, 25, 26, 35, 36, 39, 42, 49, 52, 54, 61)

Helves, Captain (SB) One of the guests of the Tauntons on the Steam Excursion. He 'gave slight descriptions of battles and duels, with a most bloodthirsty air, which made him the admiration of the women, and the envy of the men'. He was later arrested for embezzlement, leading to Mrs Taunton's complaint that she had been deceived in him. ('Tales: The Steam Excursion')

Henrietta (CS) For a short time, she was the girl friend of Tom, the pavement artist. ('Somebody's Luggage')

Henry, Mr (SB) A pawnbroker with 'curly black hair, diamond ring, and double silver watch-guard'. ('Scenes: The Pawnbroker's Shop')

Herbert, Mr (BR) Henry Herbert (1741–1811), who became the first Earl of Carnarvon in 1793, was a Member of Parliament at the time of the Gordon Riots. He objected to Lord George Gordon's sitting in the House of Commons wearing in his hat a blue cockade, the 'signal of rebellion'. (73)

Herschel, John (CS) The first cousin of the narrator of 'The Haunted House'. He was 'so called after the great astronomer' (i.e., Sir John Herschel, 1792–1871). He and his wife, 'a charming creature', were among the guests invited to solve the mystery of the ghost. ('The Haunted House')

Hexam, Charley (OMF) The son of Gaffer Hexam and brother of Lizzie. 'There was a curious mixture in the boy, of uncompleted savagery, and uncompleted civilisation. His voice was hoarse and coarse, and his face was coarse, and his stunted figure was coarse; but he was cleaner than other boys of his type; and his writing, though large and round, was good; and he glanced at the backs of the books [in the Veneerings' library], with an awakened curiosity that went below the binding.' Encouraged by Lizzie, Charley leaves home to better himself, and becomes a pupil teacher and protégé of Bradley Headstone. Petulant, moody and selfish, Charley resents Lizzie's self-sacrificing behaviour in looking after Jenny Wren. He also resents Eugene Wrayburn's arranging for her to be taught: 'I am more important to my sister than he thinks. I intend to raise myself, I intend to raise her; she knows that, and she has to look to me for her prospects.' He approves of Bradley Headstone's suit, and is angered at Lizzie's rejection of it: 'And so all my endeavours to cancel the past and to raise myself in the world, and to raise you with me, are to be beaten down by *your* low whims: are they?' He casts her aside and later, when he has become a master at another school, he rejects Bradley Headstone as well. George Gissing observed that 'of characters in the novels, there is no low-class malcontent worth mention except Charley Hexam . . . This youth has every fault that can attach to a half-taught cub of his particular world' (1974: 213). (I: 3, 6; II: 1, 6, 11, 14, 15; IV: 7)

Hexam, Gaffer (OMF) Formerly a partner of Rogue Riderhood, Jesse Hexam (always known as Gaffer) was 'a strong man with ragged grizzled hair and a sunbrowned face'. He is a 'bird of prey', who gets his living by fishing for corpses in the Thames and robbing them. He is utterly opposed to any education for his two children, Lizzie and Charley, and disowns the latter when he leaves his home in order to go to school. Hexam finds the supposed corpse of John Harmon in the river. In revenge for Hexam's breaking their partnership, Rogue Riderhood accuses him of murdering Harmon. When the Inspector, Riderhood, Mortimer Lightwood and Eugene Wrayburn go in search of Hexam, they find him dead in a boat on the river, entangled in his own rope. (I: 1, 3, 6, 12–14; II: 16)

Hexam, Lizzie (OMF) The beautiful, dark-haired daughter of Gaffer Hexam. She is an affectionate sister to Charley, whom she is anxious to see get on in life (with the ironical and cruel result that he later rejects her). After her father's death, Lizzie lodges with Jenny Wren and works in the stockroom of a seamen's outfitter. Both Eugene Wrayburn and Bradley Headstone fall in love with her. She angers her brother by her rejection of Brad-

ley Headstone's passionate declarations of love. Fully aware of the difference of social status between them, she is deeply in love with Eugene, although she cannot admit this to him or anyone else for a long time. Dickens wonderfully expresses her feelings in a moving, sympathetic passage: 'And going on at her side so gaily, regardless of all that had been urged against him; so superior in his sallies and self-possession to the gloomy constraint of her suitor [Bradley Headstone], and the selfish petulance of her brother; so faithful to her, as it seemed, when her own stock was faithless; what an immense advantage, what an overpowering influence was his that night! Add to the rest, poor girl, that she had heard him vilified for her sake, and that she had suffered for his, and where the wonder was that his occasional tones of serious interest (setting off his carelessness, as if it were assumed to calm her), that his lightest touch, his lightest look, his very presence beside her in the dark common street, were like glimpses of an enchanted world, which it was natural for jealousy and malice and all meanness to be unable to bear the brightness of, and to gird at as bad spirits might!' In order to escape both Eugene and Bradley Headstone, she leaves London to work at a paper-mill, owned by acquaintances of Riah. While there, she accidentally encounters old Betty Higden, who dies in her arms. In conversation with Bella Wilfer, Lizzie tells her of her constant fear of Bradley and indirectly of her love for Eugene. With her experience and physical skill derived from helping her father in the old days, she drags Eugene to safety from the river, after Rogue Riderhood's attack. She marries him on his sickbed, giving him new physical and moral strength. (I: 1, 3, 6, 13; II: 1, 2, 5, 6, 11, 14–16; III: 1, 2, 8, 9, 11; IV: 5–7, 9–11, 16, 17)

Heyling, George (PP) The subject of the interpolated story, 'The Old Man's Tale about the Queer Client'. He takes revenge on his father-in-law, who had had him imprisoned in the Marshalsea for debt. While Heyling was in prison, his wife, Mary, and his son died. (21)

Hicks, Septimus (SB) One of Mrs Tibbs's boarders. He was a 'tallish, white-faced young man, with spectacles, and a black ribbon round his neck instead of a neckerchief – a most interesting person; a poetical walker of the hospitals, and "a very talented young man"'. He was fond of 'lugging into conversation all sorts of quotations from [Byron's] *Don Juan*, without fettering himself by the propriety of their application; in which particular he was remarkably independent'. He marries Miss Matilda Maplesone, but deserts her. ('Tales: The Boarding-House')

Higden, Betty (OMF) Almost 80 years old, Betty Higden was 'one of those old women . . . who by dint of an indomitable purpose and a strong constitution fight out many years, though each year has come with its new knock-down blows fresh to the fight against her, wearied by it; an active old woman, with a bright dark eye and a resolute face, yet quite a tender creature too; not a logically-reasoning woman, but God is good, and hearts may count in Heaven as high as heads'. She keeps a 'a Minding-School' for children, including Sloppy, whose occupation is turning the mangle. Betty Higden is determined at all costs to keep out of the Poor House, a determination that Dickens emphasises with an apostrophe (a device he rarely uses): 'A surprising spirit in this lonely woman after so many years of hard working and hard living, my Lords and Gentlemen and Honourable Boards! What is it we call it in our grandiose speeches? British independence, rather perverted? Is that, or something like it, the ring of cant?' Mrs Boffin visits her in order to adopt her great-grandson, Johnny, who, how-

ever, dies in hospital. Knowing that Sloppy feels bound to stay with her instead of earning a good living with the Boffins, she decides to 'run away'. She wanders the roads, sells knitwear at country markets, collapses at the roadside on the bank of the Thames and dies in Lizzie Hexam's arms. In his Postscript to *Our Mutual Friend*, Dickens commented: 'In my social experiences since Mrs Betty Higden came upon the scene and left it, I have found Circumlocutional champions disposed to be warm with me on the subject of my view of the Poor Law.' Forster concisely indicated her function in the novel: 'Betty Higden finishes what Oliver Twist began' (1928: Book 9, Ch. 5). (I: 16; II: 9, 10, 14; III: 8, 9)

Hilton, Mr (SB) The 'popular Mr Hilton' was the Master of Ceremonies at the ball given by the Misses Crumpton at Minerva House. ('Tales: Sentiment')

Hominy, Mrs (MC) A pretentious 'philosopher and authoress', whom Martin Chuzzlewit meets in America. She was a 'traveller' and a 'writer of reviews and analytical disquisitions'. She 'had had her letters from abroad, beginning "My ever dearest blank", and signed "The Mother of the Modern Gracchi" (meaning the married Miss Hominy), regularly printed in a public journal, with all the indignation in capitals, and all the sarcasm in italics. Mrs Hominy had looked on foreign countries with the eye of a perfect republican hot from the model oven, and Mrs Hominy could talk (or write) about them by the hour together.' (22, 23, 34)

Honeythunder, Luke (MED) The guardian of Neville and Helena Landless and the brother-in-law of Mrs Crisparkle. He writes to Mrs Crisparkle from the chief offices of the Haven of Philanthropy concerning the education of his wards. He is immediately characterised by Dickens as a hypocrite, who takes pleasure in denouncing wrongdoers. He assumes that Neville Landless has murdered Edwin Drood, and with his booming voice tries unsuccessfully to bully Mr Crisparkle when the latter defends Neville. Mr Crisparkle finds Honeythunder's 'platform manners or platform manoeuvres' detestable, since 'they violate equally the justice that should belong to Christians, and the restraints that should belong to gentlemen'. (6, 7, 17)

Hopkins (SB) One of the candidates (with seven children) for the office of beadle. ('Our Parish: The Election for Beadle')

Hopkins, Captain (DC) A fellow-prisoner of Mr Micawber's in the King's Bench Prison. He was 'in the last extremity of shabbiness, with large whiskers, and an old, brown greatcoat with no other coat below it'. David Copperfield somehow divines that 'though the two girls with the shock heads of hair [who were also in the room] were Captain Hopkins's children, the dirty lady [who was there as well] was not married to Captain Hopkins'. (11)

Hopkins, Jack (PP) A fellow medical student of Bob Sawyer's. 'He wore a black velvet waistcoat, with thunder-and-lightning buttons; and a blue striped shirt, with a false white collar.' He astonishes Mr Pickwick with some tall stories, including one about a small boy who swallowed a necklace bead by bead: 'He's in the hospital now . . . and he makes such a devil of a noise when he walks about, that they're obliged to muffle him in a watchman's coat, for fear he should wake the patients!' (32)

Hopkins, Mr (SYG) The 'bashful young gentleman', whose 'whole face was suffused with a crimson blush, and bore that downcast, timid, retiring look, which betokens a man ill at ease with himself'. He has a 'dear sister', named Harriet.

Hortense (BH) Lady Dedlock's maid. She was 'a Frenchwoman of two-and-thirty, from somewhere in the southern country about Avignon and Marseilles – a large brown woman with black hair; who would be handsome, but for a certain feline mouth, and general uncomfortable tightness of face, rendering the jaws too eager, and the skull too prominent. There is something indefinably keen and wan about her anatomy; and she has a watchful way of looking out of the corners of her eyes without turning her head, which could be pleasantly dispensed with – especially when she is in an ill-humour and near knives. Through all the good taste of her dress and little adornments, these objections so express themselves, that she seems to go about like a very neat She-Wolf imperfectly tamed.' Infuriated by Lady Dedlock's preference for Rosa, she discharges herself from her employment, tries in vain to become Esther Summerson's maid, and is then used by Mr Tulkinghorn in his investigations into Lady Dedlock's past. She murders Tulkinghorn, who she thinks has inadequately rewarded her for her services, but her attempt to throw the blame for the murder on Lady Dedlock is frustrated by Mr and Mrs Bucket's enquiries and observations. Bucket exposes her actions to Sir Leicester Dedlock and arrests her for the crime. Hortense scornfully expresses a final defiance: 'It is but death, it is all the same. Adieu, you old man, grey. I pity you, and I des-pise you!' Dickens based Hortense on Mrs Maria Manning, a Swiss woman hanged with her husband on 13 November 1849 outside Horsemonger Lane Gaol for the murder of Patrick O'Connor. Dickens, who was present, wrote two letters to *The Times* protesting at the practice of public execution. (12, 18, 22, 23, 42, 53, 54)

Howler, the Reverend Melchisedech (DS) Mrs MacStinger attends his ministry. He had been 'discharged from the West India Docks on a false suspicion (got up expressly against him by the general enemy) of screwing gimlets into puncheons, and applying his lips to the orifices'. He held meetings in a front parlour for ladies and gentlemen of the Ranting persuasion. Having consented to give the world 'another two years of existence', the Reverend Melchisedech Howler officiates at the wedding of Captain Bunsby and Mrs MacStinger. (15, 32, 60)

Hubble, Mr and Mrs (GE) Mr Hubble, the village wheelwright, and his wife were guests at the Gargerys' Christmas dinner. 'I remember [Pip says] Mrs Hubble as a little curly sharp-edged person in sky-blue, who held a conventionally junior position, because she had married Mr Hubble – I don't know at what remote period – when she was much younger than he. I remember Mr Hubble as a tough high-shouldered stooping old man, of a sawdusty fragrance, with his legs extraordinarily wide apart: so that in my short days I always saw some miles of open country between them when I met him coming up the lane.' Mr and Mrs Hubble were among those who attended Mrs Gargery's funeral. (4, 5, 35)

Hugh (BR) The ostler at the Maypole, frighteningly fearless, coarse and brutal but yet with affection for his dog and for Barnaby Rudge. He has a gross fondness for drink and sleep. He is a naturally accomplished horseman, called the 'Centaur' by Mr Chester, who uses him as a spy on the relationship between his son, Edward, and Emma Haredale. Hugh lusts after Dolly Varden, whom he unsuccessfully waylays on one occasion and whom he and Sim Tappertit capture (with Emma and Miggs) for a while during the Gordon Riots. He is in the fore-

front of the rioters, eagerly obeying Gashford's urgings to burn down the Warren (Mr Haredale's house), and later in London wielding an axe while riding 'a brewer's horse of great size and strength, caparisoned with fetters taken out of Newgate, which clanked and jingled as he went'. Gabriel Varden learns from Dennis that Hugh was the illegitimate son of Sir John Chester and a gipsy woman (who was hanged for passing forged notes), but Chester refuses to acknowledge the parentage. On the scaffold, Hugh asks that Barnaby Rudge should be spared, curses 'that man, who in his conscience owns me for his son', hopes someone will take care of his dog, and carelessly goes to his death. (10–13, 17, 20–23, 25, 28, 29, 34, 35, 37–40, 44, 48–50, 52–55, 59, 60, 63–65, 67–69, 74–77, 79)

Humm, Anthony (PP) The president of the Brick Lane Branch of the United Grand Junction Ebenezer Temperance Association, to which Mrs Susan Weller belonged. He was 'straight-walking . . . a converted fireman, now a schoolmaster, and occasionally an itinerant preacher'. Dickens describes him rather as he described Mr Chadband in *Bleak House*: he was 'a sleek, white-faced man, in a perpetual perspiration'. He takes the chair at the monthly meeting when Sam Weller and his father are present. It is suggested that Humm was based on Mr G.J. King, who died in 1875. (33)

Humphrey, Master (MHC) A 'misshapen, deformed old man', of a kindly and gentle disposition, who founds a Club holding weekly meetings in his chambers to hear tales read by its members. The manuscripts of the tales are deposited in the case of a quaint old clock. He eventually and surprisingly reveals that he was the Single Gentleman (i.e., the brother of Little Nell's grandfather) in *The Old Curiosity Shop*. (*passim*)

Hunt (PP) Captain Boldwig's head gardener, to whom he is giving orders just before Mr Pickwick is discovered asleep in the wheelbarrow. (19)

Hunter, Horace (SB) The successful wooer of Emily Brown. He challenges his rival, Alexander Trott, to a duel, which, however, does not take place because of a series of misunderstandings. ('Tales: The Great Winglebury Duel')

Hunter, Mrs Leo (PP) A poetess, who lived at the Den, Eatanswill and who wrote an 'Ode to an Expiring Frog', published in a ladies' magazine. Dressed as Minerva, Mrs Leo Hunter holds a fête-champêtre in the form of a fancy-dress breakfast, which was attended by the members of the Pickwick Club and by Mr Jingle (under the name of Mr Charles Fitz-Marshall). Her husband was a 'grave man'. (16)

Hutley, Jem (PP) A 'care-worn looking man', who is an actor known as 'Dismal Jemmy' (according to Mr Jingle) and who relates 'The Stroller's Tale'. Mr Jingle, when a prisoner in the Fleet, reveals to Mr Pickwick that Hutley was Job Trotter's brother and was a 'clever rascal – queer fellow, hoaxing genius'. Job Trotter adds the information that Jem has emigrated to America. (3, 5, 53)

Hyppolite, Private (CS) A soldier billeted at the Perfumer's, who when off duty 'volunteered to keep shop while the fair Perfumeress stepped out to speak to a neighbour or so, and laughingly sold soap with his war-sword girded on him'. ('Somebody's Luggage')

I

Ikey (CS) The stable boy at the inn near the Haunted House. He was a 'high-shouldered young fellow, with a round red face, a short crop of sandy hair, a very broad humorous mouth, a turned-up nose, and a great sleeved waistcoat of purple bars, with mother-of-pearl buttons, that seemed to be growing upon him, and to be in a fair way – if it were not pruned – of covering his head and overrunning his boots'. ('The Haunted House')

Ikey (SB) The 'factotum' of Solomon Jacobs, the bailiff who imprisoned Mr Watkins Tottle for debt. When he calls on Gabriel Parsons, Ikey is wearing a 'coarse Petersham greatcoat, whitey-brown neckerchief, faded black suit, gamboge-coloured top-boots, and one of those large-crowned hats, formerly seldom met with, but now very generally patronised by gentlemen and coster-mongers'. ('Tales: A Passage in the Life of Mr Watkins Tottle')

Infant Phenomenon, the (NN). *See* **Crummles, Vincent, and family.**

Inspector, Mr (OMF) A calm and efficient police officer, who is concerned with the discovery of the corpse of the supposed John Harmon, the pursuit and discovery of Gaffer Hexam, and the final identification of John Harmon. (I: 3, 12–14; IV: 12)

Isaac (PP) A 'shabby man in black leggings', who accompanies Mr Jackson when the latter arrests Mrs Bardell. (46)

Izzard, Mr (MC) A member of the committee that welcomed Elijah Pogram. (34)

J

Jack (GE) A 'grizzled male creature', wearing the 'bloated' shoes of a drowned seaman, in the riverside public house where Pip, Startop and Magwitch stay overnight. He ominously reports seeing 'a four-oared galley going up with the tide'. (54)

Jack (SB) The man whose brutality to a young woman led to her death in hospital, although she claimed that her injuries were due to an accident. 'Brute as the man was, he was not prepared for this. He turned his face from the bed, and sobbed'. ('Characters: The Hospital Patient')

Jack, Dark (UT) A negro sailor. ('Poor Mercantile Jack')

Jack, Mercantile (UT) A typical merchant seaman, who was liable to be duped and ill-treated in the Liverpool docks. ('Poor Mercantile Jack')

Jackman, Major James (CS) In Mrs Lirriper's opinion, he was 'a most obliging Lodger and punctual in all respects except one irregular which I need not particularly specify' (i.e., he was late in paying his rent). Despite his military ways, there was some doubt whether he was a Major. He became the joint guardian (with Mrs Lirriper) of Jemmy Jackman Lirriper. ('Mrs Lirriper's Lodgings' and 'Mrs Lirriper's Legacy')

Jackson, Mr (CS) A former clerk in the firm of Barbox Brothers, which he eventually controlled and closed down. Because of the name on his luggage, he is invariably called 'Barbox Brothers' in the story. Stopping at Mugby Junction by chance, he meets a little girl named Polly, whose mother turns out to be his former sweetheart, Beatrice Tresham. He also hears the Signalman's ghostly story. ('Mugby Junction')

Jackson, Mr (PP) Dodson and Fogg's clerk, who serves the Pickwickians with subpoenas to attend the trial of Bardell v. Pickwick and who later arrests Mrs Bardell. He was 'an individual in a brown coat and brass buttons, whose long hair was scrupulously twisted round the rim of his napless hat, and whose soiled drab trousers were so tightly strapped over his Blucher boots, that his knees threatened every moment to start from their concealment'. (20, 31, 46)

Jacobs, Solomon (SB) The bailiff in whose sponging-house Mr Watkins Tottle is confined until he is released by the intervention of Mr Gabriel Parsons. ('Tales: A Passage in the Life of Mr Watkins Tottle')

Jacques (TTC) The name by which five of the French revolutionaries are known, including Defarge, who is 'Jacques Four'. When Monsieur the Marquis is killed by Gaspard in his bed at the château, the knife in his heart has a frill of paper round the hilt, on which is scrawled: *'Drive him fast to his tomb. This, from Jacques'.* (I: 5; II: 8, 9, 15, 16, 21–23; III: 5, 9, 12, 14, 15)

Jaggers, Mr (GE) Miss Havisham's lawyer, who was also employed by Magwitch to handle all the business connected with Pip's 'great expectations'. Pip first sees him at Satis House: 'He was a burly man of an exceedingly dark complexion, with an exceedingly large head and a corresponding large hand. He took my chin in his large hand and turned up my face to have a look at me by the light of the candle. He was prematurely bald on the top of his head, and had bushy black eyebrows that wouldn't lie down, but stood up bristling. His eyes were set very deep in his head, and were disagreeably sharp and suspicious. He had a large watch chain, and strong black dots where his beard and whiskers would have been if he had let them . . . his hand smelt of scented soap.' He has an abrupt and disconcerting manner, expressing himself with a lawyer's extreme caution; he is held in awe by his clients. This professional manner of his, according to Wemmick, his clerk, was deliberately mysterious: 'Always seems to me . . . as if he had set a man-trap and was watching it. Suddenly-quick – you're caught!' He is, says Wemmick, as deep as Australia: 'If there was anything deeper . . . he'd be it.' It somehow seems appropriate that Jaggers should have been fascinated by the uncouth Bentley Drummle, whom he called the 'Spider'. He employs as his housekeeper a woman named Molly, whose acquittal for murder he had secured (despite her guilt) and whose daughter by Magwitch was Estella, whose adoption by Miss Havisham had been arranged by Jaggers (since, as he told Pip, 'here was one pretty little child out of the heap who could be saved'). (11, 18, 20, 24, 26, 29, 30, 36, 40, 48, 49, 51, 55, 56)

James Dickens gives this name to the servant who waits at table in Mrs Tibbs's boarding-house (SB: 'Tales: The Boarding-House'), Mr Brook Dingwall's servant (SB: 'Tales: Sentiment'), and the Bayham Badgers' butler (BH 13).

James A bachelor with a twin brother, John, who is also a bachelor. In the German courier's story, he sees the phantom of John, who dies immediately afterwards. ('To be Read at Dusk')

Jane As with 'James' (see above), Dickens uses this name almost as a generic name for servants: the Kitterbells' (SB: 'Tales: The Bloomsbury Christening'), Wardle's (PP 5), Mrs Pott's (PP 13), Mr Pecksniff's (MC 31), Miss Wozenham's ('Mrs Lirriper's Lodgings'), and Mrs Orange's (HR).

Jane (SB) The 'Hebe of Bellamy's', the 'kitchen' frequented by Members of Parliament. She had 'a thorough contempt for the great majority of her visitors' and was 'no bad hand at repartees'. ('Scenes: A Parliamentary Sketch')

Janet (DC) Miss Betsey Trotwood's maidservant, who was a 'pretty blooming girl, of about nineteen or twenty, and a perfect picture of neatness'. She was 'one of a series of protégées whom [David Copperfield's aunt] had taken into her service expressly to educate in a renouncement of mankind, and who had generally completed their adjuration by marrying the baker'. Janet marries 'a thriving tavern-keeper', with the encouragement of Miss Trotwood, who crowned the marriage ceremony with her presence. (13, 14, 23, 39, 43, 60)

Jarber (CS) The reader of the manuscript of the story, 'Going into Society'.

Jarley, Mrs (OCS) The proprietor of a travelling waxworks show, who befriends Little Nell and her Grandfather on their wanderings, employing Nell to describe the waxwork figures to 'admiring audiences'. She was a kindly, good-humoured, Christian lady, 'stout and comfortable to look upon, who wore a large bonnet trembling with bows'. Although she was illiterate, Mrs Jarley recited eloquent stories concerning the exhibits, which she considered to be a 'calm and classical' form of entertainment: 'No low beatings and knockings about, no jokings and squeakings like your precious Punches, but always the same, with a constantly unchanging air of coldness and gentility.' Her 'inventive genius' included transforming the appearance of the waxwork figures to suit different audiences: for girls from a boarding-school, Grimaldi the clown was changed into a grammarian, Lindley Murray, a murderess into Hannah More, Pitt into Cowper, and 'Mary Queen of Scots in a dark wig, white shirt-collar, and male attire, was such a complete image of Lord Byron that the young ladies quite screamed when they saw it.' She later marries George, the driver of her van. In his edition of *The Old Curiosity Shop*, Paul Schlicke states that 'the most conspicuous original for Mrs Jarley was Madame Tussaud (1761–1850), who toured England for twenty-six years, between 1808 and 1834' (1995: 593–4). (26–29, 31, 32, 47, 73)

Jarndyce, John (BH) A principal party in the case of Jarndyce v. Jarndyce. He is the owner of Bleak House, which was so named by his disappointed great-uncle, Tom Jarndyce. He had 'a handsome, lively quick face, full of change and motion; and his hair was a silvered iron-grey'. Esther Summerson 'took him to be nearer sixty than fifty, but he was upright, hearty, and robust'. He adopted Esther as a child after the death of her so-called 'godmother' and then engaged her as the companion to Ada Clare. He is a benevolent, good-hearted man, who disguises any upset feelings he may have by saying that 'the wind's in the east' and retreating to the small room he calls 'the Growlery'. His two oddly assorted friends are Lawrence Boythorn and Harold Skimpole, whom he treats with remarkable tolerance. Richard Carstone spurns his well-intentioned advice. Mr

Jarndyce falls in love with Esther and despite the wide difference in their ages he asks her to marry him (to which she agrees), but he happily relinquishes her to Allan Woodcourt, when he discovers that they are deeply in love. He establishes Esther and Allan in a beautiful house, also named Bleak House, in Yorkshire, and also becomes the 'fondest father' to the widowed Ada and her baby son. In Esther's opinion, Mr Jarndyce 'is [her] husband's best and dearest friend, he is our children's darling, he is the object of our deepest love and veneration'. Edgar Johnson says that 'Mr Jarndyce probably makes amends to the nobler aspects of Dickens's father [John Dickens] for the good-humouredly derisive caricature of Micawber: even the name John Jarndyce is a softened echo of John Dickens' 1953: 767). (1, 3, 6, 8, 9, 13–15, 17, 18, 23, 24, 30, 31, 35–37, 39, 43–45, 47, 50–52, 56, 57, 60–62, 64, 65, 67)

Jarvis (CS) A clerk who works for Wilding and Co., Wine Merchants. ('No Thoroughfare')

Jasper, John (MED) The choirmaster at Cloisterham Cathedral and the uncle of Edwin Drood. He is, however, a secret opium addict, who periodically visits Princess Puffer's den in the East End of London. He 'is a dark man of some six-and-twenty, with thick, lustrous, well-arranged black hair and whiskers. He looks older than he is, as dark men often do. His voice is deep and good, his manner is a little sombre.' Although he seems to be well disposed to his nephew's relationship with Rosa, he passionately loves her himself, though at first he says nothing about this. After Edwin Drood's unexplained disappearance, Jasper terrifies Rosa by his declaration of love for her. This love of his, combined with such happenings as his exploration with Durdles of the tomb and crypt of the cathedral and his suggestions that Neville Landless was possibly guilty of Edwin

Figure 13 Edwin Drood, John Jasper and Neville Landless by Luke Fildes

Drood's apparent murder, have led most readers of the unfinished novel to believe that Jasper himself was the murderer. John Forster states that he learned from Dickens, when the novelist was planning the book, that 'the story ... was to be that of the murder of a nephew by his uncle; the originality of which was to consist in the review of the murderer's career by himself at the close, when its temptations were to be dwelt upon as if, not he the culprit, but some other man, were the tempted. The last chapters were to be written in the condemned cell, to which his wickedness, all elaborately elicited from him as if told of another, had brought him. Discovery by the murderer of the utter needlessness of the murder for its object, was to follow hard upon commission of the deed.' (1928: Book 11, Ch. 2). (1, 2, 4–10, 12–20, 23)

Jeddler, Doctor Anthony (CB) The father of Grace and Marion. He was 'a great philosopher, and the heart and mystery of his philosophy was, to look upon the world as a gigantic practical

joke; as something too absurd to be considered seriously, by any rational man'. (*The Battle of Life*)

Jeddler, Grace and Marion (CB) Grace, the elder sister, had 'home-adorning, self-denying qualities'. Marion was younger and, in her father's opinion, was a more beautiful child. When Marion, who was engaged to Alfred Heathfield, discovers that Grace truly loves him, she disappears. She has apparently eloped with Michael Warden, but in fact finds refuge with her Aunt Martha. After the marriage of Grace and Alfred, she returns and eventually marries Michael Warden. Grace and Marion are based on Georgina and Mary Hogarth, Dickens's sisters-in-law (Slater 1983: 97). (*The Battle of Life*)

Jellyby, Caddy (BH) Caroline Jellyby (always known as Caddy) was the eldest daughter of Mrs Jellyby and worked as her mother's secretary: 'a jaded, unhealthy-looking, though by no means plain girl', who sits biting the feather of her pen and is ink-stained from head to foot. But determined to improve herself, Caddy decides to learn to dance at Mr Turveydrop's Academy, where she meets his son Prince, whom she eventually marries. She is devoted to her husband and to her deaf-and-dumb child, and works hard to make a success of the Academy. (4, 5, 14, 17, 23, 30, 38, 50, 65, 67)

Jellyby, Mrs (BH) She 'was a pretty, very diminutive, plump woman, of from forty to fifty, with handsome eyes, though they had a curious habit of seeming to look a long way off'. Mrs Jellyby's whole concern was with overseas philanthropic projects, particularly in Africa, where (she said) 'we hope by this time next year to have from a hundred and fifty to two hundred healthy families cultivating coffee and educating the natives of Borrioboola-Gha, on the left bank of the Niger'. She is serenely indifferent to her chaotic domestic surroundings and to the welfare of her husband ('a mild bald gentleman in spectacles') and children. When the Borrioboola-Gha scheme fails, Mrs Jellyby takes up 'the rights of women to sit in Parliament'. Dickens based Mrs Jellyby on Mrs Caroline Chisholm, who organised the Family Colonisation Loan Society, which helped families to emigrate to Australia. Dickens visited her on 26 February 1850, and wrote to Miss Burdett Coutts: 'I dream of Mrs Chisholm, and her housekeeping. The dirty faces of her children are my continual companions' (House *et al.*, vol. VI, p. 53). (4–6, 14, 23, 30, 38, 50, 67)

Jellyby, Peepy (BH) The 'self-named' little brother of Caddy Jellyby. 'Everything the dear child wore, was either too large for him or too small.' Mr Turveydrop, Caddy's father-in-law, surprisingly takes to him and is 'constant' in his patronage of him. He eventually gets a post in the Custom House, where he does 'extremely well'. (4, 5, 14, 23, 30, 38, 50, 67)

Jem (SB) A 'sallow-faced, red-haired, sulky boy', who worked for Solomon Jacobs, the bailiff. ('Tales: A Passage in the Life of Mr Watkins Tottle')

Jemima (DS) Polly Toodle's unmarried sister, who takes charge of the Toodles family (including Polly's baby) when Polly is employed by Mr Dombey as Paul's nurse. (2, 6)

Jemmy, Dismal (PP) *See* **Hutley, Jem**.

Jenkins (SYC) An acquaintance of the Contradictory Couple. His identity and the colour of his coat cause an argument between them.

Jenkins, Miss (SB) The talented pianist at the Gattletons' Private Theatricals. ('Tales: Mrs Joseph Porter')

Jenkinson (LD) A messenger in the Circumlocution Office, who 'took it very ill indeed that [Arthur Clennam] should come back again, and who was eating mashed potatoes and gravy behind a partition by the hall fire'. (I: 10)

Jennings, Miss (MED) A pupil at Miss Twinkleton's Seminary for Young Ladies. Miss Twinkleton orders her to stand upright. (9)

Jennings, Mr (MP) Mr Tulrumble's 'new secretary, just imported from London, with a pale face and light whiskers'.

Jennings, Mr (SB) A robe-maker, who was one of Mr Dounce's friends. ('Characters: The Misplaced Attachment of Mr John Dounce')

Jenny (BH) The wife of a violent, drunken brickmaker. When Mrs Pardiggle, accompanied by Esther Summerson and Ada Clare, visit her, they see her, 'a woman with a black eye, nursing a poor little gasping baby', who dies on her lap. When Lady Dedlock goes on her last desperate journey, she exchanges clothes with Jenny in order to disguise herself. (8, 22, 31, 35, 46, 57, 59)

Jerry (OCS) A travelling showman encountered by Little Nell and her Grandfather at the Jolly Sandboys inn. He was a 'tall black-whiskered man with a velveteen coat' and was the 'manager' of five 'dancing dogs'. (18, 19, 37)

Jilkins (RP) A physician with 'a very small practice', who diagnosed Our Bore's illness as indigestion and cured him by prescribing a diet of mutton chops and sherry. Jilkins's success dated from that period. ('Our Bore')

Jingle, Alfred (PP) A strolling player with 'an indescribable air of jaunty impudence and perfect self-possession' and a staccato manner of speech. He has a fund of tall stories that seem all the more comic because of his pithy expression: 'Kent, sir – everybody knows Kent – apples, cherries, hops, and women.' He turns up on several occasions in the novel, invariably causing the Pickwickians embarrassment and annoyance. While wearing Mr Winkle's coat at a ball in Rochester, he makes Doctor Slammer jealous when he dances with Mrs Budger, with the consequence that Slammer challenges Winkle to a duel. Jingle elopes from Dingley Dell with Miss Rachael Wardle and has to be bought off by Mr Perker, acting on behalf of Mr Wardle. As Mr Charles Fitz-Marshall, he and his manservant, Job Trotter, trick Mr Pickwick and Sam Weller into thinking that he is planning another elopement, this time with an heiress from a boarding-school. Mr Pickwick finally encounters the now destitute Jingle and Job Trotter as fellow-prisoners in the Fleet Prison. Thanks to Mr Pickwick's generosity, they both start a new life in America. Norman Page suggests that Jingle's manner of speech 'may well have been modelled on that of Goldfinch, a char-

acter in Thomas Holcroft's play, *The Road to Ruin* (1792), though debts to Surtees and Hook have also been proposed' (1984: 77). Another influence on his mode of speech could have been Cophagus in *Japhet, in Search of a Father* (1834–6) by Captain Marryat, who was one of Dickens's closest friends. (2, 3, 7–10, 15, 16, 18, 20, 22, 23, 25, 42, 45, 47, 53, 57)

Jiniwin, Mrs (OCS) Mrs Quilp's mother, 'who resided with [the Quilps] and waged perpetual war with Daniel [Quilp]; of whom, notwithstanding, she stood in no slight dread'. She was 'laudably shrewish in her disposition and inclined to resist male authority', but like her daughter she is no match for Quilp's cruel and domineering ways. When Mrs Jiniwin's daughter remarries after Quilp's death, her second husband 'made it a preliminary condition that Mrs Jiniwin should be thenceforth an out-pensioner'. It has been suggested that Dickens modelled her on Mrs Hogarth, his own mother-in-law. (4, 5, 23, 49, 50, 73)

Jinkins, Mr (MC) A boarder at Mrs Todgers's. He 'was of a fashionable turn; being a regular frequenter of the Parks on Sundays, and knowing a great many carriages by sight. He spoke mysteriously, too, of splendid women, and was suspected of having once committed himself with a Countess.' He was, in fact, 'a fish-salesman's book-keeper, aged forty' and was the senior boarder. (8–11, 32, 54)

Jinkins, Mr (PP) A 'tall man – a very tall man – in a brown coat and bright basket buttons, and black whiskers, and wavy black hair', who is the suitor of the widow in 'The Bagman's Story'. Tom Smart, however, reveals to her that Jinkins is already married with six children. (14)

Jinkins, Mr and Mrs (SB) An 'unshaven, dirty, sottish-looking fellow', who is a customer of the pawnbroker's. His wife, whom he treats with brutality, is 'a wretched worn-out woman, apparently in the last stage of consumption'. ('Scenes: The Pawnbroker's Shop')

Jinkinson (MHC) The barber who is the subject of an anecdote told by Sam Weller: 'easy shavin' was his natur', and cuttin' and curlin' was his pride and glory. His whole delight wos in his trade.' (5)

Jinks, Mr (PP) A 'pale, sharp-nosed, half-fed, shabbily-clad clerk of middle age', who worked for Mr Nupkins as 'the magistrate's adviser (having had a legal education of three years in a country attorney's office)'. (24, 25)

Jip (DC) Dora's pet spaniel, whose name was short for 'Gipsy' and who is her inseparable companion. The dog 'never saw [Miss Betsey Trotwood] without immediately displaying every tooth in his head, retiring under a chair, and growling incessantly: with now and then a doleful howl, as if she really were too much for his feelings'. He dies at David Copperfield's feet at the very moment of Dora's death. (26, 33, 36–38, 41, 44, 48, 52, 53)

Jo (BH) The wretched little crossing-sweeper, befriended by Captain Hawdon (known as Nemo). 'No father, no mother, no friends. Never been to school. What's home? Knows a broom's a broom, and knows it's wicked to tell a lie. Don't recollect who told him about the broom, or about the lie, but knows both.' He 'lives – that is to say. Jo has not yet died – in a ruinous place, known to the like of him by the name of Tom-all-Alone's'. He shows the disguised Lady Dedlock the graveyard where Captain Hawdon (her former lover) was buried. The authorities are always 'moving him

on' and, harassed by them and by people (including Mr Snagsby and Inspector Bucket) enquiring about the lady he met, he makes his way to St Albans, where he infects Charley (and, through her, Esther) with the smallpox. Allan Woodcourt, seeing him in the London streets, takes him to George's Shooting Gallery, where he dies in the midst of saying the Lord's Prayer. Dickens follows his description of Jo's death with an apostrophe: 'Dead, your Majesty. Dead, my lords and gentlemen. Dead, Right Reverends and Wrong Reverends of every order. Dead, men and women, born with Heavenly compassion in your hearts. And dying thus around us every day'. Dickens possibly modelled Jo on George Ruby, a boy crossing-sweeper, who testified in a case at the Guildhall on 8 January 1850. Kathleen Tillotson has suggested that a visit Dickens paid to a Ragged School in 1852 may have stimulated him to create the pathetic figure ('*Bleak House*: Another Look at Jo', in Gibson 1989: 16–28). John Forster quotes from a letter that Dean Ramsay sent to him: 'To my mind, nothing in the field of fiction is to be found in English literature surpassing the death of Jo!' Forster also states that 'the first intention was to have made Jo more prominent in the story' (1928: Book 7, Ch. 1), but Kathleen Tillotson, in the above-mentioned article, thinks that this statement is based on a misunderstanding. (11, 16, 19, 22, 25, 31, 46, 47, 57)

Jobba, Mr (MP) At the Mechanical Science session at the first meeting of the Mudfog Association, he 'produced a forcing-machine on a novel-plan, for bringing joint-stock railway shares prematurely to a premium'.

Jobling, Doctor John (MC) The doctor who attended Anthony Chuzzlewit and Lewsome and who became the medical officer of the Anglo-Bengalee Disinterested Loan and Life Assurance Company. 'He had a portentously sagacious chin, and a pompous voice', and was highly praised by his female patients. 'But Jobling was far too knowing to connect himself with the company in any closer ties than as a paid (and well-paid) functionary, or to allow his connexion to be misunderstood abroad, if he could help it.' (19, 25, 27, 28, 38, 41, 42)

Jobling, Tony (BH) Mr Guppy's friend, who 'has the faded appearance of a gentleman in embarrassed circumstances; even his light whiskers droop with something of a shabby air'. Thanks to Guppy, he finds employment as a law writer for Mr Snagsby and lodgings in Hawdon's former rooms at Krook's. Because Jobling goes in fear of his creditors, Mr Guppy 'presents his friend [to Krook] under the impromptu name of Weevle'. Krook is due to hand over papers to Guppy and Jobling about Hawdon, but the two young men, to their horror, find only his bodily remains, as he has died of 'spontaneous combustion'. (7, 20, 32, 33, 39, 64)

Jobsons, the (UT) A family of Mormon emigrants consisting of 'an old grandfather and grandmother, their married son and his wife, and *their* family of children'. ('Bound for the Great Salt Lake')

Joby (CS) A one-eyed tramp, who had encountered the hooded woman five or six times. ('The Haunted House')

Jodd (MC) A member of the committee who welcomed Elijah Pogram. (34)

Joe (CB) The dealer who buys Scrooge's possessions after his death in the vision of the future shown to Scrooge by the Spirit of Christmas Yet to Come. He 'was a grey-haired rascal, nearly seventy years of age'. (*A Christmas Carol*)

Joe (MED) The driver of the Cloisterham omnibus. (6, 15, 20)

Joe (PP) Mr Wardle's fat pageboy, who spends most of his time sleeping and eating: his 'leaden eyes, which twinkled behind his mountainous cheeks, leered horribly upon the food as he unpacked it from the basket'. But he observes Mr Tupman and Miss Rachael Wardle kissing in a bower. On delightedly breaking the news to Mrs Wardle, he begins with the memorable words: 'I wants to make your flesh creep.' (4–9, 28, 53, 54, 56)

Joe (TTC) The guard on the coach carrying Mr Lorry to Dover. (I: 2)

Joey, Captain (OMF) A 'bottle-nosed person in a glazed hat', who was a regular customer at the Six Jolly Fellowship-Porters. (I: 6; III: 3)

John Servants with this name include the waiter at the St James's Arms (SG), Mr Lovetown's (ISHW), the Maldertons' (SB: see below), Gabriel Parsons' (SB: 'Tales: A Passage in the Life of Mr Watkins Tottle'), Emma Fielding's (SYC: 'The Young Couple'), and the waiter at The Saracen's Head (PP 51)

John James's twin brother, who appears to him as a phantom immediately before his death. ('To be Read at Dusk')

John (CS) The narrator of 'The Haunted House'.

John (DS) The very poor man, with no regular employment, observed by Florence Dombey in Fulham, who does all that he can for Martha, his beloved 'ugly, misshapen, peevish, ill-conditioned, ragged, dirty' daughter. (His behaviour therefore sharply contrasts with that of Mr Dombey.) Florence unobtrusively gives him some money. (24)

John (PP) The 'low pantomime actor' whose death is the subject of 'The Stroller's Tale'. (3)

John (RP) A smith, 56 years old with ten children, who travels to London to patent an invention. The proceedings cost him 'ninety-six pound, seven, and eightpence. No more, and no less.' His experiences can be compared to Daniel Doyce's. ('A Poor Man's Tale of a Patent')

John (SB) The Maldertons' manservant, 'who, on ordinary occasions, acted as half-groom, half-gardener; but who, as it was important to make an impression on Mr Sparkins, had been forced into a white neckerchief and shoes, and touched up, and brushed, to look like a second footman'. ('Tales: Horatio Sparkins')

John (SYG) The 'poetical young gentleman'.

Johnny (OMF) Betty Higden's great-grandson, whom the Boffins had planned to adopt. But before they could do this, Johnny was taken ill and died in the Children's Hospital, addressing his last words to John Rokesmith: 'A kiss for the boofer lady [i.e., Bella Wilfer].' (I: 16; II: 9, 10)

Johnson (DS) One of the pupils at Doctor Blimber's school. Trying to suppress a cough at the dinner table while Doctor Blimber was talking, Johnson goes blue in the attempt, bursts out into 'an overwhelming fit of coughing', and takes five minutes to recover. (12, 14, 41)

Johnson, John (SG) The man who eloped to Gretna Green with Mary Wilson.

Johnson, Tom (DS) One of Cousin Feenix's acquaintances, whom he recognises as he sits in the mourning-coach at Mrs Skewton's funeral: 'Man with cork leg from White's [Club].' (41)

Joltered, Sir William (MP) The president of the Zoology and Botany section at the second meeting of the Mudfog Association.

Jonathan (OMF) One of the regular customers at the Six Jolly Fellowship-Porters. His family name, if any, was 'unknown to mankind'. (I: 6; III: 3)

Jones (DC) David Copperfield, as a boy, is distressed to hear that Miss Shepherd has 'avowed a preference for Master Jones – for Jones! a boy of no merit whatever!' (18)

Jones (SB) One of Mr John Dounce's friends: 'the barrister's clerk – rum fellow that Jones – capital company – full of anecdote!' ('Characters: The Misplaced Attachment of Mr John Dounce')

Jones (SB) A 'little smirking man with red whiskers', who is a guest at the Buddens' dinner party. ('Tales: Mr Minns and his Cousin')

Jones, George (OMF) One of the regular customers at the Six Jolly Fellowship-Porters. He wears a 'faded scarlet jacket', and is peremptorily ordered by Miss Abbey Potterson to go home to his wife when his time is up. (I: 6)

Jones, Mary (BR) A young woman of 19, with a child at her breast, who was hanged by Dennis at Tyburn 'for taking a piece of cloth off the counter of a shop in Ludgate-hill'. This incident was based on an actual occurrence (16 October 1771), to which Dickens alludes in his Prefaces to the novel. (37)

Joram (DC) A 'good-looking young fellow', who is assistant to Mr Omer, the Yarmouth undertaker. He marries Minnie, Mr Omer's daughter, and becomes a partner in the business. (9, 21, 23, 30, 32, 51)

Jorgan, Captain Silas (CS) An American shipowner, who brings Alfred Raybrock his brother Hugh's letter found in a bottle. Dickens based Jorgan on his American friend, Captain Elisha Ely Morgan (d. 1864) of the American Merchant service. ('A Message from the Sea')

Jorkins, Mr (DC) Mr Spenlow's partner in the firm of proctors where David Copperfield is articled. He is mostly unseen, and Spenlow finds it expedient to refer to his opinion to justify his own conduct. David 'was quite dismayed by the idea of this terrible Jorkins. But I found out afterwards that he was a mild man of a heavy temperament, whose place in the business was to keep himself in the background, and be constantly exhibited as the most obdurate and ruthless of men.' When David meets him, wanting to cancel his articles with the firm, he finds that he is 'a large, mild, smooth-faced man of sixty, who took so much snuff that there was a tradition in the Commons that he lived principally on that stimulant, having little room in his system for any other article of diet'. After Spenlow's death, Jorkins lets the business decline. The relationship between Spenlow and Jorkins can be compared to that between Casby and Pancks and to that between Fledgeby and Riah. (23, 29, 33, 35, 38, 39)

Joseph (CS) The 'much-respected' head waiter at the Slamjam Coffee House in London. ('Somebody's Luggage')

Joseph and Celia (UT) Charity children shaking bits of matting in a city church and 'making love' by exchanging 'a chaste salute'. ('The City of the Absent')

Jowl, Joe (OCS) With Isaac List, he was one of the gamblers encountered by Nell and her Grandfather at the Valiant Soldier. He had a rough voice and was a 'burly fellow of middle age, with large black whiskers, broad cheeks, a coarse wide mouth, and bull neck, which was pretty freely displayed as his short collar

was only confined by a loose red neckerchief'. He later tries to induce the Grandfather to rob Mrs Jarley. (29, 42, 73)

Joy, Thomas (RP) A carpenter, with whom 'Old John' lodged in Chelsea when he came to London to patent his invention. ('A Poor Man's Tale of a Patent')

Julia (RP) The sweetheart of the narrator, who is a bachelor. But 'the father of my charming Julia objects to our union'. ('The Ghost of Art')

Jupe, Sissy (HT) The daughter of a horse-rider in Sleary's Circus, known as Signior Jupe, who has disappeared and deserted her. In the classroom at Mr M'Choakumchild's school, she is known as 'Girl Number Twenty', and makes a significant and symbolic contrast to her fellow-pupil, Bitzer, since she is 'so dark-eyed and dark-haired, that she seemed to receive a deeper and more lustrous colour from the sun, when it shone upon her'. (F.R. Leavis in *The Great Tradition,* saw an 'essentially Laurentian suggestion' about this contrast (1962: 253)). Mr Gradgrind takes charge of her, is willing to educate and provide for her, and employs her 'about Mrs Gradgrind, who is rather an invalid'. Representing the power of instinct and compassion, Sissy cannot understand the factual regime imposed by Gradgrind. For her, 'statistics' are 'stutterings'. But she has a loving influence upon the Gradgrind household, and it is to her that Louisa Bounderby (née Gradgrind) turns in her despair after leaving Bounderby: 'Forgive me, pity me, help me! Have compassion on my great need, and let me lay this head of mine upon a loving heart!' Sissy is the one who successfully urges James Harthouse to leave Louisa and Coketown and who, with Rachael, discovers Stephen Blackpool lying in the deserted mineshaft. (I: 2, 4–9, 14, 15; II: 9; III: 1–9)

K

Kags (OT) A 'returned transport', who was with Toby Crackit and Chitling in the house on Jacob's Island when Bill Sikes sought refuge there. He was a 'robber of fifty years, whose face had been almost beaten in, in some old scuffle, and whose face bore a frightful scar which might probably be traced to the same occasion'. (50)

Kate (DS) A 'beautiful girl, three or four years younger than [Florence], who was an orphan child, and who was accompanied by her aunt'. They visited the Skettles's house in Fulham when Florence was staying there. She overheard the aunt tell Kate that 'not an orphan in the wide world can be so deserted as the child who is an outcast from a living parent's love'. Although of a completely different social class, Kate serves the same symbolic function as Martha, whom Florence also saw while staying in Fulham. (24)

Kate (PP) An 'arch, impudent-looking, bewitching little person', who was the cousin of Maria Lobbs in the story of 'The Parish Clerk'. (17)

Kedgick, Captain (MC) The landlord of the National Hotel in an American town, who arranges a levee for Martin Chuzzlewit before he and Mark Tapley set off for Eden. He is annoyed when they return: 'A man ain't got no right to be a public man, unless he meets the public views. Our fashionable people wouldn't have attended his le-vee, if they had know'd it.' (22, 34)

Kenge, 'Conversation' (BH) A solicitor, known as 'Conversation Kenge', who is a partner in the law firm of Kenge and Carboy, Lincoln's Inn. He is a 'portly important-looking gentleman, dressed all in black, with a white cravat, large gold watch seals, a pair of gold eyeglasses, and large seal-ring upon his little finger'. He is Mr Jarndyce's lawyer and arranges his adoption of Esther Summerson. Richard Carstone is articled to him for a while. Kenge has no time for Mr Jarndyce's hostile attitude towards the conduct of the case of Jarndyce v. Jarndyce and towards the legal system in general: 'My dear sir, this is a very great country, a very great country. Its system of equity is a very great system, a very great system.' (3, 4, 13, 17, 18, 20, 24, 62, 65)

Kenwigs, Mr and Mrs, and family (NN) Mr Kenwigs, a turner in ivory, his wife and children are lodgers in the same house as Newman Noggs. Thanks to Noggs, Nicholas Nickleby is employed to 'instruct the four Miss Kenwigses in the French language as spoken by natives, at the weekly stipend of five shillings, current coin of the realm'. The Kenwigs's expectations of inheriting money from Mr Lillyvick are dashed by his marriage to Miss Petowker ('My children, my defrauded, swindled infants!' Mr Kenwigs exclaims), but after his wife leaves him he settles his money on the children after all. As for the eldest daughter's uncommon Christian name, Morleena, 'it had been invented and composed by Mrs Kenwigs previous to her first lying-in, for the special distinction of her eldest child, in case it should prove a daughter'. (14–16, 25, 36, 52)

Ketch, Professor John (MP) At the second meeting of the Mudfog Association, he mischievously exhibits a coconut instead of the skull of the late Mr Greenacre: 'It ain't no 'ed at all; it's a coker-nut as my brother-in-law has been a-carvin', to hornament his new baked tatur-stall wots a-comin' down 'ere vile the 'sociation's in the town.' (*See* **Greenacre, James.**) The Professor's name is a version of Jack Ketch, the notorious executioner (d. 1686).

Kettle, La Fayette (MC) The secretary of the Watertoast Association, whom Martin Chuzzlewit and Mark Tapley meet as they travel to Eden. 'He was as languid and listless in his looks, as most of the gentlemen they had seen; his cheeks were so hollow that he seemed to be always sucking them in; and the sun had burnt him, not a wholesome red or brown, but dirty yellow.' His first name is that of the Marquis de la Fayette (1757–1834), the French soldier, who had rendered military assistance to the Americans in the War of Independence. (21, 22)

Kibble, Jacob (OMF) A fellow-passenger of John Harmon on the voyage from the Cape to London. He gave evidence at the inquest on the supposed body of Harmon. (I: 3; II: 13; IV: 12)

Kidderminster (HT) He was 'a diminutive boy with an old face', who played the part of Mr E.W.B. Childers's infant son in 'his daring vaulting act as the Wild Huntsman of the North American Prairies'. 'Made up with curls, wreaths, wings, white bismuth, and carmine, this hopeful young person soared into so pleasing a Cupid as to constitute the chief delight of the maternal part of the spectators; but in private, where his characteristics were a precocious cutaway coat and an extremely gruff voice,

he became of the Turf, turfy.' He eventually married a widow old enough to be his mother. (I: 6; III: 7)

Kidgerbury, Mrs (DC) A domestic servant temporarily employed by David and Dora Copperfield. She was 'the oldest inhabitant of Kentish Town, I believe, who went out charing'. (44)

Kimmeens, Kitty (CS) 'A self-helpful, steady little child', who was a pupil at Miss Pupford's school and who was left there in the holidays because her relations and friends were in India. But the Traveller tells the Hermit that she emerged from solitude and looked abroad 'for wholesome sympathy, to bestow and to receive'. ('Tom Tiddler's Ground')

Kinch, Horace (UT) A man who suffered from Dry Rot (i.e., progressive moral deterioration), which carried him 'inside the wall of the old King's Bench prison, and . . . had carried him out with his feet foremost'. ('Night Walks')

Kindheart, Mr (UT) An 'Englishman of an amiable nature, great enthusiasm, and no discretion', who dwelt in the same Italian city as the Uncommercial Traveller. ('Medicine Men of Civilisation')

King, Christian George (CS) The negro pilot of the *Christopher Columbus*, who betrayed the colonists on Silver-Store Island to the pirates and was killed by Captain Carton. ('The Perils of Certain English Prisoners')

Kitt, Miss (DC) A 'young creature in pink, with little eyes', with whom David Copperfield desperately flirted when he saw Red Whisker 'eating his dinner at the feet of Dora' at the picnic in Norwood. (33)

Kitten, Mr (CS) A 'small, youngish, bald, botanical and mineralogical gentleman', who was the Vice-commissioner or Deputy-consul on Silver-Store Island. ('The Perils of Certain English Prisoners')

Kitterbell, Mr and Mrs (SB) Mr Charles Kitterbell was Mr Nicodemus Dumps's nephew. He asks his uncle to be his infant son's godfather at the christening in Hart Street, Bloomsbury. He 'was a small, sharp, spare man, with a very large head, and a broad, good-humoured countenance. He looked like a faded giant, with the head and face partially restored; and he had a cast in his eye which rendered it quite impossible for any one with whom he conversed to know where he was looking.' His wife, Jemima, 'was a tall, thin young lady, with very light hair, and a particularly white face – one of those young women who almost invariably, though one hardly knows why, recall to one's mind the idea of a cold fillet of veal'. ('Tales: The Bloomsbury Christening')

Klem, Mr, Mrs and Miss (UT) An elderly, dejected couple, who act as caretakers in the Uncommercial Traveller's London lodgings. They bring their bed in a bundle and sleep in the basement. The aged couple have a daughter, Miss Klem, 'apparently ten years older than either of them'. ('Arcadian London')

Knag, Miss (NN) Madame Mantalini's forewoman, 'a short, bustling, over-dressed female, full of importance'. She habitually interrupts 'the torrent of her discourse' with 'a loud, shrill, clear, "hem!"' She 'still aimed at youth, although she had shot beyond it, years ago ... she was weak and vain, and one of those people who are best described by the axiom, that you may trust them as far as you can see them, and no farther'. Miss Knag at first patronises Kate Nickleby as a new employee but becomes violently jealous of the favourable impression Kate's beauty makes upon the

clientele: 'here she is – everybody is talking about her – the belle, ladies – the beauty, the – oh, you bold-faced thing!' When the business is ruined, Miss Knag takes over the ownership. (10, 17–21, 44)

Knag, Mortimer (NN) Miss Knag's brother, who was 'an ornamental stationer and small circulating library keeper, in a by-street off Tottenham Court Road'. He was 'a tall lank gentleman of solemn features', who considers himself to be 'a miserable wretch'. According to his sister, he was once 'devotedly attached' to Madame Mantalini. He now reads and writes fashionable novels. (18)

Knight Bell (M.R.C.S.), Mr (MP) At the Anatomy and Medicine session at the first meeting of the Mudfog Assocation, he 'exhibited a wax preparation of the interior of a gentleman who in early life had inadvertently swallowed a door-key'.

Koëldwithout, Baron von (NN) The hero of 'The Baron of Grogzwig', the story told by the 'merry-faced gentleman'. (6)

Krook (BH) The keeper of a grandly titled Rag and Bottle Warehouse and a Dealer in Marine Stores. He was 'an old man in spectacles and a hairy cap'. 'He was short, cadaverous, and withered; with his head sunk sideways between his shoulders, and the breath issuing in visible smoke from his mouth, as if he were on fire within. His throat, chin, and eyebrows were so frosted with white hairs, and so gnarled with veins and puckered skin, that he looked from his breast upward, like some old root in a fall of snow.' Krook takes in lodgers, including Nemo (Captain Hawdon), Miss Flite and Tony Jobling. He is nicknamed the Lord Chancellor, has a large grey cat called Lady Jane, and drinks great quantities of raw gin. Although he is illiterate, Krook realises that he possesses letters from Lady Dedlock to Captain Hawdon, but

Figure 14 Krook and Esther Summerson by Hablot K. Browne (Phiz)

before he can hand them over to Jobling and Guppy he dies of 'spontaneous combustion' (a phenomenon which Dickens believed in). Dickens's characterisation of Krook and his description of his death have a symbolic significance, as his final words in Chapter 22 make explicit: 'The Lord Chancellor of that Court, true to his title in his last act, has died the death of all Lord Chancellors in all Courts, and of all authorities in all places under all names soever, where false pretences are made, and where injustice is done. Call the death by any name Your Highness will, attribute it to whom you will, or say it might have been prevented how you will, it is the same death eternally – inborn, inbred, engendered in the corrupted humours of the vicious body itself, and that only – Spontaneous Combustion, and none other of all the deaths that can be died.' After Krook's death, Grandfather Smallweed reveals that he was Mrs Smallweed's brother; the family therefore descends upon the building, searching for documents, which they find and use in attempts to blackmail Sir Leicester

Dedlock. In his name, nickname, life and manner of death, Krook symbolises the evils of the legal system and, more widely, those of the aspects of the society that Dickens was exposing and satirising in *Bleak House*. Peter Ackroyd tellingly alludes to the Second Law of Thermodynamics, proposed in the year before Dickens began writing the novel: the novelist shows 'how the forces of poverty and disease build up and spontaneously combust in the form of Krook' (1990: 663–4). (5, 10, 11, 14, 20, 32, 33)

Kutankumagen, Dr (MP) A physician from Moscow, who informs the Mudfog Assocation session on Anatomy and Medicine how he cured a man from constantly laughing. At the risk of spelling out the obvious, one reads the name as 'cut and come again'.

Kwakley, Mr (MP) At the session on Statistics at the second meeting of the Mudfog Association, he states the results of an inquiry into the ownership of property by Members of Parliament.

L

La Cour, Monsieur le Capitaine de (CS) An officer billeted at Madame Bouclet's. ('Somebody's Luggage')

La Creevy, Miss (NN) A 'mincing young lady of fifty', who is a miniature painter. Mrs Nickleby, Nicholas and Kate lodge with her in the Strand on their arrival in London. She was a 'little bustling, active, cheerful creature' and the 'nicest lady' Smike had ever seen. She is a kind and faithful friend to the Nicklebys, and eventually marries Tim Linkinwater. (3, 5, 10, 11, 20, 27, 31–33, 35, 38, 49, 61, 63, 65)

Ladle, Joey (CS) The Head Cellarman at Wilding and Co., Wine Merchants. He was a 'slow and ponderous man, of the drayman order of human architecture'. He becomes Marguerite's devoted servant, accompanies her to Switzerland, and helps to rescue Vendale from Obenreizer's attempt to kill him. ('No Thoroughfare')

Lady Jane (BH) Krook's fierce, grey cat, with a 'wicked mouth'. (5, 10, 11, 14, 20, 32, 33)

Lagnier (LD) One of the names used by Rigaud.

Lambert, Miss (SYG) The young lady with whom Hopkins, 'the bashful young gentleman', dances a quadrille

Lammle, Alfred and Sophronia (OMF) A 'mature young gentleman' and 'a mature young lady', who are members of the Veneering circle and who have a fashionable London wedding. Lammle has 'too much nose in his face, too much ginger in his whiskers, too much torso in his waistcoat, too much sparkle in his studs, his eyes, his buttons, his talk, and his teeth'. Each imagines that the other has property, but on their honeymoon in Shanklin on the Isle of Wight they discover that each has deceived the other and that they possess nothing. Consequently, they agree 'to work together in furtherance of [their] own schemes'. For financial reward, they plan to arrange a marriage between Fledgeby and Georgiana Podsnap, but Mrs Lammle regrets helping in the scheme and persuades Twemlow to get Mr Podsnap to put a stop to the proceedings. After the failure of that scheme, 'the happy pair of swindlers' turn their attention to Mr Boffin, hoping that he will reward them for exposing the supposed machinations of Rokesmith. Boffin sees through their plan and pays them off with a £100 note. Mrs Lammle (as she tells Twemlow) has realised that Riah is only a mask for Fledgeby's ruthless purposes and eventually Lammle beats Fledgeby up. Marcus Stone's illustration of 'The Happy Pair' on the seashore, where they discuss their mutual deceit, is a memorable image of their 'moody humour': 'the lady has prodded little spirting holes in the damp sand before her with her parasol, and the gentleman has trailed his stick after him. As if he were of the Mephistopheles family indeed, and had walked with a drooping tail.' As has sometimes been suggested, there is something Henry James-like in Dickens's portrayal of the

Figure 15 The Lammles by Marcus Stone

Lammles. (I: 2, 10, 11; II: 4, 5, 16; III: 1, 5, 12, 14, 17; IV: 2, 8)

Lamps (CS) A man in charge of the oil lamps at Mugby Junction. (The narrator prefers to know him under this name, although Lamps is willing to reveal his real name.) 'He had a peculiarly shining transparent complexion, probably occasioned by constant oleaginous application; and his attractive hair, being cut short, and being grizzled, and standing staight up on end as if it in its turn were attracted by some invisible magnet above it, the top of his head was not very unlike a lamp-wick.' He is an affectionate father to Phoebe, his crippled daughter. In his edition of Forster's *Life of Dickens*, J.W.T. Ley says that Lamps was based on a lamp foreman at Tilbury named Chipperfield (1928: 746). ('Mugby Junction')

Landless, Neville and Helena (MED) Twins, born in Ceylon, where

they had a wretched existence as orphans under the guardianship of a 'cruel brute' of a stepfather. They subsequently pass into the care of Mr Honeythunder in England, who sends them to Cloisterham for their education. They are 'an unusually handsome lithe young fellow, and an unusually handsome lithe girl; much alike; both very dark, and very rich in colour; she of almost the gipsy type; something untamed about them both; a certain air upon them of hunter and huntress; yet withal a certain air of being the objects of the chase, rather than the followers. Slender, supple, quick of eye and limb; half shy, half defiant; fierce of look; an indefinable kind of pause coming and going on their whole expression, both of face and form, which might be equally likened to the pause before a crouch or a bound.' Neville, in recounting their unhappy childhood to Mr Crisparkle, says that Helen (unlike him) was never cowed and that in their attempts to run away 'she dressed as a boy, and showed the daring of a man' (a statement that may or may not be intended as significant in the development of the novel). Neville, 'impressed' by Rosa Bud, is indignant that Edwin Drood 'should hold his prize so lightly'. The two young men antagonise each other and violently quarrel in Jasper's presence, although a reconciliation between them seems to take place, largely owing to Mr Crisparkle's persuasion. After Edwin Drood's disappearance, Jasper throws suspicion on Neville, who accordingly leaves Cloisterham for London, where Helena soon joins him. Helena, it seems, is falling in love with Mr Crisparkle. Forster says that 'Crisparkle [was to marry] the sister of Landless, who was himself, I think, to have perished in assisting Tartar to unmask and seize the murderer' (1928: Book 11, Ch. 2). (6–10, 12–17, 19–22)

Lane, Miss (NN) The governess to the Borum children. (24)

Langdale, Mr (BR) A London distiller and vintner, with whom Mr Willet, the landlord of the Maypole Inn, does business. Dickens based him on the actual Thomas Langdale (1714–90), who had a famous distillery on the south side of Holborn, at the north-west corner of Fetter Lane; as in the novel, these premises were burnt down in the Gordon Riots. In the novel, Langdale is described as 'a portly old man, with a very red, or rather purple face', encountered by Mr Haredale at the Mansion House, where Langdale is angrily but vainly asking the Lord Mayor for protection of his property. As a 'very hearty old fellow and a worthy man', he gives Mr Haredale shelter, until they are forced by the mob's attack on the distillery to escape through the wine vaults. (13, 61, 66–68)

Langley, Mr (CS) One of Madame Bouclet's lodgers. Because 'he had a British way of not opening his mouth

very wide on foreign soil, except at meals', his name was thought to be 'L'Anglais', with the consequence that he was known as 'Mr the Englishman'. ('Somebody's Luggage')

Larkey Boy, the (DS) The pugilist who severely defeated the Game Chicken, reducing his visage to a state of 'great dilapidation'. (44)

Larkins, Jem (SB) The real name of Mr Horatio St Julien, an amateur actor whose line is 'genteel comedy'. ('Scenes: Private Theatres')

Larkins, Miss (DC) The 'eldest Miss Larkins' is worshipped by the youthful David Copperfield. 'She is a tall, dark, black-eyed, fine figure of a woman. The eldest Miss Larkins is not a chicken; for the youngest Miss Larkins is not that, and the eldest must be three or four years older. Perhaps the eldest Miss Larkins is about thirty. My passion for her is beyond all bounds.' He is terribly dejected when he hears that she is going to marry Mr Chestle, a hop-grower. Her father was a 'gruff old gentleman with a double chin, and one of his eyes immoveable in his head'. (18)

Lazarus, Abraham (GE) Accused of stealing plate, he is to be prosecuted by Mr Jaggers, who abruptly dismisses his brother's attempts at bribery. (20)

Leath, Angela (CS) The sweetheart and afterwards the wife of Charley. ('The Holly-Tree Inn')

Leaver, Mr (MP) A vice-president of the Display and Mechanical Science section at the second meeting of the Mudfog Association.

Leaver, Mr and Mrs (SYC) The Loving Couple, whose demonstrative behaviour on the water-party to Twickenham exasperates the other participants.

Ledbrain, Mr X (MP) A vice-president of the Statistics session at the first meeting of the Mudfog Association. He read a communication relating to the relative numbers of human legs and chair legs in 'one great town of Yorkshire'.

Ledrook, Miss (NN) An actress in Mr Crummles's company and a friend of Miss Snevellicci. She is one of the bridesmaids at Miss Petowker's wedding to Mr Lillyvick. She 'was of a romantic turn', and at the wedding 'wore in her breast the miniature of some field-officer unknown, which she had purchased, a great bargain, not very long before'. (23–25, 30)

Leeford, Edward (OT) *See* **Monks**.

Leeford, Edwin (OT) The deceased father of Monks and Oliver Twist and a former friend of Mr Brownlow's. (49, 51) *see* **Fleming, Agnes**.

Lemon, Mrs (HR) The proprietress of a preparatory school in Miss Nettie Ashford's 'romance'.

Lenville, Mr and Mrs (NN) Actors in Mr Crummles's company. Envious of Nicholas Nickleby's popularity as an actor, Mr Lenville (prompted by Folair) sends him a challenge, requesting Nicholas to meet Lenville 'for the purpose of having his nose pulled in the presence of the company'. Nicholas confronts him, knocks him down, and compels him to apologise 'humbly and submissively'. (23, 24, 29)

Lewsome (MC) A young surgeon, whose delirious ramblings during his serious illness intrigue Mrs Gamp, who attends him as a nurse. He was 'a young man – dark and not ill-looking – with long black hair, that seemed the blacker for the whiteness of the bedclothes'. After recovering, Lewsome reveals to his friend John Westlock that he supplied a slow-acting poison to Jonas Chuzzlewit, who in exchange forgave him his debts (incurred through gaming) and paid him five pounds. Lewsome therefore assumes that he was the indirect cause of Anthony Chuzzlewit's death, since the mistaken assumption was that Jonas had poisoned him. (25, 29, 48, 49, 51)

Lightwood, Mortimer (OMF) A young lawyer with chambers in the Temple, who is Eugene Wrayburn's friend and a member of the Veneerings' circle of acquaintances. He tells Wrayburn that he has been upon 'the honourable roll of solicitors of the High Court of Chancery, and attorneys at Common Law, five years; and – except gratuitously taking instructions, on an average once a fortnight, for the will of Lady Tippins who has nothing to leave – [he has] had no scrap of business but this romantic business'. This 'romantic business' is old Harmon's will. It is through Mortimer's account of the 'business' given at the Veneerings' dinner table that we learn the outlines of the Harmon story. He appears as indolent and indifferent as Eugene Wrayburn, but he is always involved with the case. Indeed, his function in the novel is often that of a commentator and a voice of conscience. For example, Mortimer worriedly reproaches Eugene about his evident fascination with Lizzie Hexam: 'What is to come of it? What are you doing? Where are you going?' Although not 'an extraordinarily impressible man', he is haunted by the sight of Bradley Headstone's tormented face when he accompanies Eugene in the latter's goading of Headstone in the London streets. When Eugene is apparently on his deathbed, Mortimer explicitly reveals his affection for him; he is, he avows, 'the friend who has always loved you, admired you, imitated you, founded himself upon you, been nothing without you, and who, God knows, would be here in your place if he could'. In disentangling Eugene's affairs,

Mortimer 'applied himself with infinite zest to attacking and harassing Mr Fledgeby [the moneylender]'. He finally rejects the values of Society, and, in the final words of the novel, 'sees Twemlow [whom he recognises as a true gentleman] home, shakes hands with him cordially at parting, and fares to the Temple, gaily'. (I: 2–4, 8, 10, 12–14, 16; II: 6, 8, 12, 14, 16; III: 4, 10, 11, 17; IV: 9–12, 16, 17)

Lilian (CB) Will Fern's 9-year-old orphaned niece. (*The Chimes*)

Lillerton, Miss (SB) A lady 'of very prim appearance, and remarkably inanimate. She was one of those persons at whose age it is impossible to make any reasonable guess; her features might have been remarkably pretty when she was younger, and they might always have presented the same appearance.' Mr Gabriel Parsons thinks she would make a suitable wife for Mr Watkins Tottle, who discovers, however, that she is engaged to Mr Timson, the parson. ('Tales: A Passage in the Life of Mr Watkins Tottle')

Lillyvick, Mr (NN) A collector of water-rates, he was 'a short old gentleman in drabs and gaiters, with a face that might have been carved out of *lignum vitae*, for anything that appeared to the contrary'. As Mrs Kenwig's uncle, he is courted by the Kenwigs family, who assume that they will inherit his money. They are therefore angry and indignant when he marries Miss Petowker. But after she has eloped with a half-pay captain, he settles his money on the Kenwigs's children after all. Mr Lillyvick's reconciliation with the family makes Mr Kenwigs exclaim: 'This is an ewent at which Evins itself looks down!' (14–16, 25, 30, 36, 48, 52)

Limbkins, Mr (OT) The 'red-faced gentleman in the high chair', who is the chairman of the Board of Guardians of the workhouse where Oliver Twist was born. (2, 3, 7)

Limbury, Mr and Mrs Peter (ISHW) Friends of the Lovetowns. Alfred Lovetown flirts with Mrs Limbury, to the fury of her husband.

Linderwood, Lieutenant (CS) An officer on board the sloop, *Christopher Columbus*. ('The Perils of Certain English Prisoners')

Linkinwater, Tim (NN) The 'fat, elderly, large-faced clerk, with silver spectacles and a powdered head', who has kept the books of Cheeryble Brothers for over forty years, never having 'slept out of the back attic one single night'. When Nicholas Nickleby joins the firm, he finds that 'there was scarcely an object in the place, animate or inanimate, which did not partake in some degree of the scrupulous method and punctuality of Mr Timothy Linkinwater'. He becomes a kind friend of the Nickleby family, and through them becomes acquainted with Miss La Creevy, a friendship that for him was 'the happiest time in all [his life]; at least, away from the counting-house and Cheeryble Brothers', and that ends in their marriage. He has a sister, who is 'a chubby old lady'. He keeps a blind pet blackbird, named Dick, in a cage in the counting-house. (35, 37, 40, 43, 46, 48, 49, 55, 59–61, 63, 65)

Linx, Miss (CS) A 'sharply observant pupil' in Miss Pupford's school. ('Tom Tiddler's Ground')

Lion (LD) Henry Gowan's 'fine Newfoundland dog'. He becomes ferocious in the presence of Blandois (Rigaud) and is violently punished by Gowan. Soon after, Lion dies, probably poisoned by Blandois. (I: 17, 34; II: 6, 7)

Lirriper, Mrs Emma (CS) A kindly widow, who keeps a lodging-house in

Figure 16 The Brothers Cheeryble, Tim Linkinwater, and Nicholas Nickleby by
Hablot K. Browne (Phiz)

Norfolk Street, The Strand. She narrates various episodes that occurred there, in a fluently colloquial prose style, in which Dickens can be said to anticipate stream-of-consciousness literary techniques. She and Major Jackman, one of her boarders, adopt the Edsons' child, who is accordingly named Jemmy Jackman Lirriper. She has a good-for-nothing brother-in-law, Doctor Joshua Lirriper. In her edition of the *Christmas Stories*,

Ruth Glancy quotes from a review by E.S. Dallas in *The Times* (3 December 1863): he praises Dickens for seeing 'a good heart and a right honest nature under the dross, and pettifogging, and worldly ways of a lodging-housekeeper' (1966: 502). ('Mrs Lirriper's Lodgings' and 'Mrs Lirriper's Legacy')

List, Isaac (OCS) One of the gamblers encountered by Little Nell and her

Grandfather at The Valiant Soldier. He was 'stooping, and high in the shoulders – with a very ill-favoured face, and a most sinister and villainous squint'. He and Jowl persuade the old man to steal from Mrs Jarley, but Nell in her turn persuades him to leave. (29, 30, 42, 73)

Lithers, Thomas (MND) The landlord of the Water-Lily Hotel.

Littimer (DC) Steerforth's manservant, who 'had come into his service at the University, [and] who was in appearance a pattern of respectability'. David Copperfield sees him as 'taciturn, soft-footed, very quiet in his manner, deferential, observant, always at hand when wanted, and never near when not wanted; but his great claim to consideration was his respectability. He had not a pliant face, he had rather a stiff neck, rather a tight smooth head with short hair clinging to it at the sides, a soft way of speaking, with a peculiar habit of whispering the letter S so distinctly, that he seemed to use it oftener than any other man; but every peculiarity that he had he made respectable . . . Such a self-contained man I never saw. But in that quality, as in every other he possessed, he only seemed to be the more respectable. Even the fact that no one knew his Christian name, seemed to form a part of his respectability.' Littimer has a smooth and ominous presence, even when he respectfully and efficiently takes over the cooking and serving at David Copperfield's little dinner party at his lodgings at Mrs Crupp's. He helps Steerforth in his elopement from Yarmouth with Em'ly. He brings back to England the news of their wanderings and unhappiness, giving a full account of these to David, Mrs Steerforth and Rosa Dartle, including the information that Steerforth wished to pass Em'ly over to him. David finally meets him as Prisoner Twenty Eight in the prison Mr Creakle is responsible for (Uriah Heep is Prisoner Twenty Seven).

Thanks to Miss Mowcher, Littimer had been arrested robbing his current 'young master'. He was awaiting transportation, and was sententiously repentant of his wrongdoings. (21–23, 28, 31, 32, 46, 61)

Little Nell (OCS) *See* **Nell, Little.**

Lively, Mr (OT) A 'salesman of small stature', who is a fence in Field Lane and who does business with Fagin. (26)

Liz (BH) A wretchedly poor woman, ill-treated by her husband, and an affectionate friend to Jenny, the brick-maker's wife. 'She had no kind of grace about her, but the grace of sympathy.' (8, 22, 31, 46, 57)

Lobbs, Maria (PP) The attractive girl loved by Nathaniel Pipkin in Mr Pickwick's tale of 'The Parish Clerk'. She was the only daughter of 'fiery old Lobbs', a wealthy saddler. (17)

Lobley (MED) Mr Tartar's man, who looked after his boat. 'He was a jolly-favoured man, with tawny hair and whiskers, and a big red face'. His arms and breast were 'tattooed in all sorts of patterns'. (22)

Lobskini, Signor (SB) The singing-master at the Miss Crumptons' 'finishing establishment', Minerva House. ('Tales: Sentiment')

Loggins (SB) The real name of an amateur actor (the 'Macbeth of the night'), whose stage-name is Mr Beverley. ('Scenes: Private Theatres')

Long Eers, the Hon. and Rev. (MP) A member of the Mudfog Association.

Longford, Edmund (CB) A poor student, who assumes the name of Denham and is nursed in his sickness by Milly Swidger. Under the temporary evil influence of Redlaw, he repudiates her but is eventually redeemed under her beneficent influence. (*The Haunted Man*)

Lorry, Jarvis (TTC) The 60-year-old confidential clerk at Tellson's Bank. 'Very orderly and methodical he looked', dressed neatly in brown and wearing 'an odd little sleek crisp flaxen wig, setting very close to his head . . . A face habitually suppressed and quieted, was still lighted up under the quaint wig by a pair of moist bright eyes that it must have cost their owner, in years gone by, some pains to drill to the composed and reserved expression of Tellson's Bank.' A born bachelor (as Miss Pross diagnoses), he is devoted to the service of the Bank, 'whose bread', he says, 'I have eaten these sixty years' (which seems an exaggerated length of time considering that Dickens has told us his age was sixty). Because Tellson's Bank has handled all Doctor Manette's business, Lorry accompanies Lucie to France to bring her father back to England after his release from the Bastille. He becomes a devoted friend of the Manette family. At the outbreak of the French Revolution, Lorry goes to Paris to attend to Bank business, does all he can to assist Lucie and Charles Darnay in their predicament there, and accompanies them back to England after Sydney Carton has contrived Darnay's release from prison. (I: 2–6; II: 2–4, 6, 12, 16–21, 24; III: 2–6, 8, 9, 11–13)

Losberne, Mr (OT) The Maylies' surgeon, known as 'the doctor', who 'had grown fat, more from good-humour than from good living', was 'kind and hearty', and an eccentric old bachelor. He tends Oliver Twist when the Maylies take the boy in after the attempted burglary and in general he acts as a kindly and sagacious adviser. (29–36, 41, 49, 51, 53)

Louis (CS) A stupid, lumpish embezzler and murderer encountered by Charley at a little inn in Switzerland. ('The Holly-Tree Inn')

Lovetown, Mr and Mrs Alfred (ISHW) A young married couple involved in flirtations.

Lowfield, Miss (SYG) A young lady, to whom 'the throwing-off young gentleman' emphasises the importance of 'the heart'.

Lowten, Mr (PP) Mr Perker's clerk, who has just finished singing a comic song at the Magpie and Stump when Mr Pickwick first meets him. He is 'a puffy-faced young man', who makes a number of lively observations. (20, 31, 34, 40, 47, 53, 54)

Loyal Devasseur, M. (RP) A citizen and town councillor, who owns 'a compact little estate of some twenty or thirty acres on a lofty hill-side, [on which] he has built two country houses, which he lets furnished'. He is a convivial man of 'unbounded' hospitality. Dickens is said to have based him on M. Ferdinand Henri Joseph Alexandre Beaucourt-Mutuel, who was his landlord when he rented houses in Boulogne in 1853, 1854 and 1856. *See* **Mutuel, Monsieur.** ('Our French Watering-Place')

Lucas, Solomon (PP) The 'Jew in the High Street', who (in Mrs Leo Hunter's words) has 'thousands of fancy dresses'. Everything in his wardrobe 'was more or less spangled'. Influenced by his arguments about the suitability of such clothes, Tupman, Winkle and Snodgrass engaged 'to array themselves in costumes which his taste and experience induced him to recommend as admirably suited to the occasion' (i.e., Mrs Leo Hunter's fancy-dress breakfast). (15)

Lud Hudibras (PP) The King of Britain and father of Prince Bladud in 'The True Legend of Prince Bladud', which Mr Pickwick read in his bedroom in his lodgings at Bath. (36)

Luffey, Mr (PP) The 'highest ornament' of the Dingley Dell cricket team. (7)

Lukin (NN) One of Mrs Nickleby's early suitors. (41)

Lumbey, Doctor (NN) The doctor who attended Mrs Kenwigs at the birth of one of her children. 'He was a stout bluff-looking gentleman, with no shirt-collar, to speak of, and a beard that had been growing since yesterday morning; for Doctor Lumbey was popular, and the neighbourhood was prolific.' (36)

Lummy Ned (MC) Lummy (i.e., first-rate) Ned had been a guard on a stage coach. When a coach driver tells Martin Chuzzlewit that Ned had emigrated to the United States, Martin starts thinking about doing the same thing. (13)

Lupin, Mrs (MC) The landlady of the Blue Dragon, 'in outward appearance just what a landlady should be: broad, buxom, comfortable, and good-looking, with a face of clear red and white, which, by its jovial aspect, at once bore testimony to her hearty participation in the good things of the larder and cellar, and to their thriving and healthful influences. She was a widow, but years ago had passed through her state of weeds, and burst into flower again . . . She had still a bright black eye, and jet black hair; was comely, dimpled, plump, and tight as a gooseberry.' Everyone assumes that Mark Tapley, the ostler at the inn, will marry her, and indeed he finds her very attractive: 'having once looked up [at her], there was no looking down again'. But it is only after he has returned from his journey with Martin Chuzzlewit to America that Mark and Mrs Lupin get married. She is distressed by Pecksniff's dismissal of Tom Pinch, and waits for the stage-coach in her chaise so that she can give him 'a basket with a long bottle sticking out of it' to sustain him on his journey to London. (3–5, 7, 31, 35–37, 43, 44, 48, 52, 53)

M

Macey, Mr and Mrs (CS) A mine-owner and his wife (Miss Maryon's sister), who live on Silver-Store Island. ('The Perils of Certain English Prisoners')

Mackin, Mrs (SB) A slipshod, vituperative woman, who has two flat-irons to pawn. ('Scenes: The Pawnbroker's Shop')

Macklin, Mrs (SB) A woman who lives at No. 4 in a London street and screams out 'Muffins!' to the passing muffin-boy. ('Scenes: The Streets – Night')

Macmanus, Mr (RP) A midshipman on the *Halsewell*. ('The Long Voyage')

MacStinger, Mrs (DS) Captain Cuttle's irascible landlady, who is a widow with three children: Charles (known as Chowley), Juliana and Alexander. She 'resorted to a great distance every Sunday morning, to attend the ministry of the Reverend Melchisedech Howler' for 'ladies and gentlemen of the Ranting persuasion'. Mrs MacStinger hunts the Captain down when he secretly leaves his lodgings at Number Nine, Brig Place to live at the Wooden Midshipman. But Cuttle's friend, Captain Bunsby, temporarily subdues her. Nevertheless, she soon gains the upper hand over Bunsby, whom she forces to marry her, much to Captain Cuttle's consternation. 'One of the most frightful circumstances of the ceremony to the Captain, was the deadly interest exhibited therein by Juliana MacStinger; and the fatal concentration of her faculties, with which that promising child, already the image of her promising parent, observed the whole proceedings.

The Captain saw in this a succession of man-traps stretching out infinitely; a series of ages of oppression and coercion, through which the seafaring line was doomed'. (9, 15, 17, 23, 25, 32, 39, 56, 60)

Maddox, John (VQ) Rose's sweetheart.

Madgers, Winifred (CS) A maidservant at Mrs Lirriper's. She was 'what is termed a Plymouth Sister, and the Plymouth Brother that made away with her was quite right, for a tidier young woman never came into a house and afterwards called with the beautifullest Plymouth Twins'. ('Mrs Lirriper's Legacy')

Magg, Mr (RP) A member of 'our vestry', who lived in Little Winkling Street. ('Our Vestry')

Maggy (LD) The simple-minded young woman, the granddaughter of Mrs Bangham (the charwoman and messenger at the Marshalsea Prison), who looks upon Little Dorrit (her junior in years) as 'Little Mother'. 'She was about eight-and-twenty, with large bones, large features, large feet and hands, large eyes and no hair. Her large eyes were limpid and almost colourless; they seemed to be very little affected by light, and to stand unnaturally still. There was also that attentive listening expression in her face, which is seen in the faces of the blind; but she was not blind, having one tolerably serviceable eye. Her face was not exceedingly ugly, though it was only redeemed from being so by a smile; a good-humoured smile, and pleasant in itself, but rendered pitiable by being constantly

Figure 17 Arthur Clenman, Little Dorrit, and Maggy by Hablot K. Browne (Phiz)

there.' She wears 'a great white cap' and ragged clothes. At the age of 10, she had had 'a bad fever', but always joyfully remembered her stay in hospital: 'Such beds there is there! . . . Such lemonades! Such oranges! Such d'licious broth and wine! Such Chicking! Oh, AIN'T it a delightful place to go and stop at!' When the Dorrits come into their money and leave England, Maggy is looked after by the Plornishes, whom she helps in their shop. (I: 9, 14, 20, 22, 24, 31, 32, 35; II: 4, 13, 29, 33, 34)

Magnus, Peter (PP) A 'red-haired man with an inquisitive nose and blue spectacles' (which become 'green' in a later description), who travels with Mr Pickwick on the coach to The Great White Horse Inn, Ipswich, where he intends to propose marriage to Miss Witherfield, a middle-aged lady. At the inn, Mr Pickwick (in a celebrated comic scene) mistakes her bedroom for his own, with embarrassing consequences. Their mutual confusion the next day angers the jealous Magnus, who threatens Mr Pickwick with a duel. Miss Witherfield reports the quarrel to Mr Nupkins, the local magistrate, with the consequence that Mr Pickwick and his fellow-Pickwickians are brought before him as trouble-makers. (22, 24)

Magsman, Toby (CS) Christened Robert, he was the proprietor of 'Magsman's Amusements' and once occupied the House to Let. ('Going into Society')

Magwitch, Abel (GE) The escaped convict whom Pip, when a small boy, meets on the marshes. 'A fearful man, all in coarse grey, with a great iron on his leg. A man with no hat, and with broken shoes, and with an old rag tied round his head. A man who had been soaked in water, smothered in mud, and lamed by stones, and cut by flints, and stung by nettles, and torn by briars; who limped and shivered, and glared and growled; and whose teeth chattered in his head as he grabbed me by the chin.' Pip brings him food, drink and a file. Having been recaptured, with Compeyson, his enemy (but former accomplice), Magwitch is transported to Australia, where through luck and diligence he makes a fortune. In

gratitude for Pip's help, he uses the money to make Pip a gentleman, using Jaggers as his intermediary. Pip, unaware of the source of his 'great expectations', is horrified when Magwitch, having illegally returned to England, reveals the truth to him: 'Look'ee here, Pip. I'm your second father. You're my son – more to me nor any son. I've put away money, only for you to spend.' Taking the name of Provis, he is concealed by Pip and Herbert Pocket, since he would be hanged if arrested. They try to smuggle him out of the country, but Compeyson has informed the police authorities. In a fight between them, they fall overboard, and Compeyson is drowned. Magwitch is arrested, condemned to death, but dies in hospital. Just before his death, Pip reveals to him that the child he had 'loved and lost' was Estella, whom he had had by Molly, his common-law wife. Magwitch's fortune is forfeit to the Crown. Magwitch therefore has a key role in the novel: he is the origin of Pip's material and emotional expectations. (1, 3, 5, 39–43, 46, 54–56)

Malderton, Mr and Mrs (SB) 'Mr Malderton was a man whose whole scope of ideas was limited to Lloyd's, the Exchange, the India House, and the Bank. A few successful speculations had raised him from a situation of obscurity and comparative poverty, to a state of affluence. As frequently happens in such cases, the ideas of himself and his family became elevated to an extraordinary pitch as their means increased.' He and his wife are anxious to marry off their daughters, Teresa and Marianne, but they are deceived by the pretensions of Horatio Sparkins. ('Tales: Horatio Sparkins')

Maldon, Jack (DC) The cousin of Annie Strong, the young wife of Doctor Strong. He was 'a rather shallow sort of young gentleman . . . with a handsome face, a rapid utterance, and confident bold air'. Doctor Strong, for his wife's sake, finds

Figure 18 Doctor Manette, Mr Lorry, Sydney Carton, Charles Darnay, and Lucie Manette by Hablot K. Browne (Phiz)

Jack Maldon employment in India and then, on his return to England, buys him 'a little Patent place'. His attentions to Annie raise suspicions, but she convincingly clears herself of any wrongful behaviour: 'We had been little lovers once. If circumstances had not happened otherwise, I might have come to persuade myself that I really loved him, and might have married him, and been most wretched. There can be no disparity in marriage like unsuitability of mind and purpose' (words which David Copperfield ponders). For David, Jack Maldon represents a society of 'hollow gentlemen and ladies'. (16, 19, 36, 42, 45, 64)

Mallard, Mr (PP) Serjeant Snubbin's elderly clerk, 'whose sleek appearance, and heavy gold watch-chain, presented imposing indications of the extensive and lucrative practice of Mr Serjeant Snubbins'. (31, 34)

Mallett, Mr (MP) The president of the Display of Models and Mechanical Science at the second meeting of the Mudfog Association.

Mallowford, Lord (NN) Arthur Gride considers a bottle-green suit to be lucky, because the first time he put it on 'old Lord Mallowford was burnt to death in his bed, and all the post-obits fell in'. (51)

Manette, Doctor Alexandre (TTC) A French physician of Beauvais, who was imprisoned in the Bastille for eighteen years because of his knowledge of the evil doings of the aristocratic St Evrémonde family. While incarcerated, Doctor Manette lost his memory and worked as a shoemaker, but he had written a testimony concerning the St Evrémondes' cruelties and concealed it in a chimney in the cell. Having been brought back to England by Mr Lorry and Lucie, his daughter, Doctor Manette recovers his physical and mental faculties, establishes himself in Soho, and practises as a physician. Under the shock of Charles Darnay's revelation, on the morning of his wedding to Lucie, of his identity as a member of the St Evrémonde family, Doctor Manette temporarily reverts to shoemaking. He is instrumental at first in gaining Charles Darnay's release from prison in France when he is arrested as a member of the notorious St Evrémondes. But Darnay is re-arrested and condemned to death on the evidence of Doctor Manette's written testimony, which Defarge had found in the Bastille. In the vision of the future that Sydney Carton imagines on the scaffold, he sees Doctor Manette 'aged and bent, but otherwise restored, and faithful to all men in his healing office, and at peace'. (I: 3–6; II: 2–4, 6, 9, 10, 16–21; III: 2–7, 9–13)

Manette, Lucie (TTC) The beautiful daughter of Doctor Manette, first met as 'a young lady of not more than seventeen . . . [with] a short, slight, pretty figure, a quantity of golden hair, [and] a pair of blue eyes'. Stryver is intent on proposing marriage to her but is strongly dissuaded by Mr Lorry from doing so. Sydney Carton makes clear to her that he loves her but knows that he is wretchedly unworthy of her; he promises her, however, that he will do anything for her. Lucie and Charles Darnay dearly love each other; they marry and have a daughter, also named Lucie. Fulfilling his promise to help Lucie, Sydney Carton substitutes himself for Darnay, who is thereby rescued from the guillotine. In his final vision, Carton sees Lucie 'with a child upon her bosom' bearing his name. Dickens based Lucie on Lucy Stroughill, a friend of his childhood days in Chatham. See **Atherfield, Mrs.** (I: 4–6; II: 2–6, 9–13, 16–18, 20, 21, 24; III: 2–7, 9, 11–13, 15)

Mann, Mrs (OT) The 'elderly female' who is in charge of children (including Oliver Twist and Dick) 'farmed out' from the main workhouse. 'She appropriated the greater part of the weekly stipend [sevenpence-halfpenny a week for each child] to her own use, and consigned the rising parochial generation to an even shorter allowance than was originally provided for them.' (2, 17)

Manners, Miss Julia (SB) 'A buxom, richly dressed female of about forty', who because of misunderstandings elopes with Mr Trott. But both of them 'came to the conclusion that it would be a pity to have all this trouble and expense for nothing; and that as they were so far on the road already, they had better go to Gretna Green, and marry each other; and they did so'. ('Tales: The Great Winglebury Duel')

Manning, Sir Geoffrey (PP) The owner

(absent in Scotland) of the estate where Mr Wardle and the Pickwickians have a shooting party (when Mr Pickwick indulges too freely in cold punch). (18, 19)

Mansel, Miss (RP) A passenger on the wrecked East Indiaman, the *Halsewell*. ('The Long Voyage')

Mantalini, Mr and Madame (NN) Madame Mantalini is the milliner and dressmaker who employs Kate Nickleby. She is 'a buxom person, handsomely dressed and rather good-looking', who has married Mr Muntle, whose name 'had been converted, by an easy transition, into Mantalini: the lady rightly considering that an English appellation would be of serious injury to the business'. She is susceptible to the flattery lavished upon her by her husband, Alfred, who is a spendthrift, ebullient and dandified young gentleman. When Nicholas Nickleby first meets him, he is 'dressed in a gorgeous morning gown, with a waistcoat and Turkish trousers of the same pattern, a pink silk neckerchief, and bright green slippers, and had a very copious watch-chain wound round his body. Moreover, he had whiskers and a moustache, both dyed black and gracefully curled.' He has an eye for the girls and an affected manner of speaking. He gets into difficulties after borrowing money from Ralph Nickleby, who is, he says, 'the demdest, longest-headed, queerest-tempered old coiner of gold and silver ever was – demmit'. Madame Mantalini's business is ruined by her husband's extravagance and transferred to Miss Knag, her forewoman. After Mr Mantalini's bankruptcy and separation from his wife, he is sent to prison, from which he is taken by a laundress to turn a mangle in a cellar ('My life is one demd horrid grind!'). (10, 17, 18, 21, 34, 35, 44, 64)

Maplesone, Mrs (SB) She and her two daughters, Julia and Matilda, were boarders at Mrs Tibbs's. She 'was an enterprising widow of about fifty: shrewd, scheming, and good-looking', and 'was amiably anxious on behalf of her daughters'. Julia marries Mr Simpson, but elopes with a half-pay officer six weeks later. Matilda's husband, Mr Septimus Hicks, deserts her. Mrs Mapelsone herself was to have married Mr Calton, whom she sues for breach of promise. ('Tales: The Boarding-House')

Marchioness, the (OCS) The tiny, wretched and half-starved servant-girl employed by Sampson and Sally Brass. 'There never was such an old-fashioned child in her looks and manner'. According to Sampson Brass, she is a 'love-child'. She knows neither her name nor her age. Dick Swiveller catches her looking through the keyhole, befriends her, teaches her to play cribbage, and affectionately names her 'the Marchioness'. When Dick regains consciousness after three weeks' delirious fever, he discovers that the Marchioness has been nursing him, having run away from the Brasses' house. She tells Dick of the conversation that she overheard (thanks to her habit of looking and listening through keyholes) between the Brasses regarding the plot against Kit Nubbles, and is therefore indirectly responsible for proving his innocence. Dick afterwards buys her clothes, sends her to school, names her Sophronia Sphynx, and marries her when 'she was, at a moderate guess, full nineteen years of age – good-looking, clever, and good-humoured'. Dickens had originally said in the manuscript of the novel that Sally Brass was her mother and had also implied that Quilp was her father, but he decided to omit this information. Even so, he still gives some unmistakable hints in the last chapter, where Dick Swiveller debates in his own mind the 'mysterious question of Sophronia's parentage': 'Sophronia herself supposed she was an orphan; but Mr Swiveller, putting various slight circumstances together, often thought Miss Brass must know better than that; and, having heard from his wife of her strange interview with Quilp, entertained sundry misgivings whether that person, in his lifetime, might not also have been able to solve the riddle, had he chosen.' (34–36, 51, 57, 58, 64–66, 73)

Margaret, Aunt (SB) She married a poor man without her mother's consent, and had therefore been 'discarded by her friends, and debarred the society of her relatives'. She is nevertheless invited to the family Christmas dinner. ('Characters: A Christmas Dinner')

Marigold, Doctor (CS) A cheap-jack, who was named 'Doctor' out of gratitude to the doctor who attended his birth on the Queen's highway. He tells his own story and describes himself as 'a middle-aged man of a broadish build, in cords, leggings, and a sleeved waistcoat the strings of which is always gone behind'. His daughter, Sophy, and his wife having died, Marigold adopts a deaf-and-dumb child (whom he also names Sophy), has her educated, and sees her married to a deaf-and-dumb husband. ('Doctor Marigold')

Markham (DC) One of Steerforth's friends ('youthful-looking, and I should say not more than twenty'), who was one of the guests at David Copperfield's 'first dissipation'. (24)

Markleham, Mrs (DC) The scheming mother of Annie Strong. 'Our boys [at Doctor Strong's school in Canterbury] used to call her the Old Soldier, on account of her generalship, and the skill with which she marshalled great forces of relations against the Doctor [i.e., her son-in-law]. She was a little, sharp-eyed woman, who used to wear, when she was dressed, one unchangeable cap, ornamented with some artificial flowers, and two artificial butterflies supposed to be

hovering above the flowers.' Her frequent allusions to Jack Maldon, whose welfare she is keen to promote, and to the discrepancies of age between the Doctor and Annie are embarrassing and hurtful. But Annie's full explanation of everything finally disconcerts her. In the opinion of Betsey Trotwood, who gives her short shrift, 'There never would have been anything the matter, if it hadn't been for that old Animal ... It's very much to be wished that some mothers would leave their daughters alone after marriage, and not be so violently affectionate.' (16, 19, 36, 42, 45, 64)

Marks, Will (MHC) John Podgers's nephew, who was the hero of 'Mr Pickwick's Tale'.

Marley, Jacob (CB) Ebenezer Scrooge's late business partner, whose ghost, wearing the chain he 'forged in life', appears to him on Christmas Eve to warn him that he will be haunted by Three Spirits. (*A Christmas Carol*)

Maroon, Captain (LD) A 'gentleman with tight drab legs, a rather old hat, a little hooked stick, and a blue neckerchief', who is Edward (Tip) Dorrit's creditor. (I: 12)

Marshall, Mary (CS) She was betrothed to Dick Doubledick, renounces him because of his wild conduct, but marries him after he was wounded at the Battle of Waterloo. ('The Seven Poor Travellers')

Martha (DS) The daughter of the poor labourer Florence sees at Fulham, when she is staying with the Skettles. 'Ugly, misshapen, peevish, ill-conditioned, ragged, dirty – but beloved!' The relationship between her and her father thus sharply contrasts with that between Florence and Mr Dombey. See **Kate** (DS). (24)

Martha (OT) An 'old crone', who is a pauper in the workhouse where Oliver Twist was born. With Anny, she is a witness of Mrs Corney's taking the pawnbroker's receipt from Sally as she lies on her deathbed. Martha's 'body was bent by age; her limbs trembled with palsy; and her face, distorted into a mumbling leer, resembled more the grotesque shaping of some wild pencil, than the work of Nature's hand'. (23, 24, 51)

Martin (PP) A 'surly-looking man with his legs dressed like the legs of a groom, and his body attired in the coat of a coachman', who drives Benjamin Allen's aunt's private fly. (39, 48)

Martin, Miss Amelia (SB) She 'was pale, tallish, thin, and two-and-thirty'. She was a milliner and dressmaker, who made a disastrous debut as a singer. Because 'she couldn't sing out, [she] never came out'. ('Characters: The Mistaken Milliner. A Tale of Ambition')

Martin, Betsey (PP) A widow with 'one child, and one eye', who has become an abstainer and a member of the Brick Lane Branch of the United Grand Junction Ebenezer Temperance Association. (33)

Martin, Captain (LD) A former prisoner in the Marshalsea ('a rather distinguished Collegian'), whom Mr Dorrit ramblingly recalls when considering his relationship with Chivery, the turnkey. (I: 19)

Martin, Jack (PP) The bagman's uncle, who 'was one of the merriest, pleasantest, cleverest fellows that ever lived'. (49)

Martin, Miss (CS) The 'young lady at the bar as makes out our bills' at the London hotel where Christopher works. ('Somebody's Luggage')

Martin, Tom (PP) A butcher imprisoned in the Fleet. (42)

Martins, the (SYG) Dear friends of Mr Mincin. ('The Very Friendly Young Gentleman')

Marton, Mr (OCS) When Little Nell and her Grandfather first see him in the village, 'he was a pale, simple-looking man, of a spare and meagre habit, [who] sat among his flowers and beehives, smoking a pipe'. He is 'the very image of meekness and simplicity' as he sits in the midst of the din of the classroom, but he is unjustly blamed by the women of the village for bringing about the death of Harry, his favourite pupil. They agree with his grandmother that he pored over his books out of fear of the schoolmaster. Later, while making his way on foot to another village where he had been appointed schoolmaster and clerk, Mr Marton accidentally meets Nell and her Grandfather again, takes them to the village, and installs them in a cottage, where they live for the rest of their days. (24–26, 45, 46, 52–54, 71, 73)

Marwood, Alice (DS) The daughter of 'Good Mrs Brown', she had been seduced and cast off by James Carker and then later was transported for theft. Embittered and wilful, Alice returns to England. Harriet Carker, witnessing her approach on a windy, rainy night, sees 'a solitary woman of some thirty years of age; tall; well-formed; handsome; miserably dressed; the soil of many country roads in varied weather – dust, chalk, clay, grave – clotted on her grey cloak by the streaming wet; no bonnet on her head, nothing to defend her rich black hair from the rain, but a torn handkerchief . . . As her hands, parting on her sunburnt forehead, swept across her face, and threw aside the hindrances that encroached upon it, there was a reckless and regardless beauty in it: a dauntless and depraved indifference to more than weather: a carelessness of what was cast upon her bare head from Heaven or earth.' Alice angrily rejects Harriet Carker's charity when she realises that she is James Carker's sister. With her mother, Alice makes Rob the Grinder reveal, in Mr Dombey's hearing, Carker and Edith Dombey's destination in France. Repentant on her deathbed, Alice asks Harriet to read to her from the Bible, kisses and blesses her on her leaving the bedroom, 'lays her hand upon her breast, murmuring the sacred name that had been read to her', and dies peacefully. (33, 34, 40, 46, 52, 53, 58)

Mary (PP) The 'pretty servant girl' whom Sam Weller sees and admires at Mr Nupkins's house. He sends her a valentine, to the disapproval of his father. After helping to bring Mr Winkle and Arabella together, Mary enters their service as a housemaid. When Mr Pickwick's housekeeper at Dulwich dies, he 'promoted Mary to that situation, on condition of her marrying Mr Weller at once, which she did without a murmur'. She thus becomes Mary Weller, which was the name of Dickens's childhood nurse. (25, 33, 39, 47, 52, 54, 56, 57)

Mary (PP) The name of maidservants at Wardle's house (5) and the Peacock, Eatanswill (14).

Mary (SB) The dying drunkard's daughter. ('Tales: The Drunkard's Death')

Mary Anne (GE) The 'neat little girl' who was Mr Wemmick's maidservant. (25, 45)

Mary Anne (OMF) Miss Peecher's favourite pupil, 'who assisted her in her little household . . . and sufficiently divined the state of Miss Peecher's affections [towards Bradley Headstone] to feel it necessary that she herself should love Charley Hexam'. She had been 'so imbued with the class-custom of stretching out her arm, as if to hail a cab or omnibus, whenever she found she had an observation on hand to offer to Miss Peecher, that she often did it in their domestic relations'. (II: 1, 11; IV: 7)

Maryon, Captain (CS) The commander of the *Christopher Columbus*. Taken sick, he died on Silver-Store Island. Miss Marion Maryon, his sister, takes a courageous part in the struggle with the pirates. She marries Captain Carton. ('The Perils of Certain English Prisoners')

Matinter, The Misses (PP) At Bath, the two sisters, 'being single and singular, paid great court to the Master of Ceremonies, in the hope of getting a stray partner now and then'. (35)

Matthews (NN) Mr Gregsbury's servant, who was 'a very pale, shabby boy, who looked as if he had slept underground from his infancy, as very likely he had'. (16)

Maunders (OCS) According to Mr Vuffin, 'old Maunders' used to have eight male and female dwarfs in his cottage when the season was over 'waited on by eight old giants in green coats, red smalls, blue cotton stockings, and high-lows'. (19)

Mawls and Maxby (RP) The first was an 'impersonal boy' at 'our school'. The latter was favoured by the usher, who was sweet on one of his sisters. ('Our School')

Maxey, Caroline (CS) A 'good-looking black-eyed girl', who was a bad-tempered servant of Mrs Lirriper's. She was sent to prison for assaulting two of the lodgers. ('Mrs Lirriper's Lodgings')

Mayday (UT) The Uncommercial Traveller's friend, who gives unsociable birthday parties. ('Birthday Celebrations')

Maylie, Harry (OT) He was about 25 years old, with a 'frank and handsome countenance' and an 'easy and prepossessing demeanour'. He becomes a clergyman, and marries Rose, his mother's adopted daughter. (34–36, 51, 53)

Maylie, Mrs (OT) An elderly and stately lady, who affectionately gives Oliver Twist a home after the attempted burglary of her house, in which he was forced to take part with Bill Sikes and Toby Crackit. Having seen Rose Fleming by chance and taken pity on her plight, she had adopted her as her daughter. (29–31, 33, 34, 41, 51, 53)

Maylie, Rose (OT) Rose 'was not past seventeen. Cast in so slight and exquisite a mould; so mild and gentle; so pure and beautiful; that earth seemed not her element, nor its rough creatures her fit companions.' Born Rose Fleming, she was the sister of Agnes, Oliver Twist's mother, and hence his aunt (though for Oliver she would always be 'sister, my own dear sister, that something taught my heart to love so dearly from the first!'). When Nancy warns her of the evil designs on Oliver, Rose urges her, as one of her own sex, to turn to a better way of life: 'It is never too late ... for penitence and atonement.' Rose marries Harry Maylie. Dickens modelled her on Mary Hogarth. (See the Introduction.) (28, 29, 30–33, 35, 36, 40, 41, 46, 51, 53)

M'Choakumchild,   Mr   (HT) The schoolmaster   employed   by   Mr Gradgrind to teach facts. 'If he had only learnt a little less, how infinitely better he might have taught much more!' (I: 1, 2, 9, 14)

Meagles, Minnie (Pet) (LD) The Meagles's beautiful daughter. 'A fair girl with rich brown hair hanging free in natural ringlets. A lovely girl, with a frank face, and wonderful eyes; so large, so soft, so bright, set to such perfection in her kind good head. She was round and fresh and dimpled and spoilt, and there was in Pet an air of timidity and dependence which was the best dependence in the world, and gave her the only crowning charm a girl so pretty and pleasant could have been without.' Arthur Clennam is smitten by her but does not permit himself to fall in love with her. She marries Henry Gowan, and they have a baby son. He treats her with indifference, but eagerly accepts the money her parents provide her with. (I: 2, 16, 17, 26, 28, 34; II: 1, 3–9, 11, 28, 33)

Meagles, Mr and Mrs (LD) Mr Meagles is a kindly, retired and comfortably-off banker (who had worked for thirty-five years), who deeply loves his wife and daughter ('Pet'). He has adopted Tattycoram to be Pet's maid. He and his wife enjoy 'trotting about the world', but his 'invariable habit' was 'always to object to everything while he was travelling, and always to want to get back to it when he was not travelling'. Having befriended Daniel Doyce (whom he introduces to Arthur Clennam), Mr Meagles is angered by his treatment by the Circumlocution Office, especially since he himself (as Doyce says) 'is a sagacious man in business, and has had a good apprenticeship to it'. But he has a weakness for the aristocracy – 'a weakness which none of us need go into the next street to find, and which no amount of Circumlocution experience could long subdue in him'. Mr and Mrs Meagles are disturbed by Pet's fondness for – and eventual marriage to – Henry Gowan, whose snobbish mother patronises them. They are distressed, too, by Tattycoram's leaving them and Mr Meagles makes great efforts to find her. Because Mr Meagles is, after all, a 'clear, shrewd, persevering man', he does his best to find the papers that Rigaud stole and is indirectly responsible for their discovery by Tattycoram. He is also instrumental with Daniel Doyce in bringing about Arthur

Clennam's release from prison. (I: 2, 10, 12, 16, 17, 23, 26–28, 33, 34; II: 7–9, 11, 33, 34)

Mealy Potatoes (DC) A boy who works at Murdstone and Grinby's warehouse. David Copperfield discovers that his name 'had been bestowed upon him in the warehouse, on account of his complexion, which was pale or mealy'. His father was a waterman and a fireman, and some other relation (possibly Mealy's little sister) 'did Imps in Pantomimes'. Dickens based him on Paul (or Poll) Green, one of the boys who worked at Warren's Blacking warehouse when Dickens was employed there (Forster 1928: Book 1, Ch. 2). (11, 12)

Meek, George (RP) A quiet man: 'My constitution is tremulous, my voice was never loud, and, in point of stature, I have been from infancy, small.' He suffers under the domination of Mrs Bigby, his mother-in-law, and Mrs Prodgit, the nurse, before and after the birth of his son, Augustus George. ('Births. Mrs Meek, of a Son')

'Melia (DS) A maid at Doctor Blimber's school, whom Paul warmly regards as a friend. 'When Paul told her [that his mother] was dead, she took her gloves off, and did what he wanted [i.e., helped him to dress]; and furthermore rubbed his hands to warm them; and gave him a kiss; and told him whenever he wanted anything of that sort – meaning in the dressing way – to ask for 'Melia; which Paul, thanking her very much, said he certainly would.' (12, 14)

Mell, Charles (DC) One of the masters at Salem House, the school where Mr Murdstone sends David Copperfield. 'He was a gaunt, sallow young man, with hollow cheeks, and a chin almost as black as Mr Murdstone's; but there the likeness ended, for his whiskers were shaved off, and his hair, instead of being glossy, was rusty and dry. He was dressed in a suit of black clothes which were rather rusty and dry too, and rather short in the sleeves and legs; and he had a white neck-kerchief, that was not over-clean.' He takes David, on his arrival, to his mother's almshouse, where he plays the flute to them (very badly). David innocently tells Steerforth of Mr Mell's poverty, with the result that Steerforth arrogantly and publicly calls Mell a beggar. Mr Creakle, the headmaster, consequently dismisses Mell, who somehow later becomes Doctor Mell of Colonial Salem-House Grammar School, Port Middlebay, Australia. He was possibly modelled on a Mr Taylor, who was a master at the Wellington House Academy, where Dickens was a pupil in 1824–7. (5–7, 63)

Mellows, J. (UT) The landlord of the Dolphin's Head, which used to be a coaching inn but after the coming of the railways had become 'sorely shrunken'. ('An Old Stage-Coaching House')

Meltham, Mr (HD) An actuary of the Inestimable Life Assurance Company, who also uses the names of Major Banks and Mr Alfred Beckwith. He hunts down Slinkton, the murderer of his (Slinkton's) niece. Slinkton commits suicide, but Meltham himself, who had loved the niece, has no remaining purpose in life and dies not long afterwards.

Melvilleson, Miss M. (BH) A 'young lady of professional celebrity who assists at the Harmonic Meetings' at the Sol's Arms. Mrs Perkins possesses 'information that she has been married a year and a half, though announced as Miss M. Melvilleson, the noted syren, and that her baby is clandestinely conveyed to the Sol's Arms every night to receive its natural nourishment during the entertainments'. (32, 33, 39)

Mercantile Jack (UT) *See* **Jack, Mercantile.**

Mercury (BH) Sir Leicester Dedlock's footman. (2, 16, 29, 32, 40, 48, 53, 54)

Mercy (UT) The Uncommercial Traveller's childhood nurse, who used to tell him frightening stories. This 'female bard [was] descended, possibly, from those terrible old Scalds who seem to have existed for the express purpose of addling the brains of mankind when they begin to investigate languages'. ('Nurse's Stories')

Merdle, Mr (LD) A financier and banker, who lives in Harley Street. 'Mr Merdle was immensely rich; a man of prodigious enterprise; a Midas without the ears, who turned all he touched to gold. He was in everything good, from banking to building. He was in Parliament, of course. He was in the City, necessarily. He was Chairman of this, Trustee of that, President of the other. The weightiest of men has said to projectors, "Now, what name have you got? Have you got Merdle?" And, the reply being in the negative, had said, "Then I won't look at you."' But he is a taciturn, withdrawn man (much to his wife's annoyance), who strolls dismally through his mansion, feels uncomfortable in the presence of the Chief Butler, and has a habit of clasping his wrists in a 'constabulary manner'. Mr Merdle commits suicide at the 'warm baths' by cutting his jugular vein with a mother-of-pearl penknife he had borrowed from Fanny Dorrit (who had married his stepson, Edmund Sparkler). It was then discovered that he was 'simply the greatest Forger and the greatest Thief that ever cheated the gallows'. Widespread financial ruin results, with the loss of the fortunes of the Dorrits and Arthur Clennam. Dickens based the career and downfall of Merdle partly on those of George Hudson, the 'Railway King' (1800–71), who after his enterprises collapsed had left England for the Continent in 1854 (just before the serialisation of *Little Dorrit* began), and partly on those of John Sadleir (1814–56), who poisoned himself on Hampstead Heath after the collapse of an Irish bank he was running. Dickens himself indicated these sources in his Preface to the Charles Dickens edition of the novel (1868): 'If I might make so bold as to defend that extravagant conception, Mr Merdle, I would hint that it originated after the Railroad-share epoch, in the times of a certain Irish bank, and of one or two other equally laudable enterprises.' (I: 20, 21, 33; II: 3, 5–7, 12–16, 18, 24, 25, 28)

Merdle, Mrs (LD) A colonel's widow and the mother of Edmund Sparkler, she had married Mr Merdle. 'The lady was not young and fresh from the hand of Nature, but was young and fresh from the hand of her maid. She had large unfeeling handsome eyes, and dark unfeeling handsome hair, and a broad unfeeling handsome bosom, and was made the most of in every particular . . . This great and fortunate man [Mr Merdle] had provided that extensive bosom, which required so much room to be unfeeling enough in, with a nest of crimson and gold some fifteen years before. It was not a bosom to repose upon, but it was a capital bosom to hang jewels upon. Mr Merdle wanted something to hang jewels upon, and he bought it for the purpose.' Always conscious of her position in society, Mrs Merdle buys off Fanny Dorrit with a bracelet when Edmund Sparkler is smitten by her, but once the Dorrits come into their fortune she is 'charmed' (as she tells Mr Dorrit) by Edmund's affection for Fanny and approves their marriage. After Mr Merdle's suicide and the financial crash that follows, Mrs Merdle is still championed by society, and 'thus, on the whole, she came out of her furnace like a wise woman, and did exceedingly well'. She and Fanny 'arrayed themselves to fight it out in the lists of Society, sworn rivals'. (I: 20, 21, 33; II: 3, 5–7, 12, 14, 15, 18, 24, 25, 33)

Meriton, Henry (RP) The second mate of the *Halsewell*, who managed to escape from the shipwreck. ('The Long Voyage')

Merrylegs (HT) Signor Jupe's 'highly trained performing dog'. Some time after Jupe's disappearance, the dog makes its way to Sleary's circus at Chester and dies at Sleary's feet. Sleary takes this to mean that Jupe has also died. (I: 3, 5–7, 9; III: 8)

Merrywinkle, Mr and Mrs (SYC) Mr Merrywinkle is a 'rather lean and long-necked gentleman, middle-aged and middle-sized, and usually troubled with a cold in the head'. His wife is a 'delicate-looking lady, with very light hair, and is exceedingly subject to the same unpleasant disorder'. Consequently, they coddle themselves. ('The Couple who Coddle Themselves')

Mesheck, Aaron (RP) A fraudster eventually detected in New York by Sergeant Dornton because of his distinctive carpet-bag. ('The Detective Police')

Mesrour (CS) In the fantasy of the Seraglio, this was the name they gave Tabby, Miss Griffin's servant. ('The Haunted House')

Micawber, Mrs (DC) The wife of Wilkins Micawber and the mother of Wilkins junior, Emma, the twins, and a baby. She was 'a thin and faded lady, not at all young', who when David first knows her seems to be always breastfeeding one or other of her twins. Despite her memories of more prosperous days with her papa and mama in the years before her marriage and mysterious references to her 'family', Mrs Micawber is as 'elastic' in temperament as her husband, to whom she is a devoted wife: 'I never will desert Mr Micawber!' (11, 12, 17, 27, 28, 34, 36, 39, 42, 49, 52, 54, 55, 57, 60, 63)

Micawber, Wilkins (DC) David Copperfield lodges with the Micawbers when he works as a boy at Murdstone and Grinby's warehouse. Mr Micawber was 'a stoutish, middle-aged person, in a brown surtout and black tights and shoes, with no more hair upon his head (which was a large one, and very shining) than there is upon an egg, and with a very extensive face, which he turned full upon me. His clothes were shabby, but he had an imposing shirt-collar on. He carried a jaunty sort of stick, with a large pair of rusty tassels to it; and a quizzing glass hung outside his coat, – for ornament, as I afterwards found, as he very seldom looked through it, and couldn't see anything when he did.' His orotund manner of speaking is immediately displayed: 'Under the impression ... that your peregrinations in this metropolis have not yet been extensive, and that you might have some difficulty in penetrating the arcana of the Modern Babylon in the direction of the City Road – in short ... that you might lose yourself – I shall be happy to call this evening, and install you in the knowledge of the nearest way.' As he tells David, Mr Micawber is 'a man who has, for some years, contended against the pressure of pecuniary difficulties', and he gives him a memorable (and often quoted) piece of advice: 'Annual income twenty pounds, annual expenditure nineteen six, result happiness. Annual income twenty pounds, annual expenditure twenty pounds ought and six, result misery. The blossom is blighted, the leaf is withered, the God of day goes down upon the dreary scene, and – and in short you are for ever floored.' Despite moments of self-dramatised hopelessness, Mr Micawber is an optimist who enjoys life with marvellous energy and gaiety. He is briefly imprisoned for debt in the King's Bench Prison, tries to find employment in

Figure 19 Mr Micawber by Frederick Barnard

Plymouth, in London, and in the Medway Coal Trade, and moves yet again to London, where he has Traddles as his lodger and becomes the confidential clerk to Wickfield and Heep. In that last capacity, he exposes Uriah Heep's villainy in a wonderfully melodramatic scene. Following Betsey Trotwood's advice, Mr Micawber and his family emigrate to Australia, where he becomes the Port Middlebay District Magistrate. Mi-cawber was based on Dickens's father, John Dickens, who was also remarkable for what John Forster calls his 'rhetorical exuberance'. As Forster remarks, 'Nobody likes Micawber less for his follies; and Dickens liked his father more, the more he recalled his whimsical qualities' (1928: Book 6, Ch. 7). G.K. Chesterton paid tribute to Dickens's creation of Mi-cawber in hyperbolic fashion: 'Dickens was a man like ourselves; we can see where he went wrong, and study him without being stunned or getting the sunstroke. But Micawber is not a man; Micawber is the superman. We can only walk round and round Micawber wondering what we shall say. All the critics of Dickens, when all is said and done, have only walked round and round Micawber wondering what they should say. I am myself at this moment walking round and round Micawber wondering what I shall say. And I have not found out yet.' (1933: 139). (11, 12, 17, 27, 28, 34, 36, 39, 42, 49, 52, 54, 55, 57, 60, 63)

Michael (CS) A 'solitary man', who relates a story of his happy family life. But it turns out to be a fantasy, since he finally admits that his 'Castle . . . is in the Air'. ('The Poor Relation's Story')

Miff, Mrs (DS) A 'wheezy little pew-opener – a mighty dry old lady, sparely dressed, with not an inch of fulness anywhere about her'. She has a 'vinegary face . . . and a mortified bonnet, and eke a thirsty soul for sixpences and shillings'. She is on duty at the wedding of Mr Dombey and Edith and later at the wedding of Walter and Florence. (31, 57)

Miggott, Mrs (UT) The laundress ('a genteel woman') of Mr Parkle's chambers in Gray's Inn Square. ('Chambers')

Miggs, Miss (BR) Mrs Varden's domestic servant. Miggs was her mistress's 'chief aider and abettor, and at the same time her principal victim and object of wrath . . . [She] was a tall young lady, very much addicted to pattens in private life; slender and shrewish, of a rather uncomfortable figure, and though not absolutely ill-looking, of a sharp and acid visage. As a general principle and abstract proposition, Miggs held the male sex to be utterly contemptible and unworthy of notice; to be fickle, false, base, sottish, inclined to perjury, and

wholly undeserving.' Nevertheless, she is bitterly jealous of Dolly Varden for having captured Sim Tappertit's affections (though Dolly utterly rejects him). Always agitated and often hysterical, Miggs pours forth her feelings in torrents of words and in phraseology, allusions and malapropisms that anticipate Dickens's inventive powers in his rendering of Mrs Gamp's speech a few years later: 'I am a abject slave, and a toiling, moiling, constant-working, always-being-found-fault-with, never-giving-satisfactions, nor-having-no-time-to-clean-one-self, potter's wessel – an't I miss! Ho yes! My situations is lowly, and my capacities is limited, and my duties is to humble myself afore the base degenerating daughters of their blessed mothers as is fit to keep companies with holy saints but is born to persecutions from wicked relations – and to demean myself before them as is no better than infidels – an't it, miss! Ho yes! My only becoming occupations is to help young flaunting pagins to brush and comb and titivate theirselves into whitening and suppulchres, and leave the young men to think that there an't a bit of padding in it nor no pinching ins nor fillings out nor pomatums nor deceits nor earthly wanities – an't it, miss! Yes to be sure it is – ho yes!' To her angry astonishment, Miggs is dismissed from service by Mrs Varden, who after the Gordon Riots has seen the error of her ways. She becomes 'a female turnkey for the County Bridewell'. (7, 9, 13, 18, 19, 22, 27, 31, 36, 39, 41, 51, 63, 70, 71, 80, 82)

Mike (GE) One of Mr Jaggers's clients, 'who, either in his own person or in that of some member of his family, seemed to be always in trouble (which in that place meant Newgate)'. (20, 51)

Miles, Bob (RP) A London pickpocket told to 'hook it' by Rogers, one of Inspector Field's men. ('On Duty with Inspector Field')

Miles, Owen (MHC) One of Master Humphrey's friends. He was 'a most worthy gentleman'. He 'was once a very rich merchant; but receiving a severe shock in the death of his wife, he retired from business, and devoted himself to a quiet, unostentatious life'. (2)

Milkwash, Mr (SYG) The 'poetical young gentleman', who is not troubled 'with the gift of poesy in any remarkable degree' but whose 'manner is abstracted and bespeaks affliction of soul'.

Miller, Mr (PP) 'A little hard-headed, Ribston-pippin-faced' man, who was one of Mr Wardle's guests at Dingley Dell. In old Mrs Wardle's opinion, he was 'a conceited coxcomb'. (6, 28)

Miller, Mrs Jane Ann (CS) Mrs Wilding's sister, who adopts (on her behalf) a foundling. ('No Thoroughfare')

Millers (GE) One of Mrs Matthew Pocket's nursemaids. (22, 23)

Mills, Julia (DC) The 'bosom friend' of Dora Spenlow. David Copperfield learns that Miss Mills had been 'unhappy in a misplaced affection'. Although she had apparently 'retired from the world on her awful stock of experience', she still took 'a calm interest in the unblighted hopes and loves of youth'. She has a poetic turn of language, as when she advises David and Dora not to be upset by a 'trivial misunderstanding': 'The gushing fountains which sparkle in the sun, must not be stopped in mere caprice; the oasis in the desert of Sahara, must not be plucked up idly.' She keeps a journal, and used to meet David on the Common to read it or lend it to him. Miss Mills goes to India, where she marries 'a growling old Scotch Croesus with great flaps of ears'. For David, she and Jack Maldon represent a society of 'hollow gentlemen and ladies'. Julia Mills is also mentioned in 'Our English Watering Place' (in *Reprinted Pieces*) as leaving marginal notes on the pages of romances in the library there. (33, 37–39, 42, 48, 64)

Milvey, the Reverend Frank, and family (OMF) Mr and Mrs Boffin's clergyman, whom they approach when they wish to adopt an orphan. 'He was quite a young man, expensively educated and wretchedly paid, with quite a young wife [Margaretta] and half-a-dozen quite young children. He was under the necessity of teaching and translating from the classics to eke out his scanty means, yet was generally expected to have more time to spare than the idlest person in the parish, and more money than the richest. He accepted the needless inequalities and inconsistencies of his life, with a kind of conventional submission that was almost slavish.' He finds a suitable orphan in Johnny, Mrs Higden's great-grandson (who dies, however, in hospital shortly afterwards). He officiates at three ceremonies in the novel: the funeral services of Johnny and Betty Higden and the marriage service of Eugene Wrayburn and Lizzie Hexam. (I: 9, 16; II: 10; III: 9; IV: 11)

Mim (CS) A travelling showman ('a wery hoarse man'), from whom Doctor Marigold acquires Sophy, a deaf-and-dumb girl, for a pair of braces. ('Doctor Marigold')

Mincin, Mr (SYG) The 'very friendly young gentleman'.

Minns, Augustus (SB) A bachelor 'of about forty as he said – of about eight-and-forty as his friends said. He was always exceedingly clean, precise, and tidy; perhaps somewhat priggish, and the most retiring man in the world.' When his cousin, Mr Octavius Budden, invites him to dinner, he has so many unfortunate and embarrassing experiences that he leaves all the Budden family out of his will. ('Tales: Mr Minns and his Cousin')

Misty, Mr X. X. (MP) At the second meeting of the Mudfog Association, he 'communicated some remarks [to the Zoology and Botany section] on the disappearance of dancing-bears from the streets of London, with observations on the exhibition of monkeys as connected with barrel-organs'.

Mith, Sergeant (RP) A Scotland Yard detective, who is 'a smooth-faced man with a fresh bright complexion, and a strange air of simplicity' and who 'is a dab at housebreakers'. He tells 'the Butcher's story'. He is based on Detective-Sergeant M. Smith. ('The Detective Police')

Mithers, Lady (DC) A client of Miss Mowcher's: '*there's* a woman! *How* she wears!' (22)

Mitts, Mrs (UT) An inmate of Titbull's Alms-houses, who marries a one-armed Greenwich Pensioner. ('Titbull's Alms-Houses')

Mivins, Mr (PP) One of Mr Pickwick's fellow-prisoners in the Fleet, known facetiously as the Zephyr. He is dancing the hornpipe, 'with a slang and burlesque caricature of grace and lightness'. As a joke, he snatches Mr Pickwick's nightcap from his head and fixes it on the head of a drunken man sharing their room. Mr Pickwick indignantly strikes him on the chest, but the Zephyr takes it all in good part. (41, 42, 44)

Mobbs (NN) One of Squeers's pupils at Dotheboys Hall. Squeers reports that Mobbs's stepmother 'took to her bed on hearing that he wouldn't eat fat'. (8)

Moddle, Augustus (MC) The 'youngest gentleman' among the boarders at Todgers's. He is perpetually mournful, gazing lovingly and sadly at Mercy

Pecksniff, 'in such a lonely melancholy state [according to Mrs Todgers], that he was more like a Pump than a man, and might have drawed tears'. When he hears that she has married Jonas Chuzzlewit, he 'often informed Mrs Todgers that the sun had set upon him; that the billows had rolled over him; that the Car of Juggernaut crushed him; and also that the deadly Upas tree of Java had blighted him'. Moddle transfers his affections to Mercy's sister, Charity. They become engaged, but he mortifies her by jilting her on the wedding morning, sending her a dramatic letter from shipboard addressed to 'Ever-injured Miss Pecksniff'. He tells her that he is on his way to Van Dieman's Land: 'I love another. She is Another's. Everything appears to be somebody else's.' (9–11, 32, 37, 46, 54)

Molly (GE) Mr Jaggers's housekeeper. 'She was a woman of about forty, I [i.e., Pip] supposed – but I may have thought her younger than she was. Rather tall, of a lithe nimble figure, extremely pale, with large faded eyes, and a quantity of streaming hair.' Mr Jaggers makes her show her wrist, which is deeply scarred. Wemmick later tells Pip that Jaggers had obtained her acquittal at the Old Bailey of a charge of murdering another woman, taken her into his service, and 'tamed' her. It is later revealed that she was Magwitch's common-law wife and that their child was Estella. (24, 26, 48)

Monflathers, Miss (OCS) The head 'of the head Boarding and Day Establishment' in the town where Mrs Jarley has set up her waxworks exhibition. She condescends 'to take a Private View with eight chosen young ladies', and severely rebukes Little Nell for being a 'wax-work child', since such a position is 'naughty and unfeminine'. (29, 31, 32)

Monks (OT) His real name is Edward Leeford, and he is the half-brother of Oliver Twist, whom he has deprived of his inheritance. With the help of Fagin, Monks seeks first to ensure that Oliver becomes a criminal who will suffer death or transportation and then to track him down and destroy him. Mr Brownlow is instrumental in unmasking his villainous activities and forces him to execute the provisions of the will that apply to Oliver. Monks squanders his own portion of the money in the New World, and dies there in prison. At first, he appears in the novel just as a shadowy figure, but Nancy later describes him as dark, withered, and haggard, with lips 'often discoloured and disfigured with the marks of teeth' and with hands that are also wounded with teeth marks. (26, 33, 34, 37–39, 49, 51, 53)

Montague (MC) *See* **Tigg, Montague.**

Moon (RP) A physician consulted by Our Bore. Diagnosing his illness as due to 'Kidneys!' he 'gave strong acids, cupped, and blistered'. ('Our Bore')

Mooney (BH) The beadle who is summoned to Krook's house on Hawdon's death and gives evidence at the inquest. He is apparently based on a beadle named Looney, who superintended Salisbury Square (Ackroyd 1990: 653). (11)

Mooney, Mr (L) An astrologer.

Mopes, Mr (CS) The hermit who lived in a squalid and derelict dwelling on Tom Tiddler's ground. He was a misanthrope, who 'by steeping himself in soot and grease and other nastiness, had acquired great renown in all that countryside'. Dickens based him on James Lucas (1813–74), a celebrated recluse, whom Dickens himself visited in 1861. ('Tom Tiddler's Ground')

Mordlin, Brother (PP) A member of the Brick Lane Branch of the United Grand Junction Ebenezer Temperance Associ-

ation. He 'had adapted the beautiful words of "Who hasn't heard of a Jolly Young Waterman?" to the tune of the Old Hundredth'. (33)

Morfin, Mr (DS) In the offices of Dombey and Son, he is 'an officer of inferior state'. He 'was a cheerful-looking, hazel-eyed elderly bachelor: gravely attired, as to his upper man, in black; and as to his legs, in pepper-and-salt colour. His dark hair was touched here and there with specks of grey, as though the thread of Time had splashed it; and his whiskers were already white. He had a mighty respect for Mr Dombey, and rendered him due homage . . . He was a great musical amateur in his way – after business; and had a paternal affection for his violoncello, which was once in every week transported from Islington, his place of abode, to a certain club-room hard by the Bank, where quartettes of the most tormenting and excruciating nature were executed every Wednesday evening by a private party.' Mr Morfin quietly observes the evil machinations of James Carker, befriends John and Harriet Carker, and marries Harriet. (13, 33, 53, 58, 62)

Morgan, Becky (OCS) The 79-year-old woman who had died and whose grave David was preparing while Little Nell and the sexton were questioning him. (54)

Mortair, Mr (MP) A vice-president of the Anatomy and Medicine session at the second meeting of the Mudfog Association.

Mould, Mr, and family (MC) An undertaker, who was 'a little elderly gentleman, bald, and in a suit of black', whose 'queer attempt at melancholy' on his face 'was at odds with a smirk of satisfaction'. He is a placid man, contented with his wife and two daughters: 'Plump as any partridge was each Miss Mould, and

Mrs M was plumper than the two together.' He carried out the funeral of Anthony Chuzzlewit and was always ready to recommend Mrs Gamp as a nurse. (19, 25, 29, 38)

Mowcher, Miss (DC) A manicurist and hairdresser who tends Steerforth. She was 'a pursy dwarf, of about forty or forty-five, with a very large head and face, a pair of roguish grey eyes, and such extremely little arms, that, to enable herself to lay a finger archly against her snub nose as she ogled Steerforth, she was obliged to meet the finger half-way, and lay her nose against it'. On this first appearance, she is not only grotesque in appearance but is also full of cunning, suggestiveness and sly jokes, parting with the question, 'Ain't I volatile?' But when she reappears, Miss Mowcher is a more sympathetic character, grief-stricken and remorseful at being deceived by Steerforth and Em'ly and promising to do 'anything to serve the poor betrayed girl'. She later grabs the disguised Littimer (Steerforth's former confidential manservant) in the street, so enabling officers to arrest him, and gives 'her evidence in the gamest way'. Dickens had made the change in Miss Mowcher because he had received a protest during the serialisation of the novel from Mrs Seymour Hill, a dwarf who was a chiropodist and manicurist and who was a neighbour of Dickens's. He had indeed partly based Miss Mowcher on Mrs Seymour Hill, but he was so pained by the latter's distress that he promised her that he would alter the characterisation. (22, 32, 61)

Mr F's Aunt (LD) *See* **Aunt, Mr F's.**

Mudberry, Mrs (PP) Mrs Sanders testified at the trial of Bardell v. Pickwick that 'Mrs Mudberry which kept a mangle' had told her that Mrs Bardell was engaged to Mr Pickwick. (34)

Muddlebranes, Mr (MP) One of the vice-presidents of the Zoology and Botany section at the second meeting of the Mudfog Association.

Mudge, Jonas (PP) The secretary of the Brick Lane Branch of the United Grand Junction Ebenezer Temperance Association. He was a 'chandler's shop-keeper, an enthusiastic and disinterested vessel, who sold tea to the members'. (33)

Muff, Professor (MP) He related to the Anatomy and Medicine section at the first meeting of the Mudfog Association 'a very extraordinary and convincing proof of the wonderful efficacy of the system of infinitesimal doses'.

Muggs, Sir Alfred (SB) A friend of Cornelius Brook Dingwall, Esq., to whom he had recommended the Miss Crumptons' establishment. ('Tales: Sentiment')

Mull, Professor (MP) A member of the Mudfog Association.

Mullins, Jack (OMF) A customer at the Six Jolly Fellowship-Porters. (I: 6)

Mullion, John (CS) A brave seaman on the *Golden Mary*. ('The Wreck of the Golden Mary')

Mullit, Professor (MC) A 'very short gentleman . . . with [a] red nose', who is a Professor of Education seen by Martin Chuzzlewit at Mrs Pawkins's boardinghouse in New York. Jefferson Brick tells Martin that Mullit 'felt it necessary, at the last election for President, to repudiate and denounce his father, who voted in the wrong interest' and that he 'has since written some powerful pamphlets, under the signature of "Suturb", or Brutus reversed'. The reference is to Brutus, the semi-legendary founder of the Roman Republic after the expulsion of the Tarquin family. (16)

Muntle (NN) Mr Mantalini's real name. *See* **Mantalini, Mr and Madame.**

Murderer, Captain (UT) The 'first diabolical character' to intrude into the Uncommercial Traveller's youth when his young nurse, Mercy, used to tell him terrible stories. ('Nurse's Stories')

Murdstone, Edward (DC) Mrs Copperfield's second husband and hence David Copperfield's step-father. As a small boy, David observes his appearance with a kind of awe: 'His hair and whiskers were blacker and thicker, looked at so near, than even I had given them credit for being. A squareness about the lower part of his face, and the dotted indication of the strong black beard he shaved close every day, reminded me of the wax-work that had travelled into our neighbourhood some half-a-year before.' Having married David's mother, Clara, Mr Murdstone immediately proves to be harsh and unyielding as far as David's upbringing and education are concerned and insists that Clara should also take a firm attitude (to her distress). He beats David mercilessly with a cane when he cannot do his lessons satisfactorily, sends him away to board at Mr Creakle's school, and after the death of David's mother puts him to work at Murdstone and Grinby's warehouse in London. Miss Betsey Trotwood, however, defies him and his sister when they come to her house to try to take him back, accusing Murdstone of tyranny to 'the simple baby' (i.e., Clara) and of breaking her heart. David hears in later life that Mr Murdstone has married another young wife, whose spirit (according to Mr Chillip, the physician) 'has been entirely broken since her marriage' so that she has become 'all but melancholy mad'. In 'The Incompatibles', reprinted in his *Irish Essays* (1882), Matthew Arnold refers to 'that charming and instructive book, the *History of David Copperfield*'. He says that, 'Mr Murdstone may be called the natural product of a course of Salem House and of Mr Creakle, acting upon hard, stern, and narrow natures'.

Arnold also refers to Miss Murdstone's severity. 'These two people, with their hardness, their narrowness, their want of consideration for other people's feelings, their inability to enter into them, are just the type of Englishman and his civilisation as he presents himself to the Irish mind by his serious side' (1891: 47–8). (2–4, 8–10, 14, 17, 33, 59)

Murdstone, Jane (DC) Edward Murdstone's unmarried sister, who moves into Blunderstone Rookery with him when he marries David Copperfield's mother. She was 'gloomy-looking . . . dark, like her brother, whom she greatly resembled in face and voice; and with very heavy eyebrows, nearly meeting over her large nose, as if, being disabled by the wrongs of her sex from wearing whiskers, she had carried them to that account. She brought with her two uncompromising hard black boxes, with her initials on the lids in hard brass nails. When she paid the coachman she took her money out of a hard steel purse, and she kept the purse in a very jail of a bag which hung upon her arm by a heavy chain, and shut up like a bite. I had never, at that time, seen such a metallic lady altogether as Miss Murdstone was.' She takes command of the household and gives her brother complete support in his stern attitude towards David and in his attempts to instil firmness into David's mother. She meets her match in Betsey Trotwood, who virtually ignores her when she and her brother attempt to take David away from his great-aunt's house in Dover, although she threatens to knock her bonnet off and tread on it if Miss Murdstone rides a donkey again over her green. David encounters Miss Murdstone again when he discovers that she is Dora Spenlow's 'companion and protector'. Just before Mr Spenlow's death, Miss Murdstone reveals to him David's love-letters to Dora, which leads to his forbidding any relationship between them. For Matthew Arnold's comments, see the above entry on Mr Murdstone. (4, 8–10, 12, 14, 17, 26, 33, 38, 59)

Mutanhed, Lord (PP) A visitor to the Assembly Rooms at Bath. Mr Bantam, the Master of Ceremonies, informs Mr Pickwick that he is the 'richest young man in Ba-ath at this moment'. He is splendidly dressed, with long hair and a particularly small forehead, and is affectedly unable to pronounce the letter 'r'. (35, 36)

Mutuel, Monsieur (CS) A friend of Madame Bouclet's. He is 'a spectacled, snuffy, stooping old gentleman' with an 'amiable old walnut-shell countenance'. He is based on M. Ferdinand Henri Joseph Alexandre Beaucourt-Mutuel (1805–81), who was Dickens's landlord when he stayed in Boulogne in 1853, 1854 and 1856. Forster gives much information about him (1928: Book 7, Ch. 4). ('Somebody's Luggage')

Muzzle (PP) Mr Nupkins's 'undersized footman, with a long body and short legs'. Job Trotter's ambitions to marry the cook anger him, since she 'keeps company' with him, and he challenges Job to a fight – but the cook attacks Job first. (24, 25, 39)

N

Nadgett (MC) The enquiry agent employed at £1 a week by the Anglo-Bengalee Disinterested Loan and Life Assurance Company (the fraudulent organisation run by Montague Tigg). 'He was a short, dried-up, withered old man, who seemed to have secreted his very blood; for nobody would have given him credit for the possession of six ounces of it in his whole body.' Everything he does is secret. 'He was mildewed, threadbare, shabby; always had flue [i.e., fluff] upon his legs and back; and kept his linen so secret by buttoning up and wrapping over, that he might have had none – perhaps he hadn't.' Tigg asks Nadgett to collect all the possible information about Jonas Chuzzlewit, with the consequence that he discovers Jonas's attempt to poison Anthony Chuzzlewit. He also establishes Jonas's guilt regarding the murder of Tigg by fishing his bloodstained clothes from the river. Philip Collins points out that Nadgett is the earliest elaborate example of an amateur detective in Dickens's work: 'he moves in the melodramatic atmosphere of mystery, diligence, patience, and uncanny perceptiveness which Dickens later transfers to the more respectable police detectives' (1964: 215). (27–29, 38, 40, 41, 47, 48, 50, 51)

Namby, Mr (PP) The sheriff's deputy of Bell Alley, Coleman Street, who arrests Mr Pickwick 'at the suit of Bardell'. 'He was a man of about forty, with black hair, and carefully combed whiskers. He was dressed in a particularly gorgeous manner, with plenty of articles of jewellery about him – all about three sizes larger than those which are usually worn by gentlemen – and a rough great-coat to crown the whole.' (40)

Nancy (OT) A prostitute in Fagin's service, who is Bill Sikes's mistress. When Oliver Twist first sees her with Bet, we are told that 'the two girls were not exactly pretty, perhaps; but they had a great deal of colour in their faces; and looked quite stout and hearty'. Dickens first portrays her as a willing associate of Fagin, whom she helps to recapture Oliver. But later in the narrative Nancy overhears Monks telling Fagin his villainous schemes to destroy Oliver. Loathing, then, her life of vice and misdeeds, Nancy reports Monks's intentions to Rose Maylie (who adjures her to renounce her way of life) and repeats these revelations to Rose and Mr Brownlow on London Bridge, although she refuses to deliver up Fagin. Bill Sikes brutally clubs her to death when he hears of the meeting on the bridge. In his Preface to the third edition of the novel (April 1841), Dickens wrote that 'it is useless to discuss whether the conduct and character of the girl seem natural or unnatural, probable or improbable, right or wrong. It is TRUE . . . From the first introduction of that poor wretch, to her laying her bloody head upon the robber's breast, there is not one word exaggerated or over-wrought.' Kathleen Tillotson notes that in the 1841 Preface Dickens says plainly that 'the girl is a prostitute' but that these words are omitted in his 1867 Preface (1954b: 67). (9, 13, 15, 16, 18–20, 26, 39, 40, 44–47)

Nandy, John Edward (LD) Mr Nandy was the father of Mrs Plornish. He was 'a poor reedy piping old gentleman, like a worn-out bird; who had been in what he called the music-binding business, and met with great misfortunes . . . [He] had retired of his own accord to the Workhouse.' Mrs Plornish, however, loves and admires him for his talents and manners. 'The poor little old man knew some pale and vapid songs, long out of date, about Chloe, and Phyllis, and Strephon being wounded by the son of Venus; and for Mrs Plornish there was no such music at the Opera, as the small internal flutterings and chirpings wherein he would discharge himself of these ditties, like a weak, little, broken barrel-organ, ground by a baby.' On visiting his son-in-law in the Marshalsea, where he was briefly imprisoned for debt, Nandy made the acquaintance of Mr Dorrit, who loftily patronised him. Nandy left the workhouse to live with the Plornishes when Mr Dorrit bought their little business for them. (I: 31; II: 4, 13, 26, 27)

Nathan, Mr (SB) The dresser at a private theatre. He was a 'red-headed and red-whiskered Jew'. ('Scenes: Private Theatres')

Native, the (DS) Major Bagstock's Indian manservant. The Major sometimes pelts him with various objects, for he 'plumed himself on having the Native in a perfect state of drill, and visited the least departure from strict discipline with this kind of fatigue duty'. (7, 10, 20, 24, 26, 29, 58, 59)

Neckett (BH) The bailiff's man who comes to arrest Mr Skimpole for debt. When Esther Summerson sees him, he is sitting on a sofa 'in a white great-coat, with smooth hair upon his head and not much of it, which he was wiping smoother, and making less of, with a pocket-handkerchief'. Because he threatens to take Mr Skimpole to a sponging-house, Coavinses, Skimpole invariably refers to him by that name. When Neckett dies, he leaves three orphans, Charlotte (known as Charley), Emma and Tom, who are provided for by Mr Jarndyce. (6, 15, 23, 67)

Neckett, Charlotte (BH) *See* **Charley.**

Ned (OT) A chimney sweep, who kept his son small on purpose so that he could hire him out to help burglars to break into houses. Bill Sikes is angry at the Juvenile Delinquent Society's action in taking the boy away and teaching him to read and write. (19)

Neddy (PP) A turnkey at the Fleet Prison. When Mr Pickwick first sees him, he 'was paring the mud off his shoes with a five-and-twenty bladed pocket knife'. He appeared to be 'of a taciturn and thoughtful cast'. (42–44)

Neeshawts, Dr (MP) A member of the Mudfog Association. He was one of those attending the discussion in the Anatomy and Medicine section at the second meeting.

Nell, Little (OCS) The 13-year-old heroine of *The Old Curiosity Shop*. She is 'a pretty little girl' with blue eyes and light brown hair, who is as devoted to her grandfather as he is to her. She is anxiously aware of his weakness for gambling and protective of him on their wanderings. As Dickens states in his 1848 Preface to the novel, he surrounded 'the lonely figure of the child with grotesque and wild, but not impossible companions', who include the threatening figures of Quilp and Codlin and Short, the formidable but kindly Mrs Jarley, and the awkward but loving Kit Nubbles. Worn out by emotional and physical strain, Little Nell dies in the cottage where she and her grandfather had found refuge. As she lay dead, 'she seemed a creature fresh from the hand of God, and waiting for the breath of life', in 'tranquil

Figure 20 Little Nell and her Grandfather by George Cattermole

beauty and profound repose'. At the time, Dickens's portrayal of Little Nell and her death was seen by many as a supremely tragic achievement. Francis Jeffrey, who wept on reading of her death, thought her the most perfect creation in English literature since Cordelia (in *King Lear*). Other prominent contemporaries who were greatly moved by Dickens's characterisation of Little Nell included Walter Savage Landor, Daniel O'Connell and W.C. Macready. There is also the well-known story that crowds waiting on the quay in New York for the ship bringing the latest numbers of the serial called out, 'Is Little Nell dead?' (1–3, 5–7, 9–13, 15–19, 21, 24–32, 40, 42–46)

Nemo (BH) *See* **Hawdon, Captain.**

Nettingall, the Misses (DC) One of David Copperfield's early loves, Miss

Shepherd, attends their 'establishment', i.e., a school for young ladies. (18)

Newcome, Clementina (Clemency) (CB) Doctor Jeddler's servant. 'She was about thirty years old, and had a sufficiently plump and cheerful face, though it was twisted up into an odd expression of tightness that made it comical.' She is physically ungainly, 'but from head to foot she was scrupulously clean, and maintained a kind of dislocated tidiness'. She marries Benjamin Britain. (*The Battle of Life*)

Nicholas (SB) The old butler of Bellamy's (the refreshment room for Members of Parliament). He is an 'excellent servant', has a 'sleek, knowing-looking head and face', and is neatly dressed. ('Scenes: A Parliamentary Sketch')

Nickits (HT) The former owner of the country estate that Bounderby bought and typically boasts about, emphasising, as always, his supposed youthful poverty: 'When that man was a boy, he went to Westminster School. Went to Westminster School as a King's Scholar, when I was principally living on garbage, and sleeping in market baskets.' (II: 7)

Nickleby, Kate (NN) The beautiful young sister of Nicholas Nickleby. She finds employment at Madame Mantalini's dressmaking establishment, where she excites the jealousy of Miss Knag, the forewoman, because her beauty makes her so popular with the customers. She then becomes Mrs Wititterley's companion, until she is dismissed when Mrs Wititterley becomes jealous of the attentions she receives from Sir Mulberry Hawk. Sir Mulberry's amorous advances cause Kate great distress, until Nicholas Nickleby violently attacks him. Kate then lives with her mother at the cottage in Bow provided for them by the Cheeryble brothers and eventually marries Frank Cheeryble. (1, 3, 5, 8, 10, 17–21, 26–28, 31–33, 35, 37, 38, 40, 41, 43, 45, 49, 55, 58, 61, 63–65)

Nickleby, Mrs (NN) Nicholas and Kate Nickleby's scatterbrained mother, who was 'a well-meaning woman enough, but weak withal'. Her opinions and reminiscences are lengthy, rambling and sometimes irrelevant, as she cannot resist the temptation to launch out into 'sundry anecdotes'. In her streams of amusing memories and advice, often mingled with sad memories, Mrs Nickleby can be seen as a precursor of Flora Finching. Here she is, for example, agonising over the jewels and other possessions lost in the unsuccessful speculations of her late husband (who had, by the way, speculated because of her insistence): 'Four-and-twenty silver teaspoons, brother-in-law, two gravies, four salts, all the amethysts – necklace, brooch, and ear-rings – all made away with, at the same time, and I saying, almost on my bended knees, to that poor good soul, "Why don't you do something, Nicholas? Why don't you make some arrangement?" I am sure that anybody who was about us at that time, will do me the justice to own, that if I said that, once, I said it fifty times a-day. Didn't I, Kate, my dear? Did I ever lose an opportunity of impressing it on your poor papa?' Mrs Nickleby is flattered by the attentions of her eccentric neighbour at Bow (where she lives in a cottage provided by the benevolent Cheeryble brothers), a gentleman who wears 'smalls and grey worsted stockings' and who throws her cucumbers and vegetable marrows over the garden wall. Dickens based Mrs Nickleby on his mother, Elizabeth Dickens. Michael Slater points out that 'in so far as Mrs Nickleby is a portrait of Elizabeth she is a harsh caricature of some aspects of the real woman's character – her ebullience, her little vanities and worldlinesses and her often ill-grounded optimism' (1983: 17). (3, 5, 10, 11, 18–20, 21, 26–28, 38, 41, 43, 45, 55, 61, 63, 65)

Nickleby, Nicholas (NN) The eponymous hero of the novel, with 'an open, handsome, and ingenuous' face, eyes that are 'bright with the light of intelligence and spirit', and a figure 'somewhat slight, but manly and well-formed'. He is brave, active and enterprising: he works briefly as an assistant teacher at Dotheboys Hall and thrashes its owner, Mr Squeers, as punishment for his cruel treatment of Smike; he joins Mr Vincent Crummles's travelling theatre company as an actor (under the name of Johnson); and finally finds employment in the firm owned by the benevolent Cheeryble brothers. Nicholas protects his sister, Kate, from the unwanted amorous attentions of Sir Mulberry Hawk, whom he assaults with a whip handle, and rescues Madeline Bray from the machinations of Gride and Ralph Nickleby. Both Fanny Squeers and

Figure 21 Mrs Squeers, Mr Squeers, Nicholas Nickleby, Fanny Squeers, Wackford
Squeers (junior), and Smike by Hablot K. Browne (Phiz)

Miss La Creevy, in very different ways, find Nicholas an attractive young man. But he marries Madeline, with whom he fell in love at first sight. In his Preface to the first cheap edition of the novel (1848), Dickens wrote: 'If Nicholas be not always found to be blameless or agreeable, he is not always intended to appear so. He is a young man of an impetuous temper and of little or no experience; and I saw no reason why such a hero should be lifted out of nature.' (1, 3–9, 12, 13, 15, 16, 20, 22–25, 29, 30, 32, 33, 35–38, 40, 42–43, 45–46, 48–49, 51–55, 58, 61, 63–65)

Nickleby, Ralph (NN) The uncle of Nicholas and Kate Nickleby. He 'was not, strictly speaking, what you would call a merchant, neither was he a banker, nor an attorney, nor a special pleader, nor a notary. He was certainly not a tradesman, and still less could he lay any claim to the title of professional gentleman; for it would have been impossible to mention any recognised profession to which he belonged.' He lives in a spacious house in Golden Square and is, among other things, a cunning and unscrupulous moneylender, with a 'cold restless eye, which seemed to tell of cunning that would announce itself in spite of him'. People trapped in his tentacles include the members of the Nickleby family, the Mantalinis, Squeers, Gride and the Brays. After the revelation, in the presence of the Cheerybles, by Brooker, his former clerk and confidant, that Ralph Nickleby was the father of Smike, he hangs himself in a mood of 'frenzy, hatred, and despair'. (1–5, 8, 10, 19, 20, 26, 28, 31, 33–34, 38, 44–45, 47, 51–54, 56, 59, 60, 62)

Nightingale, Rosina (MND) She wishes to marry Gabblewig, but Christopher Nightingale, her uncle, disapproves.

Niner, Miss Margaret (HD) Julius Slinkton's niece, whom he plans to poison, but her life is saved by Meltham and Sampson.

Nipper, Susan (DS) Florence Dombey's maid, devoted to her young mistress. She was 'a short, brown, womanly girl of fourteen, with a little snub nose, and black eyes like jet beads'. She is disgusted at the way in which Mrs Chick and Miss Tox make a social evening of supervising the Dombey children in the nursery and relieves her feelings by 'making wry faces behind the door', curling her nose, winking, squinting, and calling out names in the passage. Susan is so angry and upset at the way Florence is treated that she dares to confront Mr Dombey, who furiously orders Mrs Pipchin, his housekeeper, to dismiss her. But she later returns to Florence's service, just before the latter's marriage to Walter Gay. Susan marries Mr Toots, who assures the Blimbers and Mr Feeder that 'she is one of the most remarkable women that ever lived'. (3, 5, 6, 9, 12, 14–16, 18–19, 22, 23, 28, 31–32, 43–44, 56–57, 60–62)

Nixon, Felix (SYG) A quiet young man, who lives with his mother, who is 'a good-humoured, bustling, little body',

who constantly vaunts her son's virtues to the unmarried girls she knows. ('The Domestic Young Gentleman')

Noakes, Mr (MP) One of the vice-presidents of the Statistics session at the second meeting of the Mudfog Association.

Noakes, Mrs (SG) The landlady of the St James's Arms.

Noakes, Percy (SB) A law student, who lives in Gray's Inn Square. He was 'smart, spoffish [i.e., fussy], and eight-and-twenty.' He organises the water-party on the Thames on board the *Endeavour*. Despite the unhappy outcome of the excursion because of the squall and other misunderstandings, Mr Noakes is as 'light-hearted and careless as ever'. ('Tales: The Steam Excursion')

Noddy, Mr (PP) A 'scorbutic youth in a long stock', who is one of Bob Sawyer's guests at his party in Lant Street. He informs Mr Gunter that 'he is no gentleman', which results in a quarrel that is speedily settled. (32)

Noggs, Newman (NN) Ralph Nickleby's clerk. He was once a gentleman who used to keep 'horses and hounds' but who squandered his money, took to drink, and consequently became destitute. He was 'a tall man of middle-age, with two goggle eyes whereof one was a fixture, a rubicund nose, a cadaverous face, and a suit of clothes (if the term be allowable when they suited him not at all) much the worse for wear, very much too small, and placed upon such a short allowance of buttons that it was marvellous how he contrived to keep them on'. He befriends Nicholas and watches Ralph Nickleby's doings so that he is able to provide the information to expose his various plots and secrets involving

Kate Nickleby, Madeline Bray and Smike. As a 'grey-haired, quiet, harmless gentleman', Newman Noggs spends his last days in 'a little cottage hard by Nicholas's house'. Dickens based him on Newman Knott, a failed farmer whom he knew as an occasional clerk who worked for Ellis and Blackmore, solicitors in Gray's Inn. (2–5, 7, 11, 14–16, 22, 26, 28, 29, 31–34, 40, 44, 47, 51–52, 56–57, 59, 63, 65)

Nogo, Professor (MP) With Professor Muff, he performs some kind of operation upon a pug-dog.

Norah (CS) Master Harry Walmers's 7-year-old cousin, with whom he 'elopes'. ('The Holly-Tree Inn')

Normandy (CS) A 'bonnet' (i.e., a swindler's accomplice) at a gaming booth. He 'went into society' with Chops, but bolted with the 'plate' Chops had bought with money he had won in a lottery. ('Going into Society')

Norris, Mr and Mrs, and family (MC) A snobbish and racist family (though claiming to be abolitionists) to whom Martin Chuzzlewit is introduced by Mr Bevan in New York. (17, 33)

Norton, Squire (VQ) He attempts to seduce Lucy Benson.

Nubbles, Kit (OCS) He was, in Master Humphrey's words, 'a shock-headed, shambling awkward lad with an uncommonly wide mouth, very red cheeks, a turned-up nose, and certainly the most comical expression of face that I ever saw'. Kit is an affectionate son and brother and always ready bravely to stand up for what he believes to be right. Employed at first as a shop-boy by Little Nell's grandfather, he is devoted to her. Little Nell gives him writing lessons: 'from the very first moment of having the pen in his hand, he began to wallow in

blots, and to daub himself with ink up to the very roots of his hair'. After the departure of Little Nell and her grandfather, Kit finds employment with the kindly Garlands. Quilp bears him a grudge for calling him an ugly dwarf, for his devotion to Nell and her grandfather and for apparently knowing something of their whereabouts. For Quilp, the honourable and affectionate lad is 'a hypocrite, a double-faced, white livered, sneaking spy'. He therefore persuades the Brasses to frame Kit on a charge of stealing a five-pound note, for which imaginary offence Kit is tried, found guilty, and imprisoned. Thanks to the Marchioness's reporting the plot to Dick Swiveller, his name is cleared. With Mr Garland and the Single Gentleman, Kit travels to the village where Little Nell and her grandfather have found refuge. Before she died, Nell expressed her wish 'to see poor Kit. She wished there was somebody to take her love to Kit.' He married Barbara, and would often tell his children 'that story of good Miss Nell who died'. (1, 3, 6, 9–11, 13–14, 20–22, 38–41, 48, 51, 56–65, 68–73)

Nubbles, Mrs (OCS) The poor, widowed mother of Kit and Jacob Nubbles and a baby. She is devoted to her children, works as a laundress and attends the Little Bethel Chapel. (10, 13, 20–22, 39–41, 47, 48, 61, 63)

Nupkins, Mr, Mrs and Miss (PP) Mr George Nupkins is the mayor of Ipswich, before whom Mr Pickwick, Mr Snodgrass, Mr Tupman, Mr Winkle and Sam Weller are brought on various charges, including planning to fight a duel and disturbing the peace. When Mr Pickwick tells him that Captain Fitz-Marshall, whose visits the Nupkinses have been encouraging, is in reality Mr Jingle, Nupkins remits all punishments in order to protect himself from shameful revelations. His wife, Mrs Nupkins, 'was a majestic female in a pink turban and a light brown wig', whereas Miss Nupkins 'possessed all her mamma's haughtiness without the turban, and all her ill-nature without the wig'. Both women invariably blame Mr Nupkins for any dilemmas in which they find themselves. (24, 25, 34)

Oakum-Head (UT) A refractory female pauper in the workhouse. ('Wapping Workhouses')

Obenreizer, Jules (CS) A Swiss agent of Wilding and Co., the wine merchants. He was a 'black-haired young man of a dark complexion, through whose swarthy skin no red glow ever shone' and was distinguished by 'a comprehensive watchfulness of everything he had in his own mind, and everything that he knew to be, or suspected to be, in the minds of other men'. Having embezzled money from the firm and fearing that Vendale may discover this, he unsuccessfully attempts to kill Vendale in an Alpine pass. Obenreizer is later killed in an avalanche. His niece, Marguerite, helps to save Vendale from death and later marries him. ('No Thoroughfare')

O'Bleary, Frederick (SB) A lodger at Mrs Tibbs's. He 'was an Irishman, recently imported; he was in a perfectly wild state; and come over to England to be an apothecary, a clerk in a government office, an actor, a reporter, or anything else that turned up – he was not particular'. He had some hopes of marrying Mrs Bloss but these were dashed, and he 'discharged himself from Mrs Tibbs's house, without going through the form of previously discharging his bill'. ('Tales: The Boarding-House')

Omer, Minnie (DC) *See* **Joram and Omer, Mr.**

Omer, Mr (DC) The 'Draper, Tailor, Haberdasher, Furnisher, &c', who lived in Yarmouth and arranged the funeral of Clara Murdstone and her baby son. He was 'a fat, short-winded, merry-looking, little old man in black, with rusty little bunches of ribbons at the knees of his breeches, black stockings, and a broad-brimmed hat'. His daughter, Minnie, marries his foreman, Joram, who becomes his business partner. He employs Emily as an apprentice dressmaker and gives David Copperfield a perceptive description of her unsettled emotional behaviour in the days before her elopement with Steerforth. As a contented old man, Omer takes pleasure in David's success as a novelist: 'when I lay that book upon the table, and look at it outside; compact in three separate and individual wollumes – one, two, three; I am as proud as Punch to think that I once had the honour of being connected with your family'. (9, 21, 23, 30–32, 51)

Onowenever, Mrs (UT) The mother of a young lady loved by the Uncommercial Traveller. The name comes from a song with words by T.H. Bayley and music by Henry Bishop: 'Oh no, we never mention her'. ('Birthday Celebrations')

Orange, Mrs (HR) One of Mrs Lemon's friends in Miss Nettie Ashford's 'romance'. Her 'husband' was James.

Orlick, Dolge (GE) Joe Gargery the blacksmith's journeyman. 'He pretended that his christian name was Dolge – a clear impossibility ... He was a broad-shouldered loose-limbed swarthy fellow of great strength, never in a hurry, and always slouching.' Orlick has always hated Pip and is bitterly resentful of Mrs Gargery, whom he calls a 'foul shrew', for calling him idle and stupid and for urging her husband to fight him. Miss Havisham later employs him as a porter, which greatly perturbs Pip. In the midst of Pip and Herbert's preparations to smuggle Magwitch out of the country, Orlick by means of an anonymous letter lures Pip to a deserted lime-kiln on the marshes, where he ties him up with the intention of killing him and burning his remains in the kiln. He admits that he was the one who brutally assaulted Mrs Gargery but blames Pip for this: 'But it warn't Old Orlick as did it; it was you. You was favoured, and he was bullied and beat.' He has also discovered the whereabouts of Magwitch and is obviously working with Compeyson to make sure that Magwitch is arrested and hanged. But in the nick of time Pip is rescued by Herbert Pocket, Startop and Trabb's boy. Because they do not wish to delay their plans in getting Magwitch away, Pip and Herbert 'relinquished all thoughts of pursuing Orlick at that time'. Pip later learns from Joe that Orlick is in the county jail for breaking into Uncle Pumblechook's house. Orlick is a puzzling and disturbing character, who has sometimes been seen as Pip's *alter ego*. Furthermore, only Dickens (in Swinburne's opinion) 'could have eluded condemnation for so gross an oversight as the escape from retribution of so important a criminal as the "double murderer and monster" whose baffled or inadequate attempts are enough to make Bill Sikes seem comparatively the gentlest and Jonas Chuzzlewit the most amiable of men' (Hyder 1972: 234). (15–17, 29, 30, 53, 57)

Our Bore (RP) The subject of a paper of that name in *Household Words* on 9 October 1852. He is 'such a generic bore, and has so many traits (as it appears to us) in common with the great bore family, that we are tempted to make him the subject of the present notes'. ('Our Bore')

Overton, Joseph (SB) A solicitor, who is the Mayor of Winglebury. He was 'a sleek man' about 50 years old. ('Tales: The Great Winglebury Duel')

Overton, Owen (SG) The mayor of a small town on the road to Gretna Green.

Owen, John (OCS) One of Mr Marton's pupils in the school in the village where Nell and her Grandfather find refuge. According to the Bachelor, he was 'a lad of good parts . . . and frank, honest temper; but too thoughtless, too playful, too light-headed by far'. (52)

P

Packer, Tom (CS) A private in the Royal Marines, who is 'a wild unsteady young fellow' and who fights valiantly against the pirates. ('The Perils of Certain English Prisoners')

Pancks (LD) Casby's rent-collector. He was 'a short dark man ... dressed in black and rusty iron grey; had jet black beads of eyes; a scrubby little black chin; wiry black hair striking out from his head in prongs, like forks or hair-pins; and a complexion that was very dingy by nature, or very dirty by art, or a compound of nature and art. He had dirty hands and dirty broken nails, and looked as if he had been in the coals; he was in a perspiration, and snorted and sniffed and puffed and blew, like a little labouring steam-engine.' He is resourceful and active, dealing decisively with Mr F's Aunt and assiduously collecting rents for his master. He enjoys acting mysteriously and making enigmatic suggestions ('Pancks the gipsy – fortune-telling' is a typical remark). Enlisting the help of Mr Rugg (in whose house he is a lodger) and John Chivery, Pancks establishes the Dorrits' right to a fortune: 'In his tracking out of the claim to its complete establishment, Mr Pancks had shown a sagacity that nothing could baffle, and a patience and secrecy that nothing could tire.' But he later thinks that Mr Merdle's prospects are 'safe and genuine', invests £1000, and persuades Arthur Clennam to invest as well, with disastrous consequences. Full of remorse, he urges Clennam to reproach him: 'Say, You fool, you villain. Say, Ass, how could you do it, Beast, what did you mean by it! Catch hold of me somewhere. Say something abusive to me!' Pancks becomes involved with Clennam in hunting down Rigaud and hence in the revelation of Mrs Clennam's secrets. Having been used as a cover for Casby's ruthless dealings, Pancks finally confronts and exposes him in Bleeding Heart Yard: 'going close up to the most venerable of men [Casby], and halting in front of the bottle-green waistcoat, [Pancks] made a trigger of his right thumb and forefinger, applied the same to the brim of the broad-brimmed hat, and, with singular smartness and precision, shot it off the polished head as if it had been a large marble'. He becomes the chief clerk in the firm of Doyce and Clennam and afterwards a partner. (I: 12–13, 23–25, 27, 29, 32, 35; II: 9, 11, 13, 20, 22, 26, 28, 30, 32, 34)

Pangloss (UT) The Uncommercial Traveller's 'official friend', who 'is lineally descended from a learned doctor of that name, who was once tutor to Candide [in Voltaire's novella of that name]; in his official capacity, he unfortunately preaches the doctrine of his renowned ancestor, by demonstrating on all occasions that we live in the best of all possible worlds'. ('The Great Tasmania's Cargo')

Pankey, Miss (DS) A girl who is the only other boarder at Mrs Pipchin's when Paul lives there. She was 'a mild little blue-eyed morsel of a child, who was shampoo'd every morning, and seemed in danger of being rubbed away, altogether'. Mrs Pipchin instructs her 'that nobody who sniffed before visitors ever went to Heaven'. (8, 11, 59)

Paragon, Mary Anne (DS) David and Dora Copperfield's first servant, who was 'a woman in the prime of life; of a severe countenance; and subject (particularly in the arms) to a sort of perpetual measles or fiery rash'. She used to get drunk and she stole the teaspoons (as David subsequently discovered). When her cousin in the Life Guards deserted, hid in the coal-hole and was arrested, David got rid of her. (44)

Pardiggle, Mrs, and family (BH) Mrs Pardiggle was one of Mrs Jellyby's associates in working for good causes and raising money for them. 'She was a formidable style of lady, with spectacles, a prominent nose, and a loud voice, who had the effect of wanting a great deal of room.' Of her five young sons, four (Egbert, Oswald, Francis and Felix) were compelled to give money to good causes, and the fifth (Alfred) 'has voluntarily enrolled himself in the Infant Bonds of Joy, and is pledged never, through life, to use tobacco in any form'. Not surprisingly, they were dissatisfied children, who were 'absolutely ferocious with discontent'. They are their mother's companions in her duties: 'I am a School lady, I am a Visiting lady, I am a Reading lady, I am a Distributing lady; I am on the local Linen Box Committee, and many general Committees; and my canvassing alone is very extensive – perhaps no one's more so.' Her husband is O.A. Pardiggle, F.R.S. Like Mrs Jellyby, Mrs Pardiggle could have been modelled on Mrs Caroline Chisholm. (8, 15, 30)

Parker (RP) A policeman, 'strapped and great-coated, and waiting in dim Borough doorway by appointment' for Inspector Field. ('On Duty with Inspector Field')

Parker, Mrs Johnson (SB) She was 'the mother of seven extremely fine girls – all unmarried'. She organised a 'ladies' bible and prayer-book distribution society'. ('Our Parish: The Ladies' Societies')

Parkes, Phil (BR) An Epping Forest ranger, who is one of the regular customers at the Maypole. (1, 11, 30, 33, 54, 56, 82).

Parkins (RP) An acquaintance of Our Bore, who makes cryptic remarks about him and his wife's sister. ('Our Bore')

Parkins, Mrs (RP) The laundress in the Temple chambers where the bachelor lives who narrates the story. She was the 'wife of Parkins the porter, then newly dead of a dropsy'. ('The Ghost of Art')

Parkle (UT) An 'esteemed friend' of the Uncommercial Traveller. He lived in a set of chambers in the same building in Gray's Inn Square. ('Chambers')

Parksop, Brother (GSE) George Silverman's grandfather.

Parsons, Gabriel (SB) A 'short elderly gentleman with a gruffish voice', who tries to arrange a marriage between Mr Watkins Tottle and Miss Lillerton and who pays off Tottle's debts on condition that he immediately proposes to her. ('Tales: A Passage in the Life of Mr Watkins Tottle')

Parsons, Miss Laetitia (SB) A pupil at the Misses Crumpton's school, Minerva House. Her 'performance [on the piano] of "The Recollections of Ireland" was universally declared to be almost equal to that of Moscheles himself'. ('Tales: Sentiment')

Parsons, Mrs (SYC) A lady whose height the contradictory couple argue about. ('The Contradictory Couple')

Passnidge (DC) One of Mr Murdstone's acquaintances, whom (with Quinion)

David Copperfield meets at Lowestoft. (2)

Patty (CS) John's maiden sister, who lives with him in the Haunted House: 'I venture to call her eight-and-thirty, she is so very handsome, sensible, and engaging.' ('The Haunted House')

Pawkins, Major and Mrs (MC) Major Pawkins was the husband (from Pennsylvania) of the landlady of the boarding-house in New York where Martin Chuzzlewit stayed. He had a 'a very large skull, and a great mass of yellow forehead . . . a heavy eye and a dull slow manner . . . He was a great politician; and the one article of his creed, in reference to all public obligations involving the good faith and integrity of his country, was, "run a moist pen slick through everything and start afresh." This made him a patriot. In commercial affairs he was a bold speculator. In plainer words he had a most distinguished genius for swindling.' Mrs Pawkins was 'very straight, bony, and silent'. (16).

Payne, Doctor (PP) A 'portly personage', who is a surgeon of the 43rd Regiment and a friend of Doctor Slammer's. (2, 3)

Pea or Peacoat (RP) A policeman (dressed in a peacoat) who accompanies the narrator in a boat on the Thames. ('Down with the Tide')

Peak (BR) Sir John Chester's manservant and valet. After his master's death, Peak 'eloped with all the cash and movables he could lay his hands on, and started as a finished gentleman on his own account'. He would have eventually married an heiress but died of jail fever. (23, 24, 32, 75, 82)

Pecksniff, Charity (MC) The elder daughter of Mr Pecksniff, Charity is more shrewish and less feather-brained

than her sister, Mercy. In the early morning, the tip of her nose 'wore, at that season of the day, a scraped and frosty look, as if it had been rasped; while a similar phenomenon developed itself in her humour, which was then observed to be of a sharp and acid quality, as though an extra lemon (figuratively speaking) had been squeezed into the nectar of her disposition, and had rather damaged its flavour'. Charity is bitterly disappointed at Jonas Chuzzlewit's unexpected proposal of marriage to her sister: 'The wretch! the apostate! the false, mean, odious villain; has before my very face proposed to Mercy!' She is again humiliated when Mr Moddle jilts her on the day he was due to marry her. (2, 4–6, 8–12, 18, 20, 24, 30–32, 37, 44, 46, 54)

Pecksniff, Mercy (MC) The younger daughter of Mr Pecksniff, often called Merry. She 'sat upon a stool because she was all girlishness, and playfulness, and wildness, and kittenish buoyancy. She was the most arch and at the same time the most artless creature, was the youngest Miss Pecksniff, that you can possibly imagine. It was her great charm.' She marries Jonas Chuzzlewit, who cruelly mistreats her. After her husband's suicide, Mercy becomes 'sadly different', chastened and reformed by her experiences. (2, 4–6, 8–12, 18, 20, 24, 26, 28, 30, 32, 37, 40, 46–47, 51, 54)

Pecksniff, Mr (MC) An architect and land-surveyor in Salisbury, a cousin of old Martin Chuzzlewit and the father of Charity and Mercy. His Christian name, seldom used, is Seth. Pecksniff is the embodiment of hypocrisy and is portrayed almost in a Jonsonian style. 'Perhaps there never was a more moral man than Mr Pecksniff: especially in his conversation and correspondence . . . He was a most exemplary man: fuller of virtuous precept than a copy-book. Some people likened him to a direction-post, which is always telling the way to a place, and

Figure 22 Merry Pecksniff, old Martin Chuzzlewit, Charity Pecksniff, and
Mr Pecksniff by Hablot K. Browne (Phiz)

never goes there: but these were his enemies; the shadows cast by his brightness; that was all. [His throat] seemed to
say, on the part of Mr Pecksniff, "There
is no deception, ladies and gentlemen, all
is peace, a holy calm pervades me." So
did his hair, just grizzled with an iron-
grey, which was all brushed off his forehead, and stood bolt upright, or slightly
drooped in kindred action with his heavy
eyelids. So did his person, which was
sleek though free from corpulence. So
did his manner, which was soft and oily.
In a word, even his plain black suit, and
state of widower, and dangling double
eye-glass, all tended to the same purpose,

and cried aloud, "Behold the moral Pecksniff!"' His professional work largely consisted in his taking pupils for money, 'ensnaring parents and guardians, and pocketing premiums'. John Westlock was articled to him, but he left after a 'little difference' between them. Westlock's place was taken by young Martin Chuzzlewit, whom Pecksniff dismissed on the orders of old Martin. Pecksniff took old Martin into his house, wrongly assuming that he was senile, and made approaches to Mary Graham with a view to marrying her, hoping to inherit her guardian's wealth. He overhears Mary's disclosure to Tom Pinch of his unwelcome advances and dismisses Tom from his service. Persuaded by Jonas Chuzzlewit to invest in Tigg Montague's fraudulent Anglo-Bengalee Assurance Company, Pecksniff is reduced to poverty when the business fails. In a dramatic confrontation with old Martin, the latter strikes Pecksniff to the ground and reveals all his villainous doings. Pecksniff becomes 'a drunken, squalid, begging-letter-writing man', reduced to borrowing money from Tom Pinch. John Forster, in a lengthy consideration of Dickens's portrayal of Pecksniff, comments: 'No conceivable position, action, or utterance finds him without the vice in which his being is wholly steeped and saturated. In his own house with his daughters he continues to keep his hand in; and from the mere habit of keeping up appearances to himself he falls into the trap of Jonas. Thackeray used to say that there was nothing finer in rascaldom than this ruin of Pecksniff by his son-in-law at the very moment when the oily hypocrite believes himself to be achieving his masterpiece of dissembling over the more vulgar avowed ruffian' (1928: Book 4, Ch. 2). G.K. Chesterton controversially suggests that Dickens loved Pecksniff: he 'is always making Pecksniff say things which have a wild poetical truth about them. Hatred allows no such outbursts of original innocence' (1933: 101). A number of origins have been suggested for Pecksniff, including Sir Robert Peel (1788–1850), Augustus Pugin (1812–52), and Samuel Carter Hall (1800–89). (2–6, 8–12, 14, 18–20, 24, 30, 31, 35, 38, 43, 44, 47, 52, 54)

Peecher, Emma (OMF) The schoolmistress in the girls' division of the school where Bradley Headstone and Charley Hexam work. 'Small, shining, neat, methodical, and buxom was Miss Peecher; cherry-cheeked and tuneful of voice. A little pincushion, a little housewife [i.e., a pocket sewing-outfit], a little book, a little workbox, a little set of tables and weights and measures, and a little woman, all in one . . . If Mr Bradley Headstone had addressed a written proposal of marriage to her, she would probably have replied in a complete little essay on the theme exactly a slate long, but would certainly have replied Yes. For she loved him.' He 'did not love Miss Peecher', and indeed was unaware of her feelings. She is a 'vigilant watchman' of all his doings, often talking about these to her favourite pupil, Mary Anne, who is aware of Miss Peecher's affections. (II: 1, 11; III: 11; IV: 7, 15)

Peepy, the Honourable Miss (RP) She was 'well known to have been the Beauty of her day and the cruel occasion of innumerable duels'. ('Our English Watering-Place')

Peerybingle, John and Mary (CB) John Peerybingle was a carrier: 'this lumbering, slow, honest John . . . so stolid, but so good!' He called Mary by the nickname, Dot, because she was small. She is instrumental in bringing together Edward Plummer and May Fielding, who was about to marry Tackleton. John wrongly suspects Dot of infidelity, but the misunderstandings are all happily resolved. (*The Cricket on the Hearth*)

Peffer   (BH) Mr Snagsby's former

business partner, who had died twenty-five years previously and who had been Mrs Snagsby's uncle. (10)

Pegg (UT) A crimp (i.e., an agent employed to decoy men into service at sea) who 'gives himself out as Waterhouse'. ('Poor Mercantile Jack')

Peggotty, Clara (DC) Simply known by her surname, Peggotty was David Copperfield's affectionate nurse and equally affectionate servant to his young mother. In David's earliest memories, she had 'no shape at all, and eyes so dark that they seemed to darken their whole neighbourhood in her face, and cheeks and arms so hard and red that I wondered the birds didn't peck her in preference to apples'. She tactfully took David to her brother's home in Yarmouth so that he was out of the way when his mother married Mr Murdstone. David therefore became acquainted with the rest of her family and Little Em'ly, who played such important parts in his life as time went on. When Mr Murdstone thrashes David and arranges for him to go away to school David fully realises Peggotty's love for him: 'From that night there grew up in my breast a feeling for Peggotty which I cannot very well define. She did not replace my mother; no one could do that; but she came into a vacancy in my heart, which closed upon her, and I felt towards her something I have never felt for any other human being. It was a sort of comical affection, too; and yet if she had died, I cannot think what I should have done, or how I should have acted out the tragedy it would have been to me.' On the death of David's mother, Peggotty was dismissed by the Murdstones but soon afterwards she marries Mr Barkis, the carrier, who had long been 'willin'' to do so. When Barkis dies, Peggotty periodically appears in the action of the novel as a comforting and helpful presence. She is even treated affectionately by Miss Betsey

Trotwood, who refuses, however, to call her 'Peggotty', which she thinks of as 'that South Sea Island name', but calls her 'Barkis' instead. Peggotty, in fact, eventually becomes Miss Trotwood's housekeeper. In his characterisation of Peggotty, Dickens, in Michael Slater's opinion, has created 'a very human, believable mother-figure' (1983: 367). Some memories of Dickens's own nurse, Mary Weller, may have gone towards his portrayal. (1–5, 8–10, 12, 13, 17, 19–23, 28, 30–35, 37, 43, 51, 55, 57, 59, 63–64)

Peggotty, Daniel (DC) A Yarmouth fisherman and brother to Clara Peggotty. He is the father-figure to a 'family' that consists of Ham (his nephew), Little Em'ly (his niece), and Mrs Gummidge (the widow of his former 'partner in a boat'), who all live together in a converted barge near the sea. Daniel Peggotty deals in lobsters, crabs and crawfish. He is 'a hairy man with a very good-natured face', hearty, affectionate and hospitable, and speaking in a broad East Anglian dialect. When Em'ly elopes with Steerforth, Mr Peggotty is heartbroken and insists that a lighted candle should be placed at the window, as if to say 'Come back, my child, come back!' Like Solomon Gills in search of Walter Gay in *Dombey and Son*, he goes to seek her 'through the world', travelling unsuccessfully through France and Switzerland on his mission. With Martha Endell's assistance, he and David eventually find her in London. He emigrates to Australia with her, Martha and Mrs Gummidge. (2, 3, 7, 10, 17, 21–22, 30–32, 40, 46–47, 50–51, 55, 57, 63)

Peggotty, Ham (DC) Daniel Peggotty's nephew. 'He was . . . a huge, strong fellow of six feet high, broad in proportion, and round-shouldered; but with a simpering boy's face and curly light hair that gave him quite a sheepish look. He was dressed in a canvas jacket, and a pair of such very stiff trousers that they would have stood quite as well alone, without any legs in them. And you couldn't so properly have said he wore a hat, as that he was covered in a-top, like an old building, with something pitchy.' He is betrothed to Emily and accordingly heartbroken when she elopes with the glamorous and gentlemanly Steerforth: 'The face he turned up to the troubled sky, the quivering of his clasped hands, the agony of his figure, remain associated with that lonely waste, in my [i.e., David Copperfield's] remembrance, to this hour. It is always night there, and he is the only object in the scene.' When later David sees Ham, he recalls nothing about his face 'but an expression of stern de-termination in it – that if ever he en-countered Steerforth he would kill him'. With tragic irony, Ham is drowned when going to the rescue of the 'solitary man' (who unknown to him is Steerforth) on board the wreck in the storm at Yar-mouth. Despite the onlookers' efforts at restoration, he 'had been beaten to death by the great wave, and his generous heart was stilled for ever'. (1–3, 7, 10, 21–22, 30–32, 40, 46, 51, 55–56, 63).

Peggy (HR) In Miss Alice Rainbird's 'romance', she was the Lord Chamber-lain to King Watkins the First.

Pegler, Mrs (HT) The old lady who turns out to be Mr Bounderby's mother. When Stephen Blackpool encounters her in the street, he sees 'an old woman, tall and shapely still, though withered by time . . . She was very cleanly and plainly dressed, had country mud upon her shoes, and was newly come from a jour-ney . . . [Everything] bespoke an old woman from the country, in her plain holiday clothes, come into Coketown on an expedition of rare occurrence.' She visits Coketown from her home fifty miles away in order secretly to look ad-miringly on her successful son. She great-ly disconcerts Mr Bounderby, who had always boasted of his rise from a wretch-

edly poor childhood, when she reveals to Mr Gradgrind, Mrs Sparsit and others that she had given him a good upbringing and that Bounderby had pensioned her off on £30 a year, 'making the condition that I was to keep down in my own part, and make no boasts about him, and not trouble him'. (I: 12; II: 6, 8; III: 5, 9)

Pell, Solomon (PP) A shady attorney in the Insolvent Court, who helps Sam Weller with his plan of voluntary im-prisonment for debt in the Fleet Prison and then helps both the Wellers with the probate of Mrs Weller's will. He was 'a fat flabby pale man, in a surtout which looked green one minute and brown the next: with a velvet collar of the same chameleon tints. His forehead was nar-row, his face wide, his head large, and his nose all on one side, as if Nature, indig-nant with the propensities she observed in him in his birth, had given it an angry tweak which it had never recovered. Being short-necked and asthmatic, however, he respired principally through this feature; so, perhaps, what it wanted in ornament, it made up in usefulness.' (43, 47, 55)

Peltirogus, Horatio (NN) A 'young gentleman,' about 4 years old, who (according to Mrs Nickleby) had enter-tained an attachment for Kate Nickleby. (55)

Peplow, Mrs (SB) She and her son, Mas-ter Peplow, live in the street where the muffin boy passes by one night. ('Scenes: The Streets – Night')

Pepper (GE) *See* **Avenger, the.**

Peps, Doctor (or, Sir) Parker (DS) He is 'one of the Court Physicians, and a man of immense reputation for assisting at the increase of great families'. He is much admired by the family surgeon, with whom he attends Mrs Dombey when she gives birth to Paul. With other doctors, he also attends Paul during his fatal illness. (1, 16)

Perch, Mr and Mrs (DS) Mr Perch is the deferential and timid messenger in the firm of Dombey and Son. His wife sometimes visits the Dombey household below stairs to gossip with the servants about the family's affairs. He is disconcerted by the interrogation by his acquaintances about the goings-on in the family and firm, including Edith's apparent elopement and the bankruptcy of the business, but finds some comfort and refuge in the company of his wife at their home at Balls Pond. When the firm collapses, 'Mr Perch alone remained of all the late establishment, sitting on his bracket looking at the accountants, or starting off it, to propitiate the head accountant, who was to get him into the Fire Office.' (13, 17, 18, 22–23, 31, 35, 46, 51, 53, 58–59)

Percy, Lord Algernon (BR) The second son (1750–1830) of the first Duke of Northumberland, who was in command of the Northumberland Militia during the Gordon Riots in London. (67)

Perker, Mr (PP) Mr Wardle's lawyer of Gray's Inn. 'He was a little high-dried man, with a dark squeezed-up face, and small restless black eyes, that kept winking and twinkling on each side of his little inquisitive nose.' A brisk and efficient man, he appears at several critical moments in the narrative: he arranges a financial settlement with Mr Jingle to prevent his intended marriage to Miss Rachael Wardle, acts as Samuel Slumkey's agent in the Eatanswill election, and looks after Mr Pickwick's interests in the case of Bardell v. Pickwick. He may have been based on Mr Ellis, a partner in the firm of Ellis and Blackmore, where Dickens was employed as a clerk in 1827–28. (10, 13, 20, 26, 31, 33–35, 40, 45–47, 53–54)

Perkins (CS) A general dealer, whose shop is opposite the Haunted House, which he wouldn't go near: 'he an't overwise, an't Perkins, but he an't such a fool as *that*'. ('The Haunted House')

Perkins, Mrs (BH) She and Mrs Piper, neighbours of Krook's, take a keen interest in all the happenings at his dwelling, especially from the discovery of Nemo's death onwards: 'Mrs Perkins, who has not been for some weeks on speaking terms with Mrs Piper, in consequence of an unpleasantness originating in young Perkins having "fetched" young Piper "a crack," renews her friendly intercourse on this auspicious occasion.' (11, 20, 32, 33, 39)

Perkinsop, Mary Anne (CS) One of Mrs Lirriper's maidservants: 'although I behaved handsomely to her and she behaved unhandsomely to me [she] was worth her weight in gold as overawing lodgers without driving them away.' Miss Wozenham enticed her away with an offer of 'one pound per quarter more' than Mrs Lirriper paid her. ('Mrs Lirriper's Lodgings')

Pessell, Mr (MP) A vice-president of the Anatomy and Medicine session at the second meeting of the Mudfog Association. His name is, of course, a pun on 'pestle'.

Peter, Lord (SB) The young peer with whom Miss Julia Manners planned to elope. Having mistaken Alexander Trott for him, she and Trott agree to marry. Lord Peter, after drinking champagne, was thrown from his horse in a steeplechase and was killed. ('Tales: The Great Winglebury Duel')

Petowker, Henrietta (NN) An actress at the Theatre Royal, Drury Lane, whom Mr Lillyvick meets at the Kenwigs's house and becomes infatuated with. She joins Vincent Crummles's theatrical company and is with them when Mr Lillyvick secretly marries her (to the disappointment and anger of the Kenwigs family). Mr Crummles later informs Nicholas Nickleby that 'Mr Lillyvick didn't dare to say his soul was his own, such was the tyrannical sway of Mrs Lillyvick who reigned paramount and extreme.' She elopes, however, with a half-pay captain, which leads Mr Lillyvick to declare: 'I turn her off, for ever.' (14–16, 25, 30, 36, 48, 52)

Pettifer, Tom (CS) Captain Jorgan's steward, who has kept a leaf of paper in his hat that helps to solve the mystery concerning an inheritance. ('A Message from the Sea')

Phenomenon, The Infant (NN) *See* **Crummles, Vincent, and family.**

Phib (NN) *See* **Phoebe** (NN).

Phibbs, Mr (RP) A haberdasher, who had sent a pair of gloves to be cleaned, which were found under the pillow of Eliza Grimwood, whose murder is investigated by Inspector Wield. ('Three "Detective" Anecdotes')

Phil (RP) The 'morose' serving man at 'Our School'. The schoolboys 'had a high opinion of his mechanical genius', but he 'had a sovereign contempt for learning'. ('Our School')

Philips (BR) A constable who the Lord Mayor of London desperately suggests might help to protect Mr Langdale during the Gordon Riots: 'he's not very old for a man at his time of life, except in his legs, and if you put him up at a window he'd look quite young by candle-light, and might frighten 'em very much.' (61)

Phoebe (CS) The crippled daughter of Lamps, who works at Mugby Junction. She is about 30 years old. Despite her disability, which means she must always lie on a couch, she is 'always working [at making lace] . . . always contented, always lively, always interested in others, of all sorts'. ('Mugby Junction')

Phoebe (NN) The Squeers's hungry maidservant, who attends Fanny in her own room. Fanny patronisingly abbreviates her name to 'Phib'. (12)

Phunky, Mr (PP) The junior to Serjeant Snubbin in the case of Bardell v. Pickwick. 'Although an infant barrister, he was a full-grown man. He had a very nervous manner, and a painful hesitation in his speech,' which was due to his timidity. He was overawed both by the Serjeant and the Judge. (31, 34)

Physician (LD) A regular guest of Mr Merdle's. He 'knew everybody . . . and everybody knew [him]'. When Bar and Bishop wonder why Mr Merdle is depressed, Physician replies that he can find nothing the matter with him. Only after Merdle's suicide does he realise what Merdle's complaint had been. (I: 21; II: 12, 25)

Pickles, Mr (HR) In Miss Alice Rainbird's 'romance', he was the fishmonger in whose shop King Watkins unknowingly encountered the Fairy Grandmarina, who was invisible to him. (Part II)

Pickleson (CS) A 'languid young man', who was exhibited by Mim as a giant under the name of Rinaldo di Velasco. He tells Doctor Marigold about Sophy's ill-treatment, which results in her adoption by Marigold. ('Doctor Marigold')

Pickwick, Samuel (PP) The founder and General Chairman of the Pickwick Club, he is a benevolent, middle-aged bachelor with 'a bald head, and circular spectacles'. In recalling his negotiations with Chapman and Hall concerning the writing of the serial novel, Dickens wrote in his Preface to the Cheap Edition (1847) that 'I thought of Mr Pickwick, and wrote the first number; from the proof sheets of which, Mr Seymour [the illustrator of that number] made his drawing of the Club, and that happy portrait of its founder, by which he is always recognised, and which may be said to have made him a reality.' Chapman wrote in a letter to John Forster that Seymour's sketch was made from Chapman's description of a friend of his at Richmond, 'a fat old beau who would wear, in spite of the ladies' protests, drab tights and black gaiters. His name was John Foster' (1928: Book 1, Ch. 5). Mr Pickwick sets forth from London with three other Pickwickians (Winkle, Snodgrass and Tupman) to observe and investigate 'the hidden countries which on every side surround' his apartment in Goswell Street. In his innocence and kindness, he becomes involved in many embarrassing situations: angering a cabman, unwittingly intruding into ladies' accommodation, falling asleep after drinking too much punch and being wheeled into a pound, and so on. Above all, he is sued by his landlady, Mrs Bardell, for breach of promise, which results in his being found guilty and being imprisoned. Like a number of heroes of picaresque novels, Mr Pickwick is aided by a quick-witted and resourceful manservant in the person of Sam Weller, who is devoted to his master's welfare. As the narrative develops, Dickens portrays Mr Pickwick as a less naïve man who shows positive qualities of integrity. Dickens, however, did not think that 'this change will appear forced or unnatural to my readers, if they will reflect that in real life the peculiarities and oddities of a man who has anything whimsical about him, generally impress us first, and that it is not until we are better acquainted with him that we usually begin to look below these superficial traits, and to know the better part of him' (Preface to the cheap edition, 1847). In his essay, 'Dingley Dell and the Fleet',

W.H. Auden thought that Pickwick 'changes from an innocent child into an innocent adult who no longer lives in an imaginary Eden of his own but in the real and fallen world' (1963: 409) (*passim*). Mr Pickwick reappears in *Master Humphrey's Clock* (3, 4)

Pidger, Mr (DC) David Copperfield discovers that Miss Lavinia Spenlow, one of Dora's aunts, 'was an authority in affairs of the heart, by reason of there having anciently existed a certain Mr Pidger, who played short whist, and was supposed to have been enamoured of her'. David privately thinks, however, that 'this was entirely a gratuitous assumption'. (41, 43)

Pierce, Captain (RP) The master of the East Indiaman, the *Halsewell*. ('The Long Voyage')

Piff, Miss (CS) One of the 'young ladies' who serve in the refreshment room at Mugby Junction. ('Mugby Junction')

Pilkins, Doctor (DS) The Dombeys' family doctor. (1, 8)

Pinch, Ruth (MC) Tom Pinch's sister. Ruth Pinch 'had a good face; a very mild and prepossessing face; and a pretty little figure – slight and short, but remarkable for its neatness. There was something of her brother, much of him indeed, in a certain gentleness of manner, and in her look of timid trustfulness.' She works as a governess for a 'lofty family' in Camberwell. After Tom Pinch's dismissal from Mr Pecksniff's employment and his move to London, he takes his sister away from the family, who have made her existence miserable, to live with him as his housekeeper. 'Pleasant little Ruth! Cheerful, tidy, bustling, quiet little Ruth! No doll's house ever yielded greater delight to its young mistress, than little Ruth derived from her glorious dominion over the triangular parlour and the two small

Figure 23 John Westlock, Tom Pinch, and Ruth Pinch by Hablot K. Browne (Phiz)

bedrooms.' John Westlock, on visiting the Pinches, is 'transfixed in silent admiration' by the sight of Ruth, who is making a beefsteak pudding. He later declares his love for her and they marry. Most modern readers will find Dickens's presentation of Ruth Pinch embarrassingly arch and sentimental, but he himself said, in a letter to Lady Holland, that Tom and Ruth Pinch were 'two of

the greatest favourites I have ever had' (House *et al.*, 1965, vol. IV, p. 145). (6, 9, 36–37, 39–40, 45–46, 48, 50, 52–54)

Pinch, Tom (MC) Mr Pecksniff's devoted assistant. He was 'an ungainly, awkward-looking man, extremely short-sighted, and prematurely bald ... He was far from handsome certainly; and was dressed in a snuff-coloured suit, of an uncouth make at the best, which, being shrunk with long wear, was twisted and tortured into all kinds of odd shapes; but notwithstanding his attire, and his clumsy figure, which a great stoop in his shoulders, and a ludicrous habit he had of thrusting his head forward, by no means redeemed, one would not have been disposed (unless Mr Pecksniff said so) to consider him a bad fellow by any means. He was perhaps about thirty, but might have been almost any age between sixteen and sixty: being one of those strange creatures who never decline into an ancient appearance, but look their oldest when they are very young, and get over it at once.' Tom Pinch plays the organ in the village church, and falls in love at first sight with Mary Graham, whom he sees in the porch listening to the music. He sadly realises that nothing can come of this because of her love for young Martin Chuzzlewit. He defends his employer against all criticism but is finally disillusioned when Mary tells him of Pecksniff's unwelcome amorous advances. Dismissed by Pecksniff, who has overheard the conversation between him and Mary, Tom goes to London and sets up house with his sister. Through the medium of Mr Fips, a lawyer, he is given employment by an unknown patron (who turns out to be old Martin Chuzzlewit), who pays him £100 a year to arrange and classify a large number of books. Dickens ends the novel with a lengthy and eloquent apostrophe to Tom Pinch, who (seated at the organ) is also the subject of Phiz's engraved frontispiece. The last words are: 'From the Present and the Past, with which she [Ruth] is so tenderly entwined in all thy thoughts, thy strain soars onward to the Future. As it resounds within thee and without, the noble music, rolling round ye both, shuts out the grosser prospect of an earthly parting, and uplifts ye both to Heaven!' A.E. Dyson argues that 'Tom Pinch stands in a line which includes Kit

Nubbles and Joe Gargery, but which has affinities with other Dickens people as well. He is a generally other-worldly person with a rich, inner consciousness; Dickens conveys the power which music, poetry, natural beauty have in his life . . . It is a triumph of Dickens's art that he could enter into a person so dissimilar to himself, and one whom he might himself have been inclined, by temperament, to despise' (1970: 91–2). (2, 5–7, 9, 12–14, 20, 24, 30–31, 33, 36–37, 39–41, 43, 45–46, 48, 50, 52–54)

Pip (GE) The hero and narrator of *Great Expectations*. 'My father's family name being Pirrip, and my christian name Philip, my infant tongue could make of both names nothing longer or more explicit than Pip. So I called myself Pip, and came to be called Pip.' He is an orphan brought up 'by hand' by his sister, who is the wife of the blacksmith, Joe Gargery. As a small boy, he has a frightening encounter on the marshes, where he lives, with an escaped convict, whom he supplies with food and a file. Through the means of Uncle Pumblechook, he is sent to play at Satis House in order to amuse Miss Havisham. There he meets Estella, with whom he falls in love at first sight. The meeting makes him ashamed of his humble circumstances: 'I thought . . . how common Estella would consider Joe, a mere blacksmith: how thick his boots, how coarse his hands. I thought how Joe and my sister were then sitting in the kitchen, and how I had come up to bed from the kitchen, and how Miss Havisham and Estella never sat in a kitchen, and were far above the level of such common doings.' When he later learns from Mr Jaggers, the lawyer, that he has 'great expectations' and is to go to London in order to become a gentleman, Pip therefore eagerly casts off his former way of life, and lives a rather idle and spendthrift existence. He is under the impression that his benefactor is Miss Havisham. But he has some uneasiness

Figure 24 Joe Gargery, Pip, and Biddy by Marcus Stone

of conscience about his behaviour towards Joe and Biddy: 'When I woke up in
the night ... I used to think, with a
weariness in my spirits, that I should

have been happier and better if I had
never seen Miss Havisham's face, and
had risen to manhood content to be
partners with Joe in the honest old

forge.' Estella continues to spurn him, although he loves her 'against reason,
against promise, against peace, against
hope, against happiness, against all dis-
couragement there could be'. She marries
Bentley Drummle despite Pip's urging
her not to do so. Pip's 'expectations'
come to a disastrous end when Magwitch, the convict he had helped on the
marshes, illegally returns from Australia
to England and reveals to Pip that he was
his benefactor. Pip at first finds him repel-
lent, but soon returns Magwitch's affection for him. He and Herbert Pocket unsuccessfully try to smuggle Magwitch
out of England. After Magwitch's trial
and sentence to death, he falls ill, is tended by Pip, and dies in hospital. Pip has
now lost his fortune, since Magwitch's
property is forfeit to the Crown. Pip himself becomes seriously ill, is looked after
by Joe, and on his recovery is filled with
remorse for his past behaviour. He determines to go to Biddy, to 'show her
how humbled and repentant' he was and
to ask her to marry him, but discovers
that she has just married Joe (which delights Pip). He sells all he possesses, quits
England for a period, eventually becomes
a partner in Clarriker and Co., lives happily and frugally with Herbert and his
wife, and maintains 'a constant correspondence with Biddy and Joe'. Dickens
had at first intended that Pip and Estella
should remain permanently separated,
but in his revised ending of the novel,
which he wrote upon the urgings of
Bulwer Lytton, they meet on the site
of the demolished Satis House eleven
years after the climactic events in Pip's
life. Estella tells Pip that they will 'continue friends apart', but Pip ends his narrative more hopefully: 'I took her hand in
mine, and we went out of the ruined
place; and, as the morning mists had
risen long ago when I first left the forge,
so, the evening mists were rising now, and
in all the broad expanse of tranquil light
they showed to me, I saw no shadow of
another parting from her.' Peter Ackroyd

interprets the 'flawed' figure of Pip as a
projection of Dickens himself: '[*Great
Expectations* is] a book of great psychological accuracy and observation, as if
Dickens were secretly examining himself
as he writes, analysing the nature of passion, of hypocrisy, of psychological meanness, all those things "low and small" of
which Pip eventually realises himself to
be guilty' (1990: 898–9) (*passim*).

Pip, Mr (MC) One of Montague Tigg's
acquaintances, who, according to the
doctor, was 'a theatrical man – capital
man to know – oh, capital man!' (28)

Pipchin, Mrs (DS) She keeps, in Miss
Tox's words, 'an infantine Boarding-
House of a very select description' in
Brighton, where little Paul Dombey is
sent. She 'was a marvellous ill-favoured,
ill-conditioned old lady, of a stooping
figure, with a mottled face, like bad marble, a hook nose, and a hard grey eye,
that looked as if it might have been
hammered on an anvil without sustaining any injury. Forty years at least had
elapsed since the Peruvian mines had
been the death of Mr Pipchin; but his
relict still wore black bombazeen, of such
a lustreless, deep, dead, sombre shade,
that gas itself couldn't light her up after
dark, and her presence was a quencher to
any number of candles.' She was 'a bitter
old lady'. Paul disconcerts her by his
forthright remarks (such as 'I'm thinking
how old you must be'), and yet there is an
'odd kind of attraction' between them.
After Mr Dombey marries Edith, he engages Mrs Pipchin as their housekeeper.
At his downfall, she unhesitatingly leaves
('I'm going to take *my*self off in a jiffy')
to return to her former professional connections in Brighton. Dickens based her
on Mrs Roylance, his landlady in Little
College Street, London, where he stayed
as a boy when his father was imprisoned
in the Marshalsea. (8, 10–12, 14, 16, 40,
42–44, 47, 51, 59)

Piper, Mrs (BH) *See* **Perkins, Mrs.**

Piper, Professor (MC) One of the deputation that formally calls on Elijah Pogram. (34)

Pipkin, Mr (MP) A member of the Mudfog Association, who at their second meeting read a 'short but most interesting communication' about homeopathy.

Pipkin, Nathaniel (PP) The parish clerk ('a harmless, inoffensive, good-natured being'), who is in love with Maria Lobbs, in Mr Pickwick's tale, 'The Parish Clerk'. (17)

Pipson, Miss (CS) A girl with 'curly light hair and blue eyes', who was one of Miss Griffin's pupils. ('The Haunted House')

Pirrip, Philip (GE) *See* **Pip.**

Pitcher (NN) One of the boys at Dotheboys Hall. Mrs Squeers reports to her husband that Pitcher has had a fever: 'whatever he has is always catching too. I say it's obstinacy, and nothing shall convince me that it isn't. I'd beat it out of him; and I told you that, six months ago.' (7)

Pitt, Jane (CS) A 'sort of wardrobe-woman' at a boarding-school. She was 'a very nice young woman' with 'a very frank, honest, bright face'. She married Old Cheeseman. ('The Schoolboy's Story')

Plornish, Mr and Mrs (LD) A poor, kindly plasterer and his wife who live with their children in Bleeding Heart Yard. 'Mrs Plornish was a young woman, made somewhat slatternly in herself and her belongings by poverty; and so dragged at by poverty and the children together, that their united forces had already dragged her face into wrinkles.' Mr Plornish was a 'smooth-cheeked, fresh-coloured, sandy-whiskered man of

thirty. Long in the legs, yielding at the knees, foolish in the face, flannel-jacketed, lime-whitened.' He had met Mr Dorrit in the Marshalsea when he himself was briefly imprisoned for debt and had retained an affection for the Dorrit family. Arthur Clennam uses him as his agent in getting Tip Dorrit's release from prison. Thanks to Clennam, John Baptist Cavaletto lives at the top of the Plornishes' house. Mrs Plornish's methods of communicating with him are much admired: she 'attained so much celebrity for saying, "Me ope you leg well soon," that it was considered in the Yard, but a very short remove indeed from speaking Italian. Even Mrs Plornish herself began to think that she had a natural call towards that language.' When Mr Dorrit comes into his money, he establishes Mrs Plornish in a small grocery and general trade shop 'at the crack end of the Yard'. She has the exterior painted to look like a rustic dwelling: 'On the door (when it was shut), appeared the semblance of a brass-plate, presenting the inscription, "Happy Cottage, T. and M. Plornish"; the partnership expressing man and wife.' Mrs Plornish is devoted to her poor old father, Mr Nandy, of whose musical gifts she is especially proud. (I: 6, 9, 12, 23–25, 31, 36; II: 4, 13, 26–27, 29, 32–33)

Pluck, Mr (NN) A 'gentleman with a flushed face and a flash air'. He and Mr Pyke are Sir Mulberry Hawk's 'toads in ordinary', who together perform several manoeuvres, including a joint, flattering visit to Mrs Nickleby, in order to assist Sir Mulberry in his campaign to seduce Kate Nickleby. (19, 27, 28, 38, 50)

Plummer, Caleb (CB) A 'little, meagre, thoughtful, dingy-faced man', who is a toy-maker employed by Gruff and Tackleton. He is devoted to Bertha, his blind daughter. His son, Edward, returns incognito from South America and with the help of Dot Peerybingle marries May Fielding. (*The Cricket on the Hearth*)

Pocket, Herbert (GE) The eldest son of Matthew Pocket, Herbert was Pip's friend, guide and companion in London. Pip had first met him at Satis House when as 'the pale young gentleman' he had challenged Pip to a fight. Pip knocked him down a number of times but he bore no animosity: he 'seemed so brave and innocent'. When Pip arrives in London, he lives with Herbert in rooms in Barnard's Inn. 'Herbert Pocket had a frank and easy way with him that was very taking. I had never seen any one then and I have never seen any one since, who more strongly expressed to me, in every look and tone, a natural incapacity to do anything secret or mean.' Because Herbert thinks that the two of them are so 'harmonious' and knows that Pip used to be a blacksmith, he re-christens Pip: 'Would you mind Handel for a familiar name? There's a charming piece of music, by Handel, called the Harmonious Blacksmith.' Herbert tactfully instructs Pip in manners: 'it is not the custom to put the knife in the mouth – for fear of accidents – and that while the fork is reserved for that use, it is not put further in than necessary. It is scarcely worth mentioning, only it's as well to do as other people do. Also, the spoon is not generally used over-hand, but under. This has two advantages. You get at your mouth better (which after all is the object), and you save a good deal of the attitude of opening oysters, on the part of the right elbow.' Pip secretly arranges a partnership for him in the firm of Clarriker and Co., thus enabling Herbert to marry his sweetheart, Clara Barley. Herbert is a stalwart ally of Pip in their endeavours to smuggle Magwitch out of the country. (11, 21–28, 31, 34, 36, 38–43, 45–47, 50–55, 58)

Pocket, Mr and Mrs Matthew (GE) Mr Matthew Pocket was Pip's tutor and the father of Herbert. He 'was a young-looking man, in spite of his perplexities and his very grey hair, and his manner seemed quite natural. I use the word natural, in the sense of its being unaffected; there was something comic in his distraught way, as though it would have been downright ludicrous but for his own perception that it was very near being so.' He 'had been educated at Harrow and at Cambridge; where he had distinguished himself; but . . . when he had had the happiness of marrying Mrs Pocket very early in life, he had impaired his prospects and taken up the calling of a Grinder [i.e., a crammer]'. He suggested to Pip that he should invest him 'with the functions of explainer and director' of all his studies. Mr Pocket was the only relative of Miss Havisham's who did not attend on her for her money. According to Joe, she left him 'a cool four thousand' in a codicil to her will because of Pip's high opinion of him. Mrs Pocket 'was the only daughter of a certain quite accidental deceased Knight' and 'had grown up highly ornamental, but perfectly helpless and useless'. She had two nursemaids to look after her seven children, most of whom spend their time 'tumbling' while she reclines on a garden chair reading a book. (22–24, 33, 39, 49, 57)

Pocket, Sarah (GE) One of Miss Havisham's relations and hangers-on, who hope to inherit some of her money. She was 'a little dry brown corrugated old woman, with a small face that might have been made of walnut shells, and large mouth like a cat's without the whiskers'. According to Joe Gargery, Miss Havisham left her 'twenty-five pound per-annium fur to buy pills, on account of being bilious'. (11, 15, 17, 19, 29)

Podder, Mr (PP) With Mr Dumkins, he is one of 'the most renowned members' of the All-Muggletonian cricket side. In the match with Dingley Dell, he is eventually 'stumped out' after a determined innings. (7)

Podgers, John (MHC) An inhabitant of Windsor, who was the hero of 'Mr Pickwick's Tale'. He was 'broad, sturdy, Dutch-built, short, and a very hard eater, as men of his figure often are'. (3).

Podsnap, Georgiana (OMF) The daughter of Mr Podsnap. This 'young rocking-horse was being trained in her mother's art of prancing in a stately manner without ever getting on. But the high parental action was not yet imparted to her, and in truth she was but an undersized damsel, with high shoulders, low spirits, chilled elbows, and a rasped surface of nose, who seemed to take occasional frosty peeps out of childhood into womanhood, and to shrink back again, overcome by her mother's head-dress and her father from head to foot – crushed by the mere weight of Podsnappery.' She is almost 18 years of age. Mr and Mrs Lammle cultivate a friendship with her with a view to arranging profitably a marriage between her and Fledgeby (a plan that fails because of Mrs Lammle's change of heart). Miss Podsnap is perturbed and yet shyly flattered by the reports the Lammles bring her of Fledgeby's apparent interest in her. When the Lammles are brought low, the 'credulous little creature' makes Mr Boffin promise that he will help her to give them financial assistance. (I: 11, 17; II: 4, 5, 16; III: 1, 17; IV: 2)

Podsnap, John (OMF) 'A too, too smiling large man, with a fatal freshness on him', who is a member of the Veneerings' circle of acquaintances. The word, 'Podsnappery' (the title of Book 1, Chapter 11 of *Our Mutual Friend*) has entered the language with the meaning of 'British Philistinism'. 'Mr Podsnap's world was not a very large world, morally; no, nor even geographically: seeing that although his business was sustained upon commerce with other countries, he considered other countries, with that important reservation, a mistake, and of their manners and customs would conclusively observe, "Not English!" when, Presto! with a flourish of the arm, and a flush of the face, they were swept away.' His other celebrated characteristic was his prudishness, an exaggeration, perhaps, of the kind of mid-Victorian 're-spectability' which was rapidly becoming established in the 1860s: 'A certain institution in Mr Podsnap's mind which he called "the young person" may be considered to have been embodied in Miss Podsnap, his daughter. It was an inconvenient and exacting institution, as requiring everything in the universe to be filed down and fitted to it. The question about everything was, would it bring a blush into the cheek of the young person?' At one of his dinner parties, he patronises an 'unfortunately-born foreigner', correcting his pronunciation: 'Our English adverbs do Not terminate in Mong and We Pronounce the "ch" as if there were a "t" before it. We say Ritch.' He brings his instruction to a climax with: 'there is in the Englishman a combination of qualities, a modesty, an independence, a responsibility, a repose, combined with an absence of everything calculated to call a blush into the cheek of a young person.' Mr Podsnap is duly disgusted with Eugene Wrayburn and Lizzie Hexam's marriage: 'my gorge arises against such a marriage'. The model for Podsnap in certain respects was John Forster, Dickens's biographer and intimate friend. (I: 2, 10–11, 17; II: 3–5; III: 1, 17; IV: 17)

Podsnap, Mrs (OMF) Mr Podsnap's wife, who would be a 'fine woman for Professor Owen [the anatomist], quantity of bone, neck and nostrils like a rocking-horse, hard features, majestic head-dress in which Podsnap has hung golden offerings'. (I: 2, 10, 11, 17; II: 3, 4; III: 1, 17; IV: 17).

Pogram, Elijah (MC) A self-important Member of Congress, much admired by his fellow-Americans. Martin Chuzzle-wit meets him on the steamboat on the way back from Eden. 'He was about five and thirty; was crushed and jammed up in a heap, under the shade of a large green cotton umbrella; and ruminated over his tobacco-plug like a cow . . . But about this gentleman there was a peculiar air of sagacity and wisdom, which convinced Martin that he was no common character; and this turned out to be the case.' Later, the boarders at the National Hotel determine to 'pounce upon the Honourable Elijah Pogram, and give *him* a le-vee forthwith'. (34)

Polly (BH) The waitress at a dining-house ('of the class known among its frequenters by the denomination Slap-Bang') visited by Mr Guppy, Mr Jobling and Young Smallweed. She was a 'bouncing young female of forty', who was 'supposed to have made some impression on the susceptible Smallweed'. (20)

Pordage, Commissioner (CS) The British consul on Silver-Store Island. 'He was a stiff-jointed, high-nosed old gentleman, without an ounce of fat on him, of a very angry temper, and a very yellow complexion. Mrs Commissioner Pordage, making allowance for difference of sex, was much the same.' Ruth Glancy points out that Dickens based Pordage on Lord Canning (1812–62), the Governor-General of India (1996: 810). ('The Perils of Certain English Prisoners')

Porkenham, Mr and Mrs, and family (PP) Mr and Mrs Sidney Porkenham and the Miss Porkenhams, were 'bosom friends' of the Nupkins family. Mr Nupkins is aghast at the possibility of their knowing the identity of Captain Fitz-Marshall (i.e., Mr Jingle). (25)

Porter, Mrs Joseph (SB) The Gattletons' neighbour, who mischievously encourages Uncle Tom to correct the performers' mistakes at the Gattletons' evening of Private Theatricals. She can thus triumphantly tell everybody that the evening was 'a complete failure'. ('Tales: Mrs Joseph Porter')

Porters, Mr (MED) A 'certain finished gentleman', who 'revealed a homage of the heart' to Miss Twinkleton at 'a certain season at Tunbridge Wells'. (3)

Potkins, William (GE) The waiter who attends Pip and Uncle Pumblechook at the Blue Boar. Pumblechook deliberately boasts in his presence of being Pip's earliest benefactor. (58)

Pott, Mr and Mrs (PP) Mr Pott is the pompous editor of the *Eatanswill Gazette*. He has 'a face in which solemn importance [is] blended with a look of unfathomable profundity'. He is, however, in terror of his wife, who (aided and abetted by her maidservant, Goodwin) becomes hysterical when he angrily confronts Mr Winkle about an anonymous verse in the rival paper, the *Independent*, which suggests that Winkle and Mrs Pott are over-fond of each other. He later has a furious quarrel and fight with his rival editor, Mr Slurk, at the Saracen's Head, Towcester, until this is stopped by the intervention of Sam Weller, who covers Pott's head and shoulders with a meal-sack. It has been suggested that Dickens based Pott on Lord Brougham (1778–1868). (13–15, 18, 51)

Potter, Thomas (SB) A city clerk and close friend of Mr Robert Smithers, another clerk. On receipt of their quarter's salary, they make a night of it. They have dinner, go to the theatre, get drunk, become riotous, are arrested, and are heavily fined. ('Characters: Making a Night of It')

Potterson, Miss Abbey (OMF) The 'sole proprietor and manager' of the tavern, the Six Jolly Fellowship-Porters, on the

River Thames. She is about 60 years old and was christened Abigail. Miss Potterson 'was a tall, upright, well-favoured woman, though severe of countenance, and had more of the air of a schoolmistress than mistress of the Six Jolly Fellowship-Porters'. She bans Gaffer Hexam and Rogue Riderhood from the tavern as potential trouble-makers. She advises Lizzie Hexam to leave her father. But after reading the document drawn up by John Rokesmith (i.e., Harmon) and signed by Rogue Riderhood she realises that she was wrong in thinking that Gaffer Hexam had murdered the man he had found dead in the Thames. Her brother, Job, a steward on the ship that brought John Harmon back to England, identified him as Rokesmith. (I: 6, 13; III: 2–3; IV: 12, 16)

Pouch, Mrs Joe (BH) Joe Pouch's widow, whom Mrs Bagnet thinks George should have married: 'If you had only settled down, and married Joe Pouch's widow when he died in North America, *she'd* have combed your hair for you.' (27)

Powlers, the (HT) Mrs Sparsit's late husband had been a 'Powler' by the mother's side. The Powlers 'were an ancient stock, who could trace themselves so exceedingly far back that it was not surprising if they sometimes lost themselves'. (I: 7; II; 1)

Pratchett, Mrs (CS) The head chambermaid at a London hotel. Her husband was in Australia, where his address was 'the Bush'. ('Somebody's Luggage')

Price, Matilda (NN) A miller's daughter, playful and vivacious, who is Fanny Squeers's firm friend and encourages her in her attempted amorous approaches to Nicholas Nickleby. She marries John Browdie. (9, 12, 39, 42, 43, 45, 64)

Price, Mr (PP) A 'coarse vulgar young

man of about thirty,' a prisoner for debt at Namby's, where Mr Pickwick encounters him. (40)

Prig, Mrs Betsey (MC) A nurse, who is the friend and colleague of Mrs Gamp, who calls her 'the best of creeters'. 'Mrs Prig was of the Gamp build, but not so fat; and her voice was deeper and more like a man's. She had also a beard.' Like Mrs Gamp, she is ruthless in dealing with patients, as in her advice to Mrs Gamp when the latter is taking over the supervision of Lewsome: 'The easy-chair an't soft enough. You'll want his piller.' She finally incurs Mrs Gamp's unforgiving wrath when she doubts whether Mrs Harris actually exists: 'I don't believe there's no sich a person!' In his Preface to the first cheap edition of *Martin Chuzzlewit* (1849), Dickens wrote: 'The hospitals of London are, in many respects, noble institutions; in others, very defective. I think it not the least among the instances of their mismanagement, that Mrs Betsey Prig is a fair specimen of a Hospital nurse.' But by the time that he wrote the Preface to the Charles Dickens edition of the novel (1868), he noted a great improvement 'through the agency of good women'. (25, 29, 46, 49, 51)

Priscilla (BH) Mrs Jellyby's maid, who drinks, as Caddy points out to Esther Summerson: 'It was as bad as a public-house, [her] waiting at dinner; you know it was!' (4, 5)

Prodgit, Mrs (RP) Mrs Meek's nurse, who imposes her authority on Mr Meek. He claims that his new-born son, Augustus George, 'is a production of Nature . . . and should be treated with some remote reference to Nature. In my opinion, Mrs Prodgit is, from first to last, a convention and a superstition. Are all the faculty afraid of Mrs Prodgit? If not, why don't they take her in hand and improve her?' ('Births. Mrs Meek, Of A Son')

Prosee, Mr (MP) At the second meeting of the Mudfog Association, he examined Mr Blank's machine in the Display of Models and Mechanical Science, but he declared 'that he was wholly unable to discover how it went on at all'.

Pross, Miss (TTC) She had been the companion of Lucie Manette since the girl was 10 years old. She is fiercely protective of her 'Ladybird', as she calls her. She was 'a wild-looking woman, whom even in his agitation, Mr Lorry observed to be all of a red colour, and to have red hair, and to be dressed in some extraordinary tight-fitting fashion, and to have on her head a most wonderful bonnet like a Grenadier wooden measure, and a good measure too, or a great Stilton cheese'. She lays 'a brawny hand upon his chest, and [sends] him flying back against the nearest wall'. Mr Lorry nevertheless realises that she is loving and true, stationing her 'much nearer to the lower Angels than many ladies immeasurably better got up both by Nature and Art'. When in France during the dangerous days for Charles and Lucie, Miss Pross is aggressively English. When Madame Defarge comes in search of Lucie, Miss Pross declares: 'I am a Briton . . . I am desperate. I don't care an English Twopence for myself. I know that the longer I keep you here, the greater hope there is for my Ladybird. I'll not leave a handful of that dark hair upon your head, if you lay a finger on me!' In the struggle, Madame Defarge is accidentally killed by her own pistol, the noise of which permanently deafens Miss Pross. Miss Pross's brother is Solomon, known as John Barsad. (I: 4; II: 6, 17–21; III: 2–3, 6–8, 11, 14)

Pross, Solomon (TTC) *See* **Barsad.**

Provis (GE) *See* **Magwitch, Abel.**

Pruffle (PP) The servant of the 'scientific gentleman' Mr Pickwick meets at Clifton. (39)

Puffer, Princess (MED) The old hag who keeps the London opium den frequented by John Jasper. She makes two mysterious, ominous visits to Cloisterham. In the first, Edwin Drood 'becomes quite aware of a woman crouching on the ground near a wicket gate in a corner' and sees that she 'is of a haggard appearance, and that her weazen chin is resting on her hands, and that her eyes are staring – with an unwinking, blind sort of steadfastness'. She tells Edwin that Ned is 'A threatened name. A dangerous name.' After Jasper pays her a visit six months after the disappearance of Edwin Drood, she secretly follows him back to Cloisterham, encounters Datchery and (according to Deputy) plans to visit the Cathedral on the next morning. (1, 14, 23)

Pugstyles, Mr (NN) A 'plump old gentleman in a violent heat', who leads the delegation that protests to Mr Gregsbury about his conduct as a Member of Parliament. (16)

Pumblechook, Uncle (GE) Joe Gargery's uncle, 'but Mrs Joe appropriated him'. He 'was a well-to-do corn-chandler in the nearest town, and drove his own chaise-cart'. He was 'a large hard-breathing middle-aged slow man, with a mouth like a fish, dull staring eyes, and sandy hair standing upright on his head, so that he looked as if he had just been all but choked, and had that moment come to'. Pumblechook is a pompous hypocrite, who is responsible for arranging for Pip to play at Miss Havisham's. When Pip hears of his 'great expectations', Pumblechook takes credit for this turn of events, assuming that Pip's benefactor is Miss Havisham: 'To think . . . that I should have been the humble instrument of leading up to this, is a proud reward.' He insists on

Figure 25 Mr and Mrs Hubble, Mr Wopsle, Joe Gargery, Uncle Pumblechook, Mrs Gargery, and Pip by Harry Furniss

continually shaking hands with Pip and hints that 'More Capital' would help him to enlarge his business. Joe tells Pip towards the end of the novel that Orlick broke into Pumblechook's house, stole money, drank his wine and ate his food, slapped his face, pulled his nose, 'tied him up to his bedpust, and they giv' him a dozen, and they stuffed his mouth full of flowering annuals to perwent his crying out'. In a final meeting with Pip, Pumblechook, the 'windy donkey' (in Pip's phrase) maintains that the 'finger of Providence' is present in Pip's downfall, signifying '*Reward of ingratitoode to earliest benefactor, and founder of fortun's.*' (4–9, 12–13, 15, 19, 35, 37, 57, 58)

Pumpkinskull, Professor (MP) At the Zoology and Botany session during the second meeting of the Mudfog Association, he wonders whether the application of bears'-grease by young gentlemen about town 'had imperceptibly infused into those unhappy persons something of the nature and quality of the bear'.

Pupford, Miss Euphemia (CS) The proprietress of an 'establishment for six young ladies of tender years'. She 'is one of the most amiable of her sex', but for professional reasons keeps sentiment 'as far out of sight as she can – which (God bless her!) is not very far'. ('Tom Tiddler's Ground')

Pupker, Sir Matthew (NN) The chairman of the United Metropolitan Improved Hot Muffin and Crumpet Baking and Punctual Delivery Company. He had 'a little round head with a flaxen wig on the top of it'. (2)

Purblind, Mr (MP) A member of the Mudfog Association.

Purday, Captain (SB) An 'old naval officer on half-pay', whose 'bluff and unceremonious behaviour' disturbs his neighbour, an old lady, and who causes trouble at vestry meetings. ('Our Parish: The Curate. The Old Lady. The Half-Pay Captain; The Election for Beadle.')

Pyegrave, Charley (DC) A duke's son, who is one of Miss Mowcher's clients. (22)

Pyke, Mr (NN) A 'sharp-faced gentleman', who with Pluck is one of Sir Mulberry Hawk's 'toads in ordinary'. *See* **Pluck, Mr** for their combined machinations on behalf of Sir Mulberry. (19, 27, 28, 38, 50)

Q

Quale, Mr (BH) A 'loquacious young man ... with large shining knobs for temples, and his hair all brushed to the back of his head', who is one of Mrs Jellyby's philanthropic circle and who is also the 'train-bearer and organ-blower to a whole procession of people', including Mrs Pardiggle and Mr Gusher. His mission 'was to be in ecstasies with everybody's mission'. He is interested in marrying Caddy Jellyby, who detests him, and is eventually 'accepted' by Miss Wisk. (4, 5, 15, 23, 30)

Quanko Samba (PP) A bowler in the West Indies cricket match described by Mr Jingle at Dingley Dell. He bowled Jingle out, but never recovered from his exertions in the heat: 'bowled on, on my account – bowled off, on his own – died, sir'. (7)

Queerspeck, Professor (MP) At the Mechanical Science session at the first meeting of the Mudfog Association, he 'exhibited an elegant model of a portable railway, neatly mounted in a green case, for the waistcoat pocket'. This would enable clerks to transport themselves to their places of work at sixty-five miles an hour.

Quickear (UT) A policeman in the Liverpool Docks. ('Poor Mercantile Jack')

Quilp, Daniel (OCS) One of the most grotesque and fearsomely comic of all Dickens's characters, Daniel Quilp was an elderly man, 'so low in stature as to be quite a dwarf, though his head and face were large enough for the body of a giant. His black eyes were restless, sly, and cunning, his mouth and chin, bristly with the stubble of a coarse hard beard; and his complexion was one of that kind which never looks clean and wholesome. But what added most to the grotesque expression of his face, was a ghastly smile, which, appearing to be the mere result of habit and to have no connection with any mirthful or complacent feeling, constantly revealed the few discoloured fangs that were yet scattered in his mouth, and gave him the aspect of a panting dog. His dress consisted of a large high-crowned hat, a worn dark suit, a pair of capacious shoes, and a dirty white neckerchief sufficiently limp and crumpled to disclose the greater portion of his wiry throat. Such hair as he had, was of a grizzled black, cut short and straight upon his temples, and hanging in a frowzy fringe about his ears. His hands, which were of a rough coarse grain, were very dirty; his finger-nails were crooked, long, and yellow.' Quilp 'could scarcely be said to be of any particular trade or calling'. At the breakfast table, 'he ate hard eggs, shell and all, devoured gigantic prawns with the heads and tails on, chewed tobacco and watercresses at the same time and with extraordinary greediness, drank boiling tea without winking, bit his fork and spoon till they bent again, and in short performed so many horrifying and uncommon acts that the women [Mrs Quilp and Mrs Jiniwin, her mother] were nearly frightened out of their wits and began to doubt if he were really a human creature'. Quilp lusts after Little Nell and

Figure 26 Sampson Brass, Daniel Quilp, and Sally Brass by Hablot K. Browne (Phiz)

gleefully torments his wife, Sampson Brass and others. When Nell's Grandfather is unable to pay back the money Quilp has loaned him, he seizes the Old Curiosity Shop. He suspects the old man has secret stores of wealth and endeavours to track him and Little Nell down in their extensive wanderings. He hates Kit Nubbles (particularly for calling him an ugly dwarf), plots against him and contrives to have him falsely imprisoned for theft. Fleeing from arrest, when the truth of his plotting is discovered, Quilp falls into the Thames and drowns. Because the inquest on his body concluded that he had committed suicide, 'he was left to be buried with a stake through his heart in the centre of four lonely roads'. We are constantly aware of Quilp's potent, evil presence in the novel. Peter Ackroyd says that 'Quilp the dwarfish figure . . . has been seen as a simulacrum of Dickens in his savage

state – even down to the detail, which the author later removed in manuscript, of the dwarf taking a shower bath in true Dickensian fashion'. (1990: 316). Paul Schlicke states that 'Quilp has clear affinities with the Vice figure of morality plays – the hunchbacked villain of *Richard III*, the malevolent Yellow Dwarf of fairy-tale, the hero of the Punch and Judy show and Harlequin of pantomime – but for all that, he is utterly distinctive as a character and unlike any other in fiction or in life' (1995: xxiv). (3–6, 11–13, 21, 23, 27, 33, 41, 48–51, 60, 62, 64, 66–67, 73)

Quilp, Mrs Betsy (OCS) Daniel Quilp's long-suffering wife, whom he describes as 'pretty Mrs Quilp, obedient, timid, loving Mrs Quilp'. Although he bullies her with great glee, she reflects that 'Quilp has such a way with him when he likes, that the best-looking woman here couldn't refuse him if I was dead, and she was free, and he chose to make love to her'. Mrs Quilp always regrets coaxing Little Nell to reveal her grandfather's doings while Quilp eavesdrops. Quilp torments his wife to the last, when she brings him the letter from Sally Brass that tells him that the plot against Kit Nubbles has been revealed: 'I'm glad you're cold. I'm glad you lost your way. I'm glad your eyes are red with crying. It does my heart good to see your little nose so pinched and frosty.' After Quilp's death, she marries a 'smart young fellow enough; and as he made it a preliminary condition that Mrs Jiniwin [her mother] should be henceforth an out-pensioner, they lived together after marriage with no more than the average amount of quarrelling, and led a merry life upon the dead dwarf's money'. (3–6, 13, 21, 23, 49–50, 67, 73)

Quinch, Mrs (UT) The oldest inhabitant of the Alms-Houses, who 'have totally lost her head'. ('Titbull's Alms-Houses')

Quinion, Mr (DC) The manager of Murdstone and Grinby's warehouse in Blackfriars, where David Copperfield is sent to work. David had first met him (with Passnidge) at Lowestoft (2, 10–12).

R

Rachael (HT) The devoted friend of Stephen Blackpool. Rachael had 'a quiet oval face, dark and rather delicate, irradiated by a pair of very gentle eyes, but further set off by the perfect order of her shining black hair. It was not a face in its first bloom; she was a woman five-and-thirty years of age.' She selflessly tends Stephen's sick, drunken wife, whom she had known since they had worked together as girls. 'As the shining stars were to the heavy candle in the window [of Mrs Blackpool's sick-room], so was Rachael, in the rugged fancy of this man [Stephen], to the common experiences of his life.' Rachael urges Stephen to 'let the laws be', and it is because of a promise to her that he refuses to join in trade union activities. She and Sissy Jupe discover him lying at the bottom of a disused mine shaft, into which he fell on his journey back to Coketown to clear his name. After Stephen's death, Rachael suffers a long illness but then continues to work among the Coketown Hands, 'a woman of pensive beauty, always dressed in black, but sweet-tempered and serene, and even cheerful; who, of all the people in the place, alone appeared to have compassion on a degraded, drunken wretch of her own sex [presumably Stephen Blackpool's widow], who was sometimes seen in the town secretly begging of her, and crying to her; a woman working, ever working, but content to do it, and preferring to do it as her natural lot, until she should be too old to labour any more'. It is relevant to note the biblical associations of her name: Jacob had to wait patiently for fourteen years before he married Rachel (Genesis, 29). (I: 10–13; II: 4, 6; III: 4–7, 9)

Rachael, Mrs (BH) Esther Summerson's nurse, who later married the Reverend Mr Chadband (q.v.).

Raddle, Mrs (PP) A 'little fierce woman', who is Bob Sawyer's landlady and the sister of Mrs Cluppins. She scornfully bullies her husband: 'Don't talk to me, don't, you brute, for fear I should be perwoked to forgit my sect and strike you!' (32, 46)

Radfoot, George (OMF) The third mate on the ship bringing John Harmon back to England. He and Harmon, who strike up a friendship, 'were alike in bulk and stature'. Radfoot obtains a drug from Rogue Riderhood, and then drugs and assaults Harmon in an attempt to rob him of his money. But Radfoot is himself murdered and thrown into the Thames, where his body is mistaken for that of Harmon. (II: 12, 13)

Rainbird, Alice (HR) The 7-year-old girl who is the 'bride' of Bob Redforth and who writes the 'romance' about Princess Alicia and the Fairy Godmother.

Rairyganoo, Sally (CS) One of Mrs Lirriper's domestic servants, whom she suspects is 'of Irish extraction'. ('Mrs Lirriper's Lodgings')

Ram Chowder Doss Azuph Al Bowlar (SB) A 'devilish pleasant fellow', who had been a particular friend of Captain Helves in the East Indies. ('Tales: The Steam Excursion')

Rames, William (CS) The second mate of the *Golden Mary*. In Mr Steadiman's opinion, he was 'as good a sailor as [he was], and as trusty and kind a man as ever stepped'. ('The Wreck of the Golden Mary')

Rampart, Sir Charles (SB) Mr Tibbs's commanding officer when he was in the volunteer corps in 1806. ('Tales: The Boarding-House')

Ramsey (PP) A 'precious seedy-looking customer', against whom Messrs Dodson and Fogg issued a writ and whose misfortunes the lawyers' clerks humorously recount in the hearing of Mr Pickwick and Sam Weller. (20)

Rarx, Mr (CS) An old gentleman, who was a passenger on the *Golden Mary*. He was 'a sordid and selfish character', who became delirious and ungovernable after the shipwreck. ('The Wreck of the Golden Mary')

Ravender, Captain (CS) The brave captain of the *Golden Mary*, who dies of exposure in the long-boat. ('The Wreck of the Golden Mary')

Raybrock, Mrs (CS) A draper and postmistress in the village of Steepways. She was 'a comely elderly woman, short of stature, plump of form, sparkling and dark of eye'. She has two sons, Alfred, a fisherman, and Hugh, a sailor, who is mistakenly thought to be lost at sea. Captain Jorgan brings Hugh's 'message from the sea' (a letter found in a bottle) to Alfred. ('A Message from the Sea')

Raymond, Cousin (GE) One of the 'toadies and humbugs' who hang around Miss Havisham at Satis House. In his opinion, Matthew Pocket (who is not one of the 'toadies') 'never had, and . . . never will have any sense of proprieties'. (11).

Redburn, Jack (MHC) An inmate of Master Humphrey's house 'these eight years past'. In Master Humphrey's words: 'He is my librarian, secretary, steward, and first minister; director of all my affairs, and inspector-general of my household. He is something of a musician, something of an author, something of an actor, something of a painter, very much of a carpenter, and an extraordinary gardener, having had all his life a wonderful aptitude for learning everything that was of no use to him.' (2)

Redforth, Bob (HR) William Tinkling's 9-year-old cousin, who assumes the part of a bloodthirsty pirate and is the 'husband' of Alice Rainbird.

Redlaw, Mr (CB) A 'learned man in chemistry', whose power of memory is removed from him by a Phantom that appears to him on Christmas Eve. He consequently loses feelings of compassion, and communicates this insensibility to others. But Milly Swidger's goodness redeems him and those he has influenced. (*The Haunted Man*)

Red Whisker (DC) The young man, three or four years older than David Copperfield, whose attentions to Dora Spenlow at her birthday picnic excite David's jealousy: 'By-and-bye, I saw him, with the majority of a lobster on his plate, eating his dinner at the feet of Dora!' (33)

Reynolds, Miss (MED) One of Miss Twinkleton's pupils, who appears 'to stab herself in the hand with a pin' when Miss Twinkleton is addressing the young ladies on the subject of the 'slight fracas between two young gentlemen' that had occurred on the previous night. (9)

Riah (OMF) An elderly Jew employed by Fledgeby. He was 'a venerable man, bald and shining at the top of his head, and long grey hair flowing down at its sides and mingling with his beard. A man who with a graceful Eastern action of homage bent his head and stretched out his hands with the palms downward, as if to deprecate the wrath of a superior.' Because Riah had got into debt with Fledgeby's father, he is ruthlessly used by Fledgeby as a cover for his moneylending business. He is kind towards Lizzie Hexam and Jenny Wren, who calls him her 'godmother'. Through him, Lizzie obtained work in the paper mill outside London. Riah is scorned by his employer, Fledgeby, and patronised by Eugene Wrayburn. He later confesses to Jenny Wren that he hated himself for his subservience: 'in bending my neck to the yoke I was willing to wear, I bent the unwilling necks of the whole Jewish people'. Jenny takes him home to live with her now that Lizzie's lodgings are empty. Dickens's sympathetic portrayal of Riah owes much to his response to a letter he received from Mrs Liza Davis, who told him that Jews thought his depiction of Fagin, in *Oliver Twist*, was 'a great wrong' to their people. She later presented Dickens with a copy of Benisch's Hebrew and English Bible in 'grateful and admiring recognition' of his 'atoning for an injury' (Johnson, 1953: 1010–12). (II: 5, 15; III: 1–3, 10, 12–13; IV: 9, 16)

Richard (CB) Meg Veck's sweetheart, who was a smith. 'A handsome, well-made, powerful youngster he was; with eyes that sparkled like the red-hot droppings from a furnace fire; black hair that curled about his swarthy temples rarely; and a smile – a smile that bore out Meg's eulogium on his style of conversation' which she had described as strong, earnest, kind and gentle. (*The Chimes*)

Richards (DS) *See* **Toodle, Polly.**

Rickitts, Miss (MED) A pupil at Miss Twinkleton's establishment. She was 'a junior of weakly constitution', who daily took 'steel drops' in cowslip wine. (13)

Riderhood, Pleasant (OMF) The daughter of Rogue Riderhood. 'Upon the smallest of small scales, she was an unlicensed pawnbroker, keeping what was popularly called a Leaving Shop, by lending insignificant sums on insignificant articles of property deposited with her as security.' She has no information why she was christened Pleasant. She 'found herself possessed of what is colloquially termed a swivel eye (derived from her father)... [but] was not otherwise positively ill-looking, though anxious, meagre, of a muddy complexion, and looking as old again as she really was [i.e., twenty-four]'. She is loved by Mr Venus but has an aversion to his business. She agrees to marry him, however, when he says he will confine his work to 'the articulation of men, children, and the lower animals'. (I: 7; II: 12; III: 3, 7; IV: 14)

Riderhood, Rogue (OMF) Roger Riderhood, who was always known as Rogue Riderhood, was Gaffer Hexam's former partner in their business of finding and robbing corpses they dragged from the Thames. He is a rough and constantly threatening man with 'a squinting leer'. In order to try to be given the reward offered by Mr Boffin, he accuses Gaffer Hexam of murdering John Harmon, but the latter, in disguise, forces him to sign a statement that the accusation was false. Riderhood is run down when in a wherry on the Thames by a foreign steamer and is almost drowned. He becomes a deputy lock-keeper. Closely observing Bradley Headstone, he realises Headstone's murderous intentions towards Eugene Wrayburn and his plan to throw the blame on Riderhood. He fishes out from the river the clothes Headstone wore when he assaulted Eugene and in a memorable scene of frightening black comedy confronts Headstone in his classroom with blackmail in mind: "' I ask your pardon, learned governor," said Riderhood, smearing his sleeve across his mouth as he laughed with relish, "tain't fair to the lambs [the schoolboys], I know. It wos a bit of fun of mine. But upon my soul I drawed this here bundle out of a river! It's a Bargeman's suit of clothes. You see, it had been sunk there by the man as wore it, and I got it up.'" Bradley later grapples with him on the snow-covered brink of the Lock: "'Let go!" said Riderhood. "Stop! What are you trying at? You can't drown Me. Ain't I told you that a man as has come through drowning can never be drowned? I can't be drowned.'" But both fall to their deaths and are found 'lying under the ooze and scum behind one of the rotting gates'. (I: 1, 6, 12–14; II 12–13, 16; III: 2–3, 8, 11; IV: 1, 7, 15)

Rigaud (LD) Sometimes calling himself Blandois and Lagnier, he was a cosmopolitan adventurer and criminal, who prided himself on living on his wits. He had close-set, glittering eyes, 'a hook nose, handsome after its kind, but too high between the eyes . . . [He] was large and tall in frame, had thin lips, where his thick moustache showed them at all, and a quantity of dry hair, of no definable colour, in its shaggy state, but shot with red.' When he laughed, 'his moustache went up under his nose, and his nose came down over his moustache, in a very sinister and cruel manner'. His father was Swiss, his mother 'French by blood, English by birth', and he was born in Belgium. We first encounter him in prison in Marseilles, sharing a cell with John Baptist Cavaletto, accused (wrongly, so he claims) of murdering his wife. Rigaud (now calling himself Blandois) becomes temporarily involved with the Gowans in Italy, where Henry Gowan takes a pleasure in setting him up 'as the type of excellence'. He pries into Mrs Clennam's affairs, obtains possession of incriminating papers, discovers her secret suppression of the codicil to Gilbert Clennam's will, and attempts to blackmail her. He is crushed to death by a 'great beam' when Mrs Clennam's house

collapses. (I: 1, 11, 29, 30; II: 1, 3, 6–7, 9–10, 17, 20, 22–23, 28, 30–31, 33)

Rinaldo di Velasco (CS) *See* **Pickleson.**

Rob the Grinder (DS) He is Robin, the eldest son of the Toodles, 'known in the family by the name of Biler, in remembrance of the steam engine' (since his father is a stoker on the railways). He was subsequently known as Rob the Grinder, after Mr Dombey had nominated him to a place in a charity school, 'called (from a worshipful company) the Charitable Grinders'. At the school, he was 'huffed and cuffed, and flogged and badged, and taught, as parrots are, by a brute jobbed into his place of schoolmaster with as much fitness for it as a hound'. Because of this treatment (which is an example of Dickens's recurrent criticism in his work of contemporary educational systems and institutions) and being 'chivied through the streets' by youths who mock his school uniform, he plays truant, falls into bad company, engages in dubious activities, and is eventually employed by Mr Carker as a spy on Captain Cuttle and Solomon Gills. He informs Mrs Brown and Alice, in Mr Dombey's hearing, of Edith and Carker's plans to go to France. Finally, Miss Tox gives him a trial at his urgent request as her 'domestic', with a view to his 'restoration to respectability'. (2, 5, 6, 20, 22–23, 25, 31–32, 38–39, 42, 46, 52, 59)

Robinson (DS) A clerk in the Counting House at Dombey and Son. He has been 'at deadly feud for months' with the 'acknowledged wit of the Counting House', but the two agree to forget their differences when the firm is faced with collapse. (51)

Robinson (SB) Mrs Tibbs's servant, who on one occasion makes her presence known by 'giving sundry hems and sniffs outside the door'. ('Tales: The Boarding-House')

Robinson, Mr (SB) A 'gentleman in a public office, with a good salary and a little property of his own', who courts all the four Miss Willises and perplexes everybody as to which of them he is going to marry. He marries the youngest and they have a baby girl. ('Our Parish: The Four Sisters')

Rodolph, Mr and Mrs Jennings (SB) Musical friends of the ornamental painter's journeyman, at whose wedding celebrations they sing and also encourage Miss Martin (a friend of the bride's) to 'come out' as a performer. ('Characters: The Mistaken Milliner. A Tale of Ambition')

Rogers (RP) A policeman under the command of Inspector Field. He is ready for action, 'strapped and great-coated, with a flaming eye in the middle of his waist, like a deformed Cyclops'. ('On Duty with Inspector Field')

Rogers, Mr (RP) The third mate of the *Halsewell*, an East Indiaman. ('The Long Voyage')

Rogers, Mr (SB) A red-faced man, who prides himself on his oratory in a London public-house and whose powerful speeches are much admired. He vehemently asserts the Englishman's right not to be 'trampled upon by every oppressor'. Dickens says he wrote the description as a kind of warning: 'A numerous race are these red-faced men; there is not a parlour, or club-room, or benefit society, or humble party of any kind, without its red-faced man. Weak-pated dolts they are, and a great deal of mischief they do to their cause, however good.' ('Characters: The Parlour Orator')

Rogers, Mrs (PP) A lodger at Mrs Bardell's. She has a servant, and 'was more gracious than intimate [with Mrs Bardell's friends], in right of her position'. (46)

Roker, Tom (PP) The turnkey who shows Mr Pickwick his accommodation at the Fleet Prison, taking a complacent pride in the room and bedstead he shows him. (40–44)

Rokesmith, John (OMF) *See* **Harmon, John.**

Rolland, Monsieur (CS) A partner in the firm of Defresnier et Cie. ('No Thoroughfare')

Rosa (BH) 'A dark-eyed, dark-haired, shy, village beauty', trained as a maidservant by Mrs Rouncewell, the housekeeper at Chesney Wold, the country seat of the Dedlocks. Much taken by her beauty, Lady Dedlock makes her her 'pet – secretary – messenger – I don't know what', thus incurring the angry jealousy of Hortense, Lady Dedlock's maid. Watt, Mrs Rouncewell's grandson, falls in love with Rosa. Watt's father, the ironmaster, at first opposes any future marriage between them. But after taking her away from Chesney Wold, Mr Rouncewell agrees to the marriage, after he has sent Rosa, with one of his own daughters, to Germany 'for a little polishing up in her education'. (7, 12, 16, 18, 28, 41, 48, 63)

Rose (SB) The girl that the 'young medical practitioner' hopes to marry when he acquires some patients. ('Tales: The Black Veil')

Rose (VQ) Lucy Benson's cousin and John Maddox's sweetheart.

Ross, Frank (SB) One of Gabriel Parsons' friends, with whom he plays cards. ('Tales: A Passage in the Life of Mr Watkins Tottle')

Rouncewell, George (BH) Known as George or Trooper George, he is 'a swarthy brown man of fifty; well-made and good-looking; with crisp dark hair, bright eyes, and broad chest. His sinewy and powerful hands, as sunburnt as his face, have evidently been used to a pretty rough life.' He is a good, honest man, but in his wild youth he left home to become a soldier and has lost touch with his mother and elder brother, who is a successful ironmaster. As a former army trooper, he is the proprietor of George's Shooting Gallery, &c., near Leicester Square and the Haymarket, where rifle-shooting, archery, fencing and boxing can be practised. Phil Squod is his assistant. George served under Captain Hawdon (Lady Dedlock's lover and Esther Summerson's father) and attended him in illness. Hence he possesses an example of his handwriting. In order to save himself and his friend Matthew Bagnet from Grandfather Smallweed's proceeding against them for debt, he surrenders the paper to Tulkinghorn. George gives shelter on different occasions to Gridley (who collapses and dies in the Gallery) and Jo (who also dies there). Bucket wrongly arrests George for Tulkinghorn's murder but he is released from prison when the real culprit, Hortense, is discovered. Thanks to Mrs Bagnet, George is reunited with his mother while in prison. In the end, he lets his shooting gallery, finds employment in attending on Sir Leicester Dedlock at Chesney Wold, and has another reunion, this time with his brother in the north of England. (7, 21, 24, 26–27, 34, 47, 49, 52, 54–56, 58, 63, 66)

Rouncewell, Mr (BH) Mrs Rouncewell's elder son, who is a thriving ironmaster in the north of England. 'He is a little over fifty, perhaps, of a good figure, like his mother; and has a clear voice, a broad forehead from which his dark hair has retired, and a shrewd, though open face. He is a responsible-looking gentleman dressed in black, portly enough, but strong and active. Has a perfectly natural and easy air, and is not in the least embarrassed by the great presence [i.e., that

of Sir Leicester and Lady Dedlock] into which he comes [at Chesney Wold].' In dignified and impressive argument with the Dedlocks, Mr Rouncewell represents the views of the new, commercial classes of the mid-nineteenth century in opposition to the views of the aristocratic Sir Leicester Dedlock. He thinks at first that Rosa, with whom Watt, his son, is in love, is an unsuitable girl for him to marry, partly because of the environment and values of Chesney Wold, where she is employed. He eventually takes her away, approves of her as a future daughter-in-law, but sends her to Germany for a while to improve her education. At the end of the novel, Mr Rouncewell has a happy reunion with George, his younger brother. (7, 28, 40, 48, 63)

Rouncewell, Mrs (BH) The housekeeper at Chesney Wold, where she has worked for fifty years. 'She is a fine old lady, handsome, stately, wonderfully neat, and has such a back and such a stomacher, that if her stays should turn out when she dies to have been a broad old-fashioned family fire-grate, nobody who knows her would have cause to be surprised.' Her younger son (who turns out to be Trooper George) 'ran wild, and went for a soldier, and never came back'. Her older son became a successful ironmaster in the north of England. His son, Watt, visits his grandmother at Chesney Wold. Owing to Mrs Bagnet's enterprise and observation, Mrs Rouncewell is reunited with George. Dickens may have based her on his paternal grandmother, who was Lord Crewe's housekeeper at Crewe Hall, Cheshire. (7, 12, 16, 26, 28, 34, 40, 52, 55–56, 58, 63, 66)

Rouncewell, Watt (BH) The son of Mr Rouncewell, the ironmaster, and the grandson of Mrs Rouncewell, the housekeeper at Chesney Wold. He is 'out of his apprenticeship, and home from a journey in far countries, whither he was sent to

Figure 27 Barnaby Rudge and Grip by Hablot K. Browne (Phiz)

enlarge his knowledge and complete his preparations for the venture of this life'. Visiting his grandmother, he meets and falls in love with Rosa, whom he eventually marries. (7, 12, 18, 28, 40, 48, 63)

Rudge, Barnaby (BR) The simple-

minded, loving son of Mrs Rudge (and Rudge, the steward, who murdered his master, Reuben Haredale). 'He was about three-and-twenty years old, and though rather spare, of a fair height and strong make. His hair, of which he had a great profusion, was red, and hanging in disorder about his face and shoulders, gave to his restless looks an expression quite unearthly – enhanced by the paleness of his complexion, and the glassy lustre of his large protruding eyes. Startling as his aspect was, the features were good, and there was something even plaintive in his wan and haggard aspect. But the absence of the soul is far more terrible in a living man than in a dead one; and in this unfortunate being its noblest powers were wanting ... The fluttered and confused disposition of all the motley scraps that formed his dress, bespoke, in a scarcely less degree than his eager and unsettled manner, the disorder of his mind, and by a grotesque contrast set off and heightened the more impressive wildness of his face.' When he was born, 'he bore upon his wrist what seemed a smear of blood but half washed out'. Barnaby, who lives with his loving mother, is harmless and affectionate, and is virtually inseparable from Grip, his pet raven, who (in Gabriel Varden's words) has 'all the wit'. He has strange fancies and visions, as when he gazes intently at the smoke rolling up the chimney: 'Why do they tread so closely on each other's heels, and why are they always in a hurry – which is what you blame me for, when I only take pattern by these busy folk about me. More of 'em! catching to each other's skirts; and as fast as they go, others come! What a merry dance it is ! I would that Grip and I could frisk like that!' When he and his mother return to London after she leaves her country refuge because of Stagg's menacing visit, Barnaby excitedly joins the Gordon Riots despite his mother's frantic pleas. He becomes an enthusiastic participant with Hugh (whom he had known in the past) and others without, of course, any understanding of the religious cause of the Riots. Barnaby is arrested and put in jail, where he meets his father, who has been imprisoned for murder. Although he and his father are released by the rioters, they are recaptured. Barnaby is sentenced to death but gains a last-minute reprieve. The shock he has sustained gives him 'a better memory and greater steadiness of purpose; but a dark cloud overhung his whole previous existence, and never cleared away'. He lives with his mother on the Maypole farm and could never be tempted to revisit London. John Forster commented that 'in Barnaby himself it was desired to show what sources of comfort there might be, for the patient and cheerful heart, in even the worst of all human afflictions' (1928: Book 2, Ch. 9). But Chesterton thought that Barnaby Rudge's 'idiot costume and his ugly raven are used for the purpose of the pure grotesque; solely to make a certain kind of Gothic sketch' (1933: 70). Literary prototypes of Barnaby Rudge include Madge Wildfire and Davie Gallatley in Scott's *The Heart of Midlothian* and *Waverley* respectively. It is also relevant to note that Edward Oxford, the 18 year-old youth who had shot at Queen Victoria on Constitution Hill, had been found guilty but insane in 1840, a year before the publication of *Barnaby Rudge* began. (3–6, 10–12, 17, 24–25, 42, 45–50, 52–53, 57–58, 60, 62, 68–69, 73, 76–77, 79, 82)

Rudge, Mr (BR) Reuben Haredale's steward, who murders him for money. He also murders the gardener, whose remains are taken to be those of Rudge. Rudge goes into hiding for many years, but re-emerges as the Stranger, who haunts and threatens Mrs Rudge. We first encounter him sitting by himself in the Maypole. Removing his hat, he discloses 'the hard features of a man of sixty or thereabouts, much weather-beaten and worn by time, and the naturally harsh expression of which was not improved by a dark handkerchief which was bound tightly round his head'. His face is scarred and his complexion 'of a cadaverous hue'. He attacks Edward Chester on the road, wanders the London streets, and falls in with Stagg, who becomes his accomplice in seeking to get money out of his wife. Mr Geoffrey Haredale seizes Rudge in the smoking ruins of the Warren, takes him to London and gets him committed to prison by Sir John Fielding, the magistrate. In prison, Rudge encounters his son, Barnaby, who has been arrested for taking part in the Gordon Riots. Although they are temporarily released by the rioters, they are recaptured. Rudge refuses his wife's pleas in prison that he should repent, and curses everyone. 'In a paroxysm of wrath, and terror, and the fear of death, he broke from her, and rushed into the darkness of his cell, where he cast himself jangling down upon the stone floor, and smote it with his ironed hands.' Rudge is duly hanged, with Mr Haredale among the witnesses of his execution. (1–3, 5–6, 16–18, 26, 33, 45–46, 55–56, 61–62, 65, 68–69, 73, 76)

Rudge, Mrs (BR) Mary Rudge was apparently the widow of Reuben Haredale's steward. 'She was about forty [in 1775, when the story opens] – perhaps two or three years older – with a cheerful aspect, and a face that had once been pretty. It bore traces of affliction and care, but they were of an old date, and Time had smoothed them. Any one who had bestowed but a casual glance on Barnaby might have known that this was his mother, from the strong resemblance between them; but where in his face there was wildness and vacancy, in hers there was the patient composure of long effort and quiet resignation.' Gabriel Varden and Mr Geoffrey Haredale are her staunch friends. Having become aware of the threatening presence of her husband who, she realises, was Reuben Haredale's murderer, she resolves to find refuge,

with Barnaby, in the country and to renounce the annuity that Mr Haredale has paid her for over twenty years. When she is later menaced by Stagg, acting as her husband's go-between, she returns to London, where, to her dismay, Barnaby joins the Gordon Riots. After Rudge's execution and her son's reprieve, she retires with Barnaby to a peaceful life on the Maypole farm. (4–6, 10, 16, 17, 24–26, 42, 45–50, 57, 62, 69, 73, 76, 79, 82)

Rugg, Anastasia (LD) The daughter of Mr Rugg, through whose agency she had successfully sued a middle-aged baker, named Hawkins, for breach of promise. With the twenty guineas she received in damages, she acquired 'a little property'. Miss Rugg had 'little nankeen spots, like shirt buttons, all over her face, and [her] yellow tresses were rather scrubby than luxuriant'. (I: 25; II: 26, 28)

Rugg, Mr (LD) He is 'a professional gentleman in an extremely small way', whose description on the fan-light of his door is: Rugg, General Agent, Accountant, Debts Recovered. He 'had a round white visage, as if all his blushes had been drawn out of him long ago, and . . . a ragged yellow head like a worn-out hearth-broom'. Mr Pancks lodges on the second floor of his house. Rugg helps Pancks to trace Mr Dorrit's fortune. When Arthur Clennam is in prison, he agrees, under protest, to carry out his request that Daniel Doyce should be publicly exonerated from any part in the collapse of the business and that Clennam should solely bear the blame. (I: 25, 32, 35–36; II: 26, 28, 32, 34)

Rummun, Professor (MP) A member of the Mudfog Association.

S

Saggers, Miss (UT) An inmate (the oldest but one) of Titbull's Alms-House. She 'has her celebrated palpitations of the heart, for the most part, on Saturday nights'. ('Titbull's Alms-House')

St Evrémonde (TTC) The French noble family of which Charles Darnay is a member. Darnay's uncle is the Marquis de St Evrémonde, often referred to as Monseigneur. 'Monseigneur had one truly noble idea of general public business, which was, to let everything go on in its own way; of particular public business, Monseigneur had the other truly noble idea that it must all go his way – tend to his own power and pocket. Of his pleasures, general and particular, Monseigneur had the other truly noble idea, that the world was made for them. The text of his order (altered from the original by only a pronoun, which is not much) ran: "The earth and the fulness thereof are mine," saith Monseigneur.' He was about 60, haughty in manner, with slightly pinched nostrils that sometimes gave 'a look of treachery, and cruelty, to the whole countenance', and a handsome and remarkable face. When driving the Marquis in his carriage recklessly through the streets, his coachman runs down and kills a child. Gaspard, the child's father, stabs the Marquis to death in his bed at his château. Charles Darnay, disgusted with the principles and practice of his family, renounces his name, his nation and his property, which (as he tells the Marquis) is 'a crumbling tower of waste, mismanagement, extortion, debt, mortgage, oppression, hunger, nakedness, and suffering'. At Charles Darnay's second trial in Paris, Doctor Manette's written testimony, which had been found by Defarge in the Bastille, gave details of the evil deeds committed over twenty years before by the Marquis and his twin brother (who was then the holder of the title but had subsequently died) involving the seduction of a peasant girl and the fatal wounding of her brother. Doctor Manette had been summoned to attend the two. The aristocratic brothers had had him imprisoned in the Bastille in order to silence him. (II: 7–9; III: 10)

Salcy, Monsieur P. (UT) He is the head of a family of 'dramatic artists, fifteen subjects in number', and has established his theatre in the Hôtel de Ville. 'The members of the Family P. Salcy were so fat and so like one another – fathers, mothers, sisters, brothers, uncles, and aunts – that I think the local audience were much confused about the plot of the piece under representation, and to the last expected that everybody must turn out to be the long-lost relative of everybody else.' ('In the French-Flemish Country')

Sally (OT) The old workhouse inmate who confesses to Mrs Corney on her deathbed that she stole the gold locket and ring that Oliver Twist's dying mother had entrusted to her (1, 23, 24).

Sam (PP) The cabman who angrily accuses Mr Pickwick, at the outset of his travels, of taking down his number. (2)

Sampson, George (OMF) A young man

who frequents the Wilfer household, first hovering about Bella (as R.W. Wilfer puts it) and then transferring his affections to Bella's sister, Lavinia. Lavinia keeps George Sampson 'possibly in remembrance of his bad taste in having overlooked her in the first instance – under a course of stinging discipline'. He dares on one occasion to protest at Mrs Wilfer's language, when she indignantly calls Lavinia a 'viper'. But George is never sure where he stands and even at the end of the narrative has to be satisfied with Lavinia's air of saying that she is his 'as yet'. (I: 4, 9; II: 14: III: 4, 16; IV: 5, 16)

Sampson, Mr (HD) The Chief Manager of a Life Assurance Office, who narrates the story, 'Hunted Down'. He helps Meltham to entrap Julius Slinkton, who has killed one of his (Slinkton's) nieces.

Sanders, Mrs (PP) A 'big, fat, heavy-faced personage', who was one of Mrs Bardell's friends. At the trial of Bardell v. Pickwick, she stated that she had always said and believed that 'Pickwick would marry Mrs Bardell'. (26, 34, 46)

Sapsea, Thomas (MED) The auctioneer in Cloisterham. 'Accepting the Jackass as the type of self-sufficient stupidity and conceit – a custom, perhaps, like some few other customs, more conventional than fair – then the purest Jackass in Cloisterham is Mr Thomas Sapsea, Auctioneer.' He is 'portentous and dull . . . much nearer sixty years of age than fifty', rather portly, and 'a credit to Cloisterham, and society'. His epitaph to his late wife (formerly, Miss Brobity, a schoolmistress) is largely self-praise, including the statement that his 'Knowledge of the World, / Though somewhat extensive, / Never brought him acquainted with / A SPIRIT / More capable of / Looking up to him.' He becomes the Mayor of Cloisterham. (4, 6, 12, 14–16, 18)

Saunders, Mr (SYC) A bachelor friend

who visits the Whifflers and their children. Mr Whiffler asks him to be the godfather of the ninth child his wife is expecting. '"Not a ninth!" cries the friend, all aghast at the idea.' ('The Couple who Dote upon their Children')

Sawyer, Bob (PP) A medical student at Guy's Hospital, Bob Sawyer has 'about him that sort of slovenly smartness, and swaggering gait, which is peculiar to young gentlemen who smoke in the streets by day, shout and scream in the same by night, call waiters by their Christian names, and do various other acts and deeds of an equally facetious description. He wore a pair of plaid trousers, and a large rough double-breasted waistcoat; out of doors, he carried a thick stick with a big top. He eschewed gloves, and looked, upon the whole, something like a dissipated Robinson Crusoe.' He lodges with Mrs Raddle in Lant Street (where Dickens lodged as a boy) but angers her through his failure to pay the rent. He and his close friend, Benjamin Allen, eventually become unsuccessful medical practitioners in Bristol ('Sawyer, late Nockemorf'). It was intended that Bob Sawyer would marry Arabella Allen, Benjamin's sister, but he is forestalled in this by Mr Winkle. Having been made bankrupt, he and Benjamin Allen take up surgical appointments in the East India Company. (30, 32, 38–39, 47–48, 50–52, 57)

Saxby, Long (DS) One of Cousin Feenix's acquaintances, a 'man of six foot ten'. (51)

Scadder, Zephaniah (MC) The rascally agent who sells Martin Chuzzlewit a worthless plot of land in Eden. Because he wore his shirt collar open, 'every time he spoke something was seen to twitch and jerk up in his throat, like the little hammers in a harpsichord when the notes are struck. Perhaps it was the Truth feebly endeavouring to leap to his lips. If

Figure 28 Benjamin Allen, Tom Cripps (the errand boy), Bob Sawyer, and Mr Winkle
by Hablot K. Browne (Phiz)

so, it never reached them.' He had deep-set grey eyes, one of which was blind, and each 'long black hair upon his head hung down as straight as any plummet line'. (21).

Scadgers, Lady (HT) An 'immensely fat old woman, with an inordinate appetite for butcher's meat, and a mysterious leg which had now refused to get out of bed

for fourteen years'. She was a relative of Mrs Sparsit, whose marriage she had arranged. After Mr Sparsit's death, his widow began a 'deadly feud' with Lady Scadgers, which continued daily when Bounderby dismissed Mrs Sparsit from his employment and she went back to live with her. (I: 7; II: 8; III: 9)

Scaley, Mr (NN) The bailiff who serves

a writ of execution on the Mantalinis, when they owe 'Fifteen hundred and twenty-seven pound, four and ninepence ha'penny.' (21)

Schutz, Mr (RP) One of the passengers on the *Halsewell*. ('The Long Voyage')

Scott, Tom (OCS) An 'amphibious boy' employed at Quilp's Wharf. He is 'of an eccentric spirit' and enjoys tumbling and standing on his head, much to Quilp's annoyance. But he shed tears at the inquest on Quilp's body. He then 'began to tumble for his bread' and for the purposes of advancement assumed an Italian name. (4–6, 11, 13, 49–51, 67, 73)

Screwzer, Tommy (DS) One of Cousin Feenix's many acquaintances, 'a man of an extremely bilious habit'. (61)

Scroo, Mr (MP) A vice-president of the Display of Models and Mechanical Science at the second meeting of the Mudfog Association.

Scrooge, Ebenezer (CB) A misanthropic money-lender, whose name (one of Dickens's most ingenious inventions) has become an eponym for 'miser'. 'Oh! but he was a tight-fisted hand at the grindstone. Scrooge! a squeezing, wrenching, grasping, scraping, clutching, covetous old sinner! Hard and sharp as flint, from which no steel had ever struck out generous fire; secret, and self-contained, and solitary as an oyster. The cold within him froze his old features, nipped his pointed nose, shrivelled his cheek, stiffened his gait; made his eyes red, his thin lips blue; and spoke out shrewdly in his grating voice. A frosty rime was on his head, and on his eyebrows, and his wiry chin. He carried his own low temperature always about with him; he iced his office in the dog-days, and didn't thaw it one degree at Christmas.' On Christmas Eve, Scrooge calls Christmas a 'humbug', and grudgingly allows Bob Cratchit, his

clerk, to have the next day off. That night he is visited by the ghost of Jacob Marley, his former partner, and then by three Spirits in succession (the Ghosts of Christmas Past, Christmas Present and Christmas Yet to Come), who show him scenes of his youth, the present day and times after his death. Scrooge is thereupon converted into a happy and generous man and immediately buys a big prize turkey for the Cratchits' Christmas dinner. 'He became as good a friend, as good a master, and as good a man, as the good old city [London] knew, or any other good old city, town, or borough, in the good old world.' (*A Christmas Carol*).

Scuttlewig, The Duke of (SYC) A nobleman with whom the egotistical husband claims to be on a familiar footing. ('The Egotistical Young Couple')

Seraphina (CS) A schoolmaster's beautiful daughter, who was the heroine of Jeremy Lirriper's tale. ('Mrs Lirriper's Lodgings')

Sharp, Mr (DC) The 'first master' at Mr Creakle's school, Salem House. 'He was a limp, delicate-looking gentleman, I [i.e., David Copperfield] thought, with a good deal of nose, and a way of carrying his head on one side, as if it were a little too heavy for him. His hair was very smooth and wavy; but I was informed by the very first boy who came back that it was a wig (a second-hand one *he* said), and that Mr Sharp went out every Saturday afternoon to get it curled.' (6, 7, 9)

Sharpeye (UT) A policeman in the Liverpool police force with 'a skilful and quite professional way of opening doors'. ('Poor Mercantile Jack').

Shepherd, Miss (DC) A boarder at the Misses Nettingall's establishment, whom the youthful David Copperfield adores

Figure 29 Ebenezer Scrooge and Marley's Ghost by John Leech

for a while. 'She is a little girl, in a spencer [i.e., a close-fitting jacket], with a round face and curly flaxen hair.' (18)

Shepherdson (RP) A thief arrested by Sergeant Mith, who had adopted the guise of a butcher. ('Our Detective Police')

Shiny Villiam (PP) The deputy hostler at the Bull, Rochester, 'so called, probably, from his sleek hair and oily countenance'. (5)

Short (OCS) With Codlin, he is an itinerant Punch and Judy showman encountered by Little Nell and her Grandfather on their travels. Unlike his surly partner, Short was 'a little merry faced man with a twinkling eye and a red nose, who seemed to have unconsciously imbibed something of his hero's character'. His real name was Harris, 'but it had gradually merged into the less euphonious one of Trotters, which, with the prefatory adjective, Short, had been conferred upon him by reason of the small size of his legs. Short Trotters, however, being a compound name, inconvenient of use in friendly dialogue, the gentleman on whom it had been bestowed was known among his intimates either as "Short," or "Trotters," and was seldom accosted at full length as Short Trotters, except in formal conversations and on occasions of ceremony.' (16–19, 37, 73)

Signalman, the (CS) The strange, solitary signalman who tells Mr Jackson ('Barbox Brothers') of the warning spectre he has twice seen and who (in fulfilment of the prophecy) is killed by a train. ('Mugby Junction')

Sikes, Bill (OT) A coarse, brutal burglar, who is one of Fagin's associates. He was 'a stoutly-built fellow of about five-and-thirty', dressed in frayed and dirty clothes, with 'a broad heavy countenance with a beard of three days' growth: and two scowling eyes'. Bill Sikes is invariably accompanied by his white, shaggy dog, Bulls-eye. With Crackit, he forces Oliver Twist to take part in the unsuccessful burglary of the Maylies' house. When Sikes hears Noah Claypole's account of Nancy's meeting with Rose Maylie and Mr Brownlow on London Bridge, he is so enraged at her apparent treachery that he clubs her to death. After the murder, his desperate flight from London ends at Jacob's Island, where in his frantic efforts to jump from a house-roof with a rope he hangs himself. His dog falls to his death at the same time. In the Preface to the third edition of the novel (April 1841), Dickens replied to those readers who thought that Sikes was overdrawn because he had no redeeming traits: 'there are such men as Sikes, who, being closely followed through the same space of time, and through the same current of circumstances, would not give, by one look or action of the moment, the faintest indication of a better nature'. (13, 15–16, 19–22, 25, 28, 39, 44, 47–48, 50)

Silverman, George (GSE) He is an orphan who was brought up by Brother Hawkyard and becomes a clergyman. He falls in love with Adelina, Lady Fareway's daughter, but unselfishly sees that she marries Granville Wharton. But Lady Fareway accuses him of hypocrisy since she accuses him of being paid by Wharton to arrange the marriage. He therefore writes his explanation 'for the relief of his [own] mind, not foreseeing whether or no it will ever have a reader'.

Simmery, Frank (PP) A 'very smart young gentleman who wore his hat on his right whisker, and was lounging over the desk, killing flies with a ruler'. He was a friend of Wilkins Flasher, with whom he exchanged bets on the possibility of Boffer's killing himself. (55)

Simmonds, Miss (NN) One of Madame Mantalini's employees, who apologises to Kate Nickleby for thoughtlessly remarking on her black shawl which she was wearing in mourning for her father. (17)

Simmons (SB) The beadle of 'our parish', who suddenly dies. 'The lamented deceased had over-exerted himself, a day or two previously, in conveying an aged female, highly intoxicated, to the strong room of the workhouse.' Simmons's death causes an election for a new beadle. Kathleen Tillotson points out that Dickens's portrait of Mr Bumble was based on the 'outline sketch' of Simmons

Figure 30 Bill Sikes by George Cruikshank

(1982: viiin) ('Our Parish: The Beadle. The Parish Engine. The Schoolmaster; The Election for Beadle')

Simmons, Mrs Henrietta (OCS) One of Mrs Quilp's friends. (4)

Simmons, William (MC) Better known as Bill, he was the driver of the van on which Martin Chuzzlewit rides to Hounslow. Simmons 'was a red-faced burly young fellow; smart in his way, and with a good-humoured countenance'. (13)

Simpson, Mr (PP) One of the men Mr Pickwick was originally supposed to share a room with in the Fleet Prison. When Mr Pickwick first sees him, Simpson is 'leaning out of window as far as he could without overbalancing himself, endeavouring, with great perseverance, to spit upon the crown of the hat of a personal friend on the parade below'. (42)

Simpson, Mr (SB) A boarder at Mrs Tibbs's. 'He was as empty-headed as the great bell of St Paul's; always dressed according to the caricatures published in the monthly fashions; and spelt Character with a K.' He married Miss Julia Maplesone, but after six weeks she eloped with an officer during Mr Simpson's 'temporary sojourn in the Fleet Prison, in consequence of his inability to discharge her little mantua-maker's bill'. But he later became an author of fashionable novels. ('Tales: The Boarding-House')

Single Gentleman, the (OCS) The mysterious stranger who becomes the Brasses' lodger. He 'was a brown-faced sun-burnt man', choleric in some respects but good-humoured in others. He befriends Dick Swiveller, who is impressed by his multi-chambered, portable 'temple' in which he makes coffee and cooks food, and is fascinated by Punch and Judy shows. Having taken an active part in tracing the whereabouts of Little Nell and her Grandfather, he reveals that he is the latter's younger brother. After the deaths of Little Nell and her Grandfather, 'it was his chief delight' to retrace their journey, 'to halt where they had halted, sympathise where they had suffered, and rejoice where they had been made glad'. In *Master Humphrey's Clock*, in the paragraphs between the ending of *The Old Curiosity Shop* and the beginning of *Barnaby Rudge*, Master Humphrey, the original narrator of the novel, identifies himself as the Single Gentleman. (34–38, 40–41, 47–48, 55–56, 66, 69–73)

Skettles, Sir Barnet (DS) A Member of Parliament and the father of one of the pupils at Doctor Blimber's school, where Paul Dombey is sent. 'Sir Barnet and Lady Skettles, very good people, resided in a pretty villa at Fulham, on the banks of the Thames . . . Sir Barnet Skettles expressed his personal consequence chiefly through an antique gold snuff-box, and a ponderous silk handkerchief, which he had an imposing manner of drawing out of his pocket like a banner, and using with both hands at once. Sir Barnet's object in life was constantly to extend the range of his acquaintance.' Florence Dombey briefly stays with them during the period of her loneliness. (14, 18, 23–24, 28, 60)

Skewton, the Honourable Mrs (DS) The mother of Edith (later, the second Mrs Dombey), whom Mr Dombey and Major Bagstock meet with her daughter in Leamington Spa: 'Although the lady was not young, she was very blooming in the face – quite rosy – and her dress and attitude were perfectly juvenile . . . Her attitude in the wheeled chair (which she never varied) was one in which she had been taken in a barouche, some fifty years before [when she was twenty], by a then fashionable artist who had appended to his published sketch the name of Cleopatra: in consequence of a discovery made by the critics of the time, that it bore an exact resemblance to that Princess as she reclined on board the galley.' Mrs Skewton affects simplicity and 'heart': 'What I have ever sighed for, has been to retreat to a Swiss farm, and live entirely surrounded by cows – and china.' On a visit to Warwick Castle, she claims to admire the Tudor past and to 'doat' on King Henry VIII: 'So bluff! . . . So burly. So truly English. Such a picture, too, he makes, with his dear little peepy eyes, and his benevolent chin!' She has an

Figure 31 Edith, Withers, Mrs Skewton, the Native, Major Bagstock, and Mr
Dombey by Hablot K. Browne (Phiz)

arch, flirtatious manner, especially when addressing Major Bagstock, but she ruthlessly schemes to ensure that her daughter marries the wealthy Mr Dombey, thus incurring Edith's bitter scorn. Mrs Skewton's appearance and speech become even more grotesque when she suffers a stroke: 'They took her to pieces in very shame, and put the little of her that was real on a bed.' She dies soon afterwards, haunted by her fear of a stone arm raised to strike her, and is forgiven by Edith. Kilton says she was based on 'a Mrs Campbell, a lady well known at Leamington' (1906: 13). (21, 26–28, 30–31, 35–37, 40–41)

Skiffins, Miss (GE) She 'was of a wooden appearance', with a 'figure very like a boy's kite', and dressed (when Pip first saw her) in an orange gown and green gloves. 'But she seemed to be a good sort of fellow, and showed a high regard for the Aged [i.e., Mr Wemmick's father].' In a memorable episode, she and Wemmick later marry at a church in Camberwell Green. (37, 55)

Skimpin, Mr (PP) Serjeant Buzfuz's junior in the trial of Bardell v. Pickwick. (34)

Skimpole, Harold (BH) A friend of Mr Jarndyce, who indulgently looks upon him as a child: 'He is grown up – he is at least as old as I am – but in simplicity, and freshness, and enthusiasm, and a fine guileless inaptitude for all worldly affairs, he is a perfect child.' Esther Summerson is at first enchanted with him: 'He was a little bright creature, with a rather large head; but a delicate face, and a sweet voice, and there was a perfect charm in him. All he said was so free from effort and spontaneous, and was said with such a captivating gaiety, that it was fascinating to hear him talk. Being of a more slender figure that Mr Jarndyce, and having a richer complexion, with browner hair, he looked younger. Indeed, he had more the appearance, in all respects, of a damaged young man, than a well-preserved elderly one.' Skimpole charmingly and ingeniously excuses his selfishness: 'I almost feel as if *you* ought to be grateful to *me*, for giving you the opportunity of enjoying the luxury of generosity.' He has three daughters, Laura, Kitty and Arethusa, who represent Beauty, Sentiment and Comedy. His wife had 'once been a beauty, but was now a delicate high-nosed invalid, suffering under a complication of disorders'. To Esther's distress, Skimpole sponges on Richard Carstone, introduces him to Mr Vholes (in exchange for £5), and encourages Richard's optimism about the outcome of the case of Jarndyce v. Jarn-

dyce. Bribed by Inspector Bucket, Skimpole enables him to take Jo away from Bleak House. At long last, a coolness arises between Mr Jarndyce and Skimpole, who in a diary and letters published after his death refers to Mr Jarndyce as 'the Incarnation of Selfishness'. Dickens based Harold Skimpole on Leigh Hunt (1784–1859). John Forster and Bryan Waller Procter ('Barry Cornwall') persuaded Dickens to tone down his first sketch of the character, but Forster still expressed his disapproval: 'Upon the whole the alterations were considerable, but the radical wrong remained. The pleasant sparkling airy talk, which could not be mistaken, identified with odious qualities a friend only known to the writer by attractive ones, and for this there was no excuse. Perhaps the only person acquainted with the original who failed to recognise the copy, was the original himself (a common case); but good-natured friends in time told Hunt everything, and painful explanations followed, where nothing was possible to Dickens but what amounted to a friendly evasion of the points really at issue' (1928: Book 6, Ch. 7). On the other hand, many readers have been delighted by Dickens's presentation. Sir Osbert Sitwell, for one, was entranced by Skimpole's 'exquisite conversations': 'Seldom, if ever, has the talk of a brilliant conversationalist been wafted across to us so naturally, so successfully from the printed page' (1948: ix). (6, 8–9, 15, 18, 31, 37, 43–44, 57, 61)

Slackbridge (HT) The demagogic orator of the United Aggregate Tribunal, who denounces Stephen Blackpool as a traitor to the workmen's union. 'An ill-made, high-shouldered man, with lowering brows, and his features crushed into an habitually sour expression, he contrasted most unfavourably, even in his mongrel dress, with the great body of his hearers in their plain working clothes.' Slackbridge later condemns Stephen as a thief and 'a fester and a wound upon the noble character of the Coketown operative'. In Raymond Williams's opinion, 'the trade unions are dismissed [by Dickens] by a stock Victorian reaction, with the agitator Slackbridge' (1961: 107). (II; 4; III: 4)

Sladdery, Mr (BH) A fashionable London librarian, who boasts of his 'high connexion'. (2, 58)

Slammer, Doctor (PP) The 'surgeon to the 97th'. He was 'a little fat man, with a ring of upright black hair round his head, and an extensive bald plain on the top of it'. He is infuriated when Jingle (wearing Mr Winkle's coat) dances with Mrs Budger, the 'little old widow' to whom Doctor Slammer has been paying devoted attention. He therefore challenges Mr Winkle to a duel but good-humouredly apologises when he discovers the mistake of identity. He is said to be based on Doctor Lamert, the second husband of Dickens's aunt, and the father of James Lamert. (2, 3)

Slang, Lord (SYC) One of the egotistical gentleman's supposed acquaintances. ('The Egotistical Couple')

Slap (MND) An actor whose stage name was Formiville and who lives by practising extortion.

Slasher, Mr (PP) A surgeon at St Bartholomew's Hospital, who, in the opinion of Jack Hopkins, is the best 'operator' alive: 'Took a boy's leg out of the socket last week – boy ate five apples and a ginger bread cake – exactly two minutes after it was all over, boy said that he wouldn't lie there to be made game of, and he'd tell his mother if they didn't begin.' This anecdote reminds us of the premium put on speed in surgical operations in those days before anaesthetics were in use. (32)

Slaughter, Lieutenant (SB) Captain

Waters' friend, who hears Mr Cymon Tuggs's cough and reveals him hiding behind a curtain. ('Tales: The Tuggses at Ramsgate')

Sleary, Mr (HT) The proprietor of 'Sleary's Horse-riding' circus. He was stout, 'with one fixed eye, and one loose eye, a voice (if it can be called so) like the efforts of a broken old pair of bellows, a flabby surface, and a muddled head which was never sober and never drunk'. Sleary was 'troubled with asthma' and his breath 'came far too thick and heavy for the letter s'. He is a kind-hearted man, willing to protect Sissy Jupe after the disappearance of her father (who was one of his circus riders) but agreeing (with some reluctance) to her going to live with the Gradgrinds. He gives refuge to Tom Gradgrind in the circus when Tom is on the run and helps him to leave the country. His final words to Mr Gradgrind are the key to Dickens's message in *Hard Times*: 'Don't be croth with uth poor vagabondth. People muth be amuthed. They can't be alwayth a working, they an't made for it. You mutht have uth, Thquire. Do the withe thing and the kind thing too, and make the beth of uth; not the wurtht!' Mr Sleary's daughter, Josephine, marries E.W.B. Childers. (I: 3, 6; III: 7–8)

Sliderskew, Peg (NN) Arthur Gride's housekeeper. She was 'a short thin weasen blear-eyed old woman, palsy-stricken and hideously ugly'. Peg Sliderskew steals a box of Gride's documents, including a will relating to Madeline Bray's inheritance. Squeers is employed to find her and retrieve the document but is foiled in the nick of time by Nicholas Nickleby and Frank Cheeryble. She is apprehended for the theft and sentenced to transportation: 'Mrs Sliderskew went beyond the seas at nearly the same time as Mr Squeers, and in the course of nature never returned.' (51, 53–54, 56–57, 59, 65)

Slingo (LD) A dealer in horses, who after his release from the Marshalsea is going to give Tip Dorrit 'a berth'. (I: 7)

Slinkton, Julius (HD) A 'well-spoken gentleman' with 'insinuating manners', who murders his niece for her insurance money, plans also to murder her sister, but commits suicide when unmasked by Meltham. It is sometimes said that Dickens based Slinkton on Thomas Wainewright (1794–1852), the notorious poisoner.

Slithers (MHC) Master Humphrey's barber, who helps his housekeeper entertain Sam and Tony Weller and whose occupation prompts Sam's story of Jinkinson. (5)

Sliverstone, Mr and Mrs (SYC) All the 'lady's egotism is about her husband [a clergyman], and all the gentleman's is about his wife'. ('The Egotistical Couple')

Sloppy (OMF) A 'love-child', found in the street, brought up in the Poor-House, and taken care of by Betty Higden. He was 'a very long boy, with a very little head, and an open mouth of disproportionate capacity that seemed to assist his eyes in staring at the visitors [Mrs Boffin and John Rokesmith] ... A considerable capital of knee and elbow and wrist and ankle had Sloppy, and he didn't know how to dispose of it to the best advantage, but was always investing it in wrong securities, and so getting himself into embarrassed circumstances. Full-Private Number One in the Awkward Squad of the rank and file of life was Sloppy, and yet had his glimmering notions of standing true to the Colours.' One of his chief occupations is turning the mangle, but he is also quite accomplished at reading the newspapers aloud, since as Betty Higden says (in words that T.S. Eliot admired and used as the title of the first version of *The Waste Land*): 'He

do the Police in different voices.' The Boffins later employ him as a servant, much to his delight. As part of Mr Boffin's plotting, Sloppy is disguised as a dustman to observe Silas Wegg's actions and after the exposure of Wegg's infamous designs Sloppy throws him into a scavenger's cart. Mr Boffin pays for Sloppy's training as a cabinet-maker. An affectionate conversational exchange between Sloppy and Jenny Wren may hint at a future marriage between them: 'there's both *my* hands, Miss, and I'll soon come back again'. (I: 16; II: 9–10, 14; III: 9; IV: 3, 14, 16)

Slout (OT) The master of the workhouse where Oliver Twist was born. On Slout's death, Mr Bumble was appointed to the position. (27)

Slowboy, Tilly (CB) A foundling who was the Peerybingles' maidservant, who was of 'a spare and straight shape'. Though she had 'several times imperilled [their baby's] short life' through her clumsiness, her actions 'were the honest results of Tilly Slowboy's constant astonishment at finding herself so kindly treated, and installed in such a comfortable home'. (*The Cricket on the Hearth*)

Sludberry, Thomas (SB) In the Court of Doctors' Commons, he was found guilty of using 'heinous and sinful expressions' to Michael Bumple (including the words 'You be blowed') and was accordingly sentenced to 'excommunication for a fortnight' and the payment of costs. ('Scenes: Doctors' Commons')

Sluffen, Mr (SB) A celebrated chimney-sweep of Adam-and-Eve Court, who made an impassioned speech at an 'anniversary dinner at White Conduit House' in defence of the practice of using climbing boys: 'and as to kerhewelty to the boys, everybody in the chimbley line know'd as vell as he did, that they liked the climbin' better nor nuffin as wos'. ('Scenes: The First of May')

Slug, Mr (MP) A member of the Mudfog Association, who was 'celebrated for his statistical researches'. At its first meeting, he reported on 'the state of infant education among the middle classes of London'.

Slum, Mr (OCS) A 'tallish gentleman with a hook nose and black hair, dressed in a military surtout very short and tight in the sleeves, and which had once been frogged and braided all over, but was now sadly shorn of its garniture and quite threadbare'. He composes verses to advertise products, although Mrs Jarley, the proprietor of the travelling waxworks show, finds him very expensive. According to John Forster, Dickens modelled Mr Slum on the poets regularly employed by the firm of Warren, in whose blacking warehouse he had been employed as a boy. (1928: Book 1, Ch. 2). In the 'Seven Dials' scene in *Sketches by Boz*, Dickens describes a 'shabby-genteel' man who 'writes poems for Mr Warren, according to rumours'.(28, 47)

Slumkey, the Hon. Samuel (PP) The Blue candidate who defeats Horatio Fizkin in the Eatanswill parliamentary election. (14)

Slummery, Mr (SYC) A 'clever painter', who is a friend of the Bobtail Widgers. ('The Plausible Couple')

Slummintowkens, The (PP) Acquaintances of the Nupkins family. (25)

Slurk, Mr (PP) The editor of the Eatanswill *Independent*. He has a furious quarrel and fight with his rival, Mr Pott (the editor of the Eatanswill *Gazette*) at the Saracen's Head, Towcester. Sam Weller manages to stop their fight by drawing a meal-sack over Pott's head and shoulders. (51)

Slyme, Chevy (MC) A relative of the Chuzzlewits and a friend of Montague Tigg, who says that Slyme's peculiarity is that 'he is always waiting round the corner'. He has 'sharp features' and 'straggling red whiskers and frowzy hair'. 'Wretched and forlorn as he looked, Mr Slyme had once been, in his way, the choicest of swaggerers . . . And now so abject and so pitiful was he – at once so maudlin, insolent, beggarly, and proud – that even his friend and parasite [Tigg], standing erect beside him, swelled into a Man by contrast.' At the end of the novel Chevy Slyme reappears as the chief officer of the party that comes to arrest Jonas Chuzzlewit. Jonas gives him £100 to let him have time to kill himself. But Slyme thrusts the money back into Jonas's pocket before he dies. (4, 7, 51)

Smalder girls, the (DS) Acquaintances of Cousin Feenix, whom he sees while sitting in the mourning coach at Mrs Skewton's funeral. (41)

Smallweed, Bart (BH) Joshua Smallweed's grandson, Bartholomew. 'Whether young Smallweed (metaphorically called Small and eke Chick Weed, as it were jocularly to express a fledgeling) were ever a boy, is much doubted in Lincoln's Inn. He is now something under fifteen, and an old limb of the law . . . He is a town-made article, of small stature and weazen features; but may be perceived from a considerable distance by means of his very tall hat. To become a Guppy is the object of his ambition.' Nevertheless, Bart occasionally advises Guppy 'on difficult points in private life'. But a coolness arises between them mainly because of Guppy and Weevle's reticence about their investigations into the mysteries relating to Captain Hawdon. (20, 21, 32, 33, 39, 55)

Smallweed, Grandfather, and family (BH) A cunning, ruthless, crippled old moneylender and dealer in bills, Joshua

Smallweed is constantly quarrelling with his decrepit wife, at whom he hurls cushions and other missiles (even including Judy, his grand-daughter, on one occasion). Dickens describes him with the same relish and touches of black comedy that he used in his depiction of Quilp. The Smallweeds live in a 'grim, hard, uncouth parlour, only ornamented with the coarsest of baize table-covers, and the hardest of sheet-iron tea-trays, and offering in its decorative character no bad allegorical representation of Grandfather Smallweed's mind'. Because of his threats to 'smash' and 'crumble' George concerning the money he (Smallweed) has lent Matthew Bagnet, George agrees to hand over Captain Hawdon's writings to Mr Tulkinghorn. Grandfather Smallweed's further involvement with Lady Dedlock comes about when he and his family find further evidence among the property of Krook (who was Mrs Smallweed's brother). But the combined efforts of him, the Chadbands and Mrs Snagsby to sell the evidence at a high price to Sir Leicester Dedlock are not as profitable as he wished, owing to Inspector Bucket's intervention. Smallweed also finds a will among Krook's papers, which Bucket (after paying him £20) forces him to yield to Mr Jarndyce. Besides his wife, the other members of Smallweed's family are Bart (Bartholomew, his grandson), who was for a time an admiring associate of Guppy, and Judy (Judith, Bart's twin sister). Doris Alexander argues that Dickens based Grandfather Smallweed on Samuel Rogers (1763–1855), the poet, who was one of his close acquaintances. Similarly, she suggests, he could have based Grandmother Smallweed on Rogers's wife (1991: 35–40). (21, 26, 27, 33, 34, 39, 54, 62)

Smangle, Mr (PP) One of the prisoners with whom Mr Pickwick shares a room on his first night in the Fleet Prison. 'There was a rakish, vagabond smart-ness, and a kind of boastful rascality, about the whole man, that was worth a mine of gold.' (41, 42, 44)

Smart, Tom (PP) The hero of 'The Bagman's Story'. (14)

Smauker, John (PP) Mr Bantam's self-important footman, who invites Sam Weller to 'a friendly swarry' in Bath. (35, 37)

Smif, Putnam (MC) A young American, who writes to Martin Chuzzlewit asking whether he knows 'any member of the Congress in England' who will pay his expenses to that country and for the following six months. (22)

Smiggers, Joseph, Esq. (PP) The Perpetual Vice-President of the Pickwick Club. (1)

Smike (NN) A pathetic, half-witted boy, whom Nicholas Nickleby encounters at Dotheboys Hall. 'Although he could not have been less than eighteen or nineteen years old, and was tall for his age, he wore a skeleton suit, such as is usually put upon very little boys.' Since nobody has paid his school fees for six years, Smike is treated as a slave by Squeers, who starts to beat him mercilessly when he is caught after trying to run away. When Nicholas leaves the school, after thrashing Squeers and so saving Smike from further punishment, Smike devotedly follows him. Rather unbelievably, Smike manages to act for Mr Crummles (the part of the Apothecary in *Romeo and Juliet*). Smike was recaptured by Squeers in London but was quickly rescued by John Browdie. He pines away and dies, having told Nicholas that he loved Kate Nickleby 'with all the ardour of a nature concentrated in one absorbing, hopeless, secret passion'. After Smike's death, it is revealed that he was the son of Ralph Nickleby and was therefore Nicholas's cousin. Smallbones, in Captain Marryat's *Snarleyyow* (1836–37), has been suggested as a prototype of

Figure 32 Mr Smith, the Poor Clerk by George Cruikshank

Smike, although the likenesses may be coincidental. (7–8, 12–13, 15–16, 20, 22–23, 25, 29–30, 32–33, 35, 37–40, 42, 45–46, 49, 55, 58–60, 65)

Smith, Mr (MP) A member of the Mud-fog Association.

Smith, Mr (SB) A new Member of Parliament with 'an air of enchanting urbanity'. ('Scenes: A Parliamentary Sketch')

Smith, Mr (SB) A 'tall, thin, pale person, in a black coat, scanty grey trousers, little pinched-up gaiters, and brown beaver gloves', who leads a lonely life as a clerk in London. 'Poor, harmless creatures such men are; contented but not happy; broken-spirited and humbled, they may feel no pain, but they never know pleasure.' ('Characters: Thoughts about People')

Smithers, Miss (PP) One of the schoolgirls who boarded at Westgate House. When she discovered Mr Pickwick behind the door, she 'proceeded to go into hysterics of four young lady power'. (16)

Smithers, Miss Emily (SB) The 'belle' of Minerva House, the 'finishing establishment for young ladies' kept by the Misses Crumpton. ('Tales: Sentiment')

Smithers, Robert (SB) The city clerk who made a night of it with his close friend, Thomas Potter. After their drunk and disorderly conduct, both men were reprimanded and fined. ('Characters: Making a Night of It')

Smithie, Mr, and family (PP) Mr and Mrs Smithie and the Miss Smithies attended the ball at Rochester. Mr Smithie, who 'bowed deferentially to Sir Thomas Clubber', was 'something in the yard [i.e., the Chatham Dockyard]'. (2)

Smorltork, Count (PP) A 'well-whiskered individual in a foreign uniform', who was one of Mrs Leo Hunter's guests at her *fête champêtre*. She informs Pickwick that he is a famous foreigner who is 'gathering materials for his great work on England'. Dickens modelled Count Smorltork on Count Puckler-Muskau (1785–1871) and Professor Friedrich von Raumer, both of whom published books on their tours of England. (15)

Smouch, Mr (PP) A 'shabby-looking man in a brown great-coat shorn of divers buttons', who was Mr Namby's

assistant when the latter arrested Mr Pickwick. (40)

Smuggins, Mr (SB) A singer at a London 'harmonic meeting'. After 'a considerable quantity of coughing by way of symphony, and a most facetious sniff or two, which afford general delight, [he] sings a comic song, with a fal-de-ral – tol-de-ral at the end of every verse, much longer than the verse itself'. ('Scenes: The Streets – Night')

Snagsby, Mr and Mrs (BH) Snagsby is a law-stationer in Cook's Court, Cursitor Street. He is 'a mild, bald, timid man with a shining head, and a scrubby clump of black hair sticking out at the back. He tends to meekness and obesity.' Snagsby is dominated by his wife. He employed Nemo (Captain Hawdon) as a law-writer and (despite his wife's angry disapproval) was a kind friend to Jo, the crossing-sweeper. Snagsby becomes involved at several points with the mystery associated with Lady Dedlock, a situation that bewilders him. He feels that 'he is a party to some dangerous secret without knowing what it is'. Hortense's 'hovering' about his offices embarrasses him and excites feelings of jealousy in his wife. Mrs Snagsby is 'something too violently compressed about the waist, and with a sharp nose like a sharp autumn evening, inclining to be frosty towards the end.' She is a follower of Mr Chadband ('"My little woman," says Mr Snagsby to the sparrows in Staple Inn, "likes to have her religion rather sharp, you see!"'). She becomes highly suspicious of her husband's involvement with the Lady Dedlock mystery, 'taking everywhere, her own dense atmosphere of dust, arising from the ceaseless working of her mill of jealousy'. (10–11, 19–20, 22, 25, 32–33, 42, 47, 54, 59)

Snap, Betsy (CS) A 'withered, hard-favoured, yellow old woman', who was

Uncle Chill's domestic servant. ('The Poor Relation's Story')

Snawley, Mr (NN) A 'sleek and sanctified gentleman', who sends his two stepsons to Dotheboys Hall and becomes a friend and confederate of Mr Squeers. Ralph Nickleby employs him to pose as Smike's father. But when Snawley is told 'that Squeers was in custody – he was not told for what – that worthy, first extorting a promise that he should be kept harmless, declared the whole tale concerning Smike to be a fiction and forgery, and implicated Ralph Nickleby to the fullest extent'. (4, 38–39, 45, 56, 59)

Snevellici, Miss (NN) One of the actresses in Mr Vincent Crummles's company. She 'could do anything, from a medley dance to Lady Macbeth, and also always played some part in blue silk knee-smalls at her benefit'. In Mr Crummles's opinion, she is 'quite a genius, that girl'. Miss Snevellici tries to flirt with Nicholas Nickleby, but she marries 'an affluent young wax-chandler who had supplied the theatre with candles'. Her father and mother were also members of the company. (23–25, 29–30, 48)

Snewkes, Mr (NN) One of the guests at the Kenwigs's party for their wedding anniversary. (14)

Snicks, Mr (PP) The Life Office Secretary, who was a guest at Mr Perker's dinner party. (47)

Sniff, Mr and Mrs (CS) They both work at Mugby Junction. The 'boy at Mugby' says that Mr Sniff is 'a regular insignificant cove', who looks after 'the sawdust department in a back room' and sometimes helps 'behind the counter [of the refreshment room] with a corkscrew'. Mrs Sniff, who works in the refreshment room, was different, and when 'Our Missis' went away she 'did hold the public in check most beautiful'. ('Mugby Junction')

Sniggs, Mr (MP) Mr Tulrumble's predecessor as Mayor of Mudfog, who dies in office.

Snigsworth, Lord (OMF) Mr Twemlow's first cousin. Because of this relationship, Twemlow's acquaintance is valued by the Veneerings. Snigsworth does not appear in the novel but his awe-inspiring presence is often felt. (I: 2; 10; II: 3, 5, 16; III: 13)

Snipe, the Hon, Wilmot (PP) An ensign of the 97th, who attends the ball at Rochester and is mistaken by Mr Tupman for a 'little boy with ... light hair and pink eyes, in a fancy dress'. (2)

Snitchey, Jonathan (CB) A partner in the law firm of Snitchey and Craggs, Doctor Jeddler's solicitors. Mrs Snitchey, his wife, 'by a dispensation not uncommon in the affairs of life, was on principle suspicious of Mr Craggs'. (*The Battle of Life*)

Snivey, Sir Hookham (MP) A member of the Mudfog Association.

Snobb, the Hon. Mr (NN) A 'gentleman with the neck of a stork and the legs of no animal in particular', who was one of the guests to whom Ralph Nickleby introduced Kate Nickleby at his dinner party. (19)

Snodgrass, Augustus (PP) A member of the Pickwick Club, Mr Snodgrass is one of Mr Pickwick's three companions on his travels, but he plays a less prominent part in the novel than Mr Tupman and Mr Winkle. He is described as 'the poetic Snodgrass' and on his first appearance is 'poetically enveloped in a mysterious blue coat with a canine-skin collar'. He falls in love with Emily Wardle, marries her, and both of them settle at Dingley Dell. (1–9, 11–15, 18–19, 22, 24–26, 28, 30–32, 34–35, 44, 47, 54, 57)

Snore, Professor (MP) He presides over the proceedings of the Zoology and Botany section at the first meeting of the Mudfog Association.

Snorflerer, the Dowager Lady (SYC) An acquaintance of the egotistical couple. ('The Egotistical Couple')

Snow, Tom (CS) The black steward on the *Golden Mary*. ('The Wreck of the Golden Mary')

Snubbin, Serjeant (PP) Mr Pickwick's counsel for defence in the trial of Bardell v. Pickwick. 'A lantern-faced, sallow-complexioned man', Snubbin has an abstracted air when he reluctantly agrees to see Mr Pickwick before the case. Although Snubbin does his best to defend Mr Pickwick, he is outshone in the courtroom by Serjeant Buzfuz. (31, 34)

Snuffim, Sir Tumley (NN) Mrs Wititterly's doctor. According to her husband, she is his favourite patient. His opinion is that Kate Nickleby 'rather disagreed with Mrs Wititterly's constitution'. (28, 33)

Snuffletoffle, Mr Q.J. (MP) At the second meeting of the Mudfog Association, he tells the Umbugology and Ditchwaterisics Section that he is unacquainted 'with no authenticated instance' of a pony's simultaneously winking his eye and whisking his tail.

Snugglewood (RP) One of the doctors consulted by Our Bore. His diagnosis is 'Brain!' ('Our Bore')

Snuphanuph, the Dowager Lady (PP) One of the ladies with whom Mr Pickwick plays whist at Bath. (35, 36)

Soemup, Doctor (MP) He presides over the Anatomy and Medicine section at the second meeting of the Mudfog Association.

Sophia (MC) The brass-and-copper founder's daughter, who is Ruth Pinch's pupil. She was 'a premature little woman of thirteen years old'. (9, 36)

Sophy (CS) Doctor Marigold's adopted deaf-and-dumb daughter, whom he bought from Mim. ('Doctor Marigold')

Sophy (CS) One of Mrs Lirriper's servants, who was 'a girl so willing that I called her Willing Sophy down upon her knees scrubbing early and late and ever cheerful but always smiling with a black face'. ('Mrs Lirriper's Lodgings')

Southcote, Mr (RP) A writer of begging-letters, who turns out to be a fraudster. ('The Begging-Letter Writer')

Sowerberry, Mr and Mrs (OT) Mr Sowerberry was the parochial undertaker, to whom Oliver Twist was apprenticed for a short time. He was 'a tall, gaunt, large-jointed man, attired in a suit of thread-bare black, with darned cotton stockings of the same colour, and shoes to answer'. Despite the melancholy nature of his occupation (and his name), Mr Sowerberry was 'in general rather given to professional jocosity'. His harsh wife fed Oliver on the 'cold bits that were put by for Trip [the dog]' and makes him sleep among the coffins in the shop. She was 'a short, thin, squeezed-up woman, with a vixenish countenance'. (4–7, 27, 51)

Sownds, Mr (DS) The 'orthodox and corpulent' beadle who officiates at the church where various ceremonies in the Dombey family take place: Paul's christening, Mr Dombey's marriage to Edith, and Walter Gay's marriage to Florence. (5, 31, 57)

Sowster (MP) The beadle of Oldcastle, where the second meeting of the Mudfog Association takes place. He is a fat, double-chinned man with 'a very red nose, which he attributes to a habit of early rising – so red, indeed, that but for this explanation I should have supposed it to proceed from occasional inebriety'.

Sparkins, Horatio (SB) A young man, who greatly impresses the Malderton family with his genteel manners and apparent connections with high society. He was the 'most gentleman-like young man' Mrs Malderton had ever seen and she has hopes of him as a suitable match for her daughter, Teresa. But the ladies' illusions are shattered when they find him working as an assistant in a linen-draper's shop. His real name turns out to be Samuel Smith. ('Tales: Horatio Sparkins')

Sparkler, Edmund (LD) A vacuous young man-about-town, who is the son of Mrs Merdle by her first marriage. Some of his utterances perfectly represent the mode of speaking cultivated by the swells of the mid-Victorian period: '"I couldn't," said Mr Sparkler, after feeling his pulse as before, "couldn't undertake to say what led to it – 'cause memory desperate loose. But being in company with the brother of a doosed fine gal – well educated too – with no biggod nonsense about her."' He becomes infatuated with Fanny Dorrit when he sees her dance on the stage but Mrs Merdle buys her off with a bracelet. But when the Dorrits have come into their money, Fanny realises that she has now become 'a rather desirable match for a noodle', and the two get married. Mr Sparkler had been made one of the Lords of the Circumlocution Office. 'It was just as well [in Mrs Merdle's opinion] that he should have something to do, and it was just as well that he should have something for doing it.' After the crash of Merdle's enterprises, Edmund Sparkler finds it difficult to keep the peace between his wife and mother but humbly inclines to 'the opinion that they were both remarkably fine women, and that there was no nonsense about either of them – for which gentle recommendation they united in falling upon him frightfully'. Nevertheless, his post in the Circumlocution Office remains secure, since the lordship 'was fortunately one of those shelves on which a gentleman is considered to be put away for life, unless there should be reasons for hoisting him up with the Barnacle crane to a more lucrative height'. (I: 20–21, 33; II: 3, 5–7, 11–12, 14–16, 18, 24, 33)

Sparks, Tom (SG) The boots at the St James's Arms.

Sparsit, Mrs (HT) The elderly lady who presides over Mr Bounderby's establishment, 'in consideration of a certain annual stipend'. She was highly connected in that her great-aunt was Lady Scadgers and her late husband had been 'by the mother's side . . . a Powler'. But after the death of her husband (who was fifteen years younger than she was), Mrs Sparsit 'fell presently at deadly feud with her only relative, Lady Scadgers; and, partly to spite her ladyship, and partly to maintain herself, went out at a salary'. Her face is remarkable for 'the Coriolanian style of nose and the dense black eyebrows which had captivated Sparsit'. Mrs Sparsit, who would like to marry the wealthy (though vulgar) Mr Bounderby, is angry and jealous because of his marriage to the youthful Louisa Gradgrind. She spies on Louisa and James Harthouse and imagines that there will be a disgraceful outcome of their apparent friendship: 'She erected in her mind a mighty Staircase, with a dark pit of shame and ruin at the bottom; and down those stairs, from day to day and hour to hour, she saw Louisa coming.' But her blunders over their supposed elopement (which never materialises) and the identity of Mrs Pegler (who turns out to be Bounderby's mother) lead Mr Bounderby to dismiss her from his service. Mrs Sparsit goes to live with Lady Scadgers, with whom she fights 'a daily fight at the points of all the weapons in the female armoury'. (I: 7, 11, 16; II: 1, 3, 6, 8–11; III: 3, 5, 9)

Spatter, John (CS) Michael's clerk, whom he takes into partnership. John Spatter proves to be a staunch friend and the 'partnership throve well'. ('The Poor Relation's Story')

Specks, Joe (UT) The schoolfellow of the Uncommercial Traveller, who preserves tender memories of him, 'forasmuch as we had made the acquaintance of Roderick Random [the eponymous hero of Smollett's novel] together'. Revisiting Dullborough, the Uncommercial Traveller renews his acquaintance with Joe, who is the doctor there and who has married Lucy Green, the narrator's childhood sweetheart. ('Dullborough Town')

Spenlow, the Misses Clarissa and Lavinia (DC) The maiden aunts of Dora Spenlow, who goes to live with them in Putney after her father's death. Miss Clarissa Spenlow was six or eight years older than Miss Lavinia Spenlow. 'They were both upright in their carriage, formal, precise, composed, and quiet.' David Copperfield discovers that 'Miss Lavinia was an authority on the affairs of the heart, by reason of there having anciently existed a certain Mr Pidger, who played short whist, and was supposed to have been enamoured of her.' After formal deliberation, they consent to David's visiting Dora at their house. (38, 41–43)

Spenlow, Dora (later, Dora Copperfield) (DC) Mr Spenlow the proctor's daughter, with whom David Copperfield falls in love at first sight: 'I was swallowed up in an abyss of love in an instant. There was no pausing on the brink; no looking down, or looking back; I was gone, headlong, before I had sense to say a word to her.' Dora is sweet, childish, affectionate and impractical, and once married to

David (who remains devoted to her) proves to be a hopelessly inefficient housewife, despite his loving attempts to 'form her mind'. She calls herself his 'child–wife', and Miss Betsey Trotwood, who becomes fond of her (despite her feelings that the marriage was imprudent) calls her 'Little Blossom'. Dora's health slowly declines. She gives birth to a still-born child, and becomes even weaker. Just before she dies, after about two years of marriage, she tells David that she knows that she was 'such a silly creature' and confidentially urges Agnes Wickfield to marry him as his second wife. Dickens undoubtedly uses memories of Maria Beadnell in his portrayal of Dora, a portrayal that delicately mingles pathos and comedy, as Michael Slater points out (1983: 100). Chesterton asserted that 'there is nowhere in fiction where we feel so keenly the primary human instinct and principle that a marriage is a marriage and irrevocable, that such things do leave a wound and also a bond as in this case of David's short connection with his silly little wife. When all is said and done, when Dickens has done his best and his worst, when he has sentimentalised for pages and tried to tie up everything in the pink tape of optimism, the fact, in the psychology of the reader, still remains. The reader does still feel that David's marriage to Dora was a real marriage; and that his marriage to Agnes was nothing, a middle-aged compromise, a taking of the second-best, a sort of spiritualised and sublimated marriage of convenience' (1933: 133). (26, 28–29, 33–39, 41–45, 48–53, 62)

Spenlow, Francis (DC) A proctor in Doctors' Commons (in partnership with Mr Jorkins), to whom David Copperfield is articled for a fee of £1000. 'He was a little light-haired gentleman, with undeniable boots, and the stiffest of white cravats and shirt-collars. He was buttoned up mighty trim and tight, and must have taken a great deal of pains with his whiskers, which were accurately curled. His gold watch-chain was so massive, that a fancy came across me [i.e., David Copperfield], that he ought to have a sinewy golden arm, to draw it out with, like those which are put up over the gold-beaters' shops. He was got up with such care, and was so stiff, that he could hardly bend himself; being obliged, when he glanced at some papers on his desk, after sitting down in his chair, to move his whole body, from the bottom of his spine, like Punch.' He blames his unseen partner, Jorkins, for any awkward decisions that have to be made. Mr Spenlow strongly disapproves of David's relationship with Dora, his daughter, and opposes any thought of marriage between them. He is found dead by the roadside, having fallen by some means out of the phaeton he was driving. Dickens seems to have founded Spenlow on George Beadnell, Maria's father. (23, 26, 29, 33, 35, 38)

Sphynx, Sophronia (OCS) The name Dick Swiveller gives to the Marchioness (q.v.).

Spiker, Mr and Mrs Henry (DC) A solicitor and his wife, to whom 'immense deference' was shown at the Waterbrooks' dinner party. Mrs Henry Spiker was 'a very awful lady in a black velvet dress, and a great black velvet hat, whom I [i.e., David Copperfield] remember as looking like a near relation of Hamlet's – say his aunt'. Mr Spiker was 'so cold a man, that his head, instead of being grey, seemed to be sprinkled with hoar-frost'. (25)

Spottletoe, Mr and Mrs (MC) Relatives of old Martin Chuzzlewit. Mr Spottletoe was bald but had 'such big whiskers that he seemed to have stopped his hair, by the sudden application of some powerful remedy, in the very act of falling off his head, and to have fastened it irrevocably

on his face'. Mrs Spottletoe was 'much too slim for her years' and was of 'a poetical constitution'. When Mr Spottletoe hears that old Martin has left Salisbury, he furiously accuses Pecksniff of connivance in this and of having summoned the family under false pretences. (4, 54)

Sprodgkin, Mrs Sally (OMF) One of the Reverend Frank Milvey's parishioners, who bothers him about theological and spiritual matters. In Mrs Milvey's words, she is a 'marplot' and *does* worry so!' (IV: 11)

Spruggins, Thomas (SB) The unsuccessful candidate in the election of a beadle. His wife solicits votes for him. ('Our Parish: The Election for Beadle')

Spyers, Jem (OT) The police officer who discovers the truth about Conkey Chickweed's robbery. (31)

Squeers, Fanny (NN) The 23-year-old daughter of Mr and Mrs Wackford Squeers, with a harsh voice inherited from her mother and from her father 'a remarkable expression of the right eye, something akin to having none at all'. Angered by Nicholas Nickleby's spurning her amorous attentions and by his thrashing her father, Fanny writes a remarkable letter (ranking with the greatest of Dickens's linguistic inventions) to Ralph Nickleby: 'I am screaming out loud all the time I write and so is my brother which takes off my attention rather and I hope will excuse mistakes.' (7–9, 13, 15, 34, 64)

Squeers, Mrs (NN) The wife of Wackford Squeers, the proprietor of Dotheboys Hall. She was 'of a large raw-boned figure', had a hoarse voice, and was as harsh as her husband in the treatment of the boys at the school. She periodically dosed them with brimstone and treacle, 'partly because if they hadn't something or other in the way of medicine they'd be always ailing or giving a world of trouble, and partly because it spoils their appetites and comes cheaper than breakfast and dinner'. After Squeers's downfall, the boys force her to kneel and 'swallow a spoonful of the odious mixture,' but she is saved from further humiliation by John Browdie. (7–9, 13, 15, 34, 64)

Squeers, Wackford (NN) The brutal and ignorant proprietor of Dotheboys Hall, a Yorkshire boarding school, where unwanted boys were sent for various reasons. He had 'but one eye, and the popular prejudice runs in favour of two', a sinister appearance, a 'harsh voice and coarse manner'. He was 'about two or three and fifty, and a trifle below the middle size'. He explains to Nicholas Nickleby, who has just been appointed as an assistant teacher, his 'practical mode of teaching'; 'C-l-e-a-n, clean, verb active, to make bright, to scour. W-i-n, win, d-e-r, der, winder, a casement. When the boy knows this out of the book, he goes and does it.' Horrified by Squeers's cruel flogging of Smike, who had tried to run away from the school, Nicholas pinned him by the throat and 'beat the ruffian till he roared for mercy'. Squeers manages to recapture Smike in London, but only briefly, and later unsuccessfully conspires with Ralph Nickleby and Snawley to claim him as Snawley's son. He tries, on Ralph Nickleby's behalf, to recover Arthur Gride's papers from Peg Sliderskew (who had stolen them), but is caught in the act by Frank Cheeryble and Nicholas Nickleby, who fells him unconscious to the floor with a carefully aimed pair of bellows. Squeers is arrested, imprisoned and transported. He is generally assumed to be based on William Shaw, who was the proprietor of Bowes Academy in Yorkshire. Dickens and Browne (Phiz) saw him when they visited Yorkshire in 1838 to gather material for *Nicholas Nickleby*. But in his Preface to the first edition of the novel (1838), Dickens said that 'Mr Squeers is

the representative of a class, and not of an individual.' (3–9, 13, 15, 34, 38–39, 42, 44–45, 56–57, 59–60, 64–65)

Squeers, Wackford (junior) (NN) The 'juvenile son and heir of Mr Squeers', who was 'a striking likeness of his father'. He was a spoiled and spiteful boy, who eagerly looked forward to taking care of the school when he grew up: '"Oh my eye, won't I give it to the boys!" exclaimed the interesting child, grasping his father's cane. "Oh, father, won't I make 'em squeak again!"' When the boys rise in their final revolt, they duck young Wackford's head in Mrs Squeers's bowl of brimstone and treacle. (89, 13, 15, 34, 38–39, 42, 64)

Squires, Olympia (UT) The Uncommercial Traveller's childhood sweetheart. ('Birthday Celebrations')

Squod, Phil (BH) George's assistant at his Shooting Gallery. He was a little, scarred, limping man 'with a face all crushed together, who appears, from a certain blue and speckled appearance that one of his cheeks presents, to have been blown up, in the way of business, at some odd time or times.' George had found him hobbling on a couple of sticks in the street and had cheerfully given him employment. 'He has a curious way of limping round the gallery with his shoulder against the wall, and tacking off at objects he wants to lay hold of, instead of going straight to them, which has left a smear all round the four walls, conventionally called "Phil's mark."' Phil eventually becomes an odd-job man at Chesney Wold, when George moves there to attend on Sir Leicester Dedlock. (21, 24, 26, 34, 47, 66)

Stables, the Honourable Bob (BH) A connection of the Dedlock family. He 'can make warm mashes with the skill of a veterinary surgeon, and is a better shot than most gamekeepers'. He is anxious to be given 'a post of good emoluments, unaccompanied by any trouble or responsibility'. In his opinion, Lady Dedlock is 'the best-groomed woman in the whole stud'. But when she runs away he admits that he had no idea she was a 'bolter'. (2, 28, 40, 58)

Stagg (BH) The blind owner of the squalid cellar where Sim Tappertit and his fellow members of the Prentice Knights meet. He had a 'ragged head' and a 'hoary bristled chin,' and wore 'an old tie-wig as bare and frowzy as a stunted hearth-broom', Having given lodgings to Rudge, he becomes his accomplice in extorting money from Mrs Rudge, whom he tracks down to her refuge in the country. He visits Rudge in prison and suggests a devious plan, involving Mrs Rudge's denial that her husband is alive, by which he could be released – but this plan comes to nothing. Stagg is shot dead by the soldiers when they arrest Barnaby, Rudge and Hugh. (8, 18, 45–46, 62, 69)

Stalker, Inspector (RP) A 'shrewd, hardheaded Scotchman – in appearance not at all unlike a very acute, thoroughly-trained schoolmaster, from the Normal Establishment at Glasgow'. Dickens was thinking of Inspector Walker of Bow Street. ('The Detective Police')

Stalker, Mrs (RP) A dubious inhabitant of the Saint Giles district of London, who is given a warning by Inspector Field. ('On Duty with Inspector Field')

Staple, Mr (PP) A 'little man with a puffy Say-nothing-to-me,-or-I'll-contradict-you sort of countenance', who as a supporter of the Dingley Dell cricket team makes a lengthy speech proposing a toast to 'the united names of "Dumkins and Podder,"' who had distinguished themselves in the match with the All-Muggletonians. (7)

Stareleigh, Mr Justice (PP) The short,

fat judge who presided at the trial of Bardell v. Pickwick. His 'temper bordered on the irritable, and brooked not contradiction.' Philip Collins states that 'Dickens was generally thought to have caught exactly, in *Pickwick Papers*, the tones and mannerisms of Mr Justice Gazelee, who was indeed very deaf, very short, and comically pompous and eccentric.' Collins also interestingly observes that 'Mr Justice Stareleigh was the only Judge shown in action in the novels' (1964: 182). (34)

Stargazer, Mr (L) He predicts that Fanny Brown will marry Tom Grig.

Starling, Alfred (CS) An 'uncommonly agreeable young fellow of eight-and-twenty', who was one of the guests at the Haunted House. ('The Haunted House')

Starling, Mrs (SYC) A 'widow lady who lost her husband when she was young, and lost herself about the same time – for by her own count she has never since grown five years older'. In her opinion, Mr and Mrs Leaver are 'a perfect model of wedded felicity'. ('The Loving Couple')

Startop (GE) A 'lively bright young fellow', who is one of Mr Matthew Pocket's pupils and a friend of Pip and Herbert Pocket. He helps them to row the boat in their unsuccessful attempt to smuggle Magwitch out of the country. (23, 25–26, 34, 52–54)

Steadiman, John (CS) The 32-year-old Chief Mate of the *Golden Mary*. He was a 'brisk, bright, blue-eyed fellow', who was a 'perfect sailor'. He took over the command of the survivors of the wreck after the Captain's death and narrates part of the story. Dickens based him on his friend, Wilkie Collins, who was also 32 at this time and who wrote Steadiman's narration in this collaborative story (Glancy 1996: 808). ('The Wreck of the Golden Mary')

Steerforth, James (DC) David Copperfield first meets Steerforth at Salem House, the boarding school where Mr Murdstone has sent him. He is the senior boy, arrogant, dominating and handsome, who patronises David: 'He was [David recalls] a person of great power in my eyes.' He publicly humiliates Mr Mell, the assistant master, by revealing that his mother lives in an alms-house (which Steerforth had learnt from David), and so brings about his dismissal. David later accidentally meets Steerforth in London and takes him to Yarmouth to meet the Peggotty family. He finds Em'ly a 'most engaging little Beauty!' She finds his gentlemanly attractions irresistible and the two elope, though each suffers agonies of conscience. David, for example, notes Steerforth's mood of 'passionate dejection' at the end of his fortnight's visit to the Peggotty household. Steerforth and Em'ly live in France, Switzerland, Italy and elsewhere, but he tires of her, leaves her and proposes that she should marry Littimer, his manservant – whereupon she slowly makes her way back to England. Steerforth is drowned, despite Ham's attempts to save him (unaware of his identity), in a shipwreck off the coast at Yarmouth. When David is taken to see his body on the shore, he sees him 'lying with his head upon his arm, as I had often seen him lie at school'. Steerforth had been idolised by his mother and passionately loved by his mother's companion, Rosa Dartle (whose lip he had scarred by hurling a hammer at her when he was a boy). (5–7, 9, 19–26, 28–29, 31–32, 46, 50, 55–56)

Steerforth, Mrs (DC) The mother of James Steerforth. She was 'an elderly lady, though not very advanced in years, with a proud carriage and a handsome face'. She was devoted to her son: 'She seemed to be able to speak or think about nothing else.' In her opinion, he 'is always generous and noble', as she proudly tells David Copperfield. His elopement with Em'ly so enrages her that all attempts by Rosa Dartle, her companion, to soothe her are ineffective: 'Let him put away his whim now, and he is welcome back. Let him not put her away now, and he never shall come near me, living or dying, while I can raise my hand to make a sign against it, unless, being rid of her for ever, he comes humbly to me and begs for my forgiveness.' Her distress greatly alters her appearance: 'Her fine figure was far less upright, her handsome face was deeply marked, and her hair was almost white.' At the news of her son's death, which she seems not to comprehend, she suffers a kind of stroke. David last sees her as a 'bent lady, supporting herself by a stick, and showing [him] a countenance in which there are some traces of old pride and beauty, feebly contending with a querulous, imbecile, fretful wandering of mind'. (20–21, 24, 29, 32, 36, 46, 56, 64)

Stiggins, Mr (PP) A 'prim-faced, red-nosed man', who is a dissenting minister and 'deputy shepherd' of the Emmanuel Chapel at Dorking. Tony Weller's second wife is one of his devoted followers. Though constantly preaching the virtues of temperance, Mr Stiggins has a fondness for rum. Thanks to Tony Weller's scheming, he arrives drunk at the Brick Lane Branch of the United Grand Junction Ebenezer Temperance Association. After Mrs Weller's death, Tony Weller literally kicks Stiggins out of the Marquis of Granby public-house (which Mrs Weller used to own) and immerses his head in a horse-trough. (22, 27, 33, 43, 45, 52)

Stiltstalking, Lord Lancaster (LD) He 'had been maintained by the Circumlocution Office for many years as a representative of the Britannic Majesty abroad. This noble Refrigerator had iced several European courts in his time, and had done it with such complete success that the very name of Englishman yet struck cold to the stomachs of foreigners who had the distinguished honour of remembering him, at a distance of a quarter of a century.' (I: 10, 26)

Stiltstalking, Tudor (LD) *See* **Barnacles, the.**

Stokes, Martin (VC) A small farmer.

Straudenheim (UT) 'A large-lipped, pear-nosed old man, with white hair, and keen eyes, though near-sighted', who was a Strasbourg shopkeeper, but whose line of business and conduct remained a mystery to the Uncommercial Traveller. ('Travelling Abroad')

Straw, Sergeant (RP) A 'little wiry Sergeant of meek demeanour and strong sense'. ('The Detective Police')

Streaker (CS) The housemaid at the Haunted House. ('The Haunted House')

Strong, Annie (DC) The 'very pretty young lady' who is married to Dr Strong, the headmaster of the school David Copperfield attends in Canterbury. She is some forty years younger than her husband. David, Mr Wickfield and Uriah Heep have various degrees of suspicion regarding her relationship with Jack Maldon, her cousin. But in an impassioned declaration of love for her husband, which she makes to him in the presence of Mr Dick (who has helped to bring about the resolution of the difficulties), her mother (Mrs Markleham), Miss Trotwood and David, she convincingly and sincerely refutes all suspicions. She expresses her thankfulness that her husband saved her from 'the mistaken impulse of my undisciplined heart', a phrase that strikes a chord with David, who is undoubtedly reflecting on his marriage to Dora. (16–19, 35–36, 39, 42, 45, 62, 64)

Strong, Doctor (DC) The headmaster of the school in Canterbury where Aunt Betsey Trotwood sends David. 'Doctor Strong looked almost as rusty, to my thinking, as the tall iron rails and gates outside the house; and almost as stiff and heavy as the great stones that flanked them . . . He was in his library . . . with his clothes not particularly well brushed, and his hair not particularly well combed; his knee-smalls unbraced; his long black gaiters unbuttoned; and his shoes yawning like two caverns on the hearth-rug. Turning upon me a lustreless eye, that reminded me of a long-forgotten blind old horse who once used to crop the grass, and tumble over the graves, in Blunderstone churchyard, he said he was glad to see me: and then gave me his hand; which I didn't know what to do with, as it did nothing for itself.' He is a benign, philanthropic and other-worldly man, idolised by the boys at the school: 'We all felt [David says] that we had a part in the management of the place, and in sustaining its character and dignity.' Doctor Strong is contemplating a new Dictionary, which (according to the calculations of Adams, the head-boy) 'might be done in one thousand six hundred and forty-nine years, counting from the Doctor's last, or sixty-second birthday'. In David's last 'retrospect', he says that the Doctor is still 'labouring at his Dictionary (somewhere about the letter D)'. Doctor Strong deeply loves his young wife and does all that he can to further the interests of her cousin, Jack Maldon. He is perturbed for a while when Uriah Heep expresses his suspicions of Annie's behaviour, but she passionately avows her faithfulness and love: 'Oh, take me to your heart, my husband, for my love was founded on a rock, and it endures!' Dickens, it appears, had no particular schoolmaster in mind when he created Doctor Strong, whose school (Philip Collins suggests) 'is based partly on [Dickens's] wish-fulfilment' (1963: 118)

Struggles, Mr (PP) An enthusiastic but unsuccessful bowler for the Dingley Dell cricket team. (7)

Stryver, Mr (TTC) The solicitor who (with Sydney Carton's indispensable help) defends Charles Darnay from charges of treason. He was 'a man of little more than thirty, but looking twenty years older than he was, stout, loud, red, bluff, and free from any drawback of delicacy, [who] had a pushing way of shouldering himself (morally and physically) into companies and conversations, that argued well for his shouldering his way up in life'. But though he was glib, unscrupulous, ready and bold, Stryver 'had not that faculty of extracting the essence from a heap of statements, which is the most striking and necessary of the advocate's accomplishments'. For that skill, he had to rely on Sydney Carton, who was his 'jackal'. Struck by Lucie Manette's 'golden-haired' beauty, Stryver thinks of asking her to marry him, as he tells Carton and Mr Lorry. Lorry, however, dissuades him from doing so on the grounds that his suit would fail. Stryver calmly accepts the situation. He eventually becomes rich, having married 'a florid widow with property and three boys'. He is based on Edward James, whom Dickens had consulted with Edmund Yates during the Garrick Club controversy in 1859. James was 'a pushing and unscrupulous barrister, who was later debarred for malpractice' (Johnson 1953: 948). (II: 3–5, 11–13, 21–24)

Stubbs, Mrs (SB) A 'dirty old woman with an inflamed countenance', who was Mr Percy Noakes's laundress. ('Tales: The Steam Excursion')

Styles, Mr (MP) A Vice-President of the Statistics section at the second meeting of the Mudfog Association.

Sullivan, Mrs (SB) According to a drunken and quarrelsome woman in Seven Dials, 'poor dear Mrs Sulliwin, as has five blessed children of her own, can't go out a-charing for one arternoon, but what hussies must be a-comin,' and 'ticing away her oun' 'usband, as she's been married to twelve year come next Easter Monday'. ('Scenes: Seven Dials')

Summerson, Esther (BH) The heroine of *Bleak House*, whose first-person narrative forms part of the novel. Esther is brought up as an orphan by her aunt, Miss Barbary (Lady Dedlock's sister), whom Esther believes is her godmother. Mr John Jarndyce adopts her, sees that she is properly educated, and then employs her as a companion to Ada Clare and Richard Carstone and as the housekeeper of Bleak House. The discovery of the secret of her birth – that she is the illegitimate daughter of Lady Dedlock and Captain Hawdon – is one of the principal strands of the narrative. Mr Jarndyce affectionately calls her by various names: 'Old Woman, and Little Old Woman, and Cobweb, and Mrs Shipton, and Mother Hubbard, and Dame Durden, and so many names of that sort, that my own name soon became lost among them.' Esther has a sincere affection for her youthful companions (and hence is anxious about Richard's fecklessness), her employer, and her servant, Charley. After nursing Charley through a dangerous illness (presumably smallpox), Esther is herself infected, and lies very ill through several weeks. Her recollection of her 'sick experiences' is typically unselfish: 'I do not recall them to make others unhappy, or because I am now the least unhappy in remembering them. It may be that if we knew more of such strange afflictions, we might be the better able to alleviate their intensity.' Esther's face is disfigured as a result, which makes Guppy hastily withdraw his attempted proposal (though he later changes his mind) and which makes her pleased that Allan Woodcourt had never declared his love for her: 'I had thought, sometimes, that if he had done so, I should have been glad of it. But how much better it was now, that this had never happened!' Esther later accepts Mr Jarndyce's proposal of marriage, but he happily relinquishes her to Woodcourt, when he realises that the two love each other: 'What happiness was ours that day [she exclaims], what joy, what rest, what hope, what gratitude, what bliss!' Michael Slater has argued that Esther Summerson's 'character, behaviour and situation resembled in many ways the character, behaviour and situation of Georgina [Hogarth, Dickens's sister-in-law]' and that the novelist's 'very conception had perhaps been largely inspired by her' (1983: 166). Literary parallels have been suggested with Jane Eyre in Charlotte Brontë's novel (1847) and with Phoebe Pynchon in Nathaniel Hawthorne's *The House of the Seven Gables* (1851) (Shatto 1988: 7) (*passim*)

Sweedlepipe, Poll (MC) A bird-fancier and barber, whose first-floor lodger is Mrs Gamp. 'He was a little elderly man, with a clammy cold right hand, from which even rabbits and birds could not remove the smell of shaving-soap.' He was as peaceful as a dove, he strutted and spoke like a pigeon, and he had a knowing look like a raven's. 'Poll had a very small, shrill, treble voice, which might have led the wags of Kingsgate Street to insist the more upon his feminine designation. He had a tender heart, too; for, when he had a good commission to provide three or four score sparrows for a shooting match, he would observe, in a compassionate tone, how singular it was that sparrows should have been made expressly for such purposes. The question, whether men were made to shoot them, never entered into Poll's philosophy.' Poll Sweedlepipe is an admirer and friend of Bailey, is distraught when he hears of his apparent death in the carriage accident (or, as Mrs Gamp puts it, 'in a nice state of confusion'), and cor-

respondingly delighted when Bailey surprisingly reappears, 'a little shook and rather giddy'. Poll takes him into partnership: 'We'll make it Sweedlepipe and Bailey. He shall have the sporting branch (what a one he'll be for the matches!) and me the shavin'.' Paul Green, one of the boys who worked at Warren's Blacking warehouse when Dickens was employed there, 'was currently believed to have been christened Poll (a belief which [Dickens] transferred, long afterwards . . . to Mr Sweedlepipe in *Martin Chuzzlewit*' (Forster 1928: Book 1, Ch. 2). (19, 26, 29, 38, 49, 52)

Sweeney, Mrs (UT) A laundress in charge of a set of chambers in Gray's Inn Square. She was 'in figure extremely like an old family-umbrella' and kept a book containing information about 'the high prices and small uses of soda, soap, sand, firewood, and such articles'. ('Chambers')

Sweet William (OCS) A travelling conjuror met by Little Nell and her Grandfather at the Jolly Sandboys. He was 'a silent gentleman who earned his living by showing tricks upon the cards, and who had rather deranged the natural expression of his countenance by putting small leaden lozenges into his eyes and bringing them out at his mouth'. He was called Sweet William probably 'as a pleasant satire upon his ugliness'. (19)

Swidger, Milly (CB) The wife of William Swidger, the lodge-keeper at Redlaw's college. Her good, loving nature counteracts the evil influence of Redlaw and indeed eventually leads to the latter's redemption. Other members of William Swidger's family are Philip (his old father), George (his dissolute brother), and Charley (his nephew). (*The Haunted Man*)

Swillenhausen, Baron von (NN) His

Figure 33 Dick Swiveller by Hablot K. Browne (Phiz)

'fair daughter' marries the Baron of Grogzwig in the interpolated story of that name told by 'the merry-faced gentleman'. (6)

Swills, Little (BH) The 'comic vocalist' who sings at the Harmonic Meetings at the Sol's Arms. (11, 19, 32, 33, 39)

Swiveller, Dick (OCS) When we first meet Dick Swiveller he is an unprepossessing young man with 'wiry hair, dull eyes, and sallow face'. His 'attire was not . . . remarkable for the nicest arrangement, but was in a state of disorder which strongly induced the idea that he had gone to bed in it.' He is fond of drink and tobacco. Dick readily falls in with Fred Trent's scheme to make Nell, Fred's

sister, his wife. Quilp considers Dick to be potentially useful in furthering his plans of revenge against Nell and her Grandfather and accordingly insists that the Brasses employ him as a clerk. But Dick's function within the novel and his character begin to change at this point, especially after he befriends the Marchioness, who nurses him through a fever and tells him of the plot against Kit Nubbles. He has her educated and eventually marries her, having come into an annuity of £150 from a deceased aunt. Dickens characterises Dick throughout with lively comedy: his apartments in the neighbourhood of Drury Lane were over a tobacconist's shop, 'so that he was enabled to procure a refreshing sneeze at any time by merely stepping out on the staircase'; he stares in perplexity at Sally Brass, 'that strange monster' and has 'horrible desires to annihilate her'; he affectionately and ironically names the Brasses' little maidservant 'the Marchioness'; and so on. Dick's speech is full of flowery phrases and quotations from popular songs: '"Fred," said Mr Swiveller, "remember the once popular melody of 'Begone dull care'; fan the sinking flame of hilarity with the wing of friendship: and pass the rosy wine!"' Mrs Oliphant, in her article, 'Charles Dickens' (*Blackwood's Magazine*, April 1855), thought that 'Dick is worthy to take his place with Sam Weller, a person as distinct and true, and worthy of universal recognition' (Collins 1971: 331). J.B. Priestley also held Dickens's creation of Dick Swiveller in high regard and devoted an appreciative chapter to him in *The English Comic Characters*.

Priestley remarked that Dick Swiveller 'enjoys his high-falutin, smacks his lips over his magnificent phrases, but knows very well that he is absurd and enjoys that fact too' (1928: 227). (2–3, 7–8, 13, 21, 23, 33–38, 48, 50, 56–66, 73)

Swoshle, Mrs Henry George Alfred (OMF) A member of fashionable society, who leaves her card at the Boffins' house in Cavendish Square. (I: 17)

Swosser, Captain (BH) A Royal Navy officer, who was Mrs Bayham Badger's first husband. (13)

Sylvia (GSE) A girl who aroused 'some childish love' in George Silverman when he was sent to live in a farmhouse. She is much annoyed when he refuses her invitation to her birthday party.

T

Tabblewick, Mrs (SYC) An acquaintance of the plausible couple, who modify their praises of her beauty when a 'lovely friend' is present. ('The Plausible Couple')

Tabby (CS) A 'grinning and good-natured soul', who was the 'serving drudge' at Miss Griffin's school, 'and had no more figure than one of the beds, and upon whose face there was always more or less black-lead'. She had to assume the part of Mesrour in the 'Seraglio'. ('The Haunted House')

Tacker (MC) Mr Mould the undertaker's chief mourner. He was obese, and had a bottle nose and a face covered with pimples. 'He had been a tender plant once upon a time, but from constant blowing in the fat atmosphere of funerals, had run to seed.' (19, 25, 38)

Tackleton (CB) The sole owner of the firm of Gruff and Tackleton, Toy-merchants. Inappropriately for his line of business, he was a 'domestic Ogre'. He had a 'dry face, and a screw in his body ... and his whole sarcastic ill-conditioned self [peered] out of one little corner of one eye, like the concentrated essence of any number of ravens'. He is engaged to be married to May Fielding, but when her sweetheart, Edward Plummer, reappears she marries him instead. At the wedding celebrations, Tackleton makes an appearance, saying that he is a reformed and sweetened character. *(The Cricket on the Hearth)*

Tadger, Brother (PP) A 'little emphatic man, with a bald head, and drab shorts', who is a member of the Brick Lane Ebenezer Temperance Association. Mr Stiggins, who is drunk himself, accuses Tadger of being drunk, hits him on the nose, and so knocks him down head first from the ladder on which he has been standing. (33)

Tamaroo (MC) An old woman who succeeded Bailey as a servant at Todgers's. Her nickname was given her by the 'jocular boarders' from a word in a popular ballad ('Ben was a hackney coachman rare'). She 'was chiefly remarkable for a total absence of all comprehension upon every subject whatever'. (32, 54)

Tangle, Mr (BH) A barrister, who 'knows more of Jarndyce and Jarndyce than anybody. He is famous for it — supposed never to have read anything else since he left school.' (1)

Tape (RP) Prince Bull's 'tyrannical old godmother', who was 'bright red all over.' She therefore symbolises the bureaucracy (or, the red tape) that hampered England's efforts in the Crimean War (1854–56). ('Prince Bull. A Fairy Tale')

Tapkins, Felix (ISHW) The bachelor who flirted with Mrs Lovetown.

Tapkins, Mrs (OMF) Mrs Tapkins and her five daughters, who leave their card at the Boffins' house in Cavendish Square. (I: 17)

Tapley, Mark (MC) The ostler at the Blue Dragon. 'He was a young fellow, of some five or six-and-twenty perhaps, and dressed in such a free and fly-away fashion, that the long ends of his loose red neckcloth were streaming out behind him quite as often as before; and the bunch of bright winter berries in the buttonhole of his velveteen coat was as visible to Mr Pinch's rearward observation, as if he had worn that garment wrong side foremost.' Mark has 'a whimsical face and very merry pair of blue eyes'. He is a determined optimist but can only find real satisfaction in being happy in adverse circumstances: 'I don't believe there ever was a man as could come out so strong under circumstances that would make other men miserable, as I could, if I could only get a chance. It's my opinion that nobody never will know half of what's in me, unless something very unexpected turns up.' He therefore leaves his employment at the Blue Dragon (despite the widespread belief that he will marry Mrs Lupin, the landlady, at some time), travels to London, meets Martin Chuzzlewit there by chance, and insists on travelling with him to America. Mark's cheerfulness there under adversity, including his own illness, is a factor in Martin's conversion from selfishness. After returning to England, he marries Mrs Lupin and delightedly renames the Blue Dragon the Jolly Tapley. (5, 7, 13–15, 17, 21–23, 33–35, 43, 48, 51–54)

Taplin, Harry (SB) A comic singer at the White Conduit, where Miss Martin made her unsuccessful debut as a singer. ('Characters: The Mistaken Milliner')

Tappertit, Simon (BR) The apprentice to Gabriel Varden, the locksmith. 'Sim, as he was called in the locksmith's family, or Mr Simon Tappertit, as he called himself, and required all men to style him out of doors, on holidays, and Sundays out, – was an old-fashioned, thin-faced, sleek-haired, sharp-nosed, small-eyed little fellow, very little more than five feet high, and thoroughly convinced in his own

mind that he was above middle size; rather tall, in fact, than otherwise. Of his figure, which was well enough formed, though somewhat of the leanest, he entertained the highest admiration; and with his legs, which, in knee-breeches, were perfect curiosities of littleness, he was enraptured to a degree, amounting to enthusiasm. He also had some majestic, shadowy ideas, which had never been quite fathomed by his most intimate friends, concerning the power of his eye. Indeed he had been known to go so far as to boast that he could utterly quell and subdue the haughtiest beauty by a simple process, which he termed "eying her over".' Sim greatly admires Dolly Varden, the locksmith's beautiful daughter, and hence is bitterly jealous of Joe Willet; this admiration of his incurs Miggs's anger, since she would like Sim to take notice of her. He is the 'captain' of a group of London apprentices, the 'Prentice Knights, and is resentful of the masters who employ them. Sim impudently defies his own employer, Gabriel Varden, at the time of the Gordon Riots, in which he takes an active part: ' "A fiery devil [is abroad] ... a flaming, furious devil. Don't put yourself in its way, or you're done for, my buck. Be warned in time, G. Varden. Farewell!" ' But with cruel irony his legs are so badly crushed during the riots that he has to have wooden legs; he finds work as a shoe-black and marries 'the widow of an eminent bone and rag collector'. Hesketh Pearson thought that 'by far the most remarkable feature of *Barnaby* is the character of Simon Tappertit'. Pearson (who was writing in 1949, when images of Hitler and Charlie Chaplin were sharp in readers' minds) said that 'Tappertit is a comical apotheosis of the "little man" a century before he came into his own' (1949: 97). (4, 7–9, 18–19, 22, 24, 27, 31, 36, 39, 48–54, 59–60, 62–63, 70–71, 82)

Tappleton, Lieutenant   (PP) Doctor

Slammer's friend, who bears his challenge to Mr Winkle. (2, 3)

Tartar, Lieutenant (MED) A former First Lieutenant in the Royal Navy, who has rooms next to Neville Landless's in Staple Inn. He was Mr Crisparkle's fag in their school days. 'A handsome gentleman, with a young face, but with an older figure in its robustness and its breadth of shoulder; say a man of eight-and-twenty, or at the utmost thirty; so extremely sunburnt that the contrast between his brown visage and the white forehead shaded out of doors by his hat, and the glimpses of white throat below the neckerchief, would have been almost ludicrous but for his broad temples, bright blue eyes, clustering brown hair, and laughing teeth.' He grows runner beans and flowers in window-boxes and moves in and out of windows on a rigging of ropes and stays. His chambers 'were the neatest, the cleanest, and the best-ordered chambers ever seen under the sun, moon, and stars'. Tartar and Rosa are immediately attracted to each other, and with his help she ascends to his 'garden in the air'. He was obviously destined to play a significant part in the novel, perhaps in helping Neville Landless 'to unmask and seize the murderer' (Forster 1928: Book 11, Ch. 2). (17, 21–22)

Tarter, Bob (CS) The 'first boy' at the school, who was the President of the Society whose aim was to 'make a set against' Old Cheeseman. His claim that his father was rich turned out to be untrue. He 'went for a soldier' and Old Cheeseman purchased his discharge. ('The Schoolboy's Story')

Tatham, Mrs (SB), An old woman who pawns a child's frock and 'a beautiful silk ankecher' for only ninepence. ('Scenes: The Pawnbroker's Shop')

Tatt, Mr (RP) A 'gentleman formerly in the public line, quite an amateur Detect-ive in his way', who is a friend of Inspector Wield's. ('Three "Detective" Anecdotes')

Tattycoram (LD) The girl adopted from Coram's Foundling Hospital by the Meagles to be Pet's maid. Mr Meagles explains to Arthur Clennam why they changed her name from Harriet Beadle: 'Now, Harriet we changed into Hattey, and then into Tatty, because, as practical people, we thought even a playful name might be a new thing to her, and might have a softening and affectionate kind of effect, don't you see? ... The name of Beadle being out of the question [because of its connotations of a Jack-in-office], and the originator of the Institution for these poor foundlings having been a blessed creature of the name of Coram, we gave that name to Pet's little maid. At one time she was Tatty, and at one time she was Coram, until we got into a way of mixing the two names together, and now she is always Tattycoram.' She is a 'handsome girl with lustrous dark hair and eyes, and very neatly dressed'. Tattycoram is often sullen and passionate, feeling a sense of inferiority to Pet, despite the Meagles's benevolent intentions. Meagles, in his unintentionally patronising way, urges her to 'count five-and-twenty' when she has one of her fits of rage. Miss Wade, who sees in her a kindred spirit, persuades her to run away from the Meagles family and to live with her as her companion. Although she refuses to return, Tattycoram still retains a partially-admitted affection for them. When Clennam sees her and Miss Wade together, he 'felt how each of the two natures must be constantly tearing each other to pieces'. In the end, Tattycoram fully repents of her action, bringing to Mr and Mrs Meagles the iron box of papers that Miss Wade had concealed and promising to reform: 'I hope I shall never be quite so bad again, and that I shall get better by very slow degrees. I'll try very hard. I won't stop at five-and-twenty, sir. I'll count five-and-twenty hundred, five-and-twenty thousand!' (I: 2, 16, 27–28; II: 9–10, 20–21, 33)

Taunton, Captain (CS) The captain of Dick Doubledick's company. The expression in his 'bright, handsome, dark eyes' remarkably affected the dissipated soldier, who felt ashamed when they looked at him. The Captain successfully urges Dick to reform and he becomes a brave soldier. But Taunton is killed at Badajos in the Peninsular War. ('The Seven Poor Travellers')

Taunton, Mrs and the Misses (SB) Mrs Taunton 'was a good-looking widow of fifty, with the form of a giantess and the mind of a child'. She has two daughters, Emily and Sophia. They and the Briggs family, 'between whom there existed a degree of implacable hatred, quite unprecedented', are among Mr Percy Noakes's guests on the Thames excursion. ('Tales: The Steam Excursion')

Testator, Mr (UT) An occupant of a set of chambers in Lyon's Inn. He borrows all the furniture he finds in a locked cellar. A mysterious visitor later claims it as his but disappears and is heard of no more. ('Chambers')

Tetterby, Adolphus (CB) A poor shopkeeper with a large family, who temporarily falls under the evil influence of Redlaw. The other members of his family are his wife, Sophia, his two sons ('Dolphus, a newsboy at a railway station, and Johnny), and his infant daughter, Sally. (*The Haunted Man*)

Théophile, Corporal (CS) 'A lithe and nimble Corporal, quite complete, from the sparkling dark eyes under his knowing uniform cap to his sparkling white gaiters.' He is the protector of Bebelle, who subsequently adopted by Mr Langley. ('Somebody's Luggage')

Thomas The name of various servants: Sir Leicester Dedlock's groom (BH 40); Mr Knag's boy (NN 18); the waiter in Sam Weller's story of the gentleman who killed himself by eating crumpets (PP 44); the waiter at the Winglebury Arms (SB: 'The Great Winglebury Duel')

Thompson, Miss Julia (SYG) She is 'a great favourite with Felix', according to his mother, Mrs Nixon. ('The Domestic Young Gentleman')

Thompson, Tally Ho (RP) A famous horse-stealer, who is the subject of Sergeant Witchem's story. ('The Detective Police')

Tibbs, Mrs (SB) The 'most tidy, fidgety, thrifty little personage that ever inhaled the smoke of London'. She keeps a boarding-house in Great Coram Street. Her husband 'was to his wife what the o is in 90 – he was of some importance *with* her – he was nothing without her'. After the unfortunate misunderstanding when she is discovered in the company of Mr Evenson, Mrs Tibbs and her husband separate. She decides to dispose of the whole of her furniture and to retire 'from a residence in which she has suffered so much'. ('Tales: The Boarding-House')

Tickit, Mrs (LD) The Meagles's cook (when they were at home) and housekeeper (when they were away). In the family's absence, Mrs Tickit wore a silk gown and put on a 'jet-black row of curls' over her reddish-grey hair. She then 'established herself in the breakfast-room, put her spectacles between two particular leaves of Doctor Buchan's Domestic Medicine, and sat looking over the blind until they came back again'. (I: 16, 34; II: 9, 33)

Tickle, Mr (MP) At the Display of Models and Mechanical Science at the second meeting of the Mudfog Association, he 'displayed his newly-invented spectacles, which enabled the wearer to discern, in very bright colours, objects at a great distance, and rendered him wholly blind to those immediately before him'.

Tiddypot, Mr (RP) A vestryman, who eloquently speaks against the hypothesis that water is 'a necessary of life.' ('Our Vestry')

Tiffey, Mr (DC) Spenlow and Jorkins's chief clerk. He was 'a little dry man, sitting by himself [in the office], who wore a stiff brown wig that looked as if it were made of gingerbread'. He breaks the news of Mr Spenlow's accidental death to David Copperfield. (23, 26, 33, 35, 38)

Tigg, Montague (MC) A disreputable adventurer, who is at first an associate of Chevy Slyme. He is shabby and down-at-heel, with a shaggy moustache and 'a vast quantity of unbrushed hair'. 'He was very dirty and very jaunty; very bold and very mean; very swaggering and very slinking, very much like a man who might have been something better, and unspeakably like a man who deserved to be something worse.' He later changes his name (to Tigg Montague) and his appearance: he now has 'a world of jet-black shining hair upon his head, upon his cheeks, upon his chin, upon his upper lip'; he wears fashionable and costly clothes and a great deal of jewellery. He sets up the fraudulent Anglo-Bengalee Disinterested Loan and Life Assurance Company. Through his agent, Nadgett, Tigg discovers his partner Jonas Chuzzlewit's murderous intentions. He blackmails him into venturing further into the business and into luring Pecksniff to invest in it. In desperation, Jonas waylays and kills him with a 'thick, hard, knotted stake' in a wood near Pecksniff's house. (4, 7, 12–13, 27, 38, 40–42, 44, 47, 49, 51–52)

Timbered, Mr (MP) A vice-president of

the Statistics session at the first meeting of the Mudfog Association.

Timberry, Snittle (NN) An actor, who presides at Mr Crummles's farewell dinner before the family leaves for America. (48)

Timkins (SB) One of the candidates for the office of beadle. ('Our Parish: The Election for Beadle')

Timpson (UT) An owner of a coach business in Dullborough 'knocked down' by Pickford's. ('Dullborough Town')

Timson, the Reverend Charles (SB) The clergyman who Mr Tottle discovers to his chagrin is engaged to be married to Miss Lillerton. ('Tales: A Passage in the Life of Mr Watkins Tottle')

Tinkler, Mr (LD) Mr Dorrit's valet. When he innocently pauses on one occasion, Mr Dorrit sees 'the whole Marshalsea and all its Testimonials in the pause' and flies at him with angry words. (II: 3, 5, 15, 19)

Tinkling, William (HR) The 8-year-old boy who writes the 'Introductory Romance' and who is 'married' to Miss Nettie Ashford.

Tiny Tim (CB) The youngest child in the Cratchit family. He is a cripple, who told his father, Bob Cratchit, on the way home from church on Christmas morning that 'he hoped the people saw him in the church, because he was a cripple, and it might be pleasant to them to remember upon Christmas Day, who made lame beggars walk, and blind men see'. At the end of the family Christmas dinner, Tiny Tim plaintively sings a song 'about a lost child travelling in the snow'. Scrooge is moved by the sight of the little boy, who will die, the Spirit of Christmas Present tells him, unless 'these shadows remain unaltered by the Future'. After Scrooge's conversion, he becomes a second father to Tiny Tim. In his depiction of Tiny Tim, Dickens may have had in mind Harry Burnett, the crippled son of his sister, Fanny. (*A Christmas Carol*)

Tip (MND) Gabblewig's servant.

Tipkisson (RP) An 'inveterate saddler', who heckles 'the honourable member for Verbosity'. ('Our Honourable Friend')

Tipp (DC) The carman at Murdstone and Grinby's, who wore a red jacket and who (like Gregory, the foreman) used to address David Copperfield as 'David' whereas the other employees called him 'the little gent' or 'the young Suffolker'. Mr Quinion planned to 'quarter' David on him when Mr Micawber announced that he and his family were going away. (11, 12)

Tippin, Mr and Mrs, and family (SB) Mrs Tippin was 'a short female, in a blue velvet hat and feathers' and her husband was a 'fat man in black tights and cloudy Berlins [i.e., knitted gloves].' With Miss Tippin and Master Tippin, they sang and played at the library in Ramsgate. ('Tales: The Tuggses at Ramsgate')

Tippins, Lady (OMF) An aristocratic old lady in the Veneerings' circle. She had an 'immense obtuse drab oblong face, like a face in a tablespoon, and a dyed Long Walk up the top of her head, as a convenient public approach to the bunch of false hair behind'. She was the 'relict of the late Sir Thomas Tippins, knighted in mistake for somebody else by His Majesty King George the Third . . . [and] has a reputation for giving smart accounts of things . . . you could easily buy all you see of her, in Bond Street: or you might scalp her, and peel her, and scrape her, and make two Lady Tippinses out of her, and yet not penetrate to the genuine article'. She surveys all social proceed-

ings through a 'large gold eye-glass'. After inspecting the corpse of the supposed John Harmon, Eugene Wrayburn whispers to Mortimer Lightwood, 'Not *much* worse than Lady Tippins.' Lady Tippins has an arch flirtatiousness and a sarcastic tongue, as when she comments on Mortimer Lightwood's remarks about Lizzie and Eugene's wedding: 'Take care of me if I faint, Veneering. He means to tell us that a horrid female waterman is graceful!' (I: 2, 3, 10, 17; II: 3, 16; III, 17; IV: 17)

Tisher, Mrs (MED) Miss Twinkleton's companion. She is 'a deferential widow with a weak back, a chronic sigh, and suppressed voice, who looks after the young ladies' wardrobes, and leads them to infer that she has seen better days'. (3, 7, 9, 13, 19)

Tix, Tom (NN) The broker who accompanies Mr Scaley when they take possession of the Mantalinis' business. He was 'a little man in brown, very much the worse for wear, who brought with him a mingled fumigation of stale tobacco and fresh onions' and who was dressed in mud-stained clothes. (21)

Toddles and Poddles (OMF) The pet names of a boy and girl 'minded' by Betty Higden. (I: 16)

Toddyhigh, Joe (MHC) A poor man, who had been a boyhood friend of the Lord Mayor of London, whom he disconcerts by making himself known to him. He awakes from a sleep in the Guildhall to hear the 'Giant Chronicles' of Gog and Magog. (1)

Todgers, Mrs M (MC) The proprietor of a Commercial Boarding House in London, which is simply known as 'Todgers's'. She was 'rather a bony and hard-featured lady, with a row of curls in front of her head, shaped like little barrels of beer; and on the top of it something made of net – you couldn't call it a cap exactly – which looked like a black cobweb. She had a little basket on her arm, and in it a bunch of keys that jingled as she came.' Despite her rule that she receives 'gentlemen boarders only', Mrs Todgers ecstatically welcomes Charity and Mercy Pecksniff as well as their father when they go to stay there on their visit to London. Charity later stays at Todgers's on her own. Mercy occasionally goes there after her marriage 'to ease her poor full heart', and after Jonas's suicide finds refuge there. (8–11, 30, 32, 37, 46, 52, 54)

Tom (CS) A pavement artist infatuated with Henrietta, who leaves him for another pavement artist. ('Somebody's Luggage')

Tom (NN) A 'lean youth with cunning eyes and a protruding chin', who is the clerk at the General Agency Office where Nicholas Nickleby and Madeline Bray come separately to seek employment. Frank Cheeryble later knocks him down in a coffee room for making disrespectful remarks about Madeline. (16, 43)

Tom (SB) A 'corpulent round-headed boy', who was the young doctor's servant. ('Tales: The Black Veil')

Tom (TTC) The driver of the coach carrying Mr Lorry to Dover. (I: 2)

Tomkinley, Mr (OCS) Abel Garland's only absence from his parents was his going to Margate 'one Saturday with Mr Tomkinley that had been a teacher at that school he went to' and coming back on the Monday. But (as Mr Garland recalls) 'he was very ill after that . . . ; it was quite a dissipation.' (14)

Tomkins (SG) The lover and eventual husband of Miss Fanny Wilson.

Tomkins, Miss (PP) The headmistress of

Westgate House girls' school, where Mr Pickwick finds himself in compromising circumstances. (16)

Tomkins, Alfred (SB) One of Mrs Tibbs's boarders. He 'was a clerk in a wine-house; he was a connoisseur in paintings, and had a wonderful eye for the picturesque'. ('Tales: The Boarding-House')

Tomlinson, Mrs (PP) The post-office keeper, who 'seemed by mutual consent to have been chosen the leader of the trade party' of guests at the Rochester ball. (2)

Tommy (SB) A 'little greengrocer with a chubby face', who argued with the red-faced orator in the public house. ('Characters: The Parlour Orator')

Tompkins (NN) The boy who tells Mr Squeers that he thinks Smike has run away. Mr Squeers thereupon beats him 'until the little urchin in his writhings actually rolled out of his hands'. (13)

Toodle, Mr (DS) Polly Toodle's husband and the father of Rob the Grinder. He is a railway stoker and later an engine-driver (one of the first of such workmen to appear in English fiction). Mr Toodle has the honour of 'stokin'' Mr Dombey and Major Bagstock down to Leamington Spa. Like his wife and children, he was 'plump and apple-faced.'. (2, 15, 20, 59)

Toodle, Polly (DS) The 'plump rosy-cheeked wholesome apple-faced young woman', who is the mother of five children, and who becomes Paul Dombey's wet-nurse after the death of his mother. Mr Dombey stipulates that Polly Toodle must change her name to Richards (which is 'an ordinary name, and convenient') and that her relationship to little Paul must be simply a business matter. (It was not uncommon for employers to insist that servants used names considered to be more suitable for various reasons.) Mr Dombey dismisses her for taking Paul and Florence to her home in Staggs's Gardens, 'into haunts and into society which are not to be thought of without a shudder'. But Paul begs her to be sent for when he lies dying. When Florence seeks refuge with Captain Cuttle at the Little Midshipman, Polly becomes the housekeeper there. Her husband is a railway stoker and later an engine driver (see the preceding entry). The Toodles's eldest son became known as Rob the Grinder. It has been suggested that Dickens based Polly on a Mrs Hayes who was a servant to his sister, Fanny (Mrs Burnett). (2, 3, 5–7, 15, 16, 20, 22, 38, 56, 59)

Toorell, Doctor (MP) The president of the Anatomy and Medicine session at the first meeting of the Mudfog Association.

Tootle, Tom (OMF) The man who submissively tells Miss Abbey Potterson that one man (who turns out to be Rogue Riderhood) has been run down in a wherry by a foreign steamer on the Thames. (III: 2)

Toots, Mr (DS) The oldest pupil at Doctor Blimber's school in Brighton, where Paul Dombey is sent. Toots 'had licence to pursue his own course of study: which was chiefly to write long letters to himself from persons of distinction, addressed "P. Toots, Esquire, Brighton, Sussex," and so preserve them in his desk with great care'. He is thoroughly kind ('there were few better fellows in the world, though there may have been one or two brighter spirits'), is devoted to Paul, falls hopelessly in love with Florence and accepts all humiliations (often saying that 'it's of no consequence'). Toots becomes friendly with Captain Cuttle, whom he calls Captain Gills: 'I feel that I'd rather think about Miss Dombey in your society than talk about her in almost anybody else's.'

Although he finds it hard to accept the engagement of Florence and Walter Gay (whom he calls Lieutenant Walters), Mr Toots soon finds complete happiness in marrying Susan Nipper. (11, 12, 14, 18, 22, 28, 31, 32, 39, 41, 44, 48, 50, 56, 57, 60, 62)

Tope, Mr and Mrs (MED) Mr Tope (whose grammar is corrected by Mr Crisparkle) is Chief Verger and Showman of Cloisterham Cathedral. His wife acts as John Jasper's housekeeper. Datchery takes lodgings with the Topes, whose dwelling communicates by an upper stair with Jasper's; he is thus able to watch Jasper's doings. Tope is said to be based on William Miles (1815–1909), a verger in Rochester Cathedral. (2, 6, 12, 14, 16, 18, 23)

Topper (CB) A bachelor, who is a guest at Scrooge's nephew Fred's Christmas dinner. (*A Christmas Carol*)

Toppit, Miss (MC) One of the literary ladies who is honoured to be introduced to Elijah Pogram. (34)

Topsawyer (DC) According to William, the waiter who served David Copperfield at the inn in Yarmouth, he had ordered a glass of ale like that ordered by David. He 'drank it, and fell dead'. (5)

Tott, Mrs Isabella (CS) Known as 'Belltott', she was a soldier's widow who fought bravely against the pirates on Silver-Store Island. ('The Perils of Certain English Prisoners')

Tottle, Watkins (SB) He 'was a rather uncommon compound of strong uxorious inclinations, and an unparalleled degree of anti-connubial timidity. He was about fifty years of age, stood four feet six inches in his socks – for he never stood in stockings at all – plump, clean, and rosy.' When he is arrested for debt, Gabriel Parsons agrees to pay it on condition that he proposes to Miss Lillerton.

Mr Watkins Tottle is on the point of doing so when he discovers that Miss Lillerton is going to marry the Reverend Mr Timson. ('Tales: A Passage in the Life of Mr Watkins Tottle')

Towlinson, Mr (DS) Mr Dombey's young footman, who is always giving his opinion below stairs on the doings of the Dombey family. In the end, he informs his fellow-servants that he and Anne, the housemaid, have resolved 'to take one another for better for worse, and to settle in Oxford Market in the general greengrocery and herb and leech line'. (5, 18, 20, 27, 28, 31, 35, 44, 51, 59)

Tox, Lucretia (DS) A close friend of Mrs Chick's. Miss Tox 'was a long lean figure, wearing such a faded air that she seemed not to have been made in what linendrapers call "fast colours" originally, and to have, by little and little, washed out. But for this she might have been described as the very pink of general propitiation and politeness.' Her 'dark little house' in Princess's Place is close to the house where Major Bagstock has furnished apartments, and for some time a 'Platonic dalliance' between her and the Major 'was effected through the medium' of the latter's 'dark servant'. But Miss Tox ambitiously transfers her hopes to Mr Dombey when he becomes a widower. She swoons at the news of his forthcoming second marriage, thus revealing her feelings to an indignant Mrs Chick: '"The idea!" said Mrs Chick, "of your having basked at my brother's fireside, like a serpent, and wound yourself, through me, into his confidence, Lucretia, that you might, in secret, entertain designs upon him, and dare to aspire to contemplate the possibility of uniting himself to *you!* Why, it is an idea," said Mrs Chick, with sarcastic dignity, "the absurdity of which, almost relieves its treachery."' After Mr Dombey's downfall, Miss Tox constantly visits his house, though she 'moves in her little orbit in

the corner of another system'. After all, 'her heart is very tender, her compassion very genuine, her homage very real'. These qualities are shown, too, in her willingness to give Rob the Grinder a trial as a domestic. (1, 2, 5–8, 10, 14, 16, 18, 20, 29, 31, 36, 38, 51, 59, 62)

Tozer (DS) A 'solemn young gentleman, whose shirt-collar curled up the lobes of his ears', who is one of the pupils at Doctor Blimber's school. Paul shares a bedroom with him and Briggs. When Doctor Blimber retires, Tozer on behalf of the boys presents him with a silver inkstand 'in a speech containing very little of the mother-tongue, but fifteen quotations from the Latin, and seven from the Greek, which moved the younger of the young gentlemen to discontent and envy'. (12, 14, 41, 60)

Tpschoffski (CS) The professional name of Chops (q.v.).

Trabb, Mr (GE) The tailor from whom Pip ordered a fashionable suit when he learned of his 'great expectations'. Trabb was also the undertaker who officiated at Mrs Gargery's funeral. (19, 35)

Trabb's Boy (GE) He works for Trabb, the tailor (see the preceding entry). He was 'the most audacious boy in all that countryside'. The boy mocks Pip's pretensions when they meet in the street, as Pip recalls: 'the knees of Trabb's boy smote together, his hair uprose, his cap fell off, he trembled violently in every limb, staggered out into the road, and crying to the populace, "Hold me! I'm so frightened!" feigned to be in a paroxysm of terror and contrition, occasioned by the dignity of my appearance. As I passed him, his teeth loudly chattered in his head, and with every mark of extreme humiliation, he prostrated himself in the dust.' But later in the action it is he who leads Herbert and Startop in the direction where Pip has fallen into the hands of Orlick. G.K. Chesterton said that 'exactly what [Thackeray and George Eliot] could never have given, and exactly what Dickens does give, is the *bounce* of Trabb's boy. It is the real unconquerable rush and energy in a character which was the supreme and quite indescribable greatness of Dickens' (1933: 202–3)

Traddles, Thomas (DC) One of David Copperfield's most devoted friends. David first meets him as a fellow pupil at Mr Creakle's school. 'In a tight sky-blue suit that made his arms and legs like German sausages or roly-poly puddings, he was the merriest and most miserable of all the boys.' He was constantly caned but found enjoyment in drawing skeletons on his slate 'before his eyes were dry'. When David accidentally meets him again as a young man, Traddles is reading for the Bar. Always optimistic and high-spirited, Traddles becomes David's inseparable friend. He is engaged to be married to Sophie Crewler, 'a curate's daughter . . . one of ten, down in Devonshire'. By coincidence, Traddles lodges with the Micawbers. Thanks to him, David gets the idea of learning shorthand and Mr Dick finds a rewarding occupation in copying legal documents. Traddles advises Mr Micawber in his exposure of Uriah Heep's machinations and between them they recover Miss Trotwood's money for her. He pays off Mr Micawber's final debts 'in the noble name of Miss Trotwood'. When David returns to England, he finds Traddles a happily married man, reading 'Law insatiably' and making merry with his wife and her sisters in the evenings. It has been suggested that Sir Thomas Talfourd (1795–1854), who became a judge and was a friend of Dickens's, was a model for Traddles, whose name echoes his. (5–7, 9, 13, 25, 27, 28, 34, 36, 38, 41, 43, 44, 48, 49, 52, 54, 57, 59, 61, 62, 64)

Trampfoot (UT) A Liverpool policeman, who is one of those patrolling the area of the docks. ('Poor Mercantile Jack')

Traveller, Mr (CS) The man who wanders around Tom Tiddler's Ground in the story of that name.

Treasury (LD) One of the great men who frequent Mr Merdle's social gatherings. (I: 21; II: 26)

Tregarthen, Mr (CS) The Cornish bailiff who had been ruined by the dishonest Clissold. His daughter, Kitty, was Alfred Raybrock's sweetheart. ('A Message from the Sea')

Trent, Frederick (OCS) Little Nell's brother, usually known as Fred. He was 'a young man of one-and-twenty or thereabouts; well made, and certainly handsome, though the expression of his face was far from prepossessing, having in common with his manner and even his dress, a dissipated, insolent air which repelled me [i.e., Master Humphrey]'. Assuming that his grandfather will leave money to Little Nell, Fred urges Dick Swiveller to marry her so that he and Dick can share the proceeds, though this plan comes to nothing. He becomes one of a group of gamblers (in a 'locomotive gambling-house' touring Great Britain), indulges in riotous living abroad, and is found drowned in Paris. (2, 3, 7, 8, 21, 23, 34, 50, 73)

Trent, Nell (OCS) *See* **Little Nell.**

Tresham, Beatrice (CS) The former sweetheart of Jackson ('Barbox Brothers'), who finds her living in poverty with her dying husband and her daughter, Polly. ('Mugby Junction')

Trimmers, Mr (NN) A 'good creature' and a 'kind soul', who is one of the best friends that the Cheeryble Brothers have because he makes deserving cases known to them. (35)

Trinkle, Mr (RP) The 'great upholsterer in Cheapside', one of whose gloves was found under the pillow of the murdered Eliza Grimwood. ('Three "Detective" Anecdotes')

Trott, Alexander (SB) A young tailor, who is challenged to a duel by Horace Hunter over Emily Brown, whom Trott's parents want him to marry. After much confusion and misunderstanding, however, Mr Trott marries Julia Manners at Gretna Green. ('Tales: The Great Winglebury Duel')

Trotter, Job (PP) A hypocritical, lachrymose 'young fellow in mulberry-coloured livery', who is Mr Jingle's man-servant and accomplice. When Sam Weller first sees him at an inn, Job Trotter is 'sitting on a bench in the yard, reading what appeared to be a hymn-book, with an air of deep abstraction'. He has 'a large, sallow, ugly face, very sunken eyes, and a gigantic head, from which depended a quantity of lank black hair'. He dupes Sam Weller into believing that Jingle is planning to elope with a schoolgirl heiress, with embarrassing consequences for Mr Pickwick. Job Trotter is later imprisoned in the Fleet with Jingle and accompanies him to the West Indies, thanks to Mr Pickwick's benevolence. (16, 20, 23, 25, 42, 45–47, 53, 57)

Trottle (CS) One of those listening to Jarber's reading the story. He discomposes Jarber by asking him to supply him with 'a date or two' in connection with the story but then quietly leaves the room ('Going into Society')

Trotwood, Miss Betsey (DC) David Copperfield's formidable, honest and kindly great-aunt. When David is born, she is so annoyed by the fact that he is not a girl that she immediately walks out of Blunderstone Rookery. When David, orphaned and wretched, runs away from Murdstone and Grinby's warehouse, he makes his way to her house in Dover, where (after her initial surprise) she takes him in and gives him a secure home. 'My aunt [David says] was a tall, hard-featured lady, by no means ill-looking. There was an inflexibility in her face, in her voice, in her gait and carriage, amply sufficient to account for the effect she had made upon a gentle creature like my mother; but her features were rather handsome than otherwise, though unbending and austere. I particularly noticed that she had a quick, bright eye.' Miss Trotwood has also given a home to Mr Dick. She often cries 'Janet! Donkeys!' (sometimes to disguise her emotions) to her young servant, who has to chase away any riders who cross the little green in front of her house. When the Murdstones arrive to try to take David away, she is forthright in her condemnation of their conduct and makes clear her determination to keep David with her. She renames David 'Trotwood Copperfield', and tells him that she wants him to be 'a fine firm fellow' with the qualities of determination, resolution, and strength of character. Miss Trotwood arranges his education at Doctor Strong's school in Canterbury and then his being articled to Mr Wickfield, the lawyer. She tries to warn him about the risks of young love and his wish to marry Dora, knowing that Agnes represents true worth (though Aunt Betsey speaks affectionately and indirectly): 'Some one that I know, Trot . . ., though of a very pliant disposition, has an earnestness of affection in him that reminds me of poor Baby [i.e., David's mother]. Earnestness is what that Somebody must look for, to sustain and improve him, Trot. Deep, downright, faithful earnestness.' (Remember that 'earnestness' was a centrally important human quality in the Victorian period.) But she has a tender affection for Dora, whom she calls 'Little Blossom'. At various points, Miss Trotwood's former husband appears; he

Figure 34 Miss Betsey Trotwood and David Copperfield by Hablot K. Browne (Phiz)

had ill-used her, had re-married, but eventually dies in hospital. She thinks that she has lost most of her money because Mr Wickfield has misappropriated it, but this is retrieved when Traddles and Micawber expose Heep's machinations and resolve Wickfield's difficulties. In David's last Retrospect, he sees his aunt 'in stronger spectacles, an old woman of fourscore years and more, but upright yet, and a steady walker of six miles at a stretch in winter weather'. (1, 12–15, 17, 19, 23, 34, 35, 37–45, 47–49, 51–55, 57, 59, 60, 62–64)

Truck, Mr (MP) At the first meeting of the Mudfog Association, he is a vice-president of the Mechanical Science section.

Trundle, Mr (PP) He marries Isabella, Mr Wardle's daughter, at Christmas at Dingley Dell. His is a non-speaking role, and he is given nothing to say even on his wedding day, although we are told that 'he was in high feather and spirits, but a little nervous withal'. (4, 6, 8, 16, 17, 19, 28, 57)

Tuckle, Mr (PP) A 'stoutish gentleman in a bright crimson coat with long tails, vividly red breeches, and a cocked hat', who takes the chair at the footmen's 'swarry' in Bath attended by Sam Weller. (37)

Tugby (CB) Sir Joseph Bowley's former porter, who married Mrs Chickenstalker. He had 'a great broad chin', a nose afflicted with 'The Snuffles', and a 'thick throat and labouring chest'. He was 'an apoplectic innocent'. (*The Chimes*)

Tuggs, Mr, and family (SB) Mr Joseph Tuggs, a grocer, was 'a little dark-faced man with shiny hair, twinkling eyes, short legs, and a body of very considerable thickness'. His amiable wife's figure was 'decidedly comfortable'. They have a daughter, Charlotte, and a son, Simon. When Mr Tuggs inherits £20,000, they become socially ambitious – for example, Simon changes his name to Cymon and Charlotte becomes Charlotta. On visiting Ramsgate, they become the dupes of Captain and Mrs Waters and Lieutenant Slaughter. ('Tales: The Tuggses at Ramsgate')

Tulkinghorn, Mr (BH) An attorney-at-law and solicitor of the High Court of Chancery, who is the Dedlocks' legal adviser. 'The old gentleman is rusty to look at, but is reputed to have made good thrift out of aristocratic marriage settlements and aristocratic wills, and to be very rich. He is surrounded by a mysterious halo of family confidences; of which he is known to be the silent depository.' Mr Tulkinghorn lives in a large house in Lincoln's Inn Fields (Dickens had John Forster's house in mind), 'among his many boxes labelled with transcendent names'. His apartment is like its owner: 'Rusty, out of date, withdrawing from attention, able to afford it.' He habitually sits beneath a 'painted ceiling, with foreshortened Allegory staring down at his intrusion as if it meant to swoop upon him'. This forbidding, sinister, secretive lawyer gradually discovers the facts about Lady Dedlock's hidden past and is about to disclose them to Sir Leicester. But soon after telling Lady Dedlock of his intentions, Mr Tulkinghorn is shot through the heart by Mademoiselle Hortense, who is angered by his insufficiently rewarding her for the information she has given him about Lady Dedlock, her former mistress. Susan Shatto notes parallels between Tulkinghorn and Roger Chillingworth and Judge Pyncheon in Nathaniel Hawthorne's *The Scarlet Letter* (1850) and *The House of the Seven Gables* (1851) respectively (1988: 41–2). (2, 7, 10–12, 16, 22, 24, 25, 27, 29, 33, 34, 36, 39–42, 47–49, 52, 54)

Tulrumble, Mr (MP) A coal merchant, who becomes the Mayor of Mudfog. He persuades the council to refuse a music licence to the Jolly Boatmen Inn on the grounds that the 'fiddle and tambourine' are demoralising influences. But his consequent unpopularity leads to his repenting his action and his relinquishing public life after only six weeks.

Tungay (DC) A 'stout man with a bull-neck, a wooden leg, overhanging temples, and his hair cut close all round his head', who is the porter at Salem House. He acts as Mr Creakle's 'inter-

Figure 35 Mr Tulkinghorn, Mr Guppy, and Lady Dedlock by Hablot K. Browne
(Phiz)

preter', as he has a strong voice whereas Mr Creakle speaks in a whisper. (5–7)

Tupman, Tracy (PP) One of Mr Pickwick's companions, Mr Tupman is a middle-aged, portly bachelor, the ruling passion of whose soul is 'admiration of the fair sex'. He and Miss Rachael Wardle are smitten with each other, and their kissing in the arbour at Dingley Dell is observed with relish by Joe, the fat boy. After Mr Jingle's apparent elopement with Rachael, Mr Tupman leaves Dingley Dell, overcome with melancholy. 'You do not know what it is,' he writes to Mr Pickwick, 'at one blow, to be deserted by a lovely and fascinating creature, and to fall a victim to the artifices of a villain.' At the end of the Pickwickians' adventures, Mr Tupman takes lodgings at

Richmond, where he 'walks constantly on the Terrace during the summer months, with a youthful and jaunty air which has rendered him the admiration of the numerous elderly ladies of single condition, who reside in the vicinity. He has never proposed again.' (1–9, 11–15, 18, 19, 24–26, 28, 30, 32, 34, 35, 44, 47, 57)

Tupple, Mr (SB) The 'charming person' and 'perfect ladies' man', who is the life and soul of the New Year quadrille party held in the house with green blinds. ('Characters: The New Year')

Turveydrop, Mr (BH) The proprietor of a Dancing Academy in Newman Street, Mr Turveydrop is 'celebrated, almost everywhere, for his Deportment', in the words of Caddy Jellyby, although (as she goes on to say) 'he don't teach anything in particular'. 'He was a fat old gentleman with a false complexion, false teeth, false whiskers, and a wig' and was dressed in an elaborate and artificial manner. 'He had a cane, he had an eyeglass, he had a snuff-box, he had rings, he had wristbands, he had everything but any touch of nature; he was not like youth, he was not like age, he was not like anything in the world but a model of Deportment.' After a brief 'severe internal struggle', Mr Turveydrop benignly agrees to the marriage of Caddy and his son, Prince, on the selfish condition that they live with him and attend to his 'few and simple' wants. As Edgar Johnson points out, he can be considered as a 'bloated parody of the Prince Regent' (1953: 768). (14, 23, 30, 38, 50, 67)

Turveydrop, Prince (BH) Mr Turveydrop's son (obviously named in honour of the former Prince Regent), who marries Caddy Jellyby. He was 'a little blue-eyed fair man of youthful appearance, with flaxen hair parted in the middle, and curling at the ends all round his head. He had a little fiddle, which we

used to call at school a kit, under his left arm, and its little bow in the same hand. His little dancing-shoes were particularly diminutive, and he had a little innocent, feminine manner, which not only appealed to me [i.e., Esther Summerson] in an amiable way, but made this singular effect on me: that I received the impression that he was like his mother, and that his mother had not been much considered or well used.' Prince and his wife, who are devoted to each other, have a deaf and dumb daughter. They work hard to make the Academy a success and prosper, although eventually the main burden falls on Caddy, since her 'excellent' husband becomes lame. (14, 23, 30, 38, 50, 67)

Twemlow, Melvin (OMF) A mild-mannered, rather pathetic but 'innocent good gentleman.' The great looking-glass in the Veneerings' dining room reflects 'Twemlow: grey, dry, polite, susceptible to east wind, First-Gentleman-in-Europe collar and cravat, cheeks drawn in as if he had made a great effort to retire into himself some years ago, and had got so far and had never got any farther.' As the second cousin to Lord Snigsworth, Twemlow is always the first to be invited to the Veneerings' gatherings. He gives away the bride, Sophronia Akersham, when she marries Alfred Lammle. When Veneering seeks Twemlow's influence with Lord Snigsworth to help him get elected to Parliament, Twemlow memorably refers to the House of Commons as 'the best club in London', but is confused and worried by Veneering's request: 'I shall either go distracted, or die of this man. He comes upon me too late in life. I am not strong enough to bear him!' Mrs Lammle confides to him the plot she and her husband had devised regarding the marriage of Georgiana Podsnap to Fledgeby. He accordingly warns Mr Podsnap. Twemlow has himself fallen into the hands of Fledgeby because of debt, although he thinks that Riah is the

Figure 36 Nancy, Oliver Twist, and Bill Sikes by George Cruikshank

money-lender. Despite the hostility of Podsnap and others at the Veneering dinner table, Twemlow speaks up in favour of Eugene Wrayburn's marriage to Lizzie as the action of a true gentleman and lady. (I: 2, 10, 17; II: 3, 16; III: 13, 17; IV: 16, 17)

Twigger, Edward (MP) A 'merry-tempered, pleasant-faced, good-for-nothing sort of vagabond, with an invincible dislike to manual labour, and an unconquerable attachment to strong beer and spirits'. He 'rejoiced in the *sobriquet* of Bottle-nosed Ned'. Dressed in a suit of armour in Mr Tulrumble's mayoral procession, he becomes incapably drunk. His wife, Mrs Twigger, blames Tulrumble for her husband's predicament.

Twinkleton, Miss (MED) The principal of the Seminary for Young Ladies at the Nuns' House in Cloisterham, where Rosa Bud is the 'pet pupil'. She has 'two distinct and separate phases of being': one as the schoolmistress, and the other at night when she becomes 'sprightlier' and indulges in gossip with Mrs Tisher, 'who looks after the young ladies' wardrobes'. She follows Rosa to London, where she achieves 'a happy compromise between her two states of existence'. She has a number of sharp exchanges with 'the Billickin', with whom they are lodging. (3, 6, 7, 9, 13, 19, 20, 22)

Twist, Oliver (OT) The eponymous young hero of the novel. Oliver Twist was an orphan, born in a workhouse and given his name by Mr Bumble, the beadle. He was the illegitimate son of Edwin Leeford and Agnes Fleming, and hence the half-brother of Monks and the nephew of Rose Maylie, but the complicated story of his identity and his family is not revealed until the end of the novel. In his early life, Oliver Twist is surrounded by miserable and evil circumstances and people. He is bullied, tormented and deceived by Mr Bumble (in the workhouse), Mrs Sowerberry and Noah Claypole (at Sowerberry the undertaker's), Fagin and Bill Sikes (in the London thieves' den), and others. His most famous utterance is 'Please sir, I want some more,' when he is chosen by lot to ask the master of the workhouse for another helping of gruel (a request that has disastrous consequences). In contrast to his many sufferings in childhood, Oliver finds a temporary refuge with Mr Brownlow, who takes him in after he was falsely accused of picking Brownlow's pocket, and later an affectionate home with the Maylie family (after he was forced by Bill Sikes to take part in the burglary of their house). But Oliver is constantly threatened by the evil machinations of Monks (assisted by Fagin), who has appropriated his inheritance. When all the problems and mysteries of his life are resolved, thanks mostly to Mr Brownlow's endeavours, he is adopted by Mr Brownlow, 'who went on, from day to day, filling the mind of his adopted child with stores of knowledge'. Dickens declared, in his Preface to the Third Edition of the novel, that he 'wished to shew, in little Oliver, the principle of Good surviving through every adverse circumstance, and triumphing at last' (*passim*).

U

Uncommercial Traveller (UT) The narrator of thirty-seven essays, tales and sketches. 'I am both a town traveller and a country traveller, and am always on the road. Figuratively speaking, I travel for the great house of Human Interest Brothers, and have rather a large connection in the fancy goods way.'

Undery, Mr (CS) The narrator's friend and solicitor, who stayed at the Haunted House. He 'came down, in an amateur capacity, "to go through with it," as he said, and [he] plays whist better than the whole Law List, from the red cover at the beginning to the red cover at the end'. Dickens's lawyer was named Fred Ouvry (Glancy 1996: 815). ('The Haunted House')

Upwitch, Richard (PP) A greengrocer, who was one of the jury in the trial of Bardell v. Pickwick. (34)

V

Valentine, Private (CS) A soldier, who acted as 'sole housemaid, valet, cook, steward, and nurse in the family of his captain, Monsieur le Capitaine de la Cour'. ('Somebody's Luggage')

Varden, Dolly (BR) The daughter of Gabriel Varden, the locksmith, and his wife. Dolly has 'a roguish face . . . a face lighted up by the loveliest pair of sparkling eyes that ever a locksmith looked upon; the face of a pretty laughing girl; dimpled and fresh, and healthful – the very impersonation of good-humour and blooming beauty'. She willingly acts as a go-between for Emma Haredale and Edward Chester and (on Mr Haredale's suggestion) becomes a companion to Emma. Sim Tappertit and Hugh, the ostler, both desire her, but her true admirer is Joe Willet. But Dolly is 'a coquette by nature, and a spoilt child'. Although she loves Joe, who declares his love for her, her flirtatious rebuffs deeply hurt him and he goes abroad to serve in the army. As soon as he left her, she 'bolted herself in, laid her head down on her bed, and cried as if her heart would break'. With Emma and Miggs, she is held captive by Sim Tappertit, Hugh and Dennis during the Gordon Riots until rescued by Edward Chester, Joe Willet and Gabriel Varden. Repentant, Dolly soon afterwards declares her love for Joe, who, she says, has taught her 'to be something better' than she was. They marry and have 'more small Joes and small Dollys than could be easily counted'. On one occasion Dolly had worn a 'a little straw hat trimmed with cherry-coloured ribbons, and worn the merest trifle on one side –

just enough, in short, to make it the wickedest and most provoking head-dress that ever malicious milliner devised'. Because of this description, a 'Dolly Varden' came to mean a certain type of hat worn by women. Pictorially, Dolly's image was popular, especially as portrayed by William Powell Frith, who was requested by Dickens to paint two companion pictures, one of Dolly Varden and the other of Kate Nickleby. Frith's painting of Dolly is now in the Victoria and Albert Museum, London. (4, 7, 13, 19–23, 27, 28, 31, 41, 59, 70–72, 78, 80, 82)

Varden, Gabriel (BR) The stalwart, honest locksmith, after whom the novel Dickens eventually entitled *Barnaby Rudge* was originally named (*Gabriel Vardon* [sic], *the Locksmith of London*). He was 'a round, red-faced, sturdy yeoman, with a double chin, and a voice husky with good living, good sleeping, good humour, and good health. He was past the prime of life . . . bluff, hale, hearty, and in a green old age: at peace with himself, and evidently disposed to be so with all the world.' Gabriel Varden patiently endures the 'uncertain temper' of his wife and is a sympathetic friend to Mrs Rudge and Mr Haredale. When the Gordon Riots break out, he plays his part in upholding the forces of law and order as a sergeant in the Royal East London Volunteers. He indicates to his wife, who had been devoted to Protestantism, that 'all good things perverted to evil purposes, are worse than those which are naturally bad', thus acting as a mouthpiece for Dickens's opinions on

Figure 37 Dolly Varden by William Powell Frith

religious fanaticism and intolerance. As Gabriel had helped to make the lock on the gate of Newgate Prison, the violent mob of rioters tried to make him force it to give them access, but he defied them: 'He had never loved his life so well as then, but nothing could move him. The savage faces that glared upon him, look where he would; the cries of those who thirsted, like wild animals, for his blood; the sight of men pressing forward, and trampling down their fellows, as they strove to reach him, and struck at him above the heads of other men, with axes and iron bars; all failed to daunt him.' He is rescued by 'a one-armed man' (i.e., Joe Willet) and another man. Gabriel Varden confronts Sir John Chester with Dennis's revelations concerning Hugh's parentage but fails to get any admission of the truth from him. After the Riots, Gabriel finds complete happiness in the reformed character of his wife, the dismissal of Miggs, his wife's maid, and the marriage of Dolly to Joe. (2–7, 13, 19, 21, 22, 26, 27, 36, 41, 42, 51, 63, 64, 71, 72, 74–76, 79, 80, 82)

Varden, Mrs Martha (BR) The wife of Gabriel Varden, the locksmith, and the mother of Dolly. 'Mrs Varden was a lady of what is commonly called an uncertain temper – a phrase which being interpreted signifies a temper tolerably certain to make everybody more or less uncomfortable. Thus it generally happened, that when other people were merry, Mrs Varden was dull; and that when other people were dull, Mrs Varden was disposed to be amazingly cheerful.' She 'did not want for personal attractions, being plump and buxom to look at, though like her fair daughter, somewhat short in stature'. Mrs Varden is a fanatical Protestant, often engaged in the study of the Protestant Manual, but the outbreak of the Gordon Riots brings about a change of heart: she 'was impressed with a secret misgiving that she had done wrong; that she had, to the utmost of her small means, aided and abetted the growth of disturbances, the end of which it was impossible to foresee'. After the end of the Riots and with the coming together of Dolly and Joe Willet, Mrs Varden grows 'quite young', is 'laughing in face and mood', and dismisses Miggs, the domestic servant who had previously been her ally. (4, 7, 13, 19, 21, 22, 27, 36, 41, 42, 51, 71, 72, 80, 82)

Veck, Meg (CB) Trotty Veck's daughter. (*The Chimes*)

Veck, Trotty (CB) Toby Veck was nicknamed Trotty 'from his pace', since he was a ticket-porter, who stood all day outside the door of an old church (usually identified as St Dunstan's in Fleet Street, London). Although he was a 'weak, small, spare old man, he was a very Hercules, this Toby, in his good intentions'. He has a dream on New Year's Eve, in which he has a gloomy vision of the future, but when he awakes he joyfully discovers that the preparations for the wedding of Meg, his daughter, to Richard, the blacksmith, are being made. (*The Chimes*)

Vendale, George (CS) A 'brown-cheeked handsome fellow', who is the partner in the business of Wilding and Co., wine merchants. He eventually becomes its owner. Jules Obenreizer, fearing that Vendale will expose his fraudulent activities, hurls him over a precipice in Switzerland and leaves him for dead. But he is saved by Marguerite Obenreizer, whom he loves and eventually marries. It is discovered that he is the long-lost heir to the Wilding business. ('No Thoroughfare')

Veneering, Hamilton and Anastasia (OMF) They were the appropriately named 'bran-new people in a bran-new house in a bran-new quarter of London. Everything about the Veneerings was spick and span new.' All the things in their house 'were in a high state of high varnish and polish. And what was observable in the furniture, was observable in the Veneerings – the surface smelt a little too much of the workshop and was a trifle sticky.' Mr Veneering was 'forty, wavy-haired, dark, tending to corpulence, sly, mysterious, filmy – a kind of sufficiently well-looking veiled-prophet, not prophesying'. Mrs Veneering was 'fair, aquiline-nosed and fingered, not so much light hair as she might have, gorgeous in raiment and jewels, enthusiastic, propitiatory, conscious that a corner of her husband's veil is over herself'. They give dinner parties, at which the guests include Twemlow, Lady Tippins, the Podsnaps, Mortimer Lightwood and Eugene Wrayburn, who represent the 'voice of society'. Using the influence of such acquaintances as Twemlow, Podsnap and Lady Tippins, Veneering gets himself elected as the MP for Pocket-Breaches. In the end, however, he makes a 'resounding smash' (i.e., he is financially ruined). The Veneerings consequently 'retire to Calais, there to live on Mrs Veneering's diamonds'. Society then discovers that it had always despised and distrusted Veneering. (I: 2, 10, 11, 17; II: 3, 16; III: 17; IV: 17)

Vengeance, the (TTC) A fierce friend and 'lieutenant' of Madame Defarge's. She was the 'short, rather plump wife of a starved grocer', and regularly attends the executions at the guillotine. (II: 22; III: 3, 5, 9, 10, 12, 14, 15)

Venning, Mrs (CS) One of the residents on Silver-Store Island, who is proud, in the opinion of Gill Davis, the narrator. ('The Perils of Certain English Prisoners')

Ventriloquist, Monsieur the (UT) A 'thin and sallow [man] . . . of a weakly aspect', who is one of the entertainers at the Fair. ('In the French-Flemish Country')

Venus, Mr (OMF) A taxidermist and dealer in bones and skeletons, whose 'little dark greasy' shop is in Clerkenwell. Mr Venus has a 'sallow face with weak eyes, surmounted by a tangle of reddish-dusty hair'. One of his acquaintances is Silas Wegg, whose amputated leg he had bought from a hospital porter. Wegg persuades Mr Venus to join him in a plot to blackmail Mr Boffin regarding the provisions of old Harmon's will. Venus, however, while pretending to go along with the plot, repents of his participation

in it and secretly informs Mr Boffin of Wegg's evil schemes. In the final exposure of Wegg's machinations, Mr Venus twice calls him a 'precious old rascal'. Mr Venus, a 32-year-old bachelor, is in love with Pleasant Riderhood, who objects to his occupation, writing that she did not wish to be regarded 'in that bony light'. But she finally agrees to marry him on condition that he confines himself to the 'articulation of men, children, and the lower animals'. Dickens based Mr Venus on J. Willis, 42 St Andrew Street, Seven Dials, London. Marcus Stone, the illustrator of *Our Mutual Friend*, took Dickens to the shop: 'although Willis himself was not there, [Dickens] took note of everything; in a novel which came to anatomise society and the confusion of human identity, this articulator of skeletons and stuffer of dead animals proved to be precisely the man he needed for the purposes of his design. And so Mr Venus was born' (Ackroyd 1990: 943–4). (I: 7; II: 7; III: 6, 7, 14; IV: 3, 14)

Verisopht, Lord Frederick (OT) One of the most crudely named of Dickens's characters, he is a young nobleman in Ralph Nickleby's 'net' and under the influence of Sir Mulberry Hawk. Ralph Nickleby thinks that by introducing Lord Frederick to Kate he will be able 'to draw him on more gently'. Although Lord Frederick is in some respects a typical 'swell' (exclaiming 'What – the – deyvle!' when he first meets Kate), he is indignant at Sir Mulberry Hawk's plan to take revenge on Nicholas, who (in Lord Frederick's opinion) had acted in a 'manly and spirited' way. His differences with Sir Mulberry end in a duel, in which he is shot dead: 'So died Lord Frederick Verisopht, by the hand which he had loaded with gifts, and clasped a thousand times.' (19, 26–28, 32, 38, 44, 50)

Vholes, Mr (BH) The legal adviser of Richard Carstone, who was introduced to him by Harold Skimpole. He was 'a sallow man with pinched lips that looked as if they were cold, a red eruption here and there upon his face, tall and thin, about fifty years of age, high-shouldered, and stooping. Dressed in black, black-gloved, and buttoned to the chin, there was nothing so remarkable in him as a lifeless manner, and a slow fixed way he had of looking at Richard.' He has 'an inward manner' of speaking. Mr Vholes emphasises his family responsibilities: that he has an aged father to support and three daughters, Emma, Jane and Caroline. His dark and stale-smelling offices are in Symond's Inn, Chancery Lane. He is considered as 'a *most* respectable man' (according to Mr Kenge), has a cool and legalistic approach to everything, and makes great play with the idea of openness in his transactions. But he draws the trusting Richard deeper and deeper into the complexities of the Jarndyce v. Jarndyce case. Dickens uses him to exemplify the essentially self-seeking nature of the legal system, as he saw it, making plain his opinion in an authorial intervention: 'In a word, Mr Vholes, with his three daughters and his father in the Vale of Taunton, is continually doing duty, like a piece of timber, to shore up some decayed foundation that has become a pitfall and a nuisance. And with a great

many people in a great many instances, the question is never one of change from Wrong to Right (which is quite an extraneous consideration), but is always one of injury or advantage to that eminently respectable legion, Vholes.' (37, 39, 43, 45, 51, 60, 62, 65)

Victualler, Mr Licensed (UT) The 'host' of a public-house in the Liverpool docks. He was a 'sharp and watchful man . . . with tight lips and a complete edition of Cocker's arithmetic in each eye'. ('Poor Mercantile Jack')

Voigt, Maître (CS) A 'rosy, hearty, handsome old man,' who was the chief notary at Neuchatel. Obenreizer deceitfully operates the clock-lock that secures the door to his safe deposit and finds the evidence of Vendale's identity. ('No Thoroughfare')

Vuffin, Mr (OCS) A travelling showman encountered by Little Nell and her Grandfather. He was 'the proprietor of a giant, and a little lady without legs or arms'. When his giants become too old to be shown, Vuffin keeps them in caravans to wait upon the dwarfs: 'Once make a giant common and giants will never draw [the public] again.' (19)

W

Wackles, Sophia (OCS) The young woman between whom and Dick Swiveller 'warm and tender sentiments have been engendered' (to use his words to Fred Trent). Miss Sophy, who is a 'fresh, good-humoured, buxom girl of twenty', lives with her mother and two sisters, Melissa and Jane, in Chelsea, where they maintain a 'very small day-school for young ladies of proportionate dimensions'. But they are not favourably inclined to Dick Swiveller, and Sophy eventually marries a 'stricken market-gardener' named Cheggs. Dick, who is disconsolate, especially when Sophy's sisters deliver a piece of the bridal cake to him, blames Quilp, who had supported Fred's scheme for a marriage between Dick and Little Nell. He imagines Sophy playing cards with her husband to 'banish her regrets' and takes to playing the flute as a 'good, sound, dismal occupation'. (7, 8, 21, 50, 58)

Wade, Miss (LD) First encountered by Arthur Clennam and the Meagles family in a Marseilles hotel, she is a 'handsome young Englishwoman, travelling quite alone, who had a proud observant face'. When Mr Meagles speculates whether a prisoner, when released, forgives his prison, she says her experience has corrected any belief that forgiveness is easy: 'If I had been shut up in any place to pine and suffer, I should always hate that place and wish to burn it down, or raze it to the ground. I know no more.' She typically sits in shadow: 'One could hardly see the face, so still and scornful, set off by the arched dark eyebrows, and the folds of dark hair, without wondering what its expression would be if a change came over it . . . Although not an open face, there was no pretence in it. I am self-contained and self-reliant; your opinion is nothing to me; I have no interest in you, care nothing for you, and see and hear you with indifference – this it said plainly. It said so in the proud eyes, in the lifted nostril, in the handsome, but compressed and even cruel mouth.' Miss Wade, fascinated by Tattycoram's passionate resentment towards the Meagles family, persuades her to leave them and to live with her in Calais, where she is fiercely protective of her. She conceals the papers relating to Little Dorrit that had fallen into Rigaud's possession, denying all knowledge of them when Mr Meagles comes in search of them. Earlier, she had given Arthur Clennam an autobiographical document: 'The History of a Self Tormentor'. This was a detailed account of the tortuous and frustrated human relationships she (an illegitimate child) had suffered, caused by her own resentments and suspicions, as a schoolgirl and governess. When Henry Gowan came into her life, she found somebody who seemed to understand her, but he left her to court Pet Meagles. At that point, Miss Wade found Tattycoram, 'in various circumstances of whose position there was a singular likeness to [her] own'. Lionel Trilling sees Miss Wade as a typical example of a certain psychological condition: 'The self-torture of Miss Wade – who becomes the more interesting if we think of her as the exact inversion of Esther Summerson in *Bleak House* – is the classic manoeuvre of the child who is unloved, or believes herself to be unloved – she refuses to be lovable, she elects to be hateful' (1952: xi). (I: 2, 16, 27, 28; II: 9, 20, 21, 33)

Waghorn, Mr (MP) A vice-president of the Mechanical Science session at the first meeting of the Mudfog Association.

Wakefield, Mr, Mrs and Miss (SB) A family who arrive late with the Fleet-woods on a wherry for the excursion on the Thames. ('Tales: The Steam Excursion')

Waldengarver, Mr (GE) *See* **Wopsle, Mr.**

Walker, Mr (SB) The auditor of the ac-counts of the Indigent Orphans' Friends' Benevolent Institution. ('Scenes: Public Dinners')

Walker, Mr (SB) A jocose horse-dealer confined for debt in the lock-up where Mr Watkins Tottle is taken. ('Tales: A Passage in the Life of Mr Watkins Tottle')

Walker, Mr and Mrs (SB) Residents of No. 5 in a London suburban street. Like her neighbours, Mrs Walker buys muf-fins from the muffin boy, who 'rings his way down the little street'. ('Scenes: The Streets – Night')

Walker, H. (PP) An unemployed tailor with a wife and two children, who is one of the converts to Temperance an-nounced by the secretary in his 'Report of the Committee of the Brick Lane Branch of the United Grand Junction Ebenezer Temperance Association'. (33)

Walker, Mick (DC) The 'oldest of the regular boys' who worked at Murdstone and Grinby's warehouse. He wore 'a rag-ged apron and a paper cap', and in-formed David Copperfield that 'his father was a bargeman, and walked, in a

black velvet head-dress, in the Lord Mayor's Show'. (11, 12)

Walmer, Harry (CS) The 'little gentle-man not eight years old', who 'eloped' with Norah, 'a fine young woman of seven', Their story is told by the Boots. ('The Holly-Tree Inn')

Warden (SB) The name of a wretched London family. One son, Henry, was shot by a gamekeeper and another son, William, is arrested for murder. The drunken father plunges to his death in the river. ('Tales: The Drunkard's Death')

Warden, Michael (CB) A 'man of thirty, or about that time of life, negligently dressed, and somewhat haggard in the face, but well-made, well-attired, and well-looking', who is a spendthrift. He is in love with Marion Jeddler, with whom he is wrongly suspected of eloping. Thanks to his lawyers, Snitchey and Craggs, his financial affairs are put into order and he marries Marion. (*The Battle of Life*)

Wardle, Mr, and his family (PP) Mr Wardle is a stout, 'jolly old gentleman', who is the congenial host at his house, Manor Farm, Dingley Dell, where Mr Pickwick and his fellow-members stay on two memorable occasions in summer and winter. He heartily presides over gener-ous meals, a shooting party, Christmas festivities, and so on. Rachael Wardle, his spinster sister, gained Mr Tupman's af-fections but was persuaded to elope by the rascally Mr Jingle. Mr Wardle, with Mr Pickwick and Mr Perker, his lawyer, confronts them both at the White Hart Inn: 'you, Rachael, at a time of life when you ought to know better, what do *you* mean by running away with a vagabond, disgracing your family, and making yourself miserable. Get on your bonnet, and come back.' He abruptly reveals her age ('you're fifty if you're an hour') and when 'the humane Mr Pickwick' asks the

Figure 38 Arabella Allen, Mr Winkle, Mr Wardle, Mr Pickwick, Mrs Wardle, Emma, Sam Weller, Emily Wardle, and Mr Snodgrass by Hablot K. Browne (Phiz)

landlady to bring her a glass of water he passionately exclaims, 'A *glass* of water! . . . Bring a bucket, and throw it all over her; it'll do her good, and she richly deserves it.' He buys Jingle off with a cheque for £120. One of his daughters, Isabella, married Mr Trundle at Christmas and the other daughter, Emily, married Mr Snodgrass. Mr Wardle's mother is deaf and occasionally given to sharp-tongued utterances. (4–10, 11, 14, 16–19, 28, 30, 54, 56, 57)

Waterbrook, Mr and Mrs (DC) Agnes Wickfield stayed with them in Ely-place, Holborn, London, since Mr Waterbrook was Mr Wickfield's agent. He was a 'middle-aged gentleman, with a short throat, and a good deal of shirt-collar, who only wanted a black nose to be the portrait of a pug-dog'. Mrs Waterbrook was a 'large lady – or . . . wore a large dress' (David Copperfield did not know 'which was dress and which was lady'). Both assert the importance of 'Blood'. Mr Waterbrook is 'able to throw something in Traddles's way' occasionally (i.e., legal business). (24, 25, 27)

Waters, Captain and Mrs (SB) A 'stoutish, military-looking gentleman' and his wife, 'a young lady in a puce-coloured silk cloak, and boots of the same; with long black ringlets, large black eyes, brief petticoats, and unexceptionable ankles'. They make the acquaintance of the

Tuggses. Cymon Tuggs is duped into a Platonic dalliance with Mrs Belinda Waters, and is conveniently 'discovered' by Lieutenant Slaughter hiding behind a curtain at a crucial moment. Mr Joseph Tuggs, his father, therefore has to pay Captain Waters £1500 to hush the matter up. ('Tales: The Tuggses at Ramsgate')

Watkins, Mr (NN) Kate Nickleby's godfather, who (according to Mrs Nickleby) jumped bail, ran away to the United States, and sent the family a pair of snow shoes, but could not repay the £50 which Mr Nickleby had had to forfeit. (18)

Watkins the First (HR) The King who was the father of Princess Alicia in Miss Alice Rainbird's 'romance'.

Watson, Mrs and the Misses (SYG) Friends of Mr Mincin. ('The Very Friendly Young Gentleman')

Watty, Mr (PP) A 'rustily-clad, miserable-looking man, in boots without toes and gloves without fingers' and with 'traces of privation and suffering – almost of despair – in his lank and careworn countenance', whom Mr Pickwick and Sam Weller see at Mr Perker's chambers. According to Lowten, 'There never was such a pestering bankrupt as that since the world began.' (31)

Wedgington, Mr and Mrs B (RP) The narrator goes to Mrs Wedgington's thinly attended benefit at the Theatre in a watering-place. They both sing, and Mr Wedgington also dances in clogs. ('Out of the Season')

Weedle, Anastatia (UT) A Mormon emigrant, who is 'a pretty girl, in a bright Garibaldi [a blouse], this morning elected by universal suffrage the Beauty of the Ship'. ('Bound for the Great Salt Lake')

Weevle (BH) *See* **Jobling.**

Wegg, Silas (OMF) A street-trader with a stall near Cavendish Square, who sells a 'few small lots of fruit and sweets' and halfpenny ballads. Wegg has only one leg; his amputated leg had been sold by a hospital porter to Mr Venus. Mr Boffin employs Wegg to read to him the 'Decline-and-Fall-Off-the Rooshan-Empire' (i.e., Gibbon's *Decline and Fall of the Roman Empire*) at five shillings a week and eventually installs him in his old residence, the Bower. Wegg is a rascally, scheming man, who cherishes the notion of making a profitable discovery: 'For when a man with a wooden leg lies prone on his stomach to peep under bedsteads; and hops up ladders, like some extinct bird, to survey the tops of presses and cupboards; and provides himself with an iron rod which he is always poking and prodding into dust-mounds; the probability is that he expects to find something.' Wegg tells Mr Venus, whom he has persuaded to be his accomplice, of his resentment that Boffin has put John Rokesmith into a superior position in his household and of his suspicion that something important or valuable has been hidden in the dust mounds. He discovers there a will in which old Mr Harmon leaves his property to the Crown, thus apparently invalidating Mr Boffin's inheritance; he therefore intends to blackmail Boffin. But Venus, who repents taking part in Wegg's plot, has revealed Wegg's intentions to Boffin. In any case, the discovery of a later will completely disconcerts Wegg and puts paid to his schemes of extortion. At the end of the scene where his villainy is exposed, Sloppy grasps him by the coat collar, lightly trots him out of the room, and shoots him into a scavenger's cart: 'A somewhat difficult feat, achieved with great dexterity, and with a prodigious splash.' (I: 5, 7, 15, 17; II: 7, 10; III: 6, 7, 14; IV: 3, 14)

Weller, Sam (PP) Mr Pickwick's manservant, whom Pickwick first encounters

Figure 39 Sam Weller, Mr Perker, Mr Wardle, and Mr Pickwick by Hablot K. Browne
(Phiz)

at the White Hart Inn in the Borough, where he is working as a 'boots'. Soon afterwards, Mr Pickwick engages Sam for £12 a year and the provision of two suits of clothes, including a 'grey coat with the P.C. [Pickwick Club] button, a black hat with a cockade to it, a pink striped waistcoat, light breeches and gaiters, and a variety of other necessaries, too numerous to recapitulate'. From then on, Sam becomes Mr Pickwick's devoted and irrepressible servant through all the vagaries that beset his master, whose innocence and naïveté are always contrasted with Sam's sharpness and resourcefulness. Sam's encounters with his father, Tony Weller, are memorable occasions for repartee and mutual advice. For Sam is characterised, above all, by his vivid Cockney speech, full of inventive comic anecdotes and imagery, which quickly became known as Wellerisms and which have found their way into dictionaries of quotations: 'Vich I calls addin' insult to injury, as the parrot said ven they not only took him from his native land, but made him talk the English langwidge arterwards,' or 'Avay with melincholly, as the little boy said ven his school missis died.' At the trial of Bardell v. Pickwick, Sam surveys everyone and everything 'with a remarkably cheerful and lively aspect' when he is called to give evidence, and disconcerts Serjeant Buzfuz and others with his calmly impudent answers: 'Yes, I have a pair of eyes ... and that's just it. If they wos a pair o' patent double million magnifyin' gas microscopes of hextra power, p'raps I might be able to see through a flight o' stairs and a deal door; but bein' only eyes, you see, my wision's limited.' He remains in protective attendance on Mr Pickwick during the latter's imprisonment in the Fleet. At the end of the novel, Sam, still in Mr Pickwick's employment, marries Mary, the 'pretty servant-girl' he had earlier met at Mr Nupkins's house and who becomes Mr Pickwick's housekeeper. There seems little doubt that Dickens's introduction of Sam Weller in Chapter 12 was one of the reasons for the enormous success of *Pickwick Papers* after a comparatively slow start to its monthly serialisation. Dickens briefly but unmemorably brings back Sam Weller (with Mr Pickwick, Tony Weller and Sam Weller's son, also named Tony) in *Master Humphrey's Clock* (3–6). John Forster expresses a universal opinion when he says that the 'pre-eminent achievement [of the novel] is of course Sam Weller; one of those people that take their places among the supreme successes of fiction.' Thinking of the picaresque nature of *Pickwick Papers*, Forster also thinks that 'Sam Weller and Mr Pickwick are the Sancho and Quixote of Londoners, as little likely to pass away as the old city itself' (1928: Book 2, Ch. 1). G.K. Chesterton goes further in seeing Sam Weller as 'the great symbol in English literature of the populace peculiar to England' (1933: 21). (10, 12, 13, 15, 16, 18–20, 22–28, 30, 31, 33–35, 37–48, 50–52, 55–57)

Weller, Mrs Tony (PP) Formerly Mrs Susan Clarke, a widow, she becomes Tony Weller's second wife and hence Sam Weller's stepmother (or, to use the terminology of the period, mother-in-law). She was a 'rather stout lady of comfortable appearance', who is the hostess of the Marquis of Granby public house, Dorking, Surrey but who has fallen under the religious influence of the Reverend Mr Stiggins. Tony Weller philosophically accepts her bursts of ill-temper. Having repented of her behaviour, she leaves her husband her property in her will as well as a small legacy to Sam. (10, 16, 20, 22, 23, 27, 33, 43, 45, 52, 55)

Weller, Tony (PP) Sam Weller's father. Tony Weller is a stage coachman of the sort that in the mid-1830s were about to become obsolete with the coming of the railway. The 'old 'un', as Sam affectionately calls him after meeting him by chance after two years, is a 'stout, red-faced, elderly man', fond of drink and tobacco. He has married a widow as his second wife and often warns Sam against the hazards of matrimony, as when he catches him writing a valentine to Mary: 'To see you married, Sammy – to see you a dilluded wictim, and thinkin' in your innocence that it's all very capital ... It's a dreadful trial to a father's feelings, that 'ere, Sammy.' Tony Weller makes a memorable intervention from the gallery in the trial of Bardell v. Pickwick when the judge asks Sam how his surname is spelt: 'Put it down a we, my lord, put it down a we.' He finally exacts revenge on Mr Stiggins, the 'deputy shepherd' who was a powerful and hypocritical influence on his wife, by ducking him in a horse trough. Tony Weller is compelled by gout to retire from coach-driving, retires on 'a handsome independence' (thanks to Mr Pickwick's good investments on his behalf), and 'lives at an excellent public-house near Shooter's Hill, where he is quite reverenced as an oracle: boasting very much of his intimacy with Mr Pickwick, and retaining a most unconquerable aversion to widows'. (10, 13, 16, 20, 22, 23, 27, 33, 34, 43, 45, 52, 55–57)

Wemmick, John (GE) The chief clerk to Mr Jaggers, the lawyer in charge of Pip's 'expectations'. Wemmick was 'a dry man, rather short in stature, with a square wooden face, whose expression seemed to have been imperfectly chipped out with a dull-edged chisel'. He wears 'at least four mourning-rings', which had been presented to him by criminals before their execution. 'His mouth was such a post-office of a mouth that he had a mechanical appearance of smiling.' Wemmick tells Pip that his 'guiding star' is 'portable property', such as the rings he wears. He divides his life into two distinct parts: 'the office is one thing, and private life is another'. He is proud of his little wooden cottage in Walworth, which he has converted into a miniature castle, with gothic windows and door, a flagstaff, a drawbridge (which is a plank), and a gun (the Stinger) that he fires every night at nine o'clock, Greenwich time. Wemmick lives there with his deaf father, whom he affectionately calls 'aged parent'. Pip noticed that as Wemmick walked from Walworth to Jaggers' office in Little Britain he 'got dryer and harder as we went along' and that once he had arrived there he looked completely unconscious of his home life. Mr Wemmick

is obviously fond, in his way, of Miss Skiffins, who was 'of a wooden appearance, and was, like her escort, in the post-office branch of the service'. With the aid of her brother, who was an accountant, Wemmick, at Pip's request, secretly arranges a business partnership for Herbert Pocket. He helps Pip and Herbert with information and advice when they are faced with the problem of making safe arrangements for Magwitch. Wemmick's marriage is a remarkably eccentric event. With a fishing rod over his shoulder, he invites Pip to walk with him to Camberwell Green, until they reach a church: '"Halloa!" said Wemmick. "Here's Miss Skiffins! Let's have a wedding!"' (20, 21, 24, 25, 32, 36, 37, 45, 48, 51, 55)

West, Dame (OCS) The grandmother of Harry West, a studious little boy at the village school. She unjustly blames the Schoolmaster for his death: 'If he hadn't been poring over his books out of fear of you, he would have been well and merry now, I know he would.' (25)

Westlock, John (MC) He was 'a good-looking youth, newly arrived at man's estate', who was Martin Chuzzlewit's predecessor as Mr Pecksniff's pupil. On leaving Pecksniff at the expiry of his term, Westlock strongly expresses his anger and contempt for the treatment he had received. He is a steady and sensible presence in the novel. He clearly perceives Pecksniff's hypocrisy, is a friend and confidant of Lewsome, and insists that Tom Pinch stays with him at Furnival's Inn when Tom is dismissed from Pecksniff's service. Westlock falls in love with Ruth Pinch at first sight, 'transfixed in silent admiration' when he sees her making a beefsteak pudding, and marries her. (2, 12, 25, 29, 36, 37, 39, 40, 45, 48–53)

Westwood, Mr (NN) One of Sir Mulberry Hawk's seconds in his duel with

Lord Frederick Verisopht. The other second is Captain Adams. (50)

Wharton, Granville (GSE) A 'young gentleman near coming of age, very well connected, but what is called a poor relation. His parents were dead . . . He was well-looking, clever, energetic, enthusiastic, bold; in the best sense of the term, a thorough Anglo-Saxon.' His tutor is George Silverman, who brings him and Adelina Fareway together, and officiates at their wedding.

Wheezy, Professor (MP) A vice-president of the Zoology and Botany session at the second meeting of the Mudfog Association.

Whiff, Miss (CS) One of the young ladies who serve in the Refreshment Room at Mugby Junction. ('Mugby Junction')

Whiffers, Mr (PP) A footman in orange-coloured livery, who announces his resignation at the 'swarry' attended by Sam Weller in Bath. Although his duties were light, 'he had been required to eat cold meat', which was a 'manly outrage on his feelings'. (37)

Whiffin (PP) The 'fat [town] crier' of Eatanswill, who rings an enormous bell to command silence during the election proceedings. (13)

Whiffler, Mr and Mrs (SYC) The 'couple who dote upon their children'.

Whilks, Mr and Mrs (MC) Prospective clients of Mrs Gamp, who when she hears Mr Pecksniff's knocking on her window exclaims: 'Don't say it's you, Mr Whilks, and that poor creetur Mrs Whilks [who is pregnant] with not even a pin-cushion ready.' (19)

Whimple, Mrs (GE) The 'motherly' landlady of the house where Mr Barley and his daughter, Clara, have lodgings. (46)

Whisker (OCS) The Garlands' 'self-willed pony who, from being the most obstinate and opinionated pony on the face of the earth, was, in [Kit Nubbles'] hands, the meekest and most tractable of animals'. (14, 20–22, 38, 40, 57, 65, 68, 73)

White (HR) One of Mrs Lemon's pupils in Miss Nettie Ashford's 'romance'. He is 'a pale, bald child, with red whiskers' in disgrace for betting on horses.

White (RP) A policeman on duty on Holborn Hill in London. ('On Duty with Inspector Field')

White (SB) A young man, who works at the gas-fitter's and whose lively way of life makes Mr Augustus Cooper envious. ('Scenes: The Dancing Academy')

White, Betsey (UT) A woman in the Liverpool docks, who 'grinds' Mercantile Jack in some way or other. She 'has been indicted three times'. ('Poor Mercantile Jack')

Wickam, Mrs (DS) A waiter's wife, who was engaged as Paul Dombey's nurse after Polly Toodle's dismissal. She was a 'meek woman, of a fair complexion, with her eyebrows always elevated, and her head always drooping; who was always ready to pity herself, or to be pitied, or to pity anybody else; and who had a surprising natural gift of viewing all subjects in an utterly forlorn and pitiable light, and bringing dreadful precedents to bear upon them, and deriving the greatest consolation from the exercise of that talent'. She later nurses Alice Marwood when she lies fatally ill. (8, 9, 11, 12, 18, 58)

Wickfield, Agnes (DC) The daughter of Mr Wickfield, Miss Trotwood's Canterbury lawyer. From an early age, Agnes has acted as the housekeeper for her widowed father. When David first sees her, he sees that she has inherited the 'placid and sweet expression of the lady [her mother]', whose picture he had just seen. 'Although her face was quite bright and happy, there was a tranquillity about it, and about her – a quiet, good, calm spirit – that I have never forgotten; that I shall never forget ... I cannot call to mind where or when, in my childhood, I had seen a stained glass window in a church. Nor do I recollect its subject. But I know that when I saw her turn round, in the grave light of the old staircase, I thought of that window; and I associated something of its tranquil brightness with Agnes Wickfield ever afterwards.' Throughout the narrative, David considers her his 'sweet sister' and his 'counsellor and friend'. Without realising that she loves him and that therefore he is causing her hurt, David confides his own troubles and loves to her. Always his 'good Angel,' she warns him against Steerforth, his 'bad Angel'. Although he asserts that her opinion is unjust, he realises that Steerforth's image has 'darkened' as a result. Agnes gives David sound practical advice: that he could work as Doctor Strong's part-time secretary and that he should gently approach Dora Spenlow by means of sometimes visiting her aunts' house. Miss Trotwood is aware of Agnes's deep love for David, and Dora, on her deathbed, urges Agnes to marry him. When David eventually asks her to be his wife, Agnes at last explicitly expresses her feelings for him: 'I have loved you all my life!' The sight of Agnes's 'solemn hand upraised towards Heaven' when Dora dies remains in David's mind and is recalled in the last words of his narrative: 'Oh, Agnes, Oh my soul, so may thy face be by me when I close my life indeed; so may I, when realities are melting from me like the shadows which I now dismiss, still find thee near me, pointing upward!' Even John Forster found Agnes hard to take: 'Of the heroines who divide so equally between them the impulsive, easily

swayed, not disloyal but sorely distracted affections of the hero, the spoilt foolishness and tenderness of the loving little child–wife, Dora, is more attractive than the too unfailing wisdom and self-sacrificing goodness of the angel–wife, Agnes' (1928: Book 6, Ch.7). Admitting that Agnes is among the less convincing characters, K.J. Fielding sees her, however, 'as standing for more than herself. Dickens presents her as a symbol of how love can lead a man's life to be fulfilled and given higher purpose' (1965: 142). As for her origins, Michael Slater states that 'Mary Hogarth's sanctified shadow falls on her just as heavily as it did on Rose Maylie' (1983: 100). (15–19, 24, 34, 35, 39, 42, 43, 52–54, 57, 58, 60, 62–64)

Wickfield, Mr (DC) The lawyer in Canterbury who handles Miss Trotwood's affairs and with whom David Copperfield lodges when a pupil at Doctor Strong's school. Mr Wickfield's 'hair was quite white now, though his eyebrows were still black. He had a very agreeable face, and, I [i.e., David] thought, was handsome. There was a certain richness in his complexion, which I had been long accustomed, under Peggotty's tuition, to connect with port wine; and I fancied it was in his voice too, and referred his growing corpulency to the same cause. He was very cleanly dressed, in a blue coat, striped waistcoat, and nankeen trousers, and his fine frilled shirt and cambric neckcloth looked unusually soft and white, reminding my strolling fancy (I call to mind) of the plumage on the breast of a swan.' Mr Wickfield succumbs more and more to drink and becomes depressed and self-pitying. Uriah Heep gains an ascendancy over him, becomes the dominant partner in the firm, and has designs to make Agnes, Mr Wickfield's daughter, his wife. Wickfield calls him his 'torturer' and declares that 'before him [he has] step by step abandoned name and reputation, peace and quiet, house and home'. But after Micawber's exposure of Heep, Mr Wickfield considerably improves. His business, clear of debt, is wound up, and he employs himself working in a garden outside the town. (15–17, 19, 25, 35, 39, 42, 52, 54, 60)

Wicks, Mr (PP) One of Dodson and Fogg's clerks, who tells a long story about the unfortunate Mr Ramsay in the hearing of Mr Pickwick and Sam Weller. (20)

Widger, Mr and Mrs Bobtail (SYC) 'They are always loving and harmonious.' ('The Plausible Couple')

Wield, Inspector Charles (RP) An officer in the Detective Force, who is a 'middle-aged man of a portly presence, with a large, moist, knowing eye, a husky voice, and a habit of emphasising his conversation by the aid of a corpulent fore-finger, which is constantly in juxtaposition with his eyes or nose'. He is modelled on Inspector Charles Field (q.v.), whom Dickens knew and admired. ('The Detective Police')

Wigsby, Mr (MP) At the meeting of the Zoology and Botany section at the first meeting of the Mudfog Association, he 'produced a cauliflower somewhat larger than a chaise-umbrella, which had been raised by no other artificial means than the simple application of highly carbonated soda-water as manure'.

Wilding, Walter (CS) The foundling who was the head of Wilding and Co., Wine Merchants. He was an 'innocent, open-speaking, unused-looking man . . . with a remarkably pink and white complexion, and a figure much too bulky for so young a man, though of a good stature. With crispy curling brown hair, and amiable blue eyes. An extremely communicative man: a man with whom loquacity was the irrestrainable outpouring of contentment and gratitude.' After Mrs Wilding's death, it was discovered that he was

not the foundling she had intended to adopt, but he himself dies in the course of his attempts to establish the truth of the matter. ('No Thoroughfare')

Wildspark, Tom (PP) Tony Weller's example of the importance of an alibi: 'Ve got Tom Vildspark off that 'ere manslaughter, with a alleybi, ven all the bigvigs to a man said as nothing couldn't save him.' (33)

Wilfer, Bella (OMF) Under the terms of old Harmon's will, John Harmon had to marry Bella in order to claim his inheritance. Old Harmon had seen her stamping and screaming when she was little, thought her 'nice' and 'promising', and therefore chose her as his son's prospective wife. But she and John Harmon have never met. She is beautiful and vivacious, seated on a rug to warm herself, when we first meet her, 'with her brown eyes on the fire and a handful of her brown curls in her mouth'. Bella lives at home in poor circumstances and is indignant that the will has been apparently invalidated by John Harmon's death. Although she thinks its provisions were absurd, 'they would have been smoothed away by the money, for I love money, and want money – want it dreadfully. I hate to be poor, and we are degradingly poor, offensively poor, miserably poor, beastly poor.' She and John Harmon (whom she knows as John Rokesmith) become members of the Boffins' household. He falls in love with her, but she affects indifference ('He has no right to any power over me, and how do I come to mind when I don't care for him?') and rejects him. But as Mr Boffin, who secretly seeks to cure her mercenary nature, seemingly becomes more and more miserly she begins to question her own trust in the power of money. In a conversation with Lizzie Hexam, Bella sits 'enchained by [Lizzie's] deep, unselfish passion' and is struck by Lizzie's telling her that she [Bella] has a heart that is never daunted.

She angrily accuses Boffin of monstrous behaviour towards John Rokesmith, leaves the Boffins' house fully reformed and repentant, and eventually marries John, not discovering his true identity until a good deal later. Their married life is blissfully happy. All the while, Bella has shown a deep love for her father, shown in her entertaining him to a dinner at Greenwich, in one of the most delightful scenes that Dickens wrote. Dickens's portrayal of Bella was praised by E.S. Dallas in an unsigned review in *The Times* (29 November 1865) – a review that so pleased the novelist that he gave Dallas the manuscript of the novel: 'Mr Dickens has never done anything in the portraiture of women so pretty and so perfect ... The little dialogues in which Mr Dickens has exhibited first her love for her father, then her love for her lover, and then the two combined, are full of a liveliness and a grace and a humour that seem to us to surpass any attempt of the same description which he has ever before made' (Collins 1971: 468). (I: 4, 9, 16, 17; II: 8–10, 13, 14; III: 4, 5, 7, 9, 15, 16; IV: 4, 5, 11–13, 16)

Wilfer, Lavinia (OMF) The pert and irrepressible sister of Bella. Lavinia is frightened of nobody and is always ready to cheek even her formidable mother, who refers to her as her 'audacious child'. When George Sampson transfers his affections from Bella to her, her behaviour to her adorer is sharp and unpredictable: 'Notwithstanding all these surroundings [of Bella and John's new house], I am yours as yet, George. How long it may last is another question, but I am yours as yet.' (I: 4, 9; II: 8; III: 4, 16; IV: 5, 16)

Wilfer, Mrs (OMF) The imposing and difficult wife of R. Wilfer and mother of Bella, Lavinia and many other children. 'Mrs Wilfer was, of course, a tall woman and an angular. Her lord being cherubic, she was necessarily majestic, according

to the principle which matrimonially unites contrasts. She was much given to tying up her head in a pocket-handkerchief, knotted under the chin. This head-gear, in conjunction with a pair of gloves worn within doors, she seemed to consider as at once a kind of armour against misfortune (invariably assuming it when in low spirits or difficulties), and as a species of full dress.' When the Boffins visit her to offer to 'adopt' Bella, she adopts, as usual, a forbidding manner, describing the Wilfers' house as 'the abode of conscious though independent Poverty'. The 'bearing of this impressive woman' is notable when she, Lavinia and George Sampson visit the Rokesmiths in their luxurious house: 'She regarded every servant who approached her, as her sworn enemy, expressly intending to offer her affronts with the dishes, and to pour forth outrages on her moral feelings from the decanters. She sat erect at table, on the right hand of her son-in-law, as half suspecting poison in the viands, and as bearing up with native force of character against other deadly ambushes. Her carriage towards Bella was as a carriage towards a young lady of good position, whom she had met in society a few years ago.' (I: 4, 9, 16; II: 8; III: 4, 16; IV: 5, 16)

Wilfer, Reginald (OMF) A poor clerk in the 'drug-house of Chicksey, Veneering, and Stobbles' and the father of Bella, Lavinia, Cecilia, John, Susan and others. Wilfer is cherubic and shyly unwilling 'to own to the name of Reginald, as being too aspiring and self-assertive a name. In his signature he used only the initial R., and imparted what it really stood for, to none but his chosen friends, under the seal of confidence ... his popular name was Rumty, which in a moment of inspiration had been bestowed upon him by a gentleman of convivial habits connected with the drug market.' He loves Bella, his favourite daughter, admiringly calling her his 'lovely woman', and is delighted to attend (without Mrs Wilfer) her secret wedding to John Harmon (whom they know as John Rokesmith). When the Harmons are finally established in prosperity, R. Wilfer resigns from the drug-house and becomes the Secretary to the Harmon property. (I: 4; II: 8, 14; III: 4, 16; IV: 4, 5, 16)

Wilhelm A German courier, who tells the ghost story of the twin brothers, James and John. ('To be Read at Dusk')

Wilkins (PP) One of Captain Boldwig's gardeners, who points out to his master that trespassers have been on his land and shows him Mr Pickwick sleeping in a wheelbarrow. (19)

Wilkins, Dick (CB) Scrooge's fellow-apprentice at Mr Fezziwig's. (*A Christmas Carol*)

Wilkins, Samuel (SB) He was a 'carpenter, a journeyman carpenter of small dimensions, decidedly below the middle size – bordering, perhaps, on the dwarfish. His face was round and shining, and his hair carefully twisted into the outer corner of each eye, till it formed a variety of that description of semi-curls, usually known as "aggerawators".' He 'keeps company' with Miss Jemima Evans. When he takes her out to a concert, with another young couple, he and the other young man get into a fight with a man in a plaid waistcoat, who had made 'divers remarks complimentary to the ankles of Miss J'mima Ivins [sic] and friend, in an audible tone'. The result, however, is that he and the friend's young man 'lay gasping on the gravel'. ('Characters: Miss Evans and the Eagle')

Willet, Joe (BR) The son of John Willet, the landlord of the Maypole in Chigwell. He was 'a broad-shouldered, strapping young fellow of twenty, whom it pleased his father still to consider a little boy, and to treat him accordingly'. Joe is in love

with Dolly Varden, whose flirtatious manner conceals her own feelings of love for him. He rebels against his father's attempted authority over him, knocks Tom Cobb (one of the regular customers at the inn, who supports John Willet's attitude towards his son) to the ground and leaves home. He declares his love for Dolly, who in coquettish mood rejects his affirmation. Joe joins the army under the name of Tom Green, loses his left arm at Savannah during the American War of Independence, and returns to England at the time of the Gordon Riots. He is now a 'gallant, manly, handsome fellow', who plays a full part in the restoration of law and order: 'let the fault be where it may [he says], it makes a man sorrowful to come back to old England, and see her in this condition'. With the help of others, Joe rescues Gabriel from the mob outside Newgate Prison, Mr Haredale and Langdale from the latter's house, and Dolly, Emma Haredale and Miggs from their captivity. Dolly and Joe marry, re-open the Maypole, and have many children. (1–4, 13, 14, 19, 21, 22, 24, 29–31, 33, 41, 58, 59, 67, 71, 72, 78, 80, 82)

Willet, John (BR) The landlord of the Maypole Inn, Chigwell. He was a 'burly, large-headed man with a fat face, which betokened profound obstinacy and slowness of apprehension, combined with a very strong reliance upon his own merits. It was John Willet's ordinary boast in his more placid moods that if he were slow he was sure; which assertion could, in one sense at least, be by no means gainsaid, seeing that he was in everything unquestionably the reverse of fast, and withal one of the most dogged and positive fellows in existence – always sure that what he thought or said or did was right, and holding it as a thing quite settled and ordained by the laws of nature and Providence, that anybody who said or did or thought otherwise must be inevitably and of necessity wrong.' He exerts his authority over his customers and his son, Joe, who rebels against him, leaves home and enlists in the army. During the Gordon Riots, the mob, on its way to burn down Mr Haredale's house, the Warren, arrive at the Maypole and in a frenzy wreck the bar in John Willet's presence and bind him in his chair. As a result, he becomes permanently stupefied. He is particularly obsessed with the loss of his son's arm: 'My son's arm – was took off – at the defence of the – Salwanners [i.e., Savannah] – in America – where the war is.' Seeing Joe and Dolly talking and kissing each other and ignoring him 'was a position so tremendous, so inexplicable, so utterly beyond the widest range of his capacity of comprehension, that he fell into a lethargy of wonder, and could no more rouse himself than an enchanted sleeper in the first year of his fairy lease, a century long'. John Willet ends his days in a cottage in Chigwell, uttering as his last words, 'I'm a-going, Joseph . . . to the Salwanners.' (1–3, 10–14, 19, 21, 29, 30, 33–35, 54–56, 72, 78, 82)

William (DC) The waiter who drinks David Copperfield's glass of ale and eats most of his dinner at the inn where the boy stops on his way to Salem House. (5)

William (DC) A coachman, who persuades David Copperfield to give up his box seat to a gentleman who breeds horses and dogs. David remarks, 'I have always considered this as the first fall I had in life.' (19)

William (SB) A lad of 18 or 19, who earns a pittance for himself and his widowed mother by 'copying writings, and translating for booksellers'. The pressure of work and the 'close crowded streets' bring about his death. ('Our Parish: Our Next-Door Neighbour')

Williams (RP) A policeman awaiting Inspector Field in Ratcliff Highway. ('On Duty with Inspector Field')

Williams, William (OMF) One of Miss Abbey Potterson's obedient regular customers at the Six Jolly Fellowship-Porters. (I: 6; III: 3)

Williamson, Mrs (SB) The 'stout landlady of the Winglebury Arms', where Mr Alexander Trott is staying. ('Tales: The Great Winglebury Duel')

Willis, the Misses (SB) The four sisters who 'settled in our parish thirteen years ago'. They are the subject of much curiosity among their neighbours, who eventually discover that it is the youngest sister who has married Mr Robinson. ('Our Parish: The Four Sisters')

Willis, Mr (SB) A 'young fellow of vulgar manners, dressed in the very extreme of the prevailing fashion . . . with a lighted cigar in his mouth and his hands in his pockets', who is one of Mr Tottle's fellow-inmates in Mr Solomon Jacobs's sponging-house. ('Tales: A Passage in the Life of Mr Watkins Tottle')

Wilson, Miss Caroline (SB) She was the 'bosom friend' of Emily Smithers, the belle of Minerva House, 'because she was the ugliest girl in Hammersmith, or out of it'. ('Tales: Sentiment')

Wilson, Mr (SB) The man who was to have played the part of Iago at the Gattletons' Private Theatricals but who was 'unavoidably detained at the Post Office' on that evening. ('Tales: Mrs Joseph Porter')

Wiltshire (UT) A 'simple fresh-coloured farm labourer, of eight-and-thirty', who is a 'widderer' with a son and daughter. They are Mormon emigrants. ('Bound for the Great Salt Lake')

Winkle, Mr, senior (PP) Mr Winkle's father, a wharfinger (i.e., the owner of a wharf), was a 'little old gentleman in a snuff-coloured suit, with a head and face the precise counterpart of those belonging to Mr Winkle, junior'. When Mr Pickwick, acting as an intermediary, conveys the information to him that his son has married Arabella Allen, he receives the news with some vexation. But when he meets Arabella, he is won over by her tender and affectionate nature and gladly accepts her as 'a very charming daughter-in-law'. (47, 50, 53, 56, 57)

Winkle, Nathaniel (PP) Apart from Mr Pickwick himself, Mr Winkle is the most prominent and the most amusing of the Pickwickians. In his Preface to the first cheap edition of the novel (1847), Dickens says, 'I connected Mr Pickwick with a club, because of the original suggestion [made by the publishers], and I put in Mr Winkle expressly for the use of Mr Seymour [the original illustrator of the novel].' According to Mr Pickwick, 'the desire of earning fame in the sports of the field, the air, and the water, was uppermost in the breast of his friend Winkle'. But Mr Winkle is accident-prone, and all his sporting endeavours, including riding, shooting and skating, are comic mishaps. At the trial of Bardell v. Pickwick, his unfortunate reference to the 'trifling occasion' of Mr Pickwick's escapade at the Great White Horse Inn in Ipswich involving Miss Witherfield is highly damaging to Mr Pickwick's case. When he left the witness box, realising that he had made a blunder, Mr Winkle 'rushed with delirious haste to the George and Vulture, where he was discovered some hours after, by the waiter, groaning in a hollow and dismal manner, with his head buried beneath the sofa cushions'. But Winkle finds happiness in his runaway marriage to Arabella Allen, who had been intended by her brother, Benjamin, for his friend Bob Sawyer. (1–5, 7, 9, 11–13, 15, 18, 19, 24–26, 28, 30–32, 34–36, 38, 39, 44, 47, 54, 56, 57)

Winks (MED) *See* **Deputy.**

Wisbottle, Mr (SB) A boarder at Mrs Tibbs's boarding-house. He 'was a clerk in the Woods and Forests Office, which he considered rather an aristocratic appointment; he knew the peerage by heart, and could tell you, off-hand, where any illustrious personage lived'. He had 'a partiality for whistling' and 'a great idea of his singing powers'. ('Tales: The Boarding-House')

Wisk, Miss (BH) Mr Quale was her 'Accepted'. Her mission, according to Mr Jarndyce, 'was to show the world that woman's mission was man's mission; and that the only genuine mission, of both man and woman, was to be always moving declaratory resolutions about things in general at public meetings'. She is a notable example of an early feminist, since she asserts that 'the only practical thing for the world was the emancipation of Woman from the thraldom of her Tyrant, Man'. (30)

Witchem, Sergeant (RP) A short, thick-set police detective, who is 'marked with the small-pox' and has 'something of a reserved and thoughtful air, as if he were engaged in deep arithmetical calculations'. Dickens based him on Sergeant Jonathan Whitcher. ('The Detective Police')

Witherden, Mr (OCS) He was the 'short, chubby, fresh-coloured, brisk, and pompous' notary, to whom Abel Garland was articled. Witherden helped to resolve the two major crises of the novel: he assisted the Single Gentleman to find Little Nell and her Grandfather and he helped to expose the conspiracy of the Brasses and Quilp to get Kit Nubbles imprisoned for theft. (14, 20, 38, 40, 41, 60, 63, 65, 66, 73)

Witherfield, Miss (PP) The 'middle-aged lady, in yellow curl-papers' in whose bedroom at the Great White Horse Inn, Ipswich, Mr Pickwick embarrassingly finds himself by mistake. She is engaged to be married to Mr Peter Magnus, who therefore angrily threatens Mr Pickwick with a duel. (22, 24, 34)

Withers (DS) Mrs Skewton's page, who pushes her in her wheelchair. He 'seemed to have in part outgrown and in part out-pushed his strength, for when he stood upright he was tall, and wan, and thin, and his plight appeared the more forlorn from his having injured the shape of his hat, by butting at the carriage with his head to urge it forward, as is sometimes done by elephants in Oriental countries'. (21, 26, 27, 30, 37, 40)

Wititterley, Henry and Julia (NN) Kate Nickleby was employed for a time as Mrs Wititterley's companion at the Wititterleys' mansion in Cadogan Place, Sloane Street. Mrs Wititterley had 'an air of sweet insipidity, and a face of en-gaging paleness; there was a faded look about her, and about the furniture, and about the house'. Her husband, who made much of his wife's delicacy and fragility, was 'an important gentleman of about eight-and-thirty, of rather ple-beian countenance, and with a very light head of hair'. One of Kate's tasks was to read aloud fashionable novels to her mis-tress. Mrs Wititterley becomes jealous of the attentions Kate unwillingly receives from Sir Mulberry Hawk and Lord Frederick Verisopht. Kate, who is desper-ately unhappy in this employment, is taken away from it by Nicholas. (21, 27, 28, 33)

Wobbler, Mr (LD) A member of the Sec-retarial Department of the Circumlocu-tion Office. When Barnacle Junior refers Arthur Clennam to him, Wobbler is sit-ting with another gentleman and is 'spreading marmalade on bread with a paper-knife'. He ignores Clennam as long as possible and then says he can't inform him: 'Never heard of it. Nothing at all to do with it. Better try Mr Clive,

second door on the left in the next passage.' (I: 10)

Wolf, Mr (MC) One of Montague Tigg's guests at the dinner attended by Jonas Chuzzlewit. According to Tigg, Wolf is a 'literary character – you needn't mention it – remarkably clever weekly paper – oh, remarkably clever!' (28)

Woodcourt, Allan (BH) A young doctor, who first appears as the 'dark young man' from whom Nemo (Captain Hawdon) bought opium and who diag-noses the cause of Hawdon's death as an overdose of the drug. He is Miss Flite's doctor. Having fallen in love with Esther Summerson but not declaring his feel-ings, Woodcourt goes to China and India as a ship's surgeon. His heroic deeds in a shipwreck in the East Indian seas are re-counted to Esther by Miss Flite. On his return to England, Woodcourt appears at various crucial points in the narrative: on Esther's urging, he befriends and advises Richard Carstone; he looks after Jo in his sickness and is present at his death-bed in George's Shooting Gallery; and he tends Caddy Jellyby in her illness. Mr Jarndyce, aware of the love that exists between Woodcourt and Esther, relin-quishes Esther (who was to be Jarndyce's wife) to him, and presents them with an-other Bleak House in Yorkshire. Esther pays her husband affectionate tribute: 'I never go into a house of any degree, but I hear his praises, or see them in grateful eyes. I never lie down at night, but I know that in the course of that day he has alleviated pain, and soothed some fellow-creature in the time of need. I know that from the beds of those who were past recovery, thanks have often, often gone up, in the last hour, for his patient ministration. Is not this to be rich?' (11, 13, 14, 17, 30, 35, 45–47, 50–52, 59–61, 64, 65, 67)

Woodcourt, Mrs (BH) The mother of Allan Woodcourt. Esther Summerson tells us that she was 'a pretty old lady, with bright black eyes, but she seemed proud. She came from Wales; and had had, a long time ago, an eminent person for an ancestor, of the name of Morgan ap-Kerrig – of some place that sounded like Gimlet – who was the most illustrious person that was ever known, and all of whose relations were a sort of Royal Family.' Mrs Woodcourt is anxious that her son should form an alliance at least equal to such a pedigree. But thanks to Mr Jarndyce's tactful and kindly intercession, she fondly accepts Esther as a suitable daughter-in-law. (17, 30, 60, 62, 64)

Woodensconce, Mr (MP) The president of the Statistics section at the first meeting of the Mudfog Association.

Woolford, Miss (SB) A graceful equestrian performer at Astley's. ('Scenes: Astley's')

Wopsle, Mr (GE) A parish clerk and a friend of the Gargery family. 'Mr Wopsle, united to a Roman nose and large shining bald forehead, had a deep voice which he was uncommonly proud of; indeed it was understood among his acquaintance that if you could only give him his head, he would read the clergyman into fits; he himself confessed that if the Church was "thrown open," meaning to competition, he would not despair of making his mark in it.' He becomes an actor under the name of Waldengarver. Pip and Herbert Pocket, as young men in London, go to see him in the title role of *Hamlet*. His performance is greeted throughout by peals of laughter: 'I laughed in spite of myself all the time [Pip confesses], the whole thing was so droll; and yet I had a latent impression that there was something decidedly fine in Mr Wopsle's elocution – not for old associations' sake, I'm afraid, but because it was very slow, very dreary, very up-hill and down-hill, and very unlike

any way in which any man in any natural circumstances of life or death ever expressed himself about anything.' On a later occasion, Pip again sees him on the stage. After the performance, Wopsle tells Pip that he had seen Compeyson in the audience, sitting behind him. (4–7, 10, 13, 15, 18, 31, 47)

Wosky, Doctor (SB) Mrs Bloss's obsequious doctor, who calls on her at Mrs Tibbs's boarding-house. 'He was a little man with a red face – dressed of course in black with a stiff white neckerchief. He had a very good practice, and plenty of money, which he had amassed by invariably humouring the worst fancies of all the females of all the families he had ever been introduced to.' ('Tales: The Boarding-House')

Wozenham, Miss (CS) Mrs Lirriper's rival as a lodging-house keeper. Despite their differences, Mrs Lirriper lends Mrs Wozenham £40 when she is about to be 'sold up' for debt. ('Mrs Lirriper's Lodgings' and 'Mrs Lirriper's Legacy')

Wrayburn, Eugene (OMF) A briefless young barrister of an idle and cynical disposition, who has been a friend of Mortimer Lightwood's ever since they met at their public school and a member of the Veneerings' social circle. He tells Lightwood that he was called to the Bar seven years previously, has had no business at all and will never have any: 'If there is a word in the dictionary under any letter from A to Z that I abominate, it is energy.' Through his curiosity about the Harmon case, Eugene meets Lizzie, to whom he is immediately attracted and for whom he arranges private tuition. He incurs the jealous hatred of Bradley Headstone, whom he disdainfully taunts in various ways. Mortimer Lightwood and Jenny Wren both have their doubts about Eugene's behaviour, suspecting that he is merely indulging in upper-class dalliance with a working-class girl. Lizzie

Figure 40 Eugene Wrayburn, Mortimer Lightwood, Charley Hexam, and Bradley Headstone by Marcus Stone

herself has fallen in love with him, but decides to leave London to escape his attentions and those of Bradley Headstone. Eugene learns her whereabouts from Mr Dolls, Jenny Wren's father, confronts her and avows his love and the power of her influence over him: 'You don't know how the cursed carelessness that is over-officious in helping me at every other turning of my life, WON'T help me here. You have struck it dead, and I sometimes wish you had struck me dead along with it.' When he falls, terribly injured, into the river after Bradley Headstone has assaulted him, Lizzie rescues him. Apparently on the point of death, Eugene is married while on his sickbed to Lizzie by the Reverend Frank Milvey. But he slowly recovers his health. 'Sadly wan and worn was the once gallant Eugene, and walked resting on his wife's arm, and leaning heavily upon a stick. But he was daily growing stronger and better, and it was declared by the medical attendants that he might not be much disfigured by-and-by.' He is de-

termined to outface the opinion of Society, represented by Lady Tippins: 'Now my wife is something nearer to my heart, Mortimer, than Tippins is, and I owe her a little more than I owe to Tippins, and I am rather prouder of her than I ever was to Tippins. Therefore, I will fight it out to the last gasp, with her and for her, here in the open field.' Stephen Gill sees 'a symbolic fitness in Eugene's end. When he is plunged into the river and left for dead, he enters the element which from time immemorial has spoken of cleansing and rebirth as often as death and dissolution. The Eugene who emerges from prolonged sickness, making feeble gestures for life, is one who has suffered the extreme test of identity. He is a new man' (1972: 29). (I: 2, 3, 8, 10, 12–14; II: 1, 2, 6, 11, 14–16; III: 1, 9, 10, 11, 17; IV: 1, 6, 7, 9–11, 16)

Wren, Jenny (OMF) A dolls' dressmaker, who becomes a close friend of Lizzie Hexam's. She was 'a child – a dwarf – a girl – a something', crippled and with a 'bad' back. 'The queer little figure, and the queer but not ugly little face, with its bright grey eyes, were so sharp, that the sharpness of manner seemed unavoidable.' Her real name was Fanny Cleaver, but she had renamed herself Jenny Wren. Like a mother, she looks after her pathetic, drunken father (her 'troublesome, bad child'), whom Eugene Wrayburn calls 'Mr Dolls'. To comfort herself in her poverty and pain, Jenny has 'pleasant fancies': the smell of flowers, bird song, numbers of blessed, white-clad children. She is always alert and perceptive, especially concerning the relationship between Lizzie and Eugene. She helps to tend Eugene when he is lying desperately ill after Bradley Headstone's assault: 'all softened compassion now, [she] watched him with an earnestness that never relaxed'. Through whispering the word, 'wife', in Mortimer Lightwood's ear, so that he in turn can say it to Eugene when he comes round from a period of unconsciousness, Jenny Wren seems to start Eugene's process of recovery. Earlier, she had taken pleasure in sprinkling pepper on the plasters of brown paper and vinegar she had applied to Fledgeby's back after Lammle had assaulted him. In a curious encounter with Sloppy towards the end of the novel, she refers to a future possible husband: 'He is coming from somewhere or other, I suppose, and he is coming some day or other, I suppose.' They both laugh heartily, Sloppy says that he will soon come back again, and so the reader is left to imagine that the two will marry. (II: 1, 2, 5, 11, 15; III: 2, 3, 10, 13; IV: 8–10, 16)

Wrymug, Mrs (NN) A 'genteel female', who is a client at the General Agency Office, thinks that a post with Mrs Wrymug would suit her. Mrs Wrymug keeps 'three serious footmen' as well as a cook, housemaid and nursemaid. Each female servant is required 'to join the Little Bethel Congregation three times every Sunday – with a serious footman. If the cook is more serious than the footman, she will be expected to improve the footman; if the footman is more serious than the cook, he will be expected to improve the cook.' (16)

Wugsby, Mrs Colonel (PP) One of the ladies 'of an ancient and whist-like appearance' with whom Mr Pickwick plays cards at Bath. She indignantly refuses permission for her daughter, Jane, to dance with the youngest Mr Crawley (since 'his father has eight hundred a-year, which dies with him'), but is delighted that Lord Mutanhed has been introduced to her older daughter. (35, 36)

Y

Yawler (DC) A friend of Traddles's ('with his nose on one side') from his schooldays at Salem House. Through his help and recommendations, Traddles embarks on a career in the law. (27)

Young Blight (OMF) *See* **Blight.**

Z

Zephyr, The (PP) *See* **Mivins, Mr.**

Bibliography

Note: the publication dates are those of the editions or reprints used in this volume.

Ackroyd, P. (1990) *Dickens*, London: Sinclair-Stevenson.

Alexander, D. (1991) *Creating Characters with Charles Dickens*, University Park, Pennsylvania: The Pennsylvania State University Press.

Arnold, M. (1891) *Irish Essays*, London: Smith, Elder and Co.

Auden, W.H. (1963) *The Dyer's Hand and Other Essays*, London: Faber.

Bentley, N., Slater, M. and Burgis, N. (1988), *The Dickens Index,* Oxford: Oxford University Press.

Butt, J. and Tillotson, K. (1957) *Dickens at Work*, London: Methuen.

Chesterton, G.K. (1933) *Criticisms and Appreciations of the Works of Charles Dickens,* London: Dent.

Collins, P. (1963) *Dickens and Education*, London: Macmillan.

Collins, P. (1964) *Dickens and Crime*, 2nd edition, London: Macmillan.

Collins, P. (ed.) (1971) *Dickens: The Critical Heritage*, London: Routledge and Kegan Paul.

Collins, P. (1981) *Dickens: Interviews and Recollections*, 2 vols, London: Macmillan.

Collins, P. (ed.) (1983) *Charles Dickens: Sikes and Nancy and Other Public Readings*, Oxford: Oxford University Press.

De Castro, J.P. (1926) *The Gordon Riots*, London: Oxford University Press.

Dexter, W. (1983) 'Dickensian peeps into *Punch*' *The Dickensian*, vol. 31, pp. 264–6.

Dyson, A.E. (1970) *The Inimitable Dickens*, London: Macmillan.

Fielding, K.J. (1965) *Charles Dickens: A Critical Introduction*, 2nd edition, London: Longmans.

Forster, J. (1928), *The Life of Charles Dickens*, edited by J.W.T. Ley, London: Cecil Palmer (first edition 1872–4).

Gibson, C. (ed.) (1989) *Art and Society in the Victorian Novel*, London: Macmillan.

Gill, S. (ed.) (1972) 'Introduction', in: Dickens, C., *Our Mutual Friend*, Harmondsworth: Penguin.

Gissing, G. (1974) *Charles Dickens: A Critical Study*, New York: Haskell House Publishers Ltd.

Glancy, R. (ed.) (1996) 'Introduction' and notes, in: Dickens, C., *The Christmas Stories*, London: Dent.

Hardwick, M. and Hardwick, M. (1973) *The Charles Dickens Encyclopedia*, Reading: Osprey Publishing Ltd.

Hayward, A.L. (1924) *The Dickens Encyclopaedia*, London: Routledge and Kegan Paul.

House, H. (1942) *The Dickens World*, 2nd edition, London: Oxford University Press.

House, H. (1955) *All in Due Time*, London: Hart-Davis.

House, M., Storey, G., and Tillotson, K., *et al.* (eds) (1965) *The Pilgrim Edition of the Letters of Charles Dickens*, Oxford: Clarendon Press.

Hyder, C.K. (1972) *Swinburne as Critic*, London: Routledge and Kegan Paul.

Innes, M. (1950) 'Introduction', in: Dickens, C., *The Mystery of Edwin Drood*, London: John Lehmann.

Johnson, E. (1953) *Charles Dickens: His Tragedy and Triumph*, 2 volumes, London: Gollancz.

Kaplan, F. (1988) *Charles Dickens: A Biography*, London: Hodder and Stoughton.

Kitton, F. G. (1906) *Charles Dickens: His Life, Writings, and Personality*, London and Edinburgh: T.C. and E.C. Jack.

Laurence, D.H. and Quinn, M. (1985) *Shaw on Dickens*, New York: Frederick Ungar Publishing Co.

Leavis, F.R. (1962) *The Great Tradition*, Harmondsworth: Penguin.

Newlin, G. (1995) *Everyone in Dickens*, 3 volumes, Westport, Connecticut and London: Greenwood Press.

Page, N. (1984) *A Dickens Companion*, London: Macmillan.

Pearson, H. (1949) *Dickens: His Character, Comedy, and Career*, London: Methuen.

Pierce, G.A. and Wheeler, W.A. (1892) *The Dickens Dictionary*, new edition, London: Chapman and Hall.

Priestley, J.B. (1928) *The English Comic Characters*, London: John Lane.

Pugh, E. (1912) *The Dickens Originals*, London and Edinburgh: T.N. Foulis.

Santayana, G. (1922) *Soliloquies in England and Later Soliloquies*, London: Constable.

Schlicke, P. (ed.) (1995) 'Introduction' and notes, in: Dickens, C., *The Old Curiosity Shop*, London: Dent.

Shatto, S. (1988) *The Companion to Bleak House*, London: Unwin Hyman.

Sitwell, O. (1948) 'Introduction', in: Dickens, C., *Bleak House*, Oxford: Oxford University Press.

Slater, M. (1983) *Dickens and Women*, London: Dent.

Tillotson, K.(1954a) 'Introduction', in: Dickens, C., *Barnaby Rudge*, Oxford: Oxford University Press

Tillotson, K. (1954b) *Novels of the Eighteen-Forties*, London: Oxford University Press

Tillotson, K. (1982) 'Introduction', in: Dickens, C., *Oliver Twist*, Oxford: Oxford University Press

Trilling, L. (1952) 'Introduction', in: Dickens, C., *Little Dorrit*, Oxford: Oxford University Press

Walder, D. (1981) *Dickens and Religion*, London: Allen and Unwin.

Ward, A.W. (1882) *Dickens*, London: Macmillan.

Williams, R. (1961) *Culture and Society 1780–1950*, Harmondsworth: Penguin.